UCEED

Entrance Exam

Latest Edition
Practice Kit

10 Tests
10 Mock Test

Based On Real Exam Pattern

✓ Thoroughly Revised and Updated
✓ Detailed Analysis of all MCQs

Title : UCEED Entrance Exam
Author Name : Mr. Rohit Manglik
Published By : EduGorilla Community Pvt. Ltd.
Publishers Address : 12/651, First Floor Opp. Arvindo Park, Near Jama Masjid, Indira Nagar, Lucknow, Uttar Pradesh-226016, India

Copyright EduGorilla

ISBN : 978-93-90239-20-7

Second Edition

Disclaimer EduGorilla

Compiled and created by EduGorilla Community Pvt. Ltd

Printed By EduGorilla Community Pvt. Ltd.

ROHIT MANGLIK
CEO, EduGorilla

Editor's Note

Dear Applicants,

People say *"Success comes to those who work hard."* But I've seen people working hard for their exams day in and day out for marginal success. While others succeed in their examinations by putting in just half the work. So are they God Gifted? No! I believe that it's because they work *smart* and not just *hard*. Similarly, for your exams, you should strategize your preparation so as to increase the likelihood of success. Well with EduGorilla get ready to increase your *chances of selection* in your exam by *16x*.

EduGorilla helps you in not only working *hard* but also working in a *smart and strategic* manner. With EduGorilla's preparation package, you get a chance to make your exam preparation easy, and a fun learning path towards selection. Finding the right path to your preparations can be difficult if you don't know in which direction to head. Don't worry, we have you covered! EduGorilla will be your guide to success in your journey. With our Preparation Package, you can prepare strategically and beat the exam in just one attempt.

EduGorilla's Preparation Package includes-

- **Test Series**
- **Books**

Our preparation package is handcrafted as per the latest changes, expert opinions, and students' discretion. Thus, enabling you to get through each stage of the selection process for your exam.

Our Books are designed by the teachers and experts of the respective exam with a combined 150+ years of experience; to provide you with easy, efficient, and effective learning. Our books are smart, in the sense that not only do they give you the answers to the questions but also provide similar questions for practice.

EduGorilla's competent Test Series gives you real-time experience and confidence through which you can clear your offline or online exam in just one attempt. We currently host 83,000+ mock tests for 1,440+ competitive and academic exams.

Thus, EduGorilla misses no chance to assist you in your preparation and covers all stages of the exam, so that you don't have to look anywhere else.

We provide complete preparation packages for defense, banking, teaching, and other National & State-Level exams. Hence, it doesn't matter which exam you aspire to because you will reach your success.

ALL THE BEST !

Let EduGorilla be your Guide to Success.

Rohit Manglik,
Founder and CEO, EduGorilla

INTRODUCTION

EduGorilla focuses on guiding students to succeed in their examinations. With that in mind, our book, titled "UCEED : Entrance Exam", has been drafted through the collective efforts of our distinguished experts with 150+ years of combined experience. This book consists of questions that are created following the latest changes in the syllabus and exam pattern. We compiled the book on the basis of questions that are most likely to appear in the UCEED. Through EduGorilla's "UCEED : Entrance Exam" your chances of success will increase 16x.

EduGorilla does this through our Complete Preparation Package. This package consists of well-conceptualized and structured content in the form of questions that are tailor-made according to your needs and will help you practice for exams in a smart way by pinpointing all the necessary information. It also provides hints and solutions, along with a smart answer sheet for your self-evaluation. You can assess your shortcomings and work accordingly on areas that may require more of your attention.

EduGorilla promises to help you succeed in your examination and accomplish your dream goals. We believe in our aspirants and see them at the top of the merit list. And the first step towards the top is to start preparing with us. EduGorilla's "UCEED : Entrance Exam" includes the following attributes.

➤ Well-Researched Content

➤ Top-Notch Quality

➤ Detailed Answers and Analysis

➤ Smart Answer Sheet

➤ Exam Relevant Questions

Therefore, EduGorilla fortifies your preparation and makes it durable enough to help you stand tall and beat the examination.

UCEED

Scan QR code for Eligibility, Exam Pattern, Syllabus and more.

Book ID: 0290

TABLE OF CONTENTS

Mock Test 01

Numerical Answer Type (NAT)

Q.1 In a certain code language, MUSIC is coded as 60, and TUNE is coded as 56. How will LYRIC be coded as in that language?

Q.2 Direction: A piece of paper is folded and punched as shown below in the question figures. From the given answer figures, indicate how it will appear when opened?

Question figure:

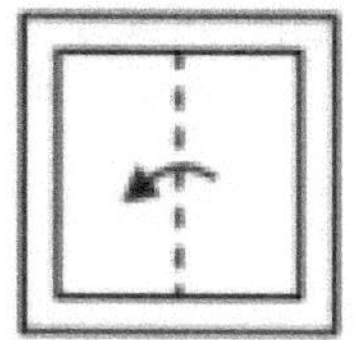

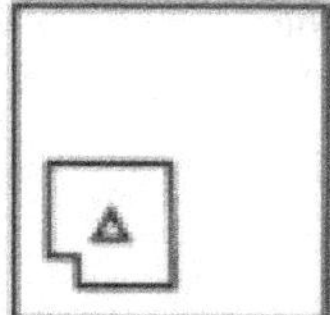

Answer figures:

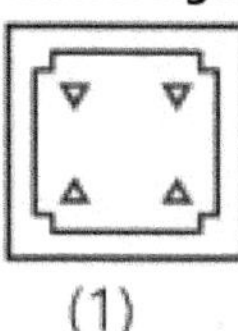
(1)

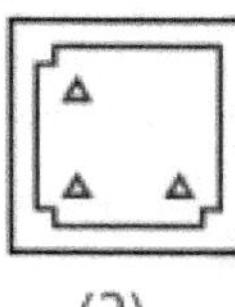
(2)

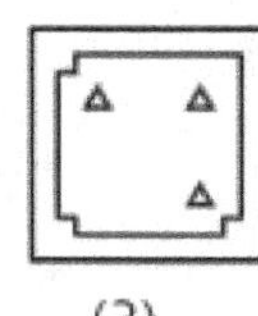
(3)

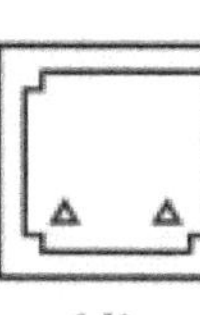
(4)

Q.3 Direction: Study the information given below carefully and answer the question that follows.

Point U is $8\ m$ east of point R. Point P is $3\ m$ north of point Q. Point U is $10\ m$ north of point V. Point W is $8\ m$ west of point V. Point R is exactly between point S and point T. Point R is $4\ m$ east of point Q. Point T is in $8\ m$ south of point S.

What is the shortest distance between point P and point R?

Q.4 In the following question, find the number which can be placed at the sign of the question mark (?).

	3	
2	31	1
	5	

	4	
2	145	6
	3	

	2	
1	?	7
	5	

Q.5 In the following question, write the related number.

$101 : 10201 :: 107 : ?$

Q.6 A cuboid shaped wooden block has 4 cm length, 3 cm breadth and 5 cm height. Two sides measuring 5 cm x 4 cm are colored in red. Two faces measuring 4 cm x 3 cm are colored in blue. Two faces measuring 5 cm x 3 cm are colored in green. Now the block is divided into small cubes of side 1 cm each. How many small cubes will have three faces colored ?

Q.7 Kirti is facing in the East direction. First, she turned $180°$ clockwise and then turned $90°$ anti-clockwise. In which direction is she facing now?

Q.8 Count the number of cubes in the following figure :

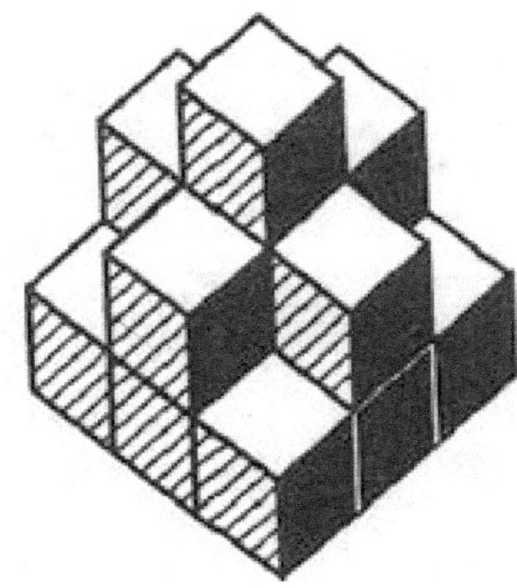

Q.9 In the following question find out the alternative which will replace the question mark.

$7 : 48 :: 12 : ?$

Q.10 What will replace the ? sign in the question given below:
16 : 56 :: 32 : ?

Q.11 Find the area of the shaded portions in the figure, where $ABCD$ is a square of side $7\ cm$.

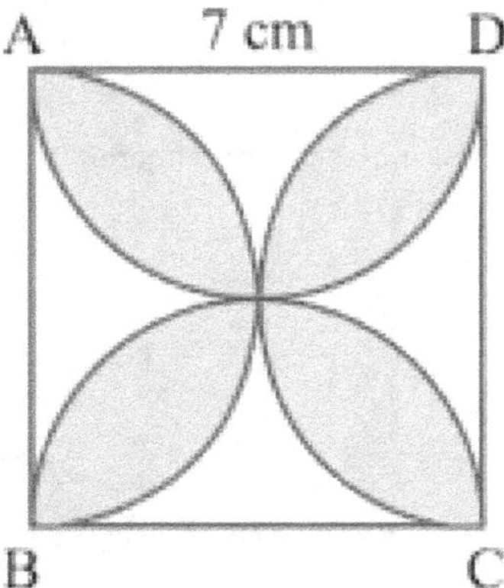

Q.12 Identify the car company shown in this picture below (Write answer in capital letters):

Q.13 If a pack of playing cards measures $1.3\ cm$ when viewed sideways, what would be the measurement if all the aces were removed(write the answer up to one decimal places)?

Q.14 In the following question, find the correct letters according to previous relation:

TRACK : MECTV : : POND : ?

Q.15 Kavya's birthday is on Tuesday 4th July. On what day of the week will be Anika's Birthday in the same year, if Anika was born on 15th August? (all letters of the answer should be in uppercase)

Q.16 In the following question, select the missing number from the given series.

6, 9, 15, 24, 39, 63,?

Q.17 Find the number that will come into the place of the question mark (?).

3	4	6
5	7	3
1	2	7
35	69	?

Q.18 How many squares are there in the following figure?

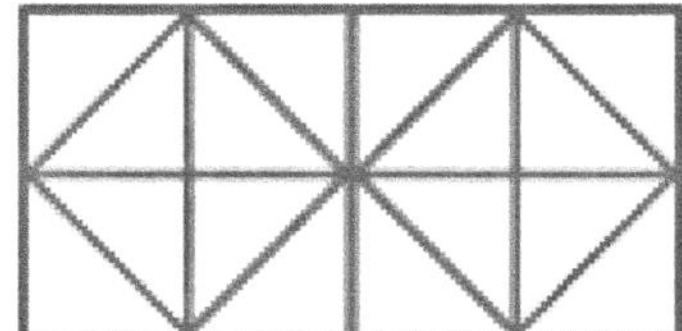

Multiple Select Questions (MSQ)

Q.19 Select all statements about Gautam Buddha that are true:

A. Gautam Buddha was an ancient sage and the founder of Buddhism. The meaning of Buddha is the awakened one. He was born in Lumbini, Nepal around 563 BCE on a Poornima. That's why his anniversary is celebrated as a 'Buddha Poornima'.

B. When he was born, astrologers predicted that he would be either a great king or a great holy man. His father tried to hide him from the religious teachings and the sufferings of daily life. One day when he was travelling in his chariot he saw an old man, a sick person, a corpse. This introduced him to the world of suffering. He left the palace for the search of the truth and to find the meaning of life. He was only 29 at that time.

C. At the age of 35, under a pipal tree (now known as bodhi tree), near Bodh Gaya, Nepal, he ultimately found what he was searching for.

D. At first he was not interested in teaching the Dharma because it was too difficult to teach in words what he learned. He thought people will misunderstand his teachings. At last he was convinced by Brahmā Sahampati to teach his dharma. He gave his first sermon at Sarnath, Uttar Pradesh. Buddha travelled all over the India to teach his lessons until his death at age 80. He died in 483 BCE at Kushinagar, India.

Q.20 What are the common "Perceptual channels"?

A. Tactile
B. Visual
C. Auditory
D. Kinesthetic

Q.21 Light bulbs are usually filled with inert gases. Which of the following can be used.

A. Argon
B. Carbon dioxide
C. Methane
D. Oxygen

Q.22 The figures show four different schematics of two flexible strings. If all the ends are pulled tight, which of the figures will form a knot?

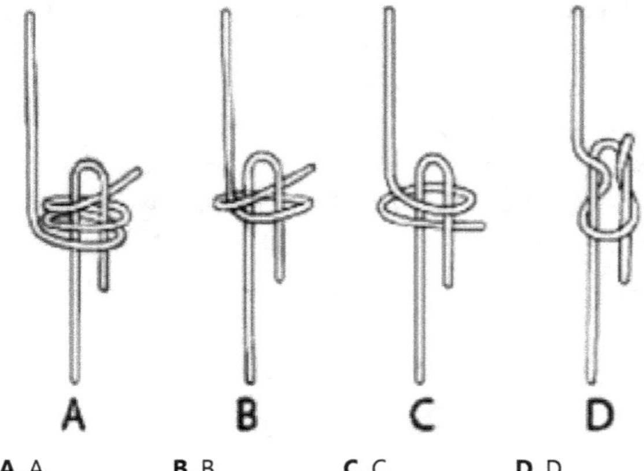

A. A
B. B
C. C
D. D

Q.23 Question given below consists of a statement, followed by three arguments numbered I , II and III. You have to decide which of the arguments is a 'strong' argument.

Statement: Should the income generated out of agricultural activities be taxed?

Arguments:

I. No. Farmers are otherwise suffering from natural calamities and low yield coupled with low procurement price and their income should not be taxed.

II.Yes. Majority of the population is dependent on agriculture and hence their income should betaxed to augment the resources.

III.Yes. Many big farmers earn much more than the majority of the service earners and they shouldbe taxed to remove the disparity.

A. Only I is strong
B. Only I and II are strong
C. Only II and III are strong
D. All are strong

Q.24 Fleas are perfectly designed by nature to feast on anything containing blood. Like a shark in the water or a wolf in the woods, fleas are ideally equipped to do what they do, making them very difficult to defeat. The bodies of these tiny parasites are extremely hardy and well suited for their job. A flea has a very hard exoskeleton, which means the body is covered by a tough, tile-like plate called a sclerite. Because of these plates, fleas are almost impossible to squish. The exoskeletons of fleas are also waterproof and shock resistant, and therefore fleas are highly resistant to the sprays and chemicals used to kill them. Little spines are attached to this plate. The spines lie flat against the flea's thin, narrow body as the flea scurries through an animal's fur in search of food. However, if anything (like fingers or a self- grooming pet) tries to pull a flea off through the hair coat, these spines will extend and stick to the fur like Velcro. Fleas are some of the best jumpers in the natural world. A flea can jump seven inches, or 150 times its own length, either vertically or horizontally. An equivalent jump for a person would be 555 feet, the height of the Washington Monument. Fleas can jump 30,000 times in a row without stopping, and they are able to accelerate through the air at an incredibly high rate—a rate which is over ten times what humans can withstand in an airplane. Fleas have very long rear legs with huge thigh muscles and multiple joints. When they get ready to jump, they fold their long legs up and crouch like a runner on a starting block. Several of their joints contain a protein called resilin, which helps catapult fleas into the air as they jump, similar to the way a rubber band provides momentum to a slingshot. Outward facing claws on the bottom of their legs grip anything they touch when they land.The adult female flea mates after her first blood meal and begins producing eggs in just 1 to 2 days. One flea can lay up to 50 eggs in one day and over 2,000 in her lifetime. Flea eggs can be seen with the naked eye, but they are about the size of a grain of salt. Shortly after being laid, the eggs begin to transform into cocoons. In the cocoon state, fleas are fully developed adults, and will hatch immediately if conditions are favorable. Fleas can detect warmth, movement, and carbon dioxide in exhaled breath, and these three factors stimulate them to emerge as new adults. If the flea does not detect appropriate conditions, it can remain dormant in the cocoon state for extended periods. Under ideal conditions, the entire life cycle may only take 3 weeks, so in no time at all; pets and homes can become infested. Because of these characteristics, fleas are intimidating opponents. The best way to control fleas, therefore, is to take steps to prevent an infestation from ever occurring.

According to the **passage**, which of the following statements is true?

A. Fleas extend their little spines if threatened.
B. Fleas have the ability to jump higher than humans.
C. Humans can jump higher if they consume foods containing resilin.
D. The resilin found in fleas is used to make rubber bands.

Q.25 The question below is given a statement followed by three assumptions numbered I, II and III. You have

to consider the statement and the following assumptions and decide which of the assumptions is

implicit in the statement.

Statement: "We do not want you to see our product on newspaper, visit our shop to get a full

view." - An advertisement.

Assumptions:

I. People generally decide to purchase any product after seeing the name in the advertisement.

II. Uncommon appeal may attract the customers.

III. People may come to see the product.

A. None is implicit
B. Only I and II are implicit
C. Only II and III are implicit
D. All are implicit

Q.26 Identify the paintings of Cezanne from the following:

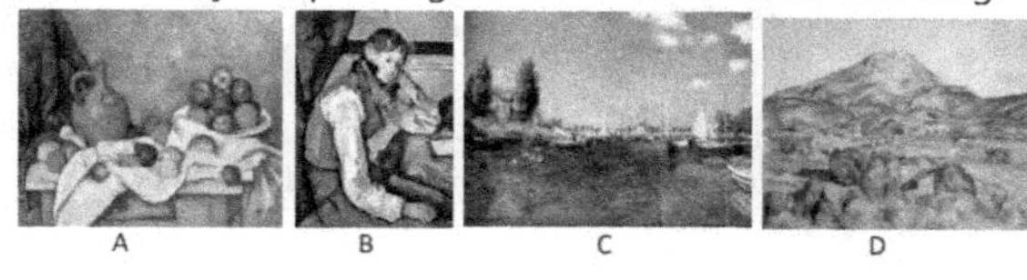

A. A **B.** B **C.** C **D.** D

Q.27 Which of the following is by the Indian artist Abanindranath Tagore:

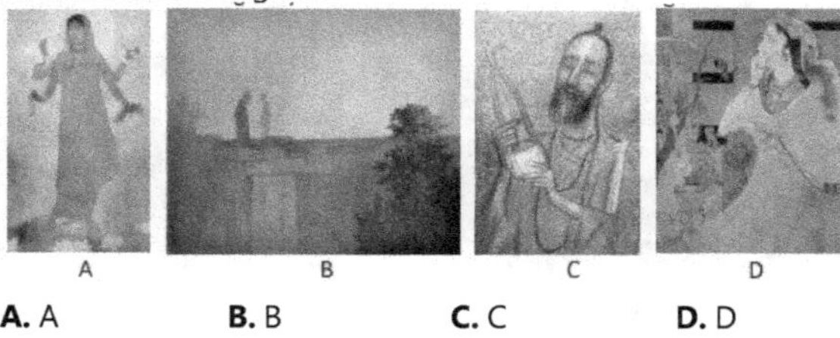

A. A **B.** B **C.** C **D.** D

Q.28 Identify the Indian traditional Art below

A. Kalamkari
B. Phad paintings
C. Mata ni pachedi
D. None of these

Q.29 In this question identify the new shape that could be constructed if the two example shapes were combined. No other change should be made to the two shapes other than combining them.

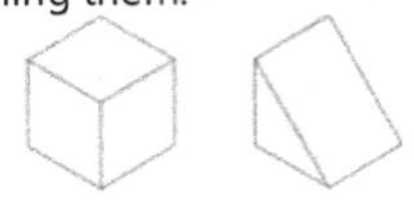

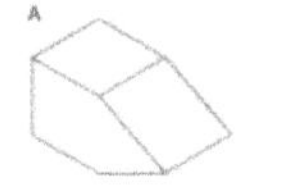 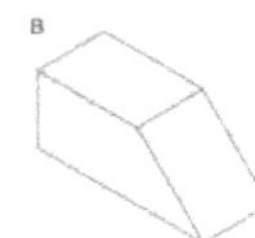 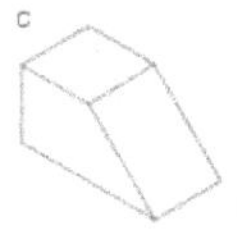 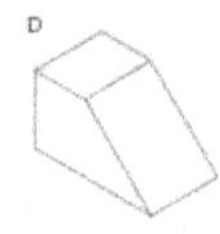

A. A **B.** B **C.** C **D.** D

Q.30 Direction: In the following question, select the related words/letters/numbers from the given alternatives.

$86:62::49:?$

A. 29 **B.** 49 **C.** 35 **D.** 42

Q.31 Identify the answer shape, which has been rotated but is otherwise the same as the question shape.

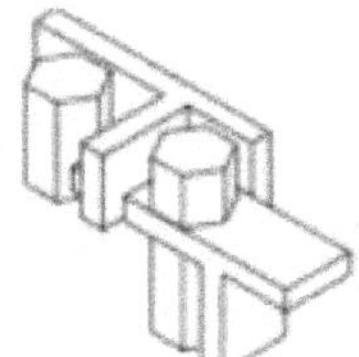

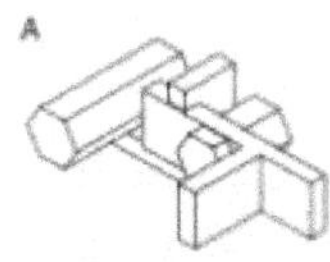 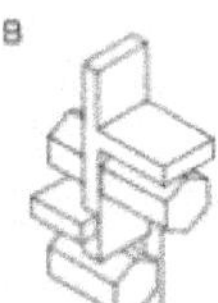 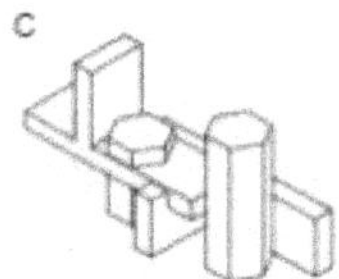

A. A **B.** B
C. C **D.** None of the above

Q.32 Identify the mirror image of the question shape.

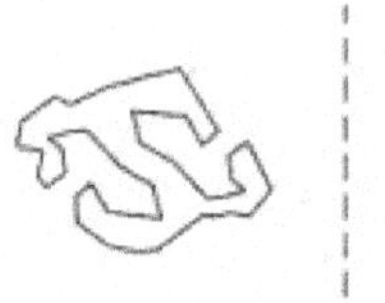

A. A **B.** B
C. C **D.** None of the above

Q.33 If a mirror is placed to the right of the figure, indicate the correct mirror image of the given figure.

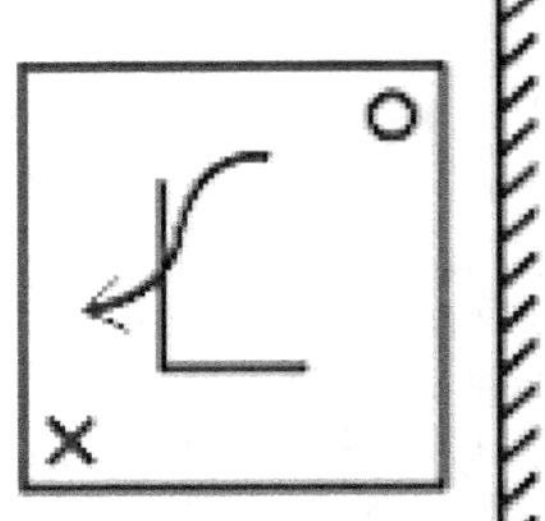

A. 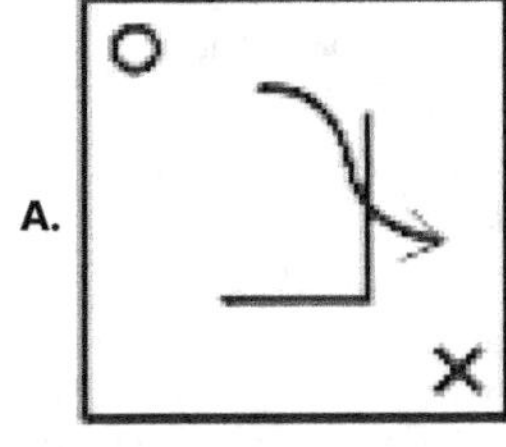

B. 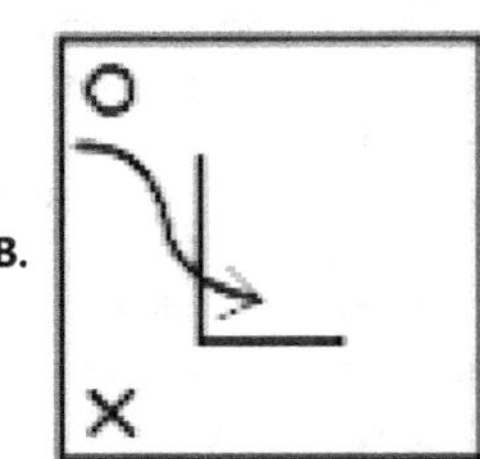

C. 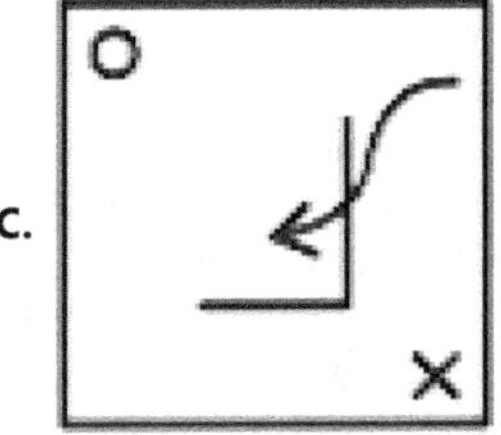

D. 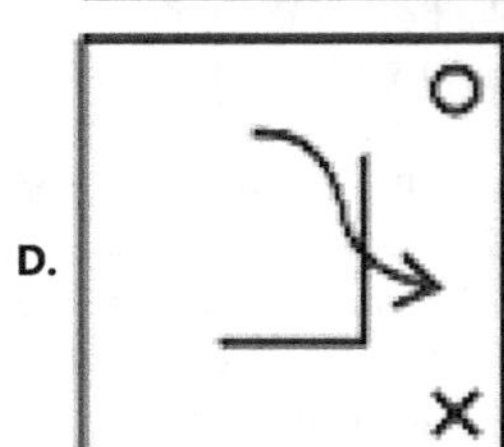

Q.34 4–5 pieces are given. Choose the answer choice that represents a figure comprised of ALL pieces.Pieces may be rotated and/or reflected.

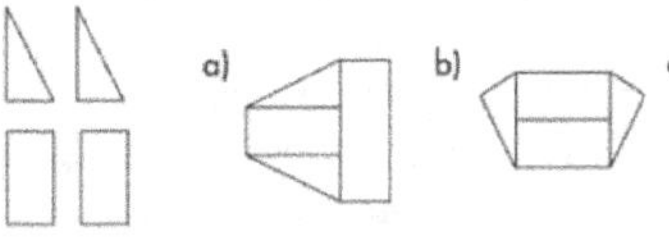 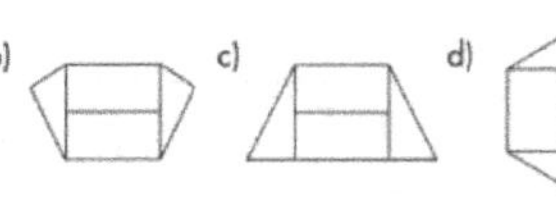

A. a **B.** b **C.** c **D.** d

Q.35 A square is cut into 7 pieces as shown on the extreme left of the image. Identify which of theoptions can be made using all 7 pieces.

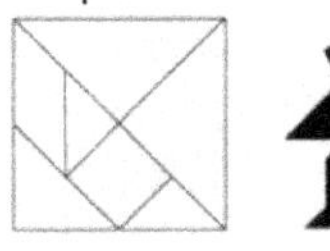    

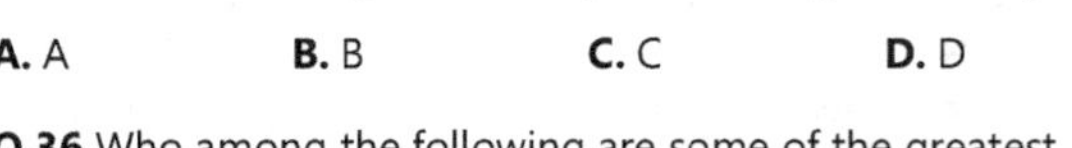

A. A **B.** B **C.** C **D.** D

Q.36 Who among the following are some of the greatest designers of all time?

A. Charlie Parrish **B.** Pierre Cardin
C. Jonathan Ive **D.** Dieter Ram

Multiple Choice Questions (MCQ)

Q.37 Identify the famous personality shown in the picture below:

A. Sir CV Raman
B. Jagadeesh Chandra Bose
C. Dr Homi Bhabha
D. Subash Chandra Bose

Q.38

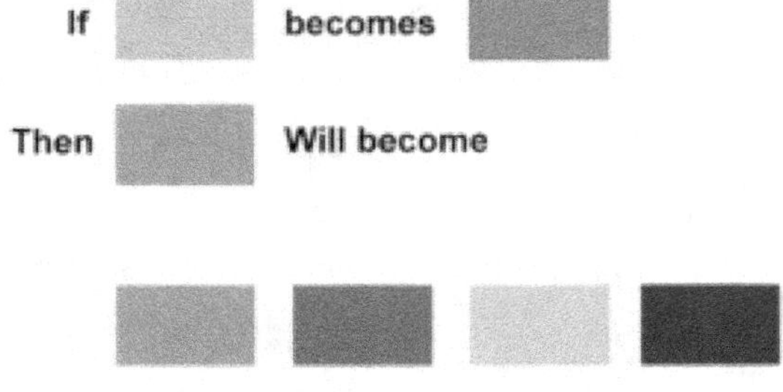

A. A **B.** B **C.** C **D.** D

Q.39 Select the option that correctly represents the relationship among the following.
Gujarat, India, Ahmedabad

A. 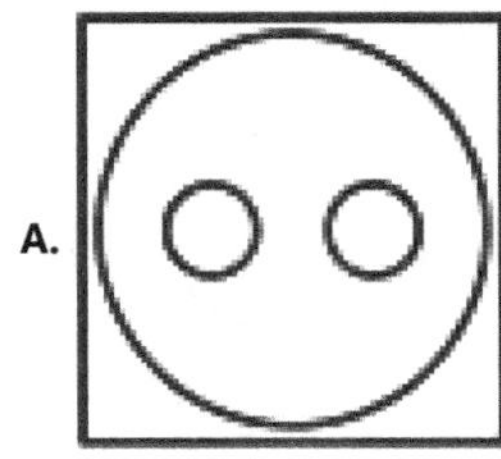

B. 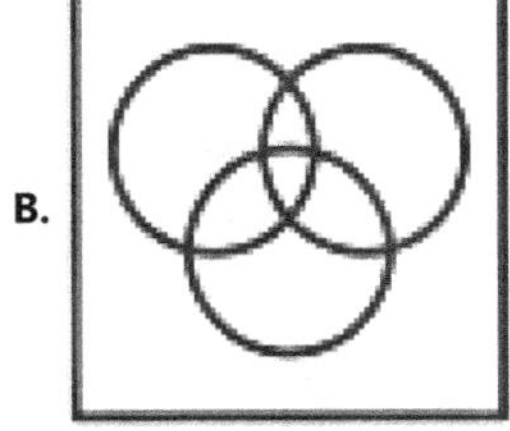

C. 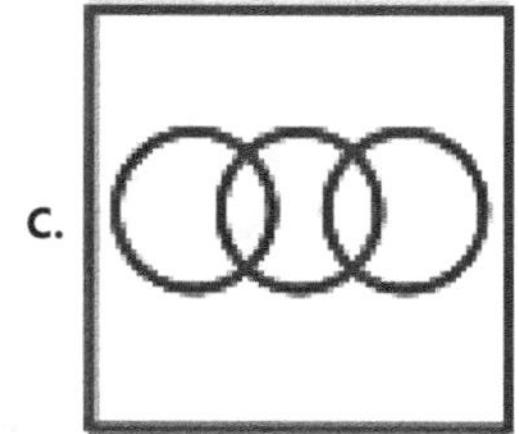

D. 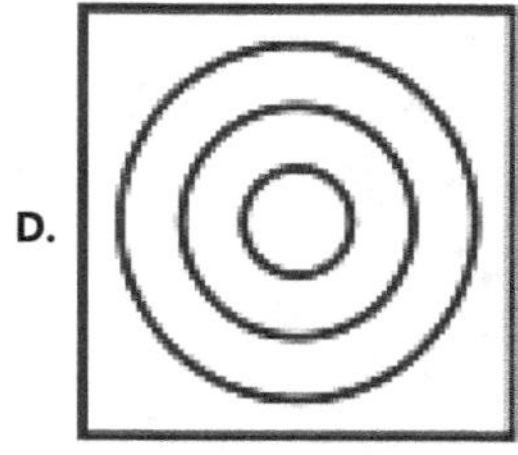

Q.40 Select the option that correctly represents the relationship among the following:
Birds, Ostrich, Albatross

A. 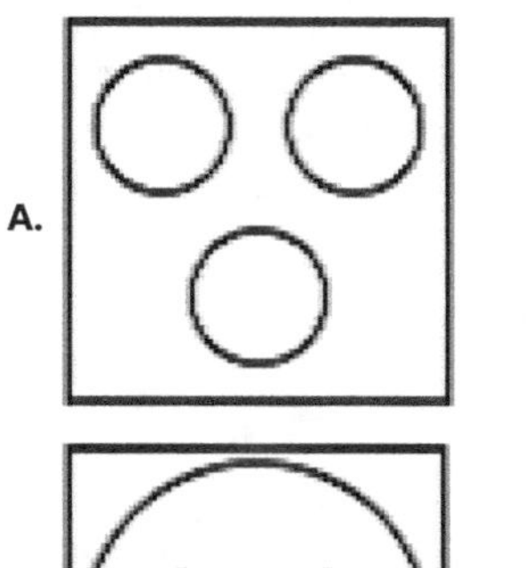

B. 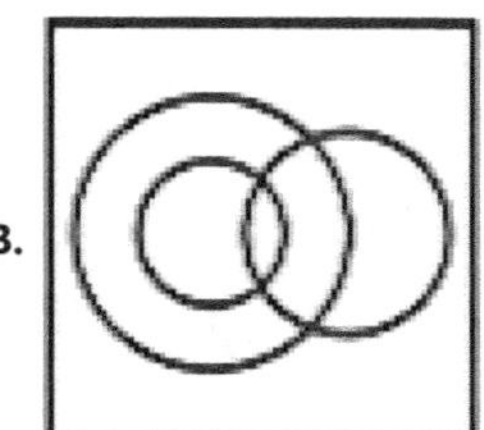

C. 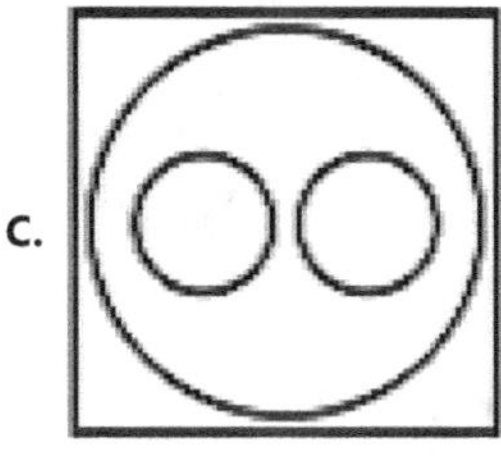

D. 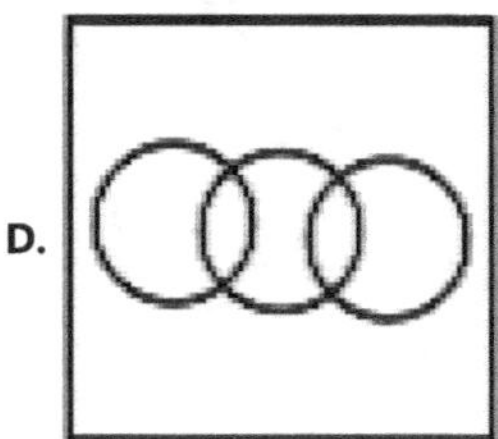

Q.41 Identify the correct art techniques sequence with which the following paintings have been made.

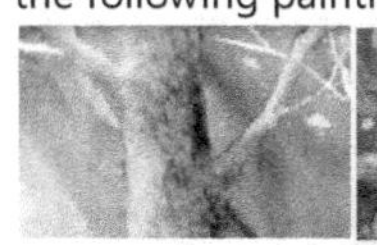 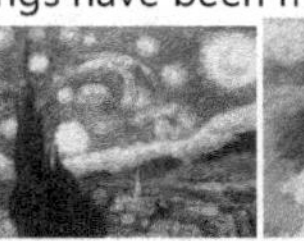 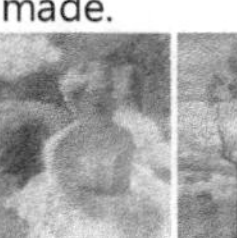 

A. Crayon, Acrylic, Watercolor, Oil
B. Acrylic, Crayon, Water color, Oil
C. Crayon, Oil, Pastel, Water Color
D. Crayon, Oil, Watercolor, Pastel

Q.42 Canon released the highest pixel camera recently, select the correct range of its megapixels (MP):

A. 30-40 MP **B.** 20-30 MP
C. 65-70 MP **D.** 50-55 MP

Q.43 Which is the odd one out?

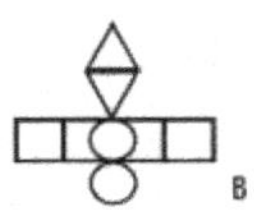

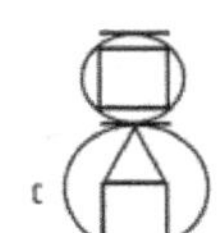

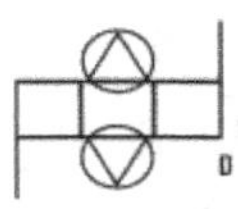

A. A **B.** B **C.** C **D.** D

Q.44

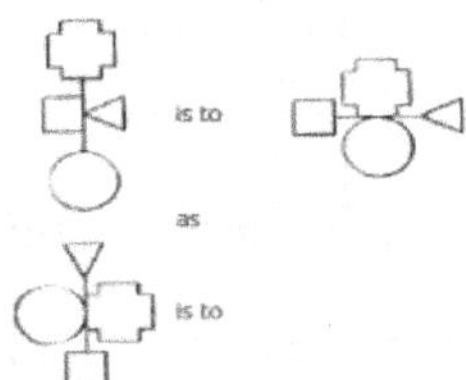

A. A **B.** B **C.** C **D.** D

Q.45 How many triangles are possible in the picture shown below?

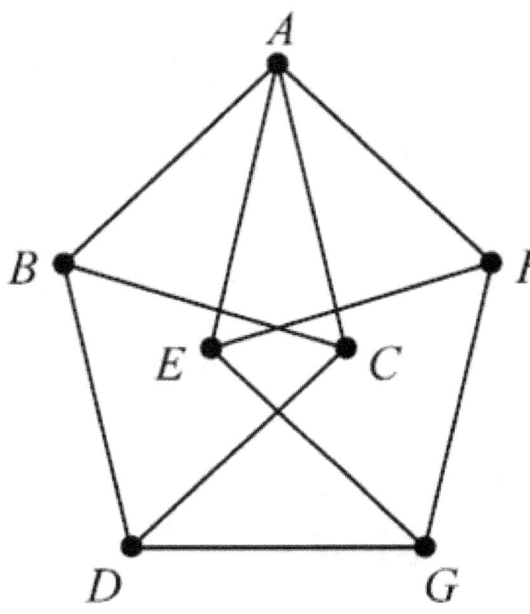

A. 1 **B.** 9 **C.** 11 **D.** 10

Q.46 Which of the sectors below – A, B, C or D – should fill the empty sector in the circle?

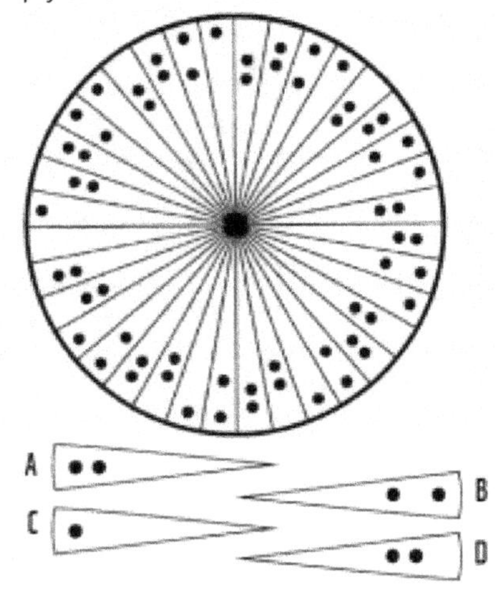

A. A **B.** B **C.** C **D.** D

Q.47 A sheet of paper is folded in half and cuts made into it. The paper is then unfolded to reveal thisshape. Which of the figures – A. B. C or D – shows the original cuts?

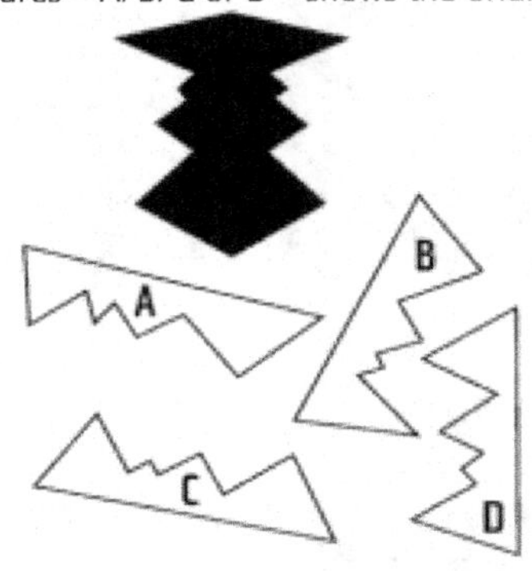

A. A **B.** B **C.** C **D.** D

Q.48 Which design is the odd one out?

A. 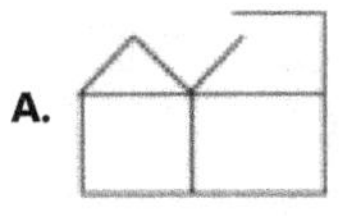

B. 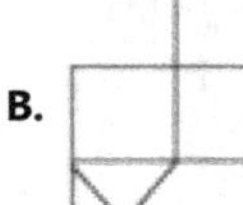

C. 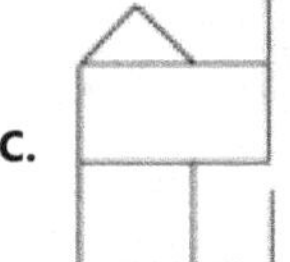

D. 

Q.49 Complete the series

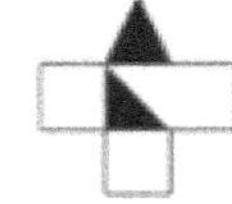   

A. 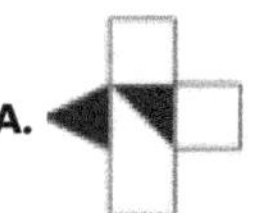

B. 

C. 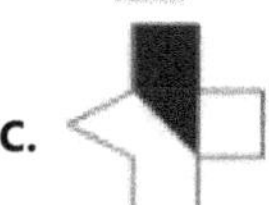 

D. 

Q.50 Complete the series

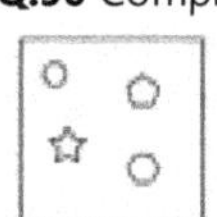 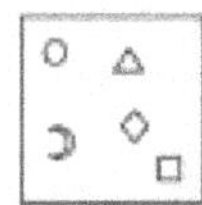  

A. 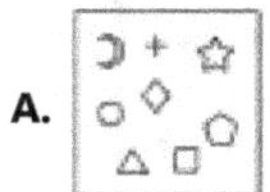

B. 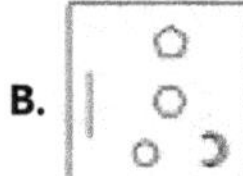

C. 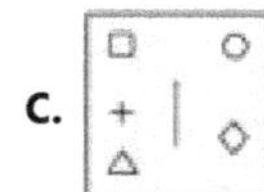

D. 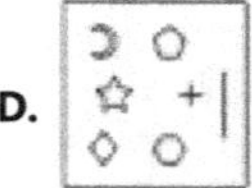

Q.51 Complete the series

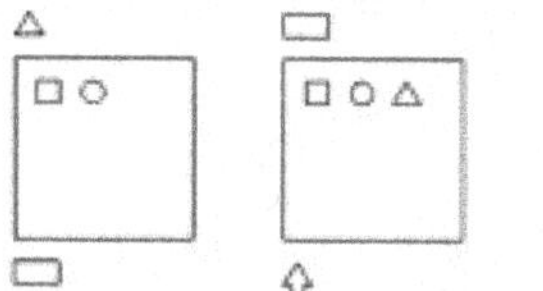

A. 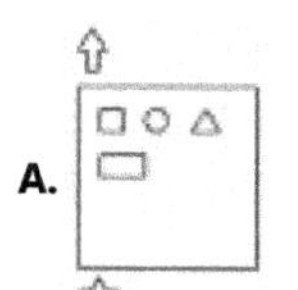 B. 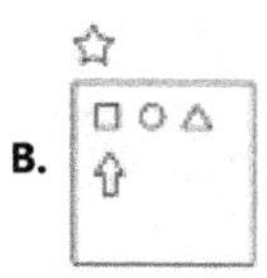 C. 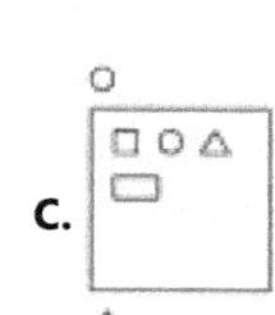 D. 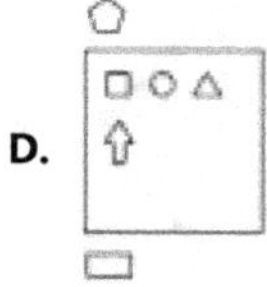

Q.52 Identify the quality in common.

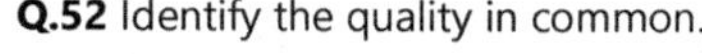
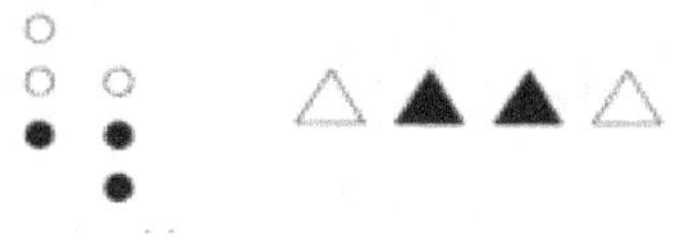

A. 

B. 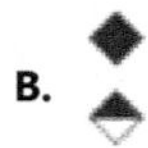

C. 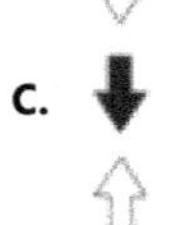

D. 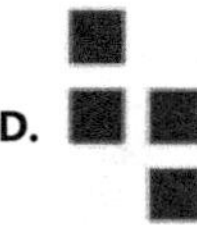

Q.53 Complete the series

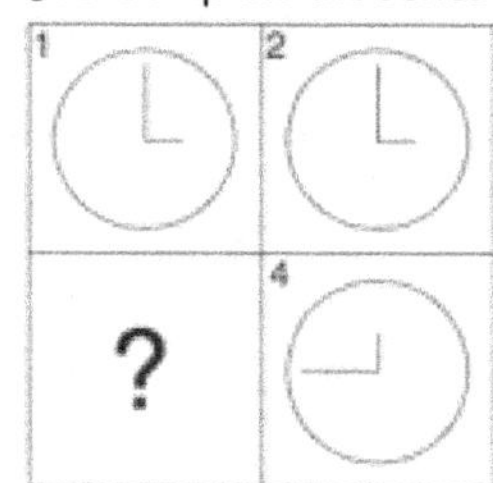

A. 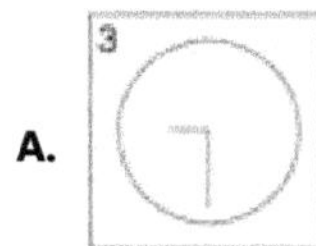

B. 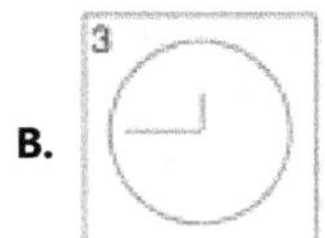

C. 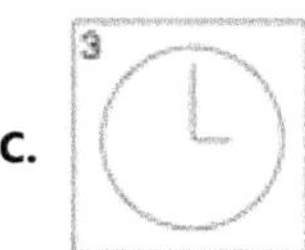

D. 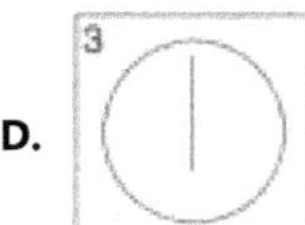

Q.54 Complete the series

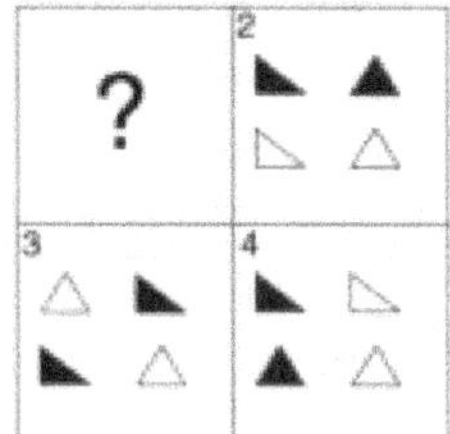

A. 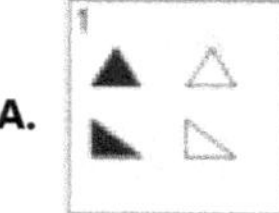

B. 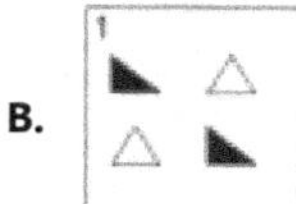

C. 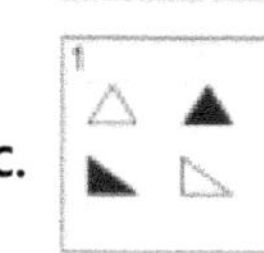

D. 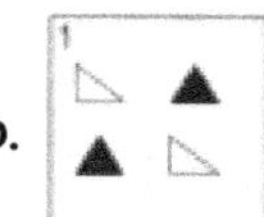

Q.55 The below shown Logo is used for:

A. National Indian child welfare
B. National Literacy mission
C. Children medical foundtion
D. NABARD

Q.56 There are eight rules which when applied to the sequence will transform it to one of the four options shown below. Identify the correct option.

- ■ Cancel all shading
- ○ Shade the second and last shapes
- ● Exchange the second and fourth shapes
- □ Reverse the sequence of shapes
- ⬇ Change all circles to shaded squares
- ⇩ Replace all shaded shapes with unshaded triangles (with the apex at the top)
- ▲ Replace the first shape with a shaded triangle with its apex pointing downwards
- △ Change the middle shape to an unshaded circle

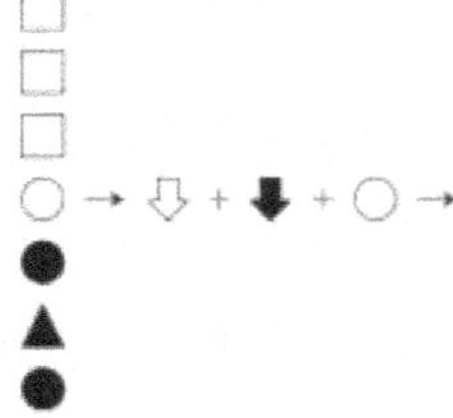

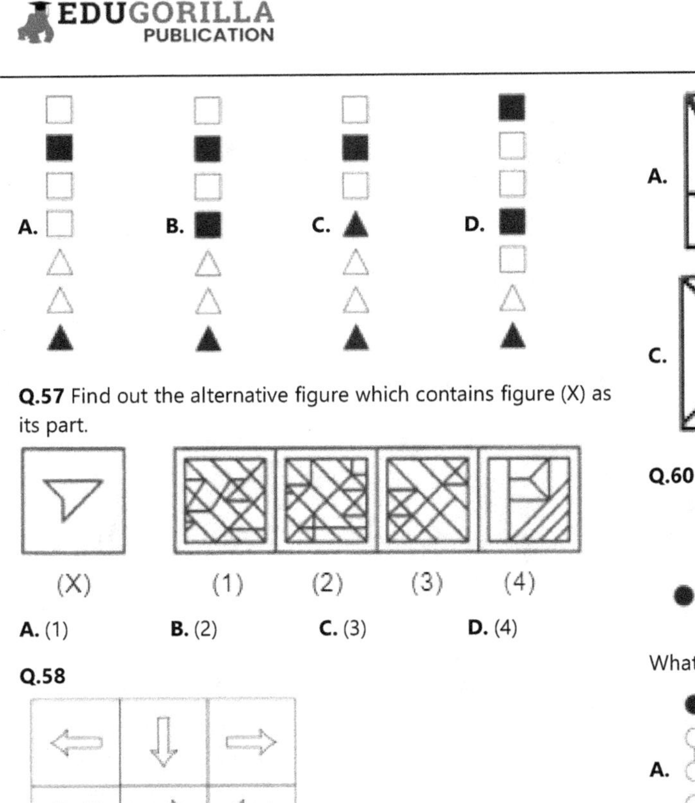

Q.57 Find out the alternative figure which contains figure (X) as its part.

(X) (1) (2) (3) (4)

A. (1) **B.** (2) **C.** (3) **D.** (4)

Q.58

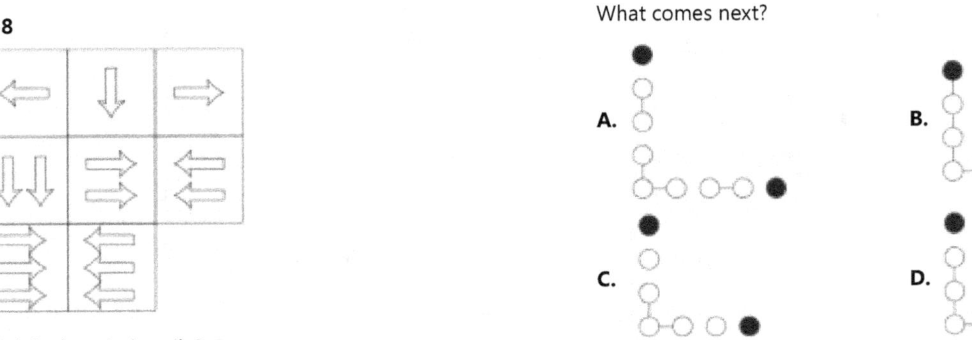

Which is the missing tile?

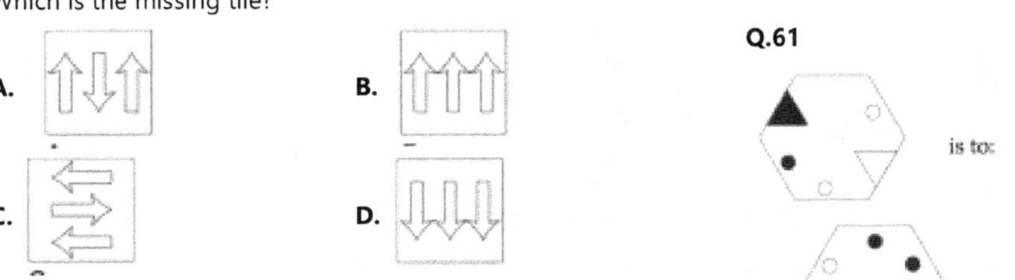

Q.59 Which answer figure will complete the pattern in the following question figure?

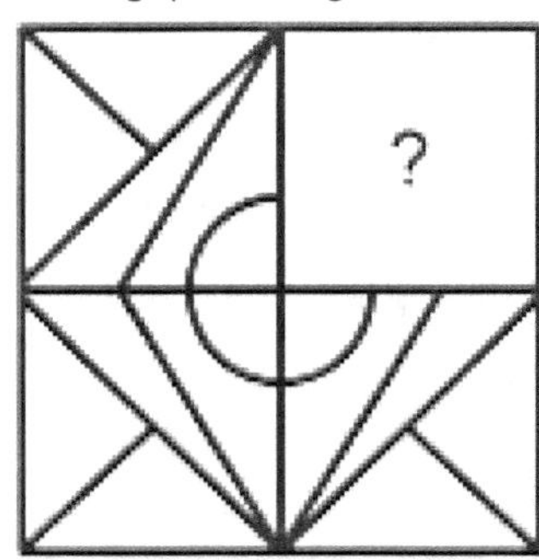

A. **B.** **C.** **D.**

Q.60

What comes next?

A. **B.** **C.** **D.**

Q.61

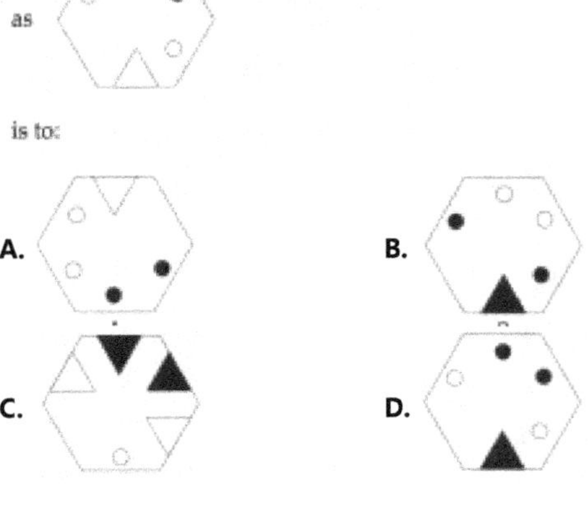

A. **B.** **C.** **D.**

Q.62 Which is the missina section?

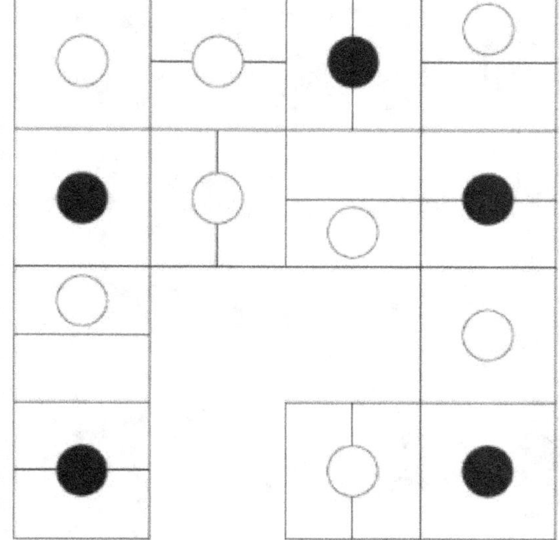

A.

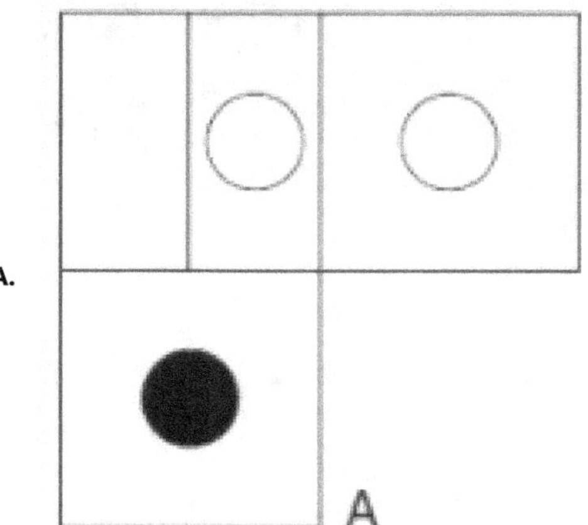

B.

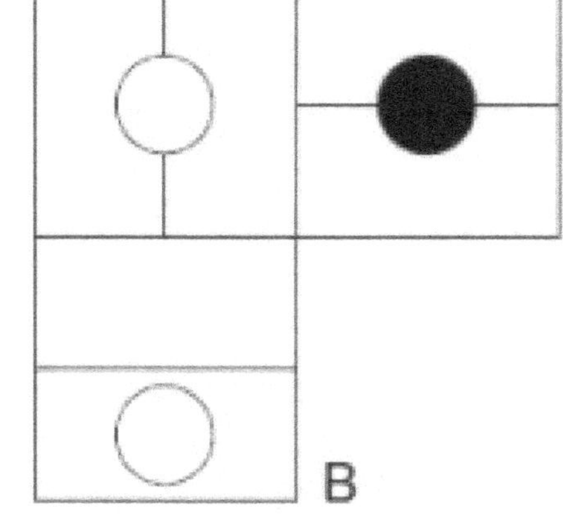

C.

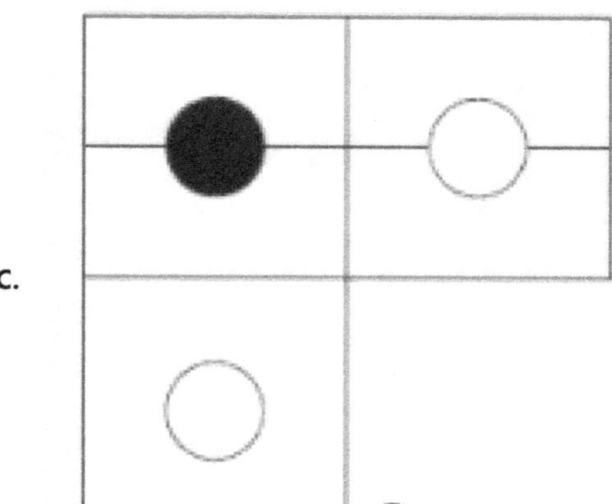

D.

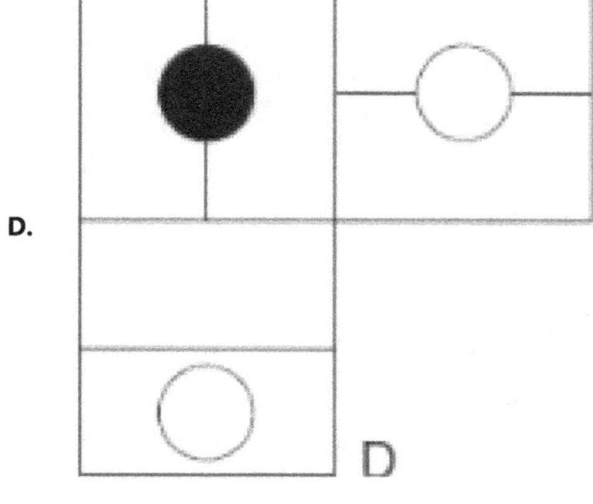

Q.63

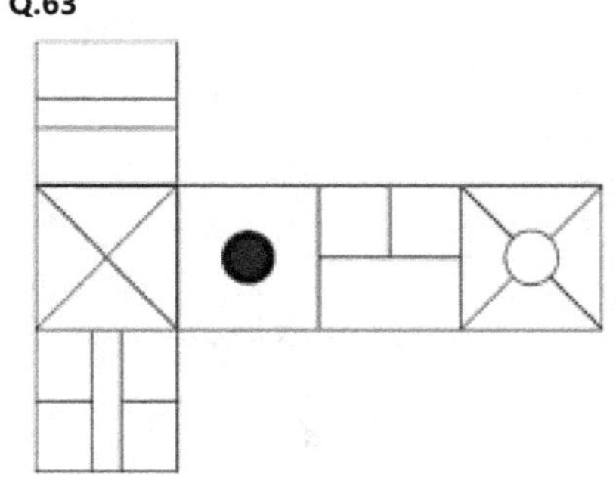

When the above is folded to form a cube, which is the only one of the following that can be produced?

A.

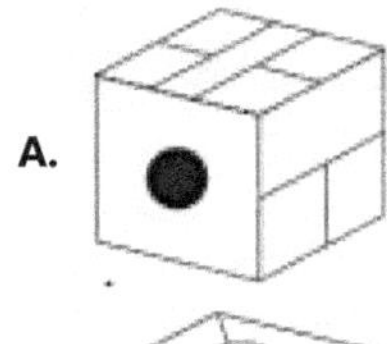

B.

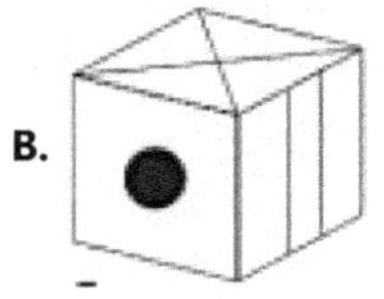

C.

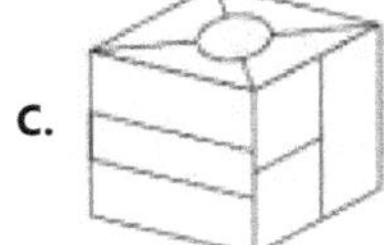

D.

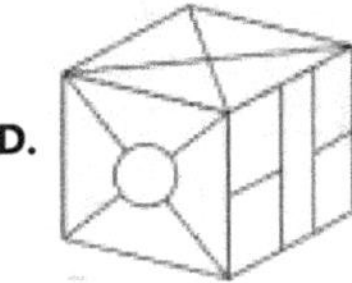

Q.64

A. 

B. 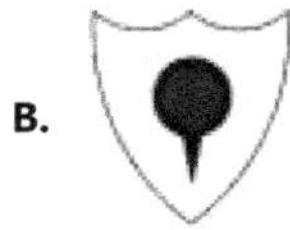

C. 

D. 

Q.65 Which is the missing segment?

A. 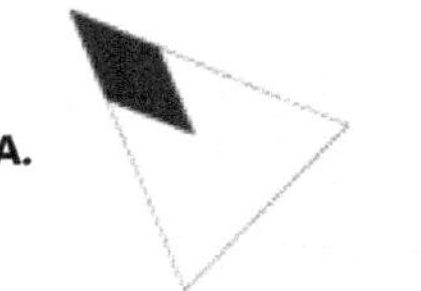

B. 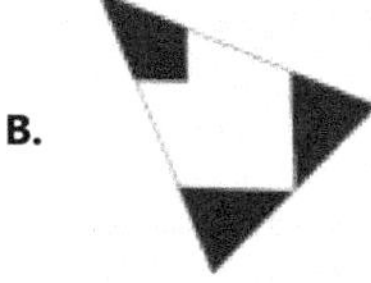

C. 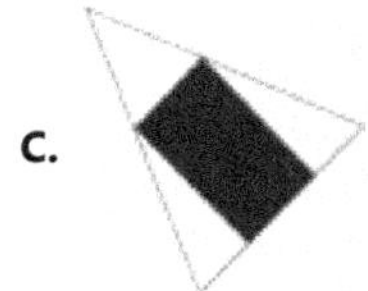

D. 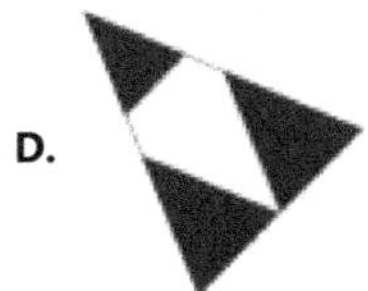

Q.66 A boat can travel with a speed of $13\ km/hr$ in still water. If the speed of the stream is $4\ km/hr$, find the time taken by the boat to go $68\ km$ downstream.

A. 2 hours **B.** 3 hours **C.** 4 hours **D.** 5 hours

Q.67 A boat can travel with a speed of 22 km/hr in still water. If the speed of the stream is 5 km/hr, find the time taken by the boat to go 54 km downstream?

A. 3 hr **B.** 5 hr **C.** 4 hr **D.** 2 hr

Q.68 Identify the famous painter who created the painting shown below:

A. Rabindranath Tagore
B. Manjit Bava
C. Raja Ravi Verma
D. Amrita Sher Gil

// Smart Answer Sheet //

Correct Indicates percentage of students who answered questions correctly.

Skipped Indicates percentage of students who skipped questions.

Q.	Ans.	Correct	Skipped
1	62	14.84 %	10.69 %
2	1	59.93 %	15.01 %
3	5	49.7 %	18.39 %
4	71	35.33 %	16.46 %
5	11449	26.15 %	21.77 %
6	8	36.6 %	27.22 %
7	#	26.9 %	23.65 %
8	15	40.94 %	23.38 %
9	143	24.0 %	27.17 %
10	112	30.62 %	27.02 %
11	28	8.01 %	27.18 %
12	#	10.07 %	27.08 %
13	#	22.13 %	26.98 %
14	#	23.2 %	24.52 %
15	#	23.13 %	25.78 %
16	#	28.26 %	32.19 %
17	94	21.04 %	28.27 %
18	#	35.43 %	29.56 %
19	B, A, D, C	44.62 %	28.43 %
20	B, D, C	32.31 %	28.09 %
21	A	39.98 %	34.51 %
22	B, D	26.33 %	32.73 %
23	C	13.33 %	32.9 %
24	A	13.05 %	36.9 %
25	C	24.37 %	33.62 %
26	B, A, D	32.11 %	36.2 %
27	B, A, D	38.54 %	33.47 %
28	A	37.27 %	33.5 %
29	C	43.67 %	31.44 %
30	B	18.51 %	33.97 %
31	B	43.45 %	33.32 %
32	A	57.2 %	30.19 %
33	A	49.28 %	32.28 %
34	C	25.88 %	32.18 %
35	B, A, C	33.18 %	35.33 %
36	B, D, C	29.18 %	36.65 %
37	C	44.81 %	25.31 %
38	B	36.97 %	25.04 %
39	D	48.88 %	28.69 %
40	C	46.55 %	25.96 %
41	C	37.69 %	28.76 %
42	D	28.54 %	29.25 %
43	C	32.8 %	30.38 %
44	C	54.47 %	29.95 %
45	C	34.86 %	29.68 %
46	B	57.05 %	30.12 %
47	B	35.33 %	31.34 %
48	B	31.86 %	30.67 %
49	C	29.58 %	32.21 %
50	D	35.46 %	34.66 %
51	A	49.98 %	32.7 %
52	A	38.81 %	33.57 %
53	A	34.94 %	31.46 %
54	D	14.34 %	35.49 %
55	A	32.13 %	36.55 %
56	B	22.41 %	38.56 %
57	A	30.02 %	33.16 %
58	D	50.07 %	31.64 %
59	A	44.32 %	36.8 %
60	D	43.8 %	33.35 %
61	B	49.28 %	33.1 %
62	D	19.58 %	37.99 %
63	D	23.1 %	36.16 %
64	D	52.01 %	34.49 %
65	D	38.88 %	33.5 %
66	C	34.54 %	36.06 %
67	D	35.46 %	33.77 %
68	C	44.84 %	34.69 %

#

Q.	Answer
7	South
12	PORSCHE
13	1.2
14	FPQR
15	TUESDAY

16	102
18	13

Performance Analysis	
Avg. Score (%)	**31.67%**
Toppers Score (%)	**115.0%**
Your Score	

//Hints and Solutions//

1. According to the alphabetical positions of the letters, the pattern followed here is that the sum of position values of all the terms – Number of terms = Code

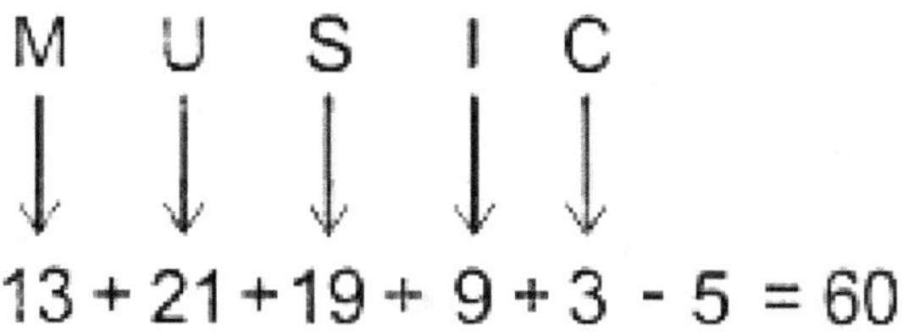

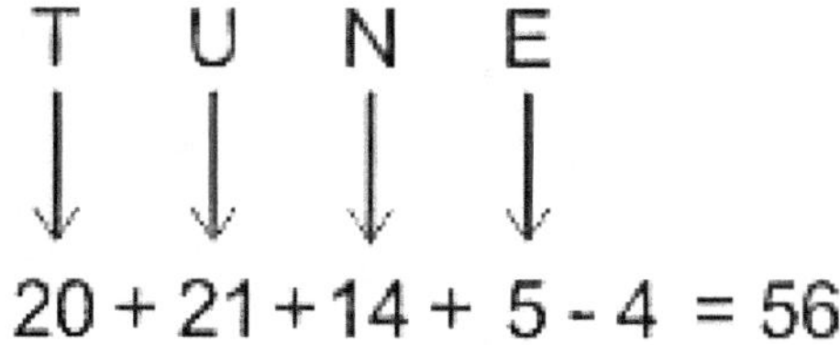

Similarly,

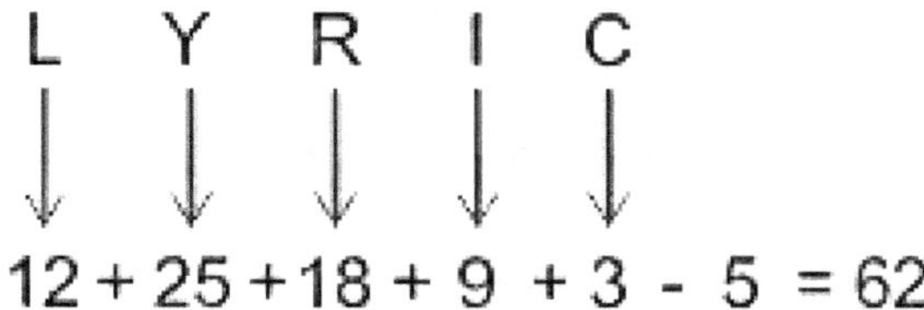

Hence, the correct answer is '62'.

2. The correct unfolded pattern will be figure (1).

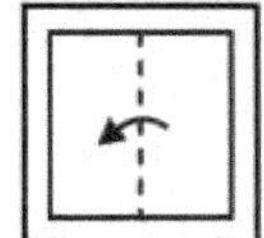 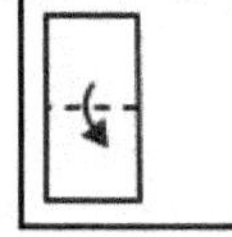 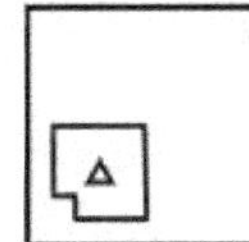 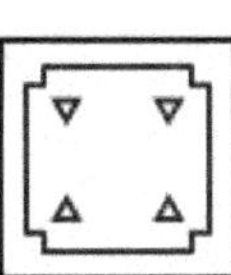

Hence, the correct answer is (1).

3. According to the given information, we get the following figure,

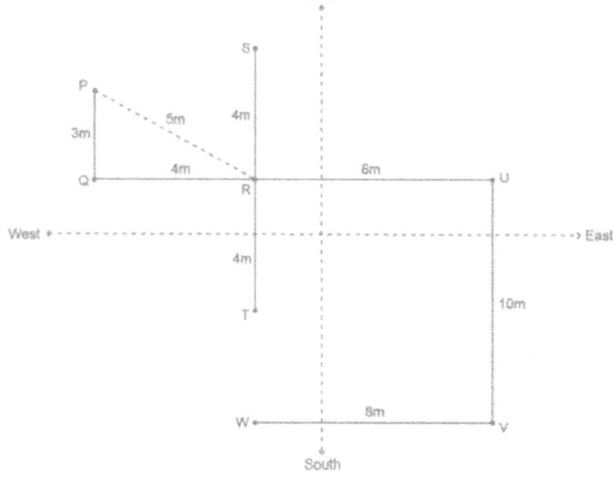

By using Pythagoras theorem,

Shortest distance between P and $R = \sqrt{(3^2 + 4^2)}$

$= \sqrt{(9 + 16)}$

$= \sqrt{25}$

$= 5$

Hence, the correct answer is $5\ m$.

4. As,

$2 \times 3 \times 1 \times 5 + 1 = 30 + 1 = 31$

$2 \times 4 \times 6 \times 3 + 1 = 144 + 1 = 145$

Similarly,

$1 \times 2 \times 7 \times 5 + 1 = 70 + 1 = 71$

71 will be the number that can be placed at the sign of the question mark (?).

Hence, the correct answer is 71.

5. From the question we can see that,

$(101)^2 = 10201$

The next term is obtained on squaring the first term.

Similarly,

$(107)^2 = 11449$

Hence, the correct answer is 11449.

6.

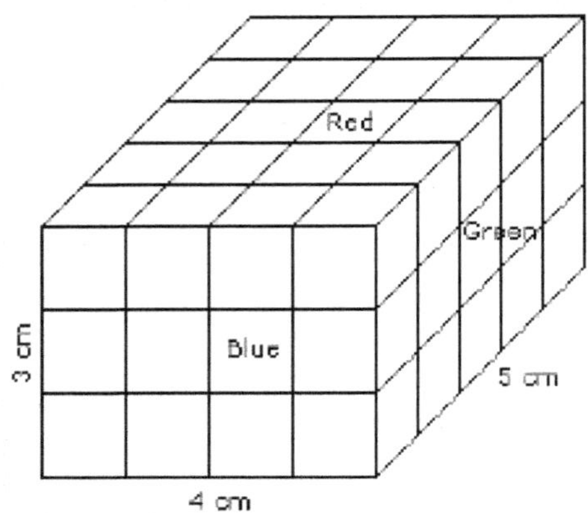

Such cubes are related to the corners of the cuboid and in the cuboid there are 8 corners. Hence, the required number of small cubes is 8.

7. According to the given information, we can draw the following diagram,

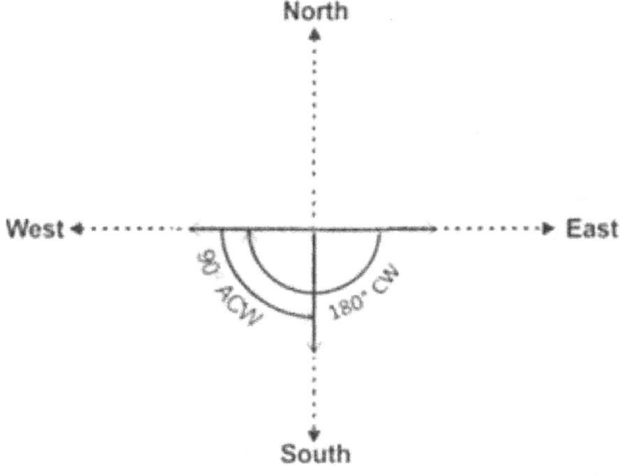

Therefore Kirti is facing in the South direction.

8. On the bottom surface, there are a total of 9 cubes (3×3).

On the middle surface, there are 5 cubes.

On the top surface there is only 1 cube.

Total number of cubes in the figure = $9 + 5 + 1$

= 15

Hence, the correct answer is 15.

9. The pattern here is,

$48 = 7^2 - 1$

Similarly,

$143 = 12^2 - 1$

Hence, the correct answer is 143.

10. As,

16:56=(2/7)

Similarly,

32:112=(2/7)

Hence, the correct answer is 112.

11. Let us mark the unshaded portions by I, II, III, and IV as shown in the figure.

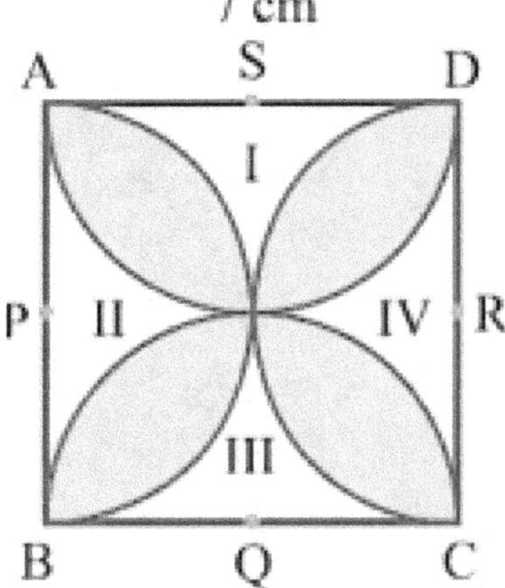

Let P, Q, R and S be the midpoints of AB, BC, CD and DA respectively.

Side of the square, $a = 7\ cm$

Radius of the semicircle, $r = \frac{7}{2}\ cm$

Area of I $+$ Area of III, $=$ Area of a square $ABCD$ $-$ Area of two semicircles with centres P and R

$= a^2 - 2 \times \frac{1}{2} \times \pi r^2$

$= 7 \times 7 - 2 \times \frac{1}{2} \times \frac{22}{7} \times \frac{7}{2} \times \frac{7}{2}$

$\therefore$ Area of I $+$ Area of III $= \left(49 - \frac{77}{2}\right) cm^2 = \frac{21}{2}\ cm^2$

Similarly, we have,

Area of II $+$ Area of IV $= \left(49 - \frac{77}{2}\right) cm^2 = \frac{21}{2}\ cm^2$

Area of the shaded portions $=$ Area of the square $ABCD -$ (Area of I $+$ Area of II $+$ Area of III $+$ Area of IV)

$= 49 - \left(\frac{21}{2} + \frac{21}{2}\right)$

$= 49 - 21$

$= 28\ cm^2$

Hence, the correct Answer is $28\ cm^2$.

12. The car company shown in this picture is PORSCHE.

PORSCHE is a German automobile manufacturer specializing in high-performance sports cars, SUVs and sedans, headquartered in Stuttgart, Baden-Württemberg, Germany. The company is owned by Volkswagen AG, a controlling stake of which is owned by Porsche Automobil Holding SE.

Hence, the correct answer is PORSCHE.

13. There are 52 playing cards, in which there are 4 aces.

If all aces are removed then the remaining cards are $48.$

According to the question,

52 cards measure $1.3\ cm.$

Then using the unitary method,

48 cards measure $= \frac{1.3}{52} \times 48 = 1.2\ cm$

Hence, the correct answer is $1.2.$

14. $T \overset{+2}{\rightarrow} V$

$R \overset{+2}{\rightarrow} T$

$A \overset{+2}{\rightarrow} C$

$C \overset{+2}{\rightarrow} E$

$K \overset{+2}{\rightarrow} M$

⇒TRACK→MECTV

Similarly

$P \overset{+2}{\rightarrow} R$

$O \overset{+2}{\rightarrow} Q$

$N \overset{+2}{\rightarrow} P$

$D \overset{+2}{\rightarrow} F$

POND → FPQR

Hence, the correct answer is FPQR.

15. 4th July = Tuesday (Given)

8th July = Saturday

29th July = Saturday

1st August = Tuesday

15th August = Tuesday

Anika's birthday will be on Tuesday.

Hence, the correct answer is TUESDAY.

16. The pattern here is:

6+9=15

9+15=24

15+24=39

24+39=63

39+63=102

Hence, the missing number is 102.

17. The pattern followed here is:

Column 1: $3^2 + 5^2 + 1^2 = 9 + 25 + 1 \rightarrow 35$

Column 2: $4^2 + 7^2 + 2^2 = 16 + 49 + 4 \rightarrow 69$

Similarly,

Column 3: $6^2 + 3^2 + 7^2 = 36 + 9 + 49 \rightarrow 94$

Hence, the correct answer is 94.

18. The number of squares in the above figure can be counted as:

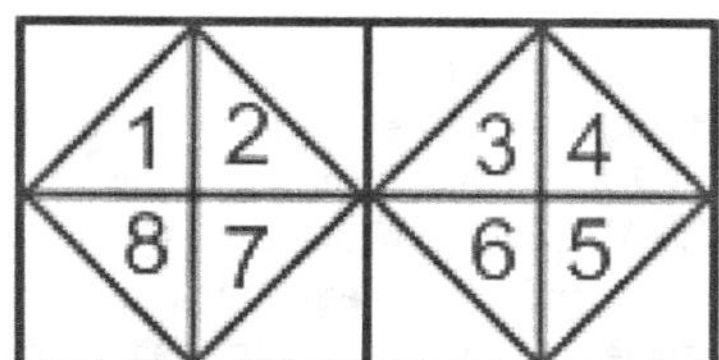

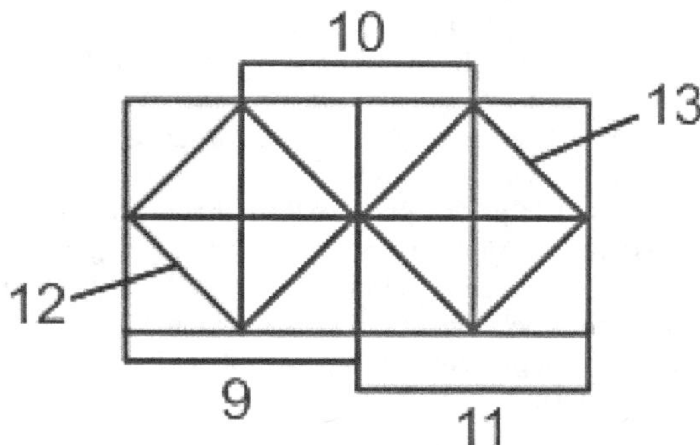

Hence, the correct answer is 13.

19. All the statements written about Gautam Buddha are true.

Hence, the correct options are A, B, C, D.

20. Visual, Auditory and Kinesthetic are the common "Perceptual channels".

Visual represents - what is seen like printed materials, fascial expressions, body language.

Auditory relates to spoken words, sounds,(what is heard and said), etc.

Kinesthetics relates to Emotions, actions, movement, taste, smell ...... (something that is felt), etc.

Hence, the correct option is (B, C, D).

21. Argon is a commonly used gas, used to fill incandescent light bulbs. It increases the bulb life by preventing the tungsten filament from deteriorating too quickly. Other gases such as helium, neon nitrogen and krypton are also used in lightning. Inert gases are reactive towards the burning filament of the bulb. Therefore we have to use either inert gases like Argon or inactive nitrogen.

Hence, the correct option is (A).

22. The figures show four different schematics of two flexible strings. If all the ends are pulled tight, Then the figures B and D will form a knot.

Hence, the correct options are (B) and (D).

23. Clearly, if the income of farmers is not adequate, they cannot be brought under the net of taxation as per rules governing the Income Tax Act. So, I is not strong. Besides, a major part of the population is dependent on agriculture and such a large section, if taxed even with certain concessions, would draw in huge funds, into the government coffers. Also, many big landlords with substantially high incomes from agriculture are taking undue advantage of this benefit. So, both arguments II and III hold strong.

24. In paragraph 3, we learn that fleas have little spines that normally lie flat, but "if anything (likefingers or a self-grooming pet) tries to pull a flea off through the hair coat, these spines will extendand stick to the fur like Velcro." From this we can understand that if a flea is threatened bysomething trying to remove it, it will extend its spines in order to stick to the fur. This means that(A) is correct. In paragraph 4, we learn that "a flea can jump seven inches, or 150 times its ownlength." This means that fleas are able to jump higher in proportion to their body sizes thanhumans are, but fleas can only jump 7 inches. A human can jump higher than 7 inches, so (B) is incorrect. There is no reference in the passage to humans consuming resilin, which makes (C)incorrect. In paragraph 5, we learn that resilin "helps catapult fleas into the air as they jump, similarto the way a rubber band provides momentum to a slingshot." This means the resilin found in fleasjoints helps them spring in a way similar to rubber bands, but the passage does not state thatrubber bands contain resilin. Therefore (D) is incorrect.

25. It can be inferred from the statement that people also like to see a product before buying. So, I isnot implicit. Also, the statement is just an attempt to arouse the people to come and see the shop.So, both II and III are implicit.

26. The artistic career of Cezanne panned more than forty years, from roughly 1860 to 1906. A prolific artist, he produced more than 900 oil paintings and 400 water colors .In the following figure a,b,d is also their paintings .

27. In the figure a,b,d is made by Abanindra nath Tagore .He was the principal artist and creator of the "Indian Society of Oriental Art".

28. Following figure is a Kalamkari painting. Kalamkari is a type of hand-painted or block-printed cotton textile, produced in Indian states of Andhra Pradesh and Telangana. Only natural dyes are used in Kalamkari and it involves twenty three steps.

29.

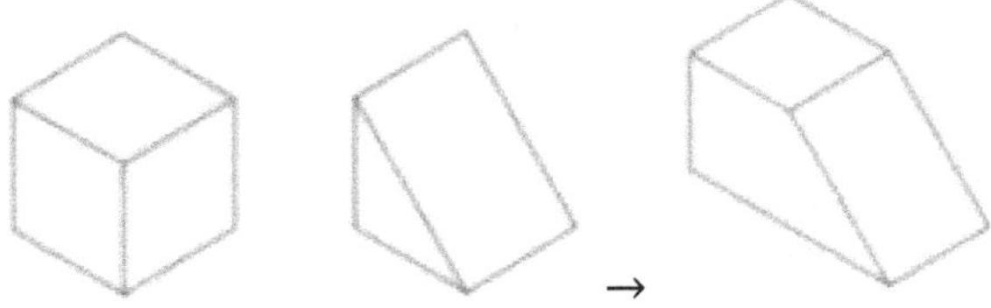

In a) the triangular shape has been deformed, and in b) and d) the cube has been deformed.

So Option c will be right choice.

30. Here, the pattern is,

$$86 = (8 \times 6) + (8 + 6) = 48 + 14 = 62$$

Similarly,

$$49 = (4 \times 9) + (4 + 9) = 36 + 13 = 49$$

Thus, 49 is related to 49.

Hence, the correct option is (B).

31.

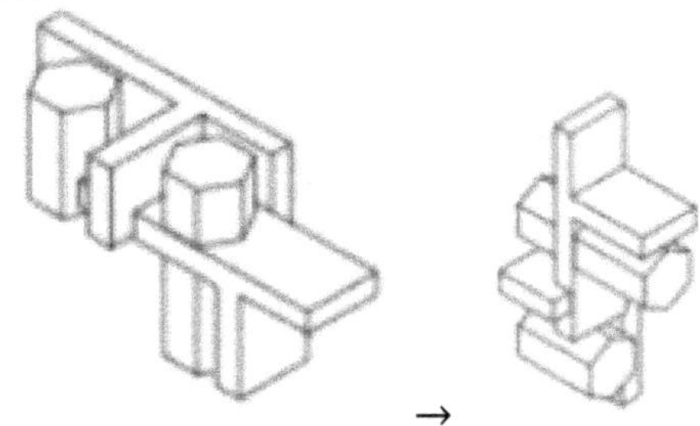

In A) and C) the two prisms have been inverted. But b is the same as the question shape.

32.

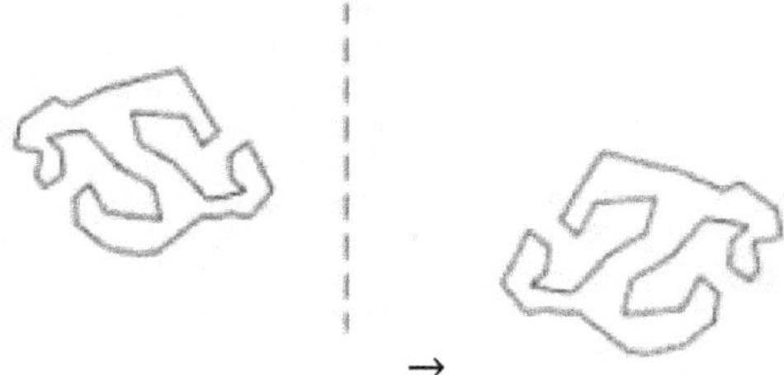

b) has been reflected vertically, and c) has been rotated.

33. Given,

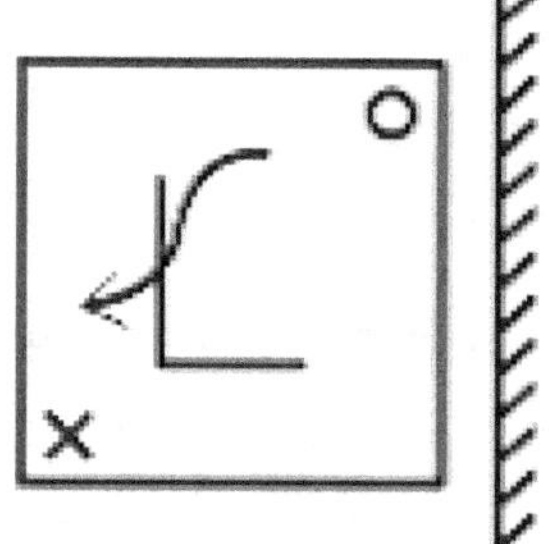

In the mirror image, the top and bottom part of the figure remains the same, and the left and right part of the figure interchange.

Therefore,

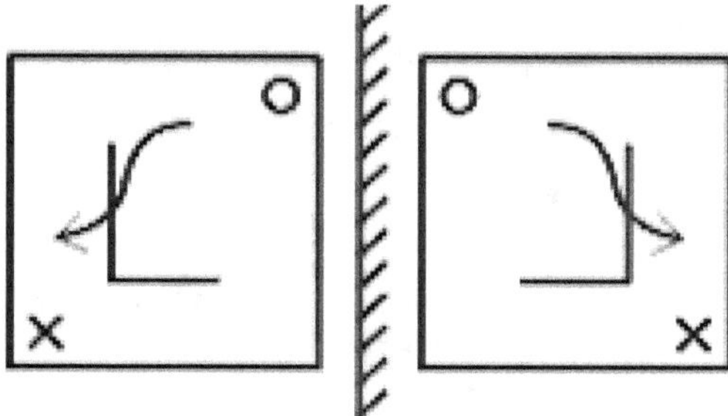

Therefore, the mirror image is,

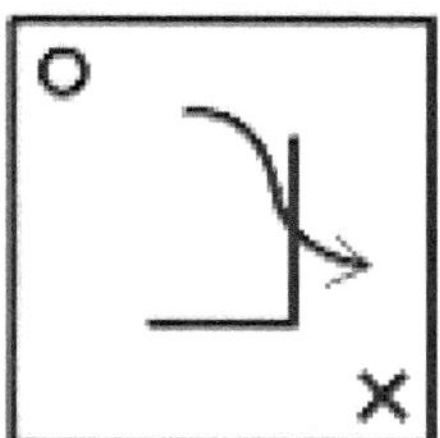

Hence, the correct option is (A).

34.

c

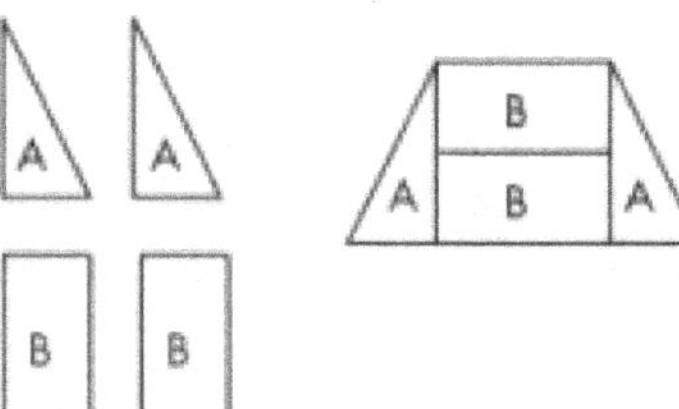

35.

→

Option a,b,c can be made using all 7 pieces.

36. The following are some of the greatest designers of all time-

Pierre Cardin - Pierre Cardin is an Italian fashion designer naturalized French. He is known for his avant-garde style and his Space Age designs

Jonathan Ive - Sir Jonathan Paul "Jony" Ive, KBE, HonFREng, RDI is a British industrial, product and architectural designer who is the former Chief Design Officer of Apple Inc., and the serving Chancellor of the Royal College of Art in London.

Dieter Ram - Dieter Rams is a German industrial designer and retired academic closely associated with the consumer products company Braun, the furniture company Vitsœ, and the functionalist school of industrial design.

37. Homi Jehangir Bhabha (30 October 1909 – 24 January 1966) was an Indian nuclear physicist, founding director, and professor of physics at the Tata Institute of Fundamental Research (TIFR). Colloquially known as "father of the Indian nuclear programme",Bhabha was also the founding director of the Atomic Energy Establishment, Trombay (AEET) which is now named the Bhabha Atomic Research Centre in his honour. TIFR and AEET were the cornerstone of Indian development of nuclear weapons which Bhabha also supervised as director.

Bhabha was awarded the Adams Prize (1942) and Padma Bhushan (1954). He was also nominated for the Nobel Prize for Physics in 1951 and 1953–1956.

38.

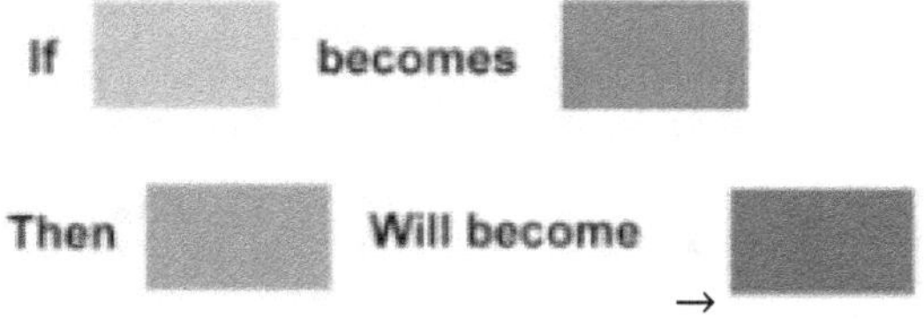

→

39. Ahmedabad lies in Gujarat.

Gujarat lies in India.

The correct Venn diagram representation is,

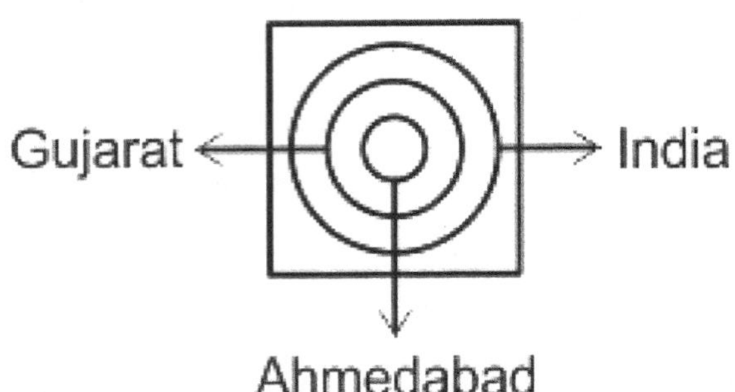

Hence, the correct option is (D).

40. Ostrich and Albatross are birds.

Thus, the following Venn diagram best describes this relationship:

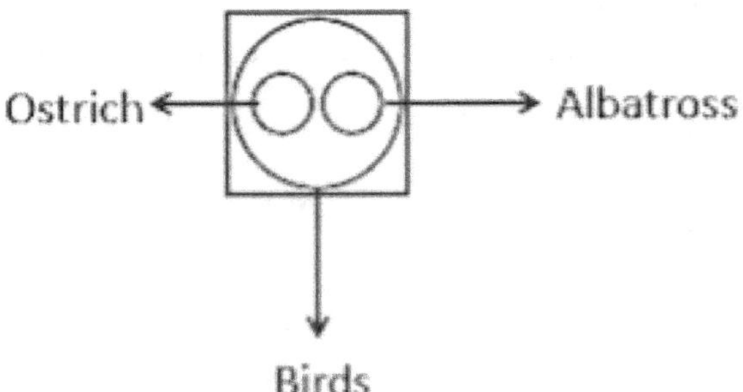

Hence, the correct option is (C).

41. Crayon, Oil, Pastel, and Watercolor art techniques sequence are used to make these paintings.

Hence, the correct option is (C).

42. The EOS 5DS R camera features Canon's newest full-frame CMOS sensor. At 50.6 Megapixels, it's the highest resolution sensor in the history of EOS.

43.

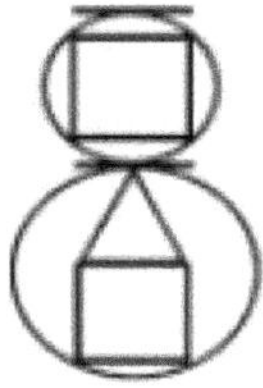

A, B and D all contain two circles, two squares, two straight lines and two triangles. In C there isonly one triangle.

44.

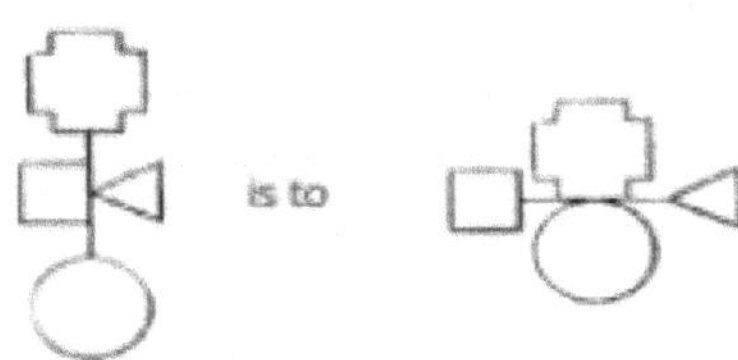

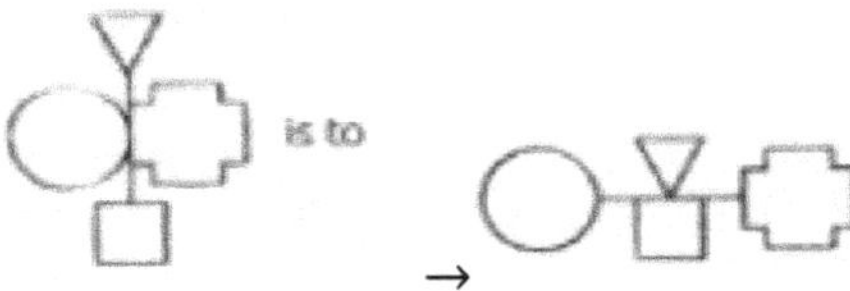

→

The figures are transposed in the same way as in the example at the top.

45. There are 11 triangles are possible in the picture shown below.

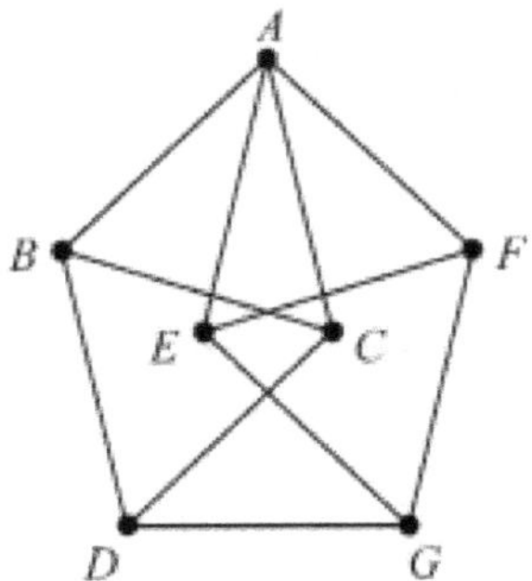

46. The position of the spots is repeated in every 4th sector.So figure (b) fill the empty sector in the circle.

47.

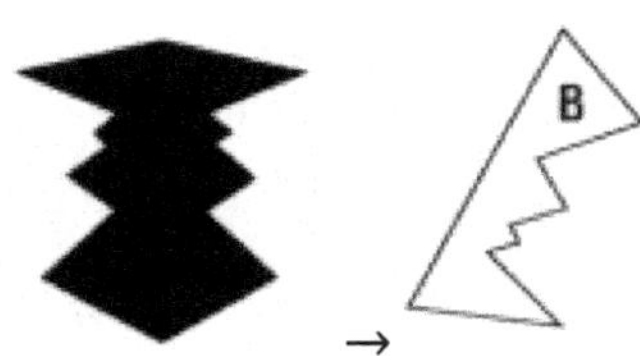

→

Following figure shows the original cuts.

48. Other than in (B), the designs are made up of a square, a triangle, a rectangle, a right angle, and a line. In (B), there are two squares but no rectangle.

Hence, the correct option is (B).

49. The shape is rotating anticlockwise, but the shaded area remains at the top and theshaded segment of the centre of the shape is alternating.

50. The type of shapes is irrelevant to the question, and the number of shapes is increased by one each step of the series.

51. At each step the shape at the top of the previous diagram moves into the box and theshape at the bottom takes its place.

52. Half the number of shapes making up the question shapes are shaded, as is the case in suggested answer A

53. The clock shape (displaying 3 o'clock) is first rotated by 360 degrees, then by 180 degrees, and finally by 90 degrees.

On applying this logic, we have the first option figure -

in place of ?

Hence, the correct option is (A).

54. The series of shapes is made from right-angled and equilateral triangles, and the shading follows the sequence one right-angled triangle and one equilateral triangle (box 2), two right-angled triangles (box 3), one right-angled triangle and one equilateral triangle (box 4) and then two equilateral triangles (box 1).

55. The National Indian Child Welfare Association (NICWA) evolved from the Northwest Indian Child Welfare Institute, which was developed in 1983 in response to the need for trained Indian child welfare workers in both reservation- and urban-based Indian child welfare programs.

56.

57. On looking carefully at the question figure, we find that figure (X) is embedded in figure (1).

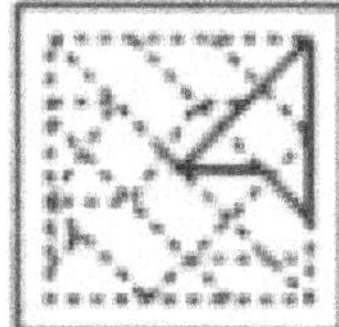

Hence, the correct option is (A).

58. in each line across and down the arrows point in each of three directions left, right and down. The number of arrows increases 1, 2, 3 in each row.

59.

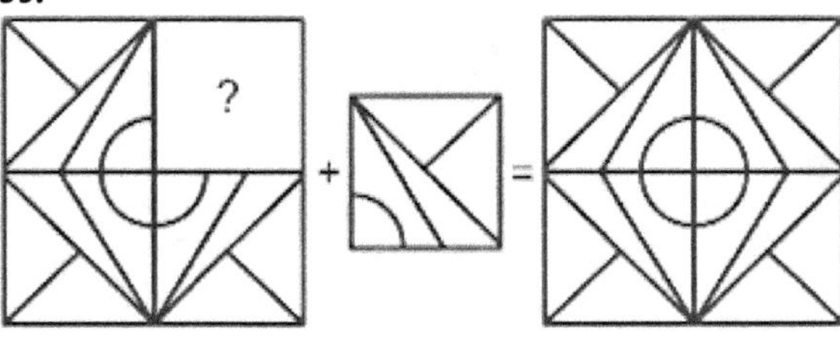

So, the figure in option (A) will complete the pattern.

Hence, the correct option is (A).

60.

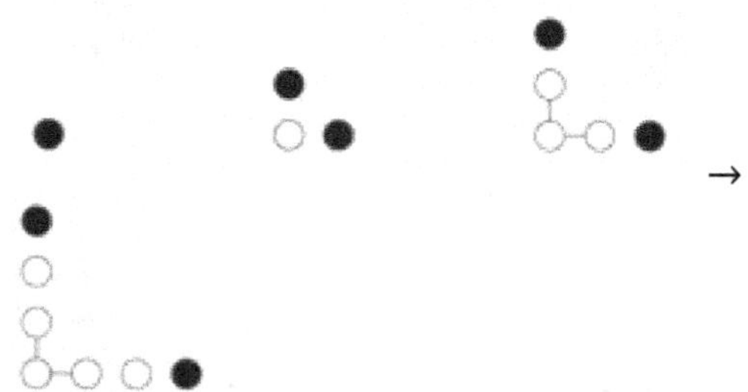

the number of white dots is increased by one each time, both vertically and horizontally, and all white dots are connected

61.

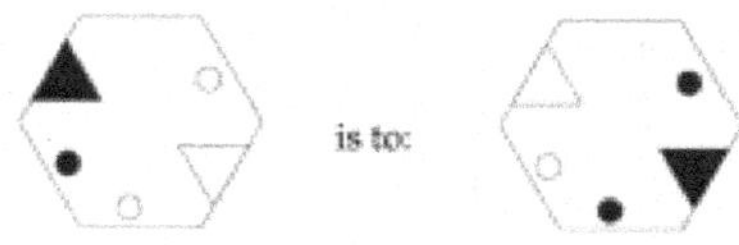

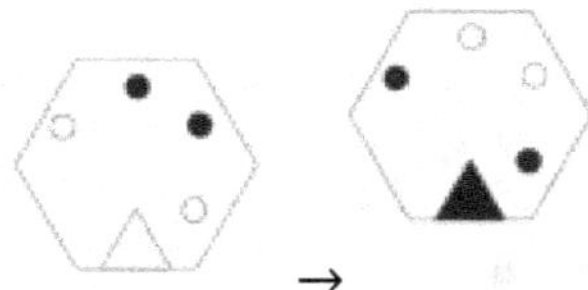

black objects turn to white and vice versa

62. The last two rows of figures repeat the first rows of figures in reverse.

Hence, the correct option is (D).

63.

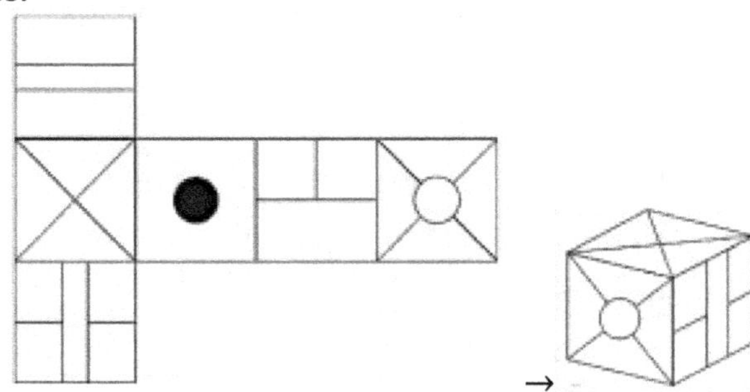

When the above is folded to form a cube, This is the only one of the following that can be produced .

64.

each line across and down contains one each of the three symbols. In each line one symbol is black, and one is upside down

65.

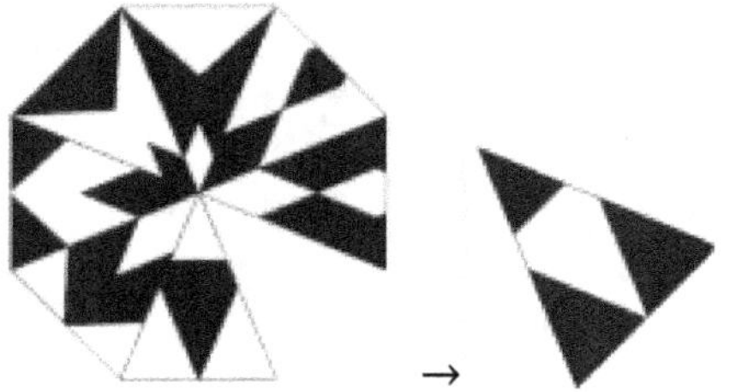

so that looking round the octagon at segments in pairs, there are four identical pairs with black/white reversal

66. Speed downstream $= (13 + 4) km/hr$
$= 17\ km/hr$

Time taken to travel $68\ km$ downstream $= \frac{68}{17}$ hours
$= 4$ hours

Hence, the correct option is (C).

67. Speed of the boat in still water = 22 km/hr

speed of the stream = 5 km/hr

Speed downstream = (22+5) = 27 km/hr

Distance travelled downstream = 54 km

Time taken = $\frac{distance}{speed} = \frac{54}{27}$

= 2 hours

68. Raja Ravi Verma created the painting shown above.

Raja Ravi Verma was born into an aristocratic family in Kerala. He taught himself the intricacies of oil painting and the practices of European naturalism.

'Woman Holding a Fruit' shows Raja Ravi Verma's mastery over the idioms of a new visual language in India. In the naturalistic depiction of the young woman, Raja Ravi Verma lyrically combines eroticism with innocence. His handling of colors – mostly soft pinks and browns – heightens the tenderness evoked in this painting.

Hence, the correct option is (C).

Mock Test 02

Numerical Answer Type (NAT)

Q.1 How many triangles are there in the following figure?

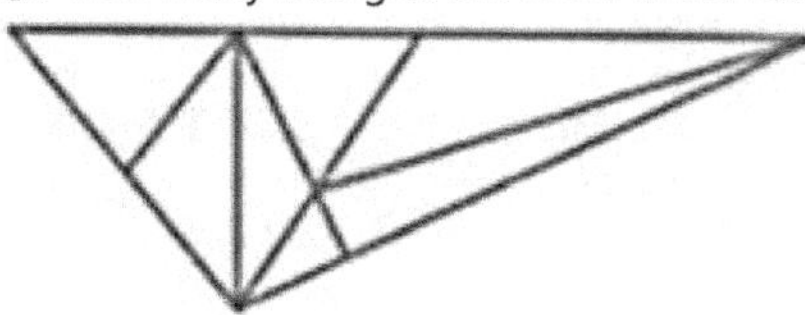

Q.2 Which number should come next in this series:

26,24,20,18,14,……

Q.3 Reena walked from A to B in the East 10 feet. Then she turned to the right and walked 3 feet. Again she turned to the right and walked 14 feet. How far is she from A?

Q.4 How many squares are there here?

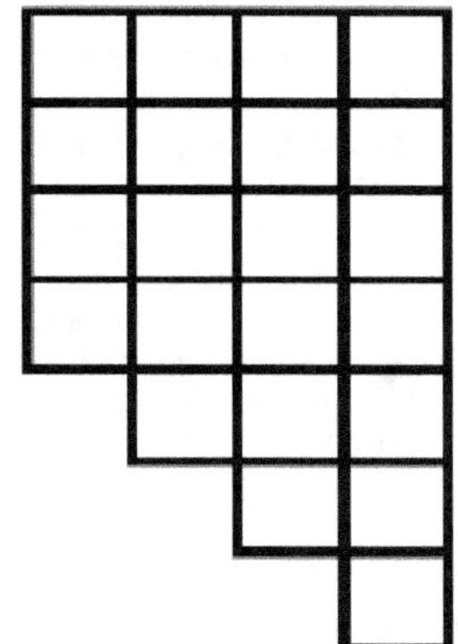

Q.5 Imagine letters are extruded into three-dimensional objects, as shown in the figure on the left (the letter A). If the word PURE (shown on the right) were to be extruded, how many surfaces would it have?

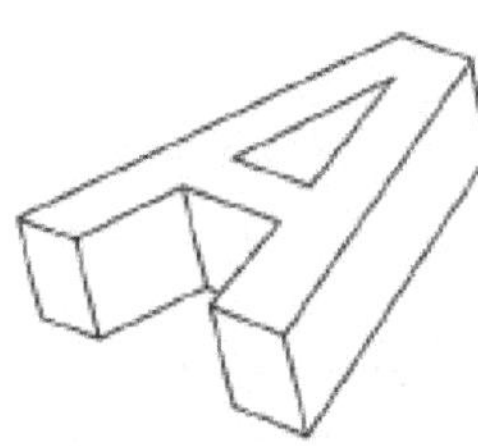

PURE

Q.6 A cuboid shaped wooden block has 4 cm length, 3 cm breadth and 5 cm height. Two sides measuring 5 cm x 4 cm are coloured in red. Two faces measuring 4 cm x 3 cm are coloured in blue. Two faces measuring 5 cm x 3 cm are coloured in green. Now the block is divided into small cubes of side 1 cm each. How many small cubes will have no faces coloured?

Q.7 Three coins are tossed in the air at the same time. What is the chance that at least two of the coins will finish heads up ?

Q.8 What is the minimum number of colours required to fill the spaces in the given diagram without any two adjacent spaces having the same colour?

Q.9 Count the number of cubes in the given figure.

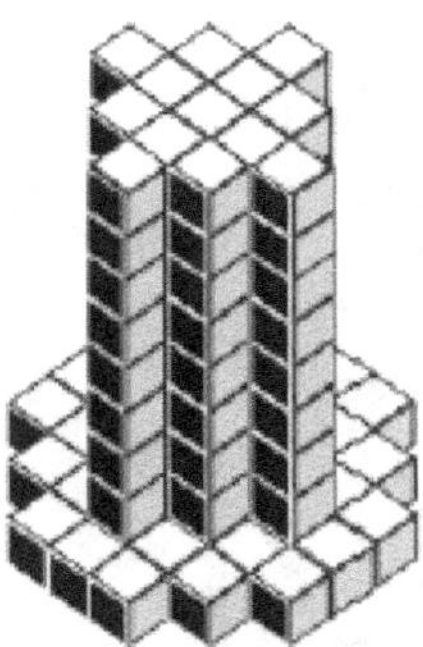

Q.10 If '$' means 'Multiplication'. '@' means 'Addition', '#' means 'Division', and '©' means 'Subtraction', then 35 @ 35 © 35 # 5 $ 7 =?

Q.11 What is the average of first five multiples of 9 ?

Q.12 A man has 53 socks in his drawer: 21 identical blue, 15 identical black and 17 identical red. The lights are fused and he is completely in the dark. How many socks must he take out to make 100 per cent certain he has a pair of black socks?

Q.13 What number should replace the question mark?

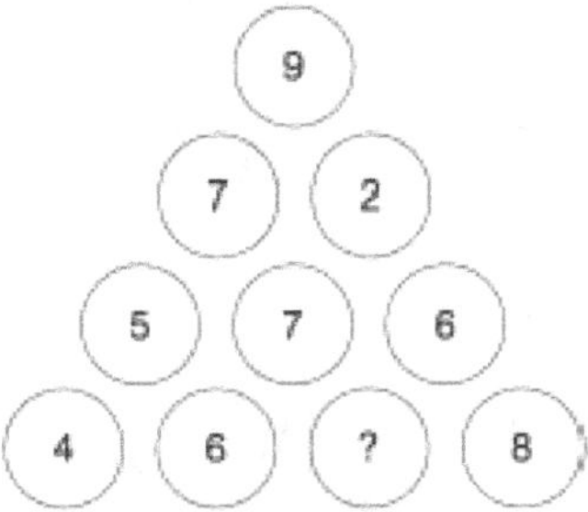

Q.14 You have 59 cubic blocks. What is the minimum number that needs to be taken away in order to construct a solid cube with none left over?

Q.15 Identify the bank whose logo is mentioned below(write the answer in small letters):

Q.16 Identify to which organization the below-mentioned logo belongs(write abbreviation in capital letters)?

Q.17 5 6 3 2 9 7 1 4 2 6 8 7 5 7 1

Delete all the numbers that appear more than once in the above list; then multiply the remaining numbers together. What is the answer?

Q.18 The average weight of A, B and C is 45 kg. If the average weight of A and B be 40 kg and that of B and C be 43 kg, then the weight of B is:

Multiple Select Questions (MSQ)

Q.19 Select all statements about Indian National flag that are true:

A. Indian National flag (also referred as "Tiranga" or "Tricolour") consists three bands of color (saffron at top, White at middle, Green at bottom) and a navy blue color ashok chakra (with 24 spokes) at middle.

B. Tricolour was adopted as Indian national flag on 22 July 1947 by constituent assembly.PingaliVenkayya designed Indian flag.

C. The ratio of width to length of the flag is3:2. All the three-color bands in the flag should be of equal length. The saffron color of the flag stands for courage, Sacrifice and spirit of Renunciation; White stands for Truth and Purity; Green stands for faith and fertility; Ashok chakra represents the wheel of law.

D. There are many laws and protocols, according to which the flag should be used. Some of the laws are- Flag Code of India, 2002; The Emblems and Names (Prevention of Improper Use) Act, 1950; Prevention of Insults to National Honour Act, 1971. Before 2002, Private Citizens were not allowed to display Indian flag except on national days. After a PIL lodged by Naveen Jindal in court, a revision to the 'flag code of India' was introduced in 2002, which suppressed the restriction.

Q.20 Which type of materials is/are recyclable completely or partly

A. Coke bottles, Coke tins

B. Tennis ball, Aquafina water bottle

C. Incandescent light Bulbs, CFL bulbs

D. Foam plates

Q.21 Which of the following statements is/are true?

A. Alan Watts was a well-known British philosopher, writer and speaker, best known for his interpretation of Eastern philosophy for Western audiences.

B. German scientist Christiane Nusslein-Volhard has been one of the leading researchers in the field of genetics and embryology.

C. Aldous Leonard Huxley was a well-known writer, essayist and screenwriter. When he was introduced to meditation, vegetarianism and Vedanta, he became an active member of Vedanta Society of Southern California.

D. Ustad Ali Akbar Khan was one of the most renowned santoor maestros.

Q.22 From the options below, select the Indian author/s writing in English whose works are represented below:

1. A suitable boy
2. An idealist view of life
3. Broken wings
4. Beastly tales
5. The Hindu view of life
6. Search for truth.

A. Dr. S. Radhakrishnan

B. Sarojini Naidu

C. Vikram Seth

D. Rabindranath Tagore

Q.23 Question given below consists of a statement, followed by three arguments numbered I, II and III. You have to decide which of the arguments is a 'strong' argument. Statement: Should the system of LokAdalats and mobile courts be encouraged in India? Arguments:

I. Yes. It helps to grant speedy justice to the masses.

II. Yes. The dispensing of minor cases at this level would reduce the burden on the higher courts.

III. No. These courts are usually partial in justice.

A. Only I and II are strong

B. Only II and III are strong
C. Only I and III are strong
D. All are strong

Q.24 When you imagine the desert, you probably think of a very hot place covered with sand. Although this is a good description for many deserts, Earth's largest desert is actually a very cold place covered with ice: Antarctica.In order for an area to be considered a desert, it must receive very little rainfall. More specifically, it must receive an average of less than ten inches of precipitation—which can be rain, sleet, hail, or snow—on the ground every year. Antarctica, the coldest place on earth, has an average temperature that usually falls below the freezing point. This is evident in the low precipitation statistics recorded for Antarctica. For example, the central part of Antarctica receives an average of less than 2 inches of snow every year. The coastline of Antarctica receives a little bit more—between seven and eight inches a year. Because Antarctica gets so little precipitation every year, it is considered a desert.When precipitation falls in hot deserts, it quickly evaporates back into the atmosphere. The air over Antarctica is too cold to hold water vapor, so there is very little evaporation. Due to this low rate of evaporation, most of the snow that falls to the ground remains there permanently, eventually building up into thick ice sheets. Any snow that does not freeze into ice sheets becomes caught up in the strong winds that constantly blow over Antarctica. These snow-filled winds can make it look as if it is snowing. Even though snowfall is very rare there, blizzards are actually very common on Antarctica. According to the final paragraph, any snow that falls over Antarctica

I. becomes part of the Antarctic ice sheet

II. is blown around by strong winds

III. evaporates back into the atmosphere

A. I only **B.** I and II only
C. II and III only **D.** I, II, and III

Q.25 Question below is given a statement followed by three assumptions numbered I, II and III. You have to consider the statement and the following assumptions and decide which of the assumptions is implicit in the statement. Statement: "X-chocolate is ideal as a gift for someone you love." - An advertisement. Assumptions:

I. People generally give gifts to loved ones.

II. Such advertisements generally influence people.

III. Chocolate can be considered as a gift item.

A. Only I and II are implicit
B. Only II and III are implicit
C. Only I and III are implicit
D. All are implicit

Q.26 Which of these paintings is / are by Roy Lichtenstein

A. 

B. 

C. 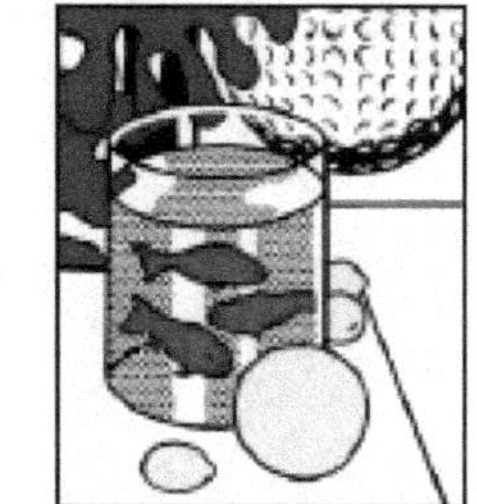

D. 

Q.27 Identify the paintings by Anolie Ela Menon from the following

A. 

B. 

C. 

D. 

Q.28 Identify the Indian traditional Art below

A. Gond **B.** Phad paintings
C. Mata ni pachedi **D.** None of these

Q.29 In this question identify the new shape that could be constructed if the two example shapes were combined. No other change should be made to the two shapes other than combining them.

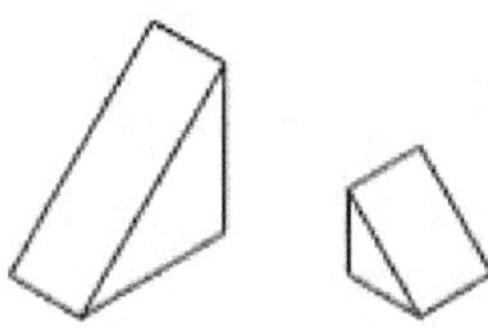

A. 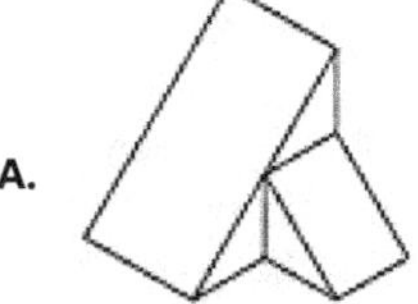 **B.** 

C. 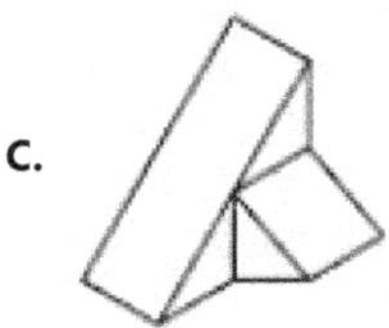 **D.** 

Q.30 Identify the 3D shape's net.

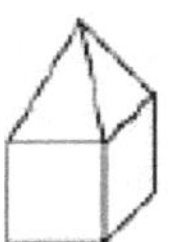

A. 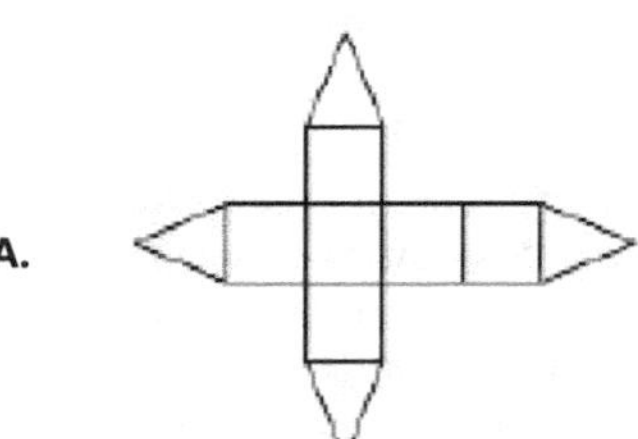

B. 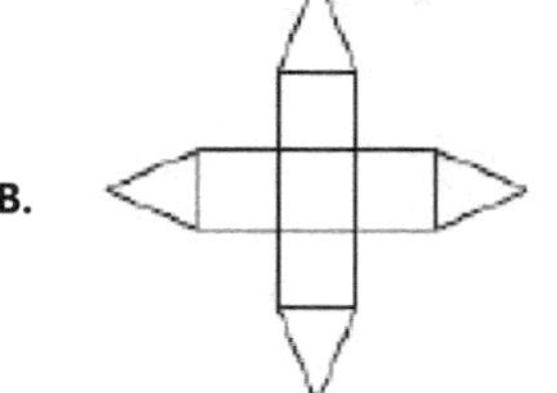

C. 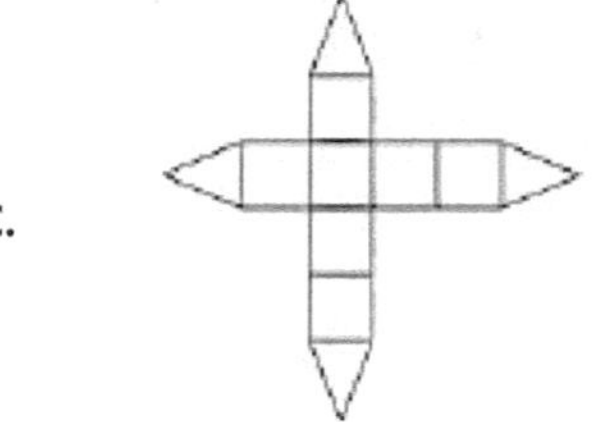

D. None of the above

Q.31 From the given answer figures, select the one in which the question figure is hidden/embedded.

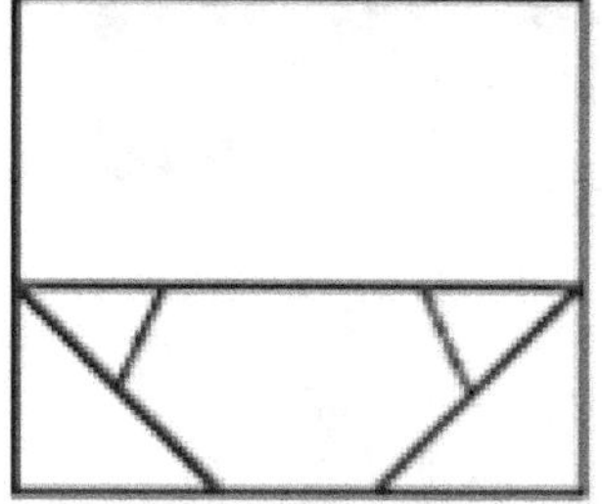

A. 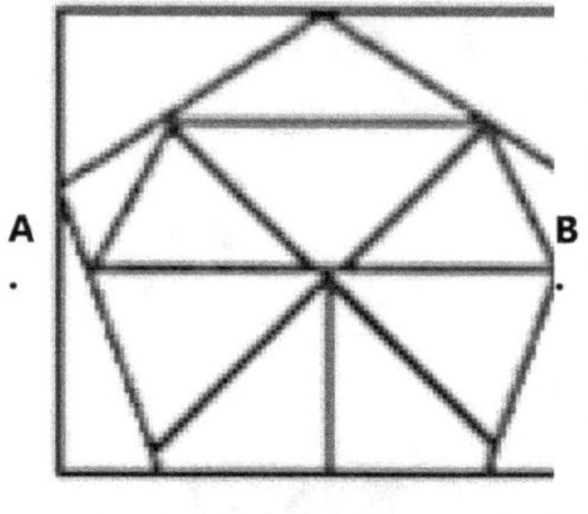

B. 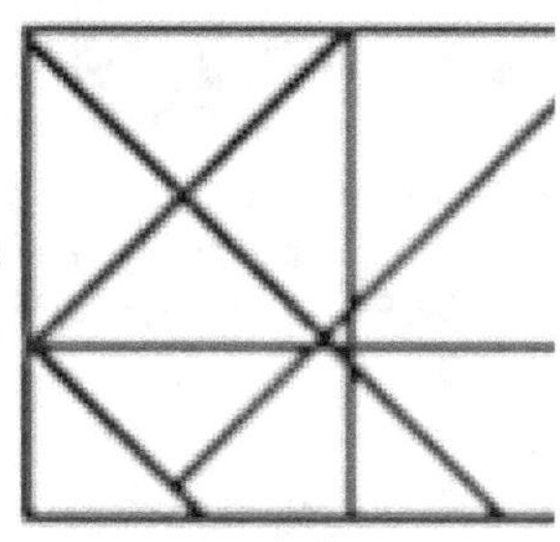

C. 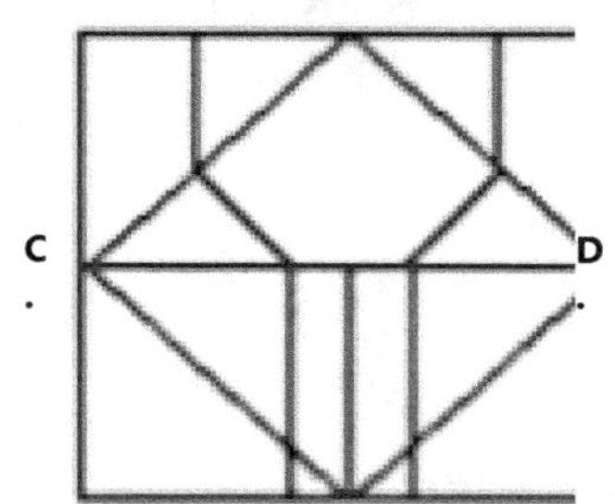

D. 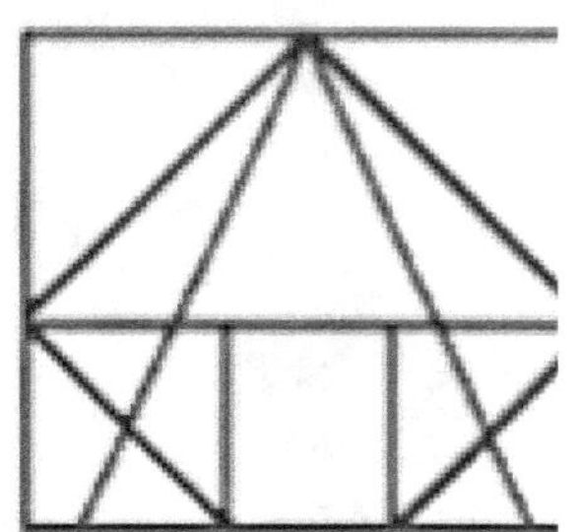

Q.32 Identify the mirror image of the question shape.

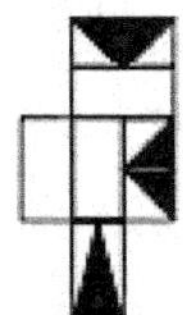

A. 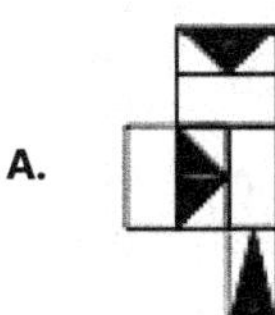

B. 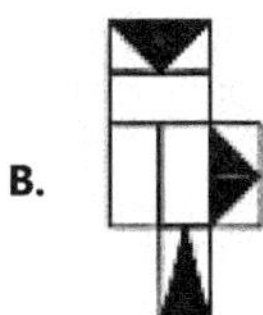

C. 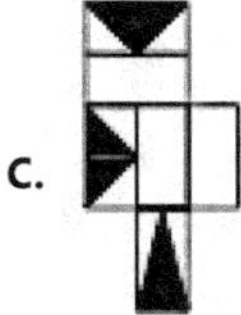

D. None of the above

Q.33 Observe the image below, and and identify the things that could possibly be made from the pattern.

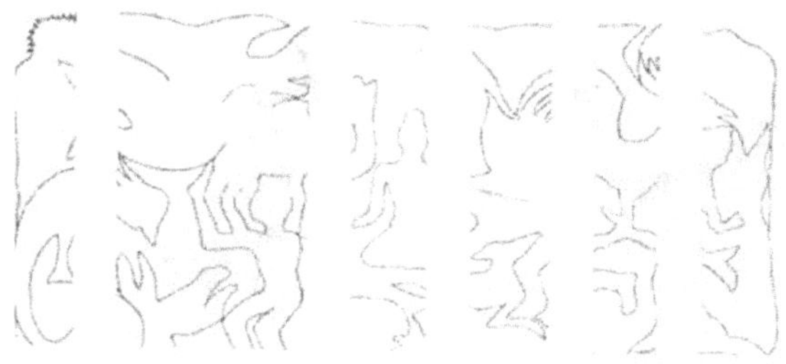

A. Elephant
B. Human
C. Hen/cock
D. Zebra

Q.34 4–5 pieces are given. Choose the answer choice that represents a figure comprised of ALL pieces. Pieces may be rotated and/or reflected.

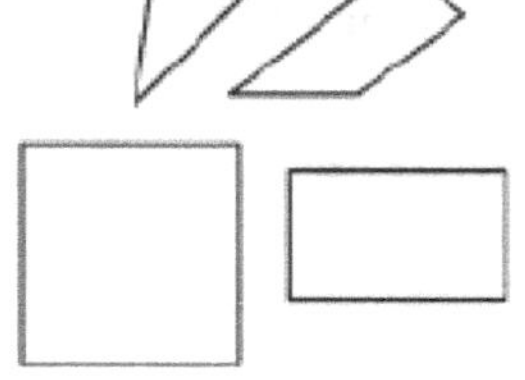

A. 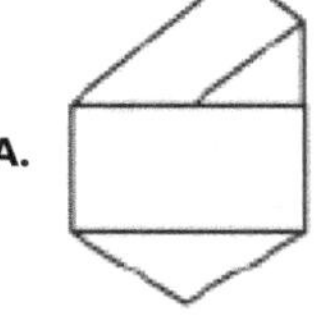

B. 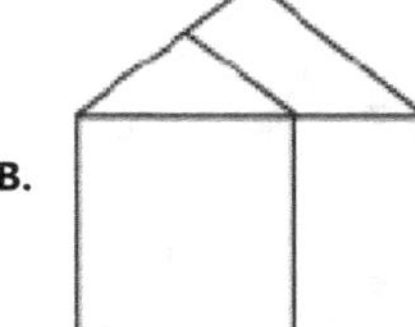

C. 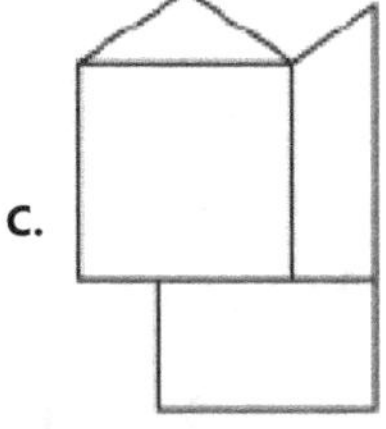

D. 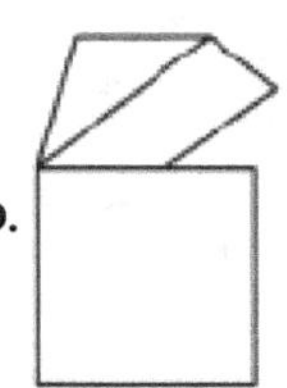

Q.35 A square is cut into 7 pieces as shown on the extreme left of the image. Identify which of the options can be made using all 7 pieces.

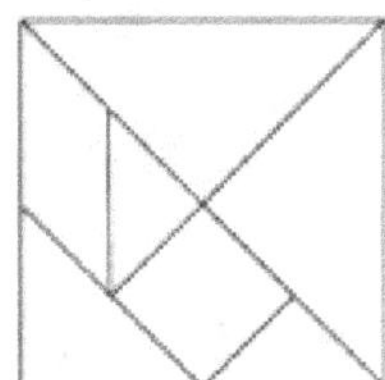

A. 

B. 

C. 

D. 

Q.36 Which of the following terms are related to photography ?

A. Aperture **B.** Bokeh
C. AI servo **D.** Histogram

Multiple Choice Questions (MCQ)

Q.37 From the following options, choose the set of colors, which is present in the painting below

Q.38 Identify the correct art techniques with which the following paintings have been made.

A. Crayon, Pastel, Oil, Acrylic
B. Oil, Crayon, Pastel, Water Color
C. Oil, Pastel, Acrylic, Crayon
D. Oil, Crayon, Acrylic, Watercolor

Q.39

If  becomes 

Then  Will become

A. 

B. 

C. 

D. 

Q.40 Given below are a few images. Identify the odd image among the options.

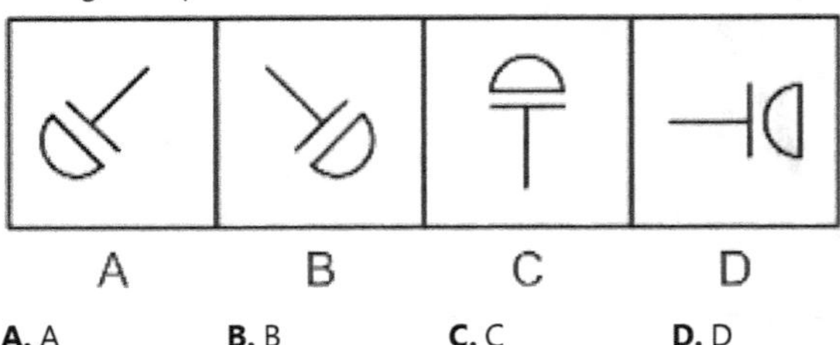

A. A **B.** B **C.** C **D.** D

Q.41 For the given pulley system shown below, if mass M_2, goes down by 10 cm, choose the correct choice (if M_1 and M_2 are equal)

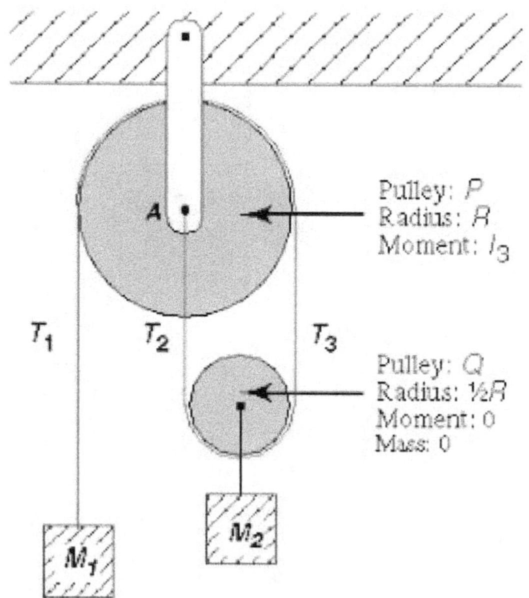

A. Mass M_1 goes down by 10cm
B. Mass M_1 goes up by 10cm
C. Mass M_1 goes up by 5cm
D. Mass M_1 goes up by 20cm

Q.42 Identify the famous personality whose image is shown below:

A. Hrishikesh Mukherjee
B. Dadasaheb Phalke
C. Satyajit Ray
D. Kamal Amrohi

Q.43 Which row is the odd one out?

Q.44 Which of the figures at the bottom A, B or C, should take the place of number 3?

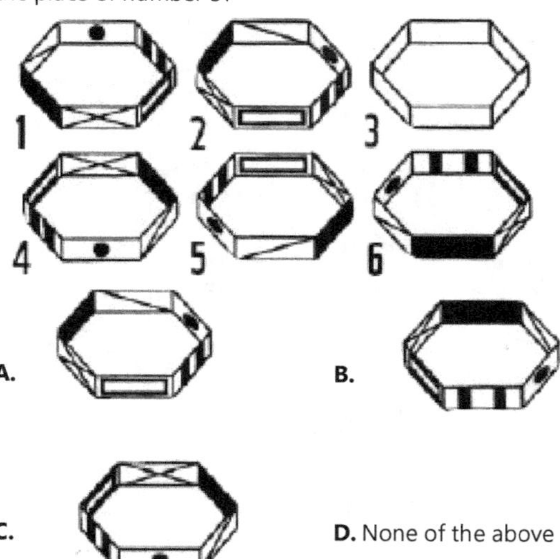

D. None of the above

Q.45 If the figure below were held in front of a mirror, which of the figures, A, B, C, D would be reflected?

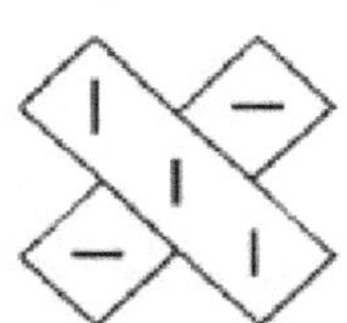

A.
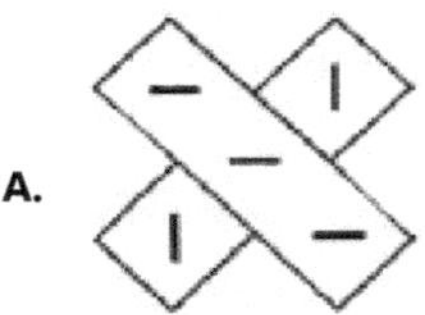

B.
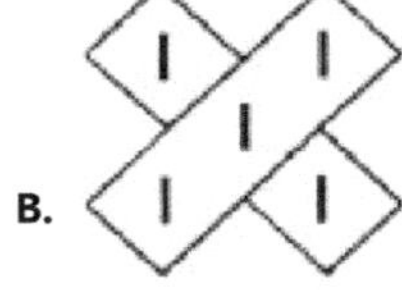

C.
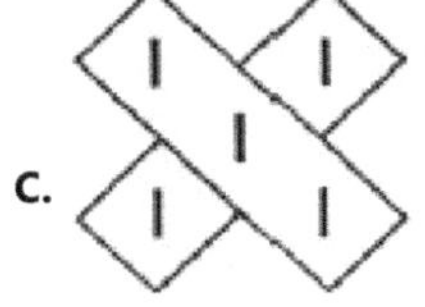

D.
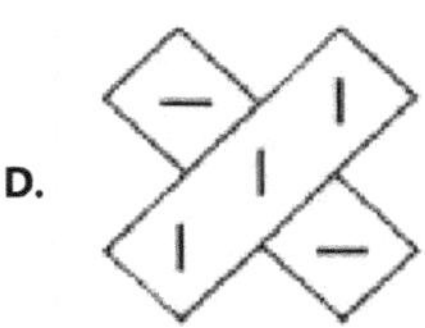

Q.46 What is the fourth color in the rainbow?
A. Blue **B.** Yelow **C.** Green **D.** Purple

Q.47 Identify the quality in common.

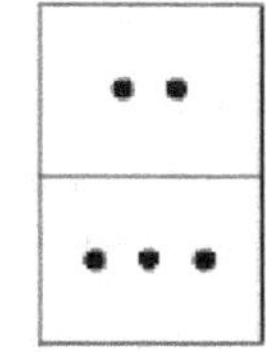 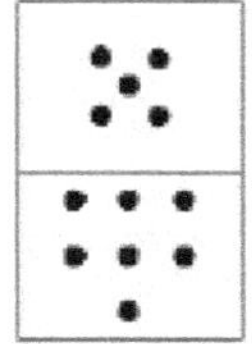

A.

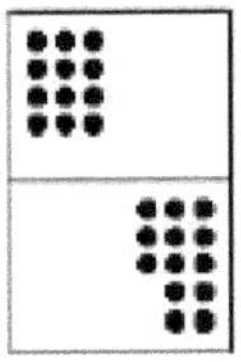

B.

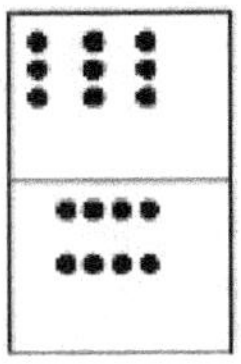

C.

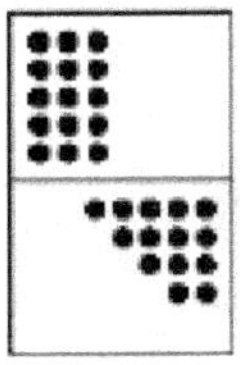

D.

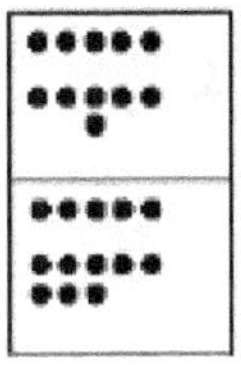

Q.48 Complete the series

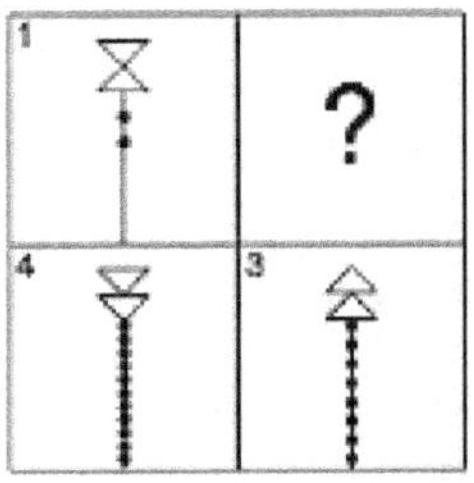

A.

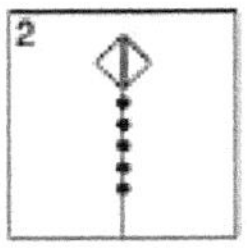

B.

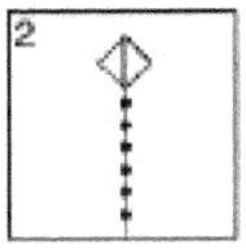

C.

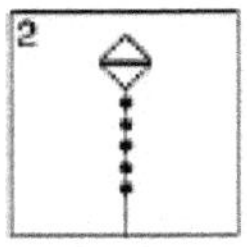

D.

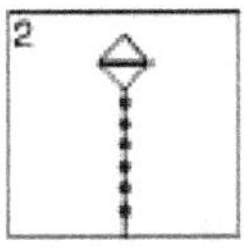

Q.49 Complete the sequence

A.

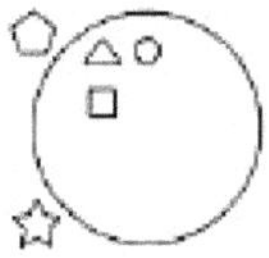

B.

C.

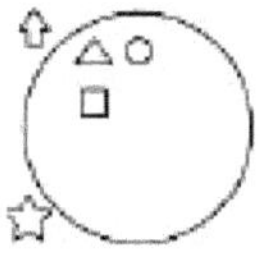

D.

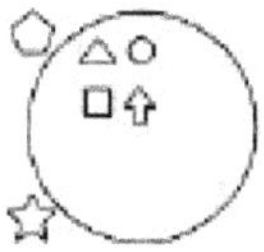

Q.50 Complete the sequence.

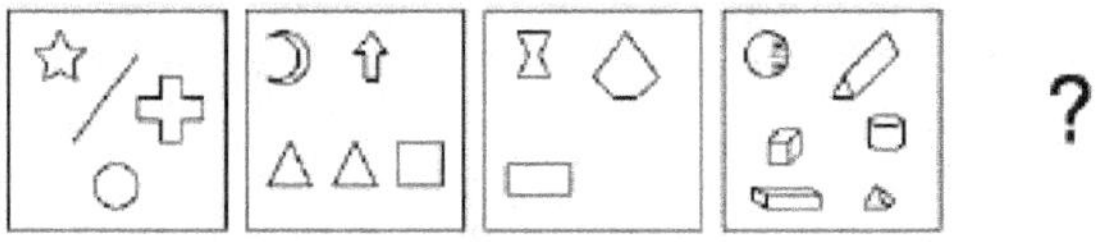

A.

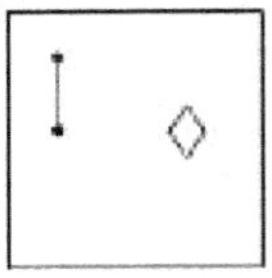

B.

C.

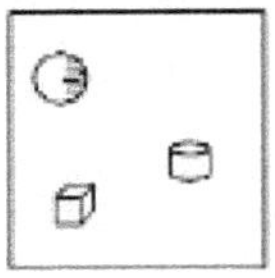

D.

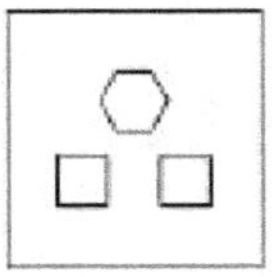

Q.51 Complete the sequence

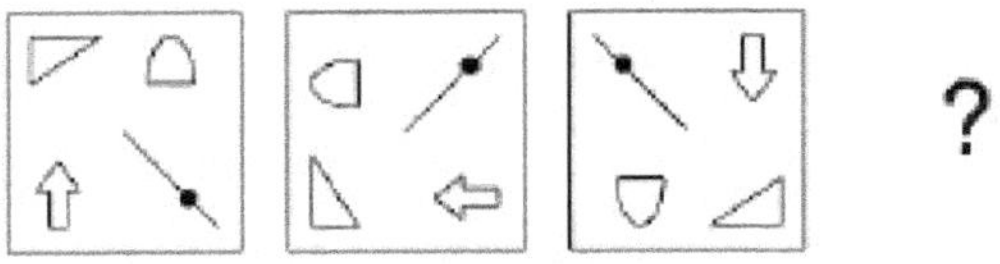

A.

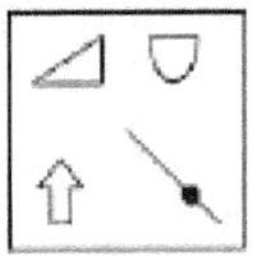

B.

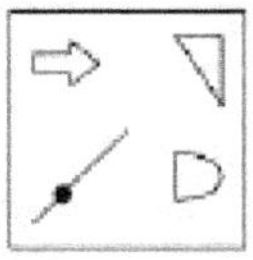

C.

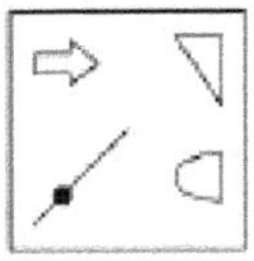

D.

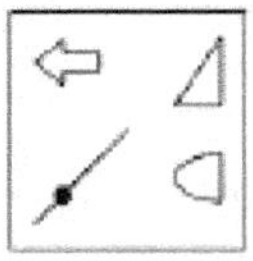

Q.52 Direction: Out of the four given figures, three-figure are similar in a certain way, one figure is not like the others. Find out the figure which doe not belong to the group.

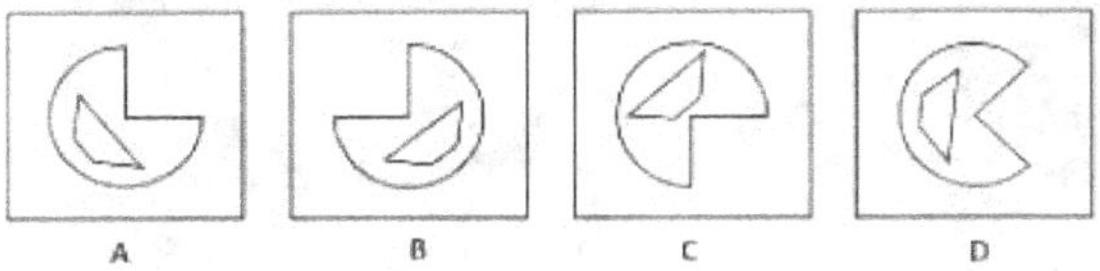

A B C D

A. A **B.** B **C.** C **D.** D

Q.53 There are eight rules which when applied to the sequence will transform it to one of the four options shown below. Identify the correct option.

- ■ Cancel all shading
- ○ Shade the second and last shapes
- ● Exchange the second and fourth shapes
- □ Reverse the sequence of shapes
- ⬇ Change all circles to shaded squares
- ⇩ Replace all shaded shapes with unshaded triangles (with the apex at the top)
- ▲ Replace the first shape with a shaded triangle with its apex pointing downwards
- △ Change the middle shape to an unshaded circle

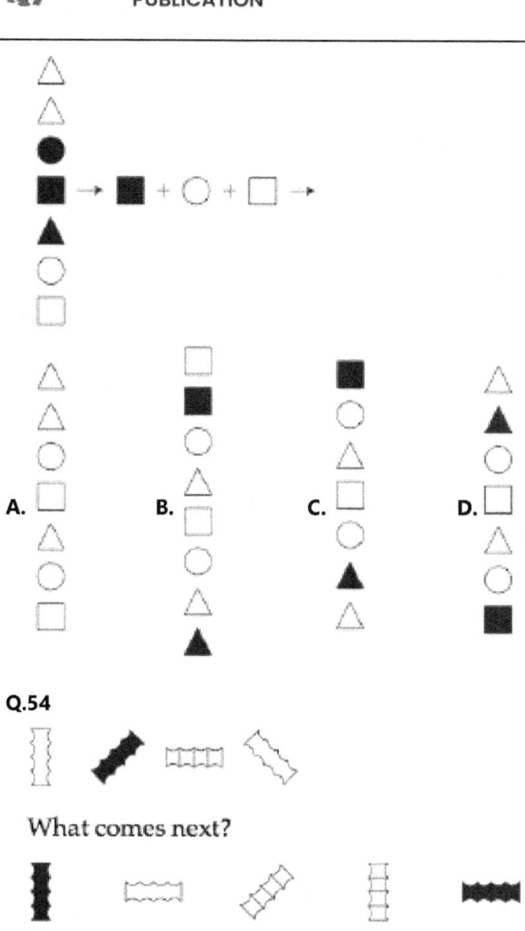

Q.54

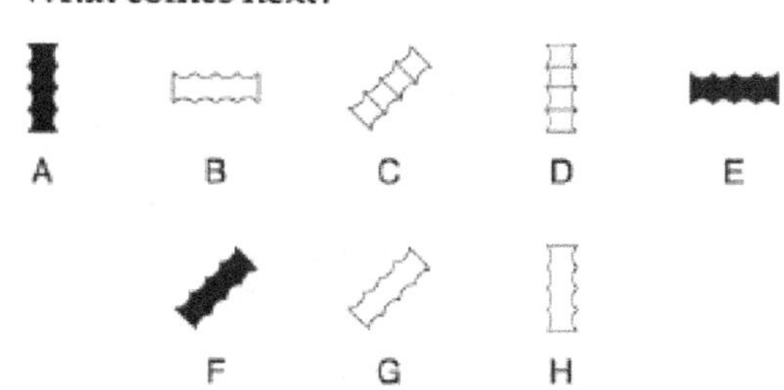

What comes next?

A B C D E

F G H

A. A
B. C
C. G
D. None of the above

Q.55

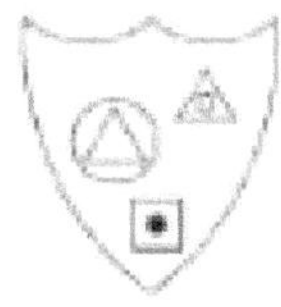

Which shield below has most in common with the shield above?

A. 

B. 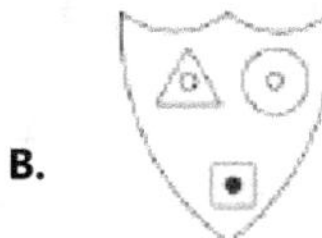

C. 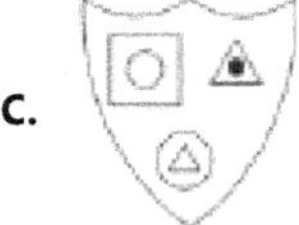

D. 

Q.56 To which hexagon below can a dot be added so that it then meets the same conditions as in the hexagon above?

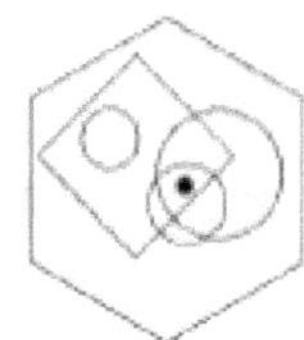

A. 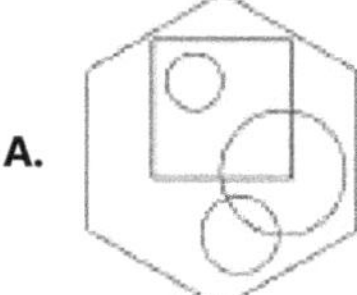

B. 

C. 

D. 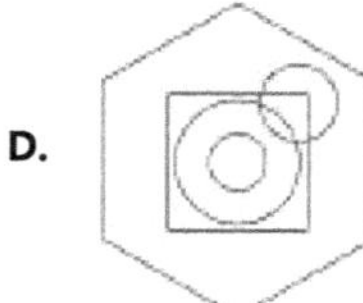

Q.57 Choose the box that is similar to the box formed from the given sheet of paper (X).

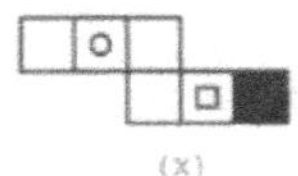    

(X) (1) (2) (3) (4)

A. 1 and 2 only
B. 3 and 4 only
C. 2 and 3 only
D. 1 and 4 only

Q.58

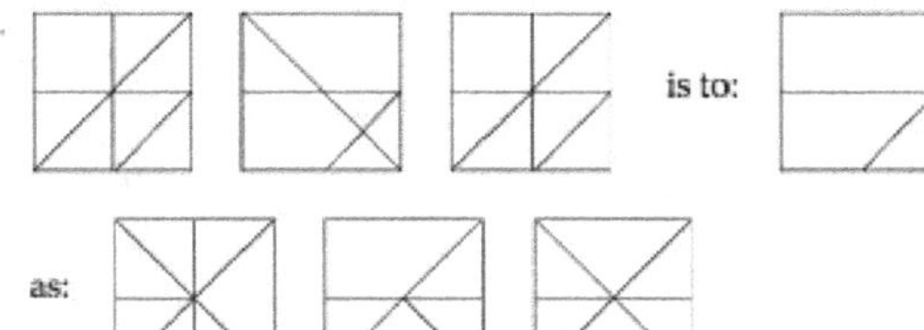

is to:

A. 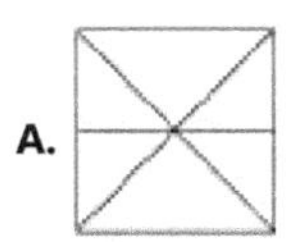

B. 

C. 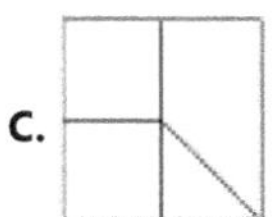

D. 

Q.59

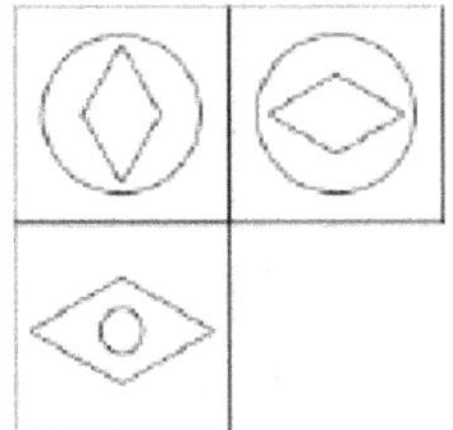

Which is the missing tile?

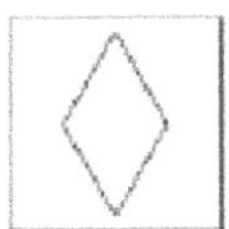

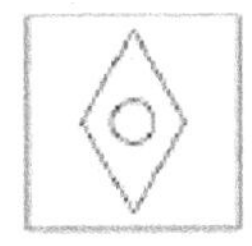
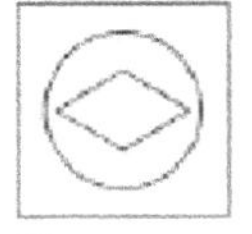

A B C D

A. A **B.** B **C.** C **D.** D

Q.60

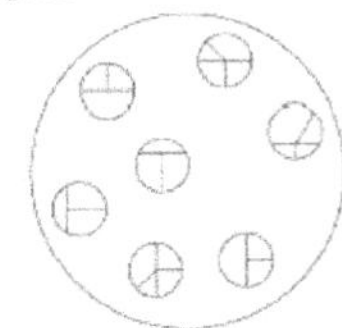

Which circle below should be placed in the large circle above?

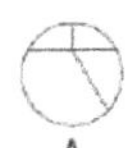

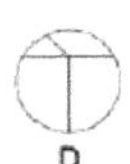

A B C D

A. A **B.** B **C.** C **D.** D

Q.61 Direction: Select a suitable figure from the four alternatives that would complete the figure matrix.

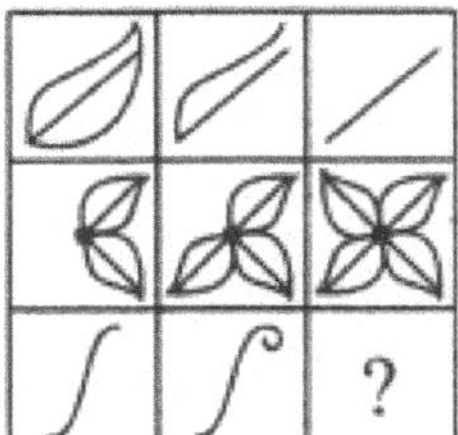

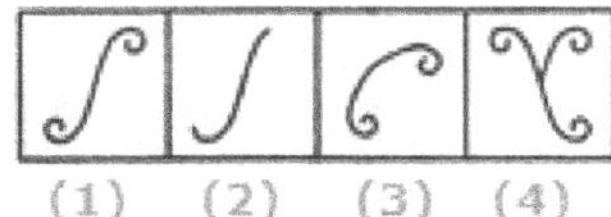

A. 1 **B.** 2 **C.** 3 **D.** 4

Q.62

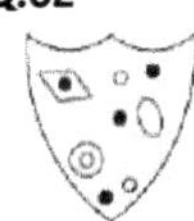

Which shield below has most in common with the shield above?

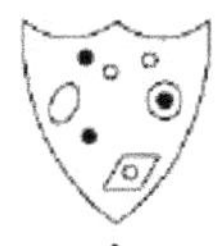

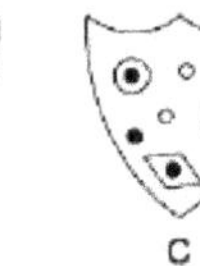

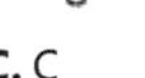
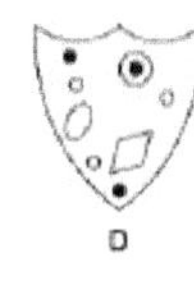

A B C D

A. A **B.** B **C.** C **D.** D

Q.63 Which is the missing tile from the following?

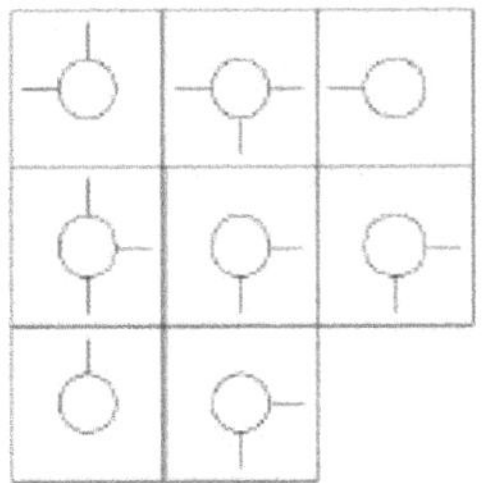

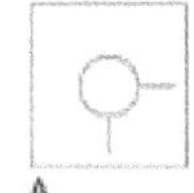

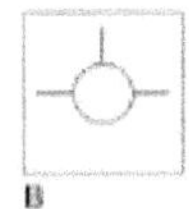

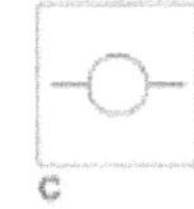

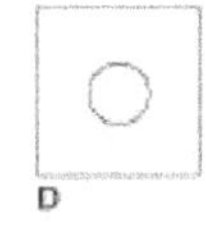

A. A **B.** B **C.** C **D.** D

Q.64 To which hexagon below can a dot be added so that it then meets the same conditions as in the hexagon above?

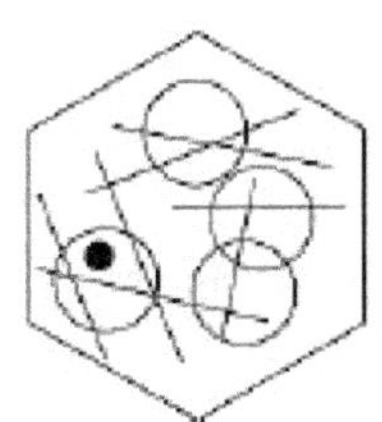

A. 

B. 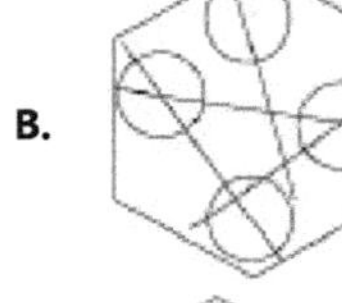

C. 

D. 

Q.65 Find the odd picture out:

A. 

B. 

C. 

D. 

Q.66 Which is the missing segment?

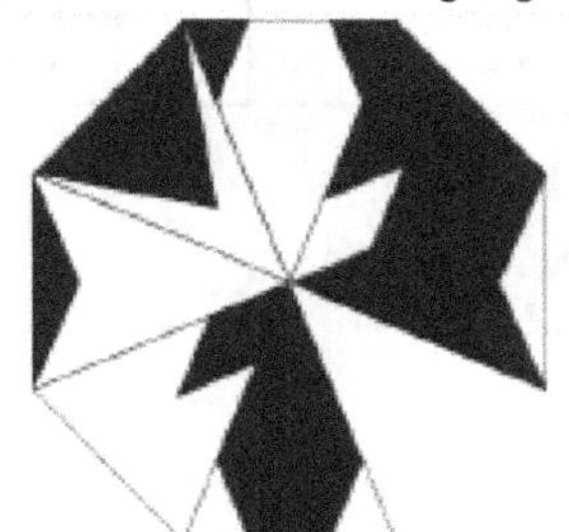

A. 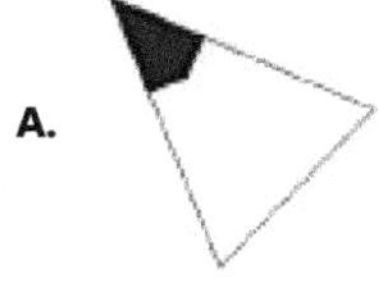

B. 

C. 

D. 

Q.67 Which of the following are true related to Paint brush.

a) Two basic types of bristles: natural and synthetic

b) Only one type: made from animal hair

c) synthetic bristles are made from nylon

d) synthetic bristles are made from Polyster

e) Natural bristles are made from hog or badger

A. b,e **B.** a,c,e **C.** a,c,d,e **D.** b,c,d

Q.68 Find out from amongst the four alternatives as to how the pattern would appear when the transparent sheet is folded at the dotted line.

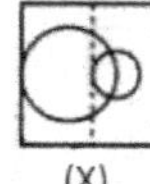
(X)

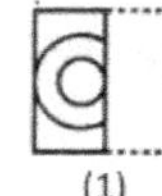
(1)

(2)

(3)

(4)

A. 1 **B.** 2 **C.** 3 **D.** 4

// Smart Answer Sheet //

Correct — Indicates percentage of students who answered questions correctly.

Skipped — Indicates percentage of students who skipped questions.

Q.	Ans.	Correct	Skipped
1	15	32.0 %	11.53 %
2	12	58.12 %	21.88 %
3	5	64.71 %	20.47 %
4	40	32.71 %	18.35 %
5	39	32.0 %	22.82 %
6	6	32.94 %	28.0 %
7	0.5	14.35 %	23.77 %
8	3	62.35 %	21.65 %
9	141	53.18 %	21.41 %
10	21	19.06 %	31.76 %
11	27	43.29 %	25.42 %
12	40	19.29 %	30.59 %
13	0	19.76 %	27.06 %
14	32	33.18 %	24.94 %
15	#	15.06 %	27.53 %
16	#	17.88 %	23.3 %
17	#	25.88 %	21.41 %
18	31	47.06 %	26.12 %
19	B, A, D	20.0 %	24.94 %
20	B, A, C	39.53 %	21.65 %
21	B, A, C	14.12 %	40.47 %
22	B, A, C	26.12 %	33.41 %
23	A	44.24 %	27.52 %
24	B	38.12 %	32.0 %
25	D	27.06 %	28.0 %
26	A, D, C	36.94 %	33.41 %
27	B, A, C	41.88 %	35.06 %
28	A	42.82 %	30.36 %
29	D	64.24 %	24.47 %
30	B	67.76 %	24.48 %
31	D	38.82 %	26.12 %
32	C	70.82 %	23.77 %
33	B, A, C	59.53 %	25.65 %
34	B	45.41 %	24.47 %
35	B, A, D	38.82 %	32.0 %
36	B, A, D, C	69.41 %	26.12 %
37	B	60.0 %	21.41 %
38	B	37.41 %	21.18 %
39	C	62.35 %	21.65 %
40	D	73.18 %	22.35 %
41	C	44.94 %	22.82 %
42	B	39.29 %	24.71 %
43	D	37.88 %	28.47 %
44	B	71.06 %	22.59 %
45	D	67.76 %	23.3 %
46	C	67.76 %	22.83 %
47	D	40.24 %	30.58 %
48	C	40.71 %	25.17 %
49	D	69.88 %	22.83 %
50	A	44.24 %	30.58 %
51	B	66.82 %	23.3 %
52	C	51.29 %	28.71 %
53	C	48.71 %	29.88 %
54	A	64.24 %	25.17 %
55	D	55.76 %	26.12 %
56	D	57.65 %	25.17 %
57	B	44.0 %	25.88 %
58	D	52.24 %	28.0 %
59	C	70.59 %	23.29 %
60	C	35.29 %	26.83 %
61	A	34.82 %	31.77 %
62	C	53.88 %	26.59 %
63	D	24.47 %	28.94 %
64	D	60.0 %	28.24 %
65	A	57.88 %	28.47 %
66	C	68.24 %	23.76 %
67	C	35.76 %	25.18 %
68	D	60.71 %	24.7 %

#

Q.	Answer
15	andhra bank
16	WHO
17	864

Performance Analysis	
Avg. Score (%)	46.67%
Toppers Score (%)	96.67%
Your Score	

//Hints and Solutions//

1. There are 15 triangles in the figure.

According to the given figure, the triangles are:

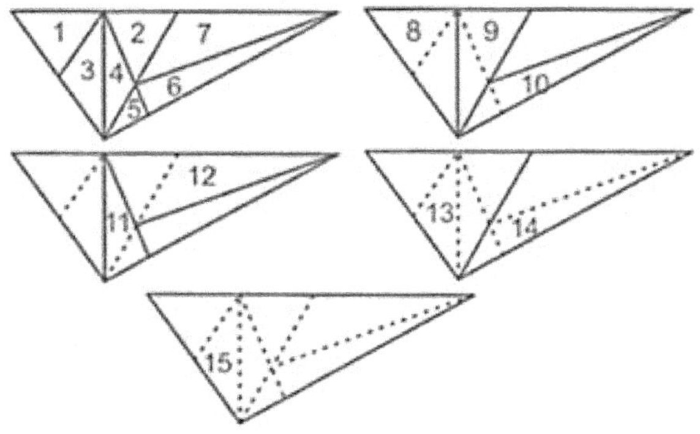

Hence, the correct answer is 15.

2. The pattern here is,

$26 - 2 = 24$

$24 - 4 = 20$

$20 - 2 = 18$

$18 - 4 = 14$

So,

$14 - 2 = 12$

Hence, the correct answer is 12.

3.

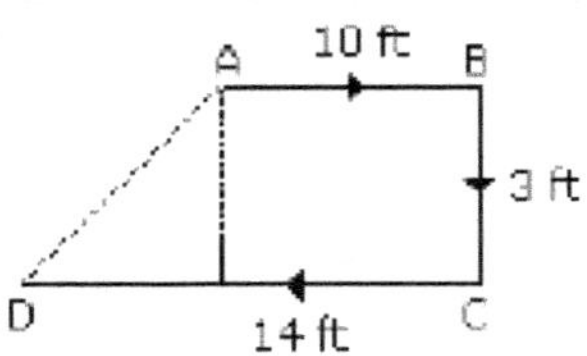

$$\text{Required distance} = AD$$
$$= \sqrt{3^2 + (14 - 10)^2}$$
$$-\sqrt{9 + 16}$$
$$= 5ft$$

4. There are 40 square presents in the given figure.

5. There are 39 surfaces required to represent the PURE letter of the word (to shown on the right).

6.

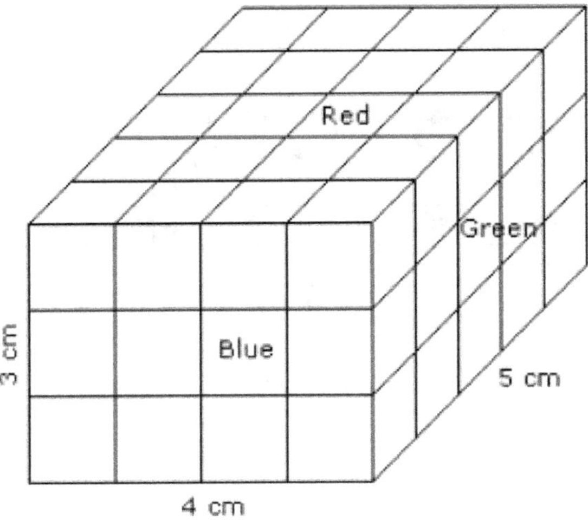

Required number of small cubes = (5 - 2) x (4 - 2) x (3 - 2) = 3 x 2 x 1 = 6

7. When three coins are tossed simultaneously, the possible outcomes:

HHH, HHT, HTH, HTT, THH, THT, TTH, TTT

Probability of getting atleast 2 heads = $\frac{4}{8}$ (HHH, HHT, HTH, THH)

$= \frac{1}{2}$

$= 0.5$

Hence, the correct answer is 0.5

8. The figure may be labeled as shown.

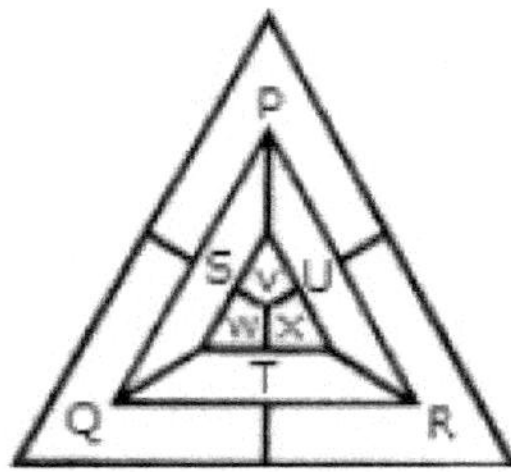

The spaces P, Q and R have to be shaded by three different colours definitely (since each of these three spaces lies adjacent to the other two). Now, in order that no two adjacent spaces be shaded by the same colour, the spaces T, U and S must be shaded with the colours of the spaces P, Q and R respectively. Also the spaces X, V and W must be shaded with the colours of the spaces S, T and U respectively i.e. with the colours of the spaces R, P and Q respectively. Thus, minimum three colours are required.

9. There are 141 cubes in this given figure.

10. Given equation:

35 @ 35 © 35 # 5 $ 7

After converting:

$35 + 35 - 35 \div 5 \times 7$

Using BODMOS rule,

$= 35 + 35 - 7 \times 7$

$= 35 + 35 - 49$

$= 70 - 49$

$= 21$

Hence, the correct answer is 21.

11. Required average

$= \frac{Sum\ of\ the\ first\ five\ multiples\ of\ 9}{5}$

$= \frac{9+18+27+36+45}{5}$

$= \frac{135}{5}$

$= 27$

Hence, the correct answer is 27.

12. If he takes out 38 socks, although it is very unlikely, it is possible they could all be blue and red. To make 100 per cent certain that he also has a pair of black socks he must take out a further two socks

13. Looking at lines of numbers from the top: 9×8=72; 72×8= 576; 576 × 8 = 4608

14. the next cube number below 64 (4 × 4 × 4) is 27 (3 × 3 × 3). In order to construct a solid cube, therefore, with none left over, 59 – 27 = 32 blocks need to be taken away

15. This is the logo of andhra bank.

Andhra Bank was a medium-sized public sector bank (PSB) of India, with a network of 2885 branches, 4 extension counters, 38 satellite offices and 3798 automated teller machines. During 2011–12, the bank entered the states of Tripura and Himachal Pradesh. It operated in 25 states and three union territories. It had its headquarters in Hyderabad, Telangana, India. Along with Corporation Bank, Andhra Bank was merged with Union Bank of India in April 2020.

Hence, the correct answer is andhra bank.

16. This is the logo of the World Health Organization (WHO). It is a specialized agency of the United Nations that is concerned with international public health. It was established on 7th April 1948 and is headquartered in Geneva, Switzerland. The WHO is a member of the United Nations Development Group. Its predecessor, the Health Organization, was an agency of the League of Nations.

Hence, the correct answer is WHO.

17. 5 6 3 2 9 7 1 4 2 6 8 7 5 7 1 after deleting the repeated number we get,

4 8 3 9, then after multiply those numbers we will get,

4 x 8 x 3 x 9 = 864

18. Let A, B, C represent their respective weights.

Then, we have: A + B + C = (45 x 3) = 135 .... (i)

A + B = (40 x 2) = 80 .... (ii)

B + C = (43 x 2) = 86 ....(iii)

Adding (ii) and (iii),

we get: A + 2B + C = 166 .... (iv)

Subtracting (i) from (iv),

we get : B = 31. B's weight = 31 kg.

19. The ratio of width to length of the flag is 2:3.

20.

1. Coke bottles, Coke tins
2. Tennis ball, Aquafina water bottle
3. Incandescent light Bulbs, CFL bulbs

21. Alan Watts was a well-known British philosopher, writer and speaker, best known for his interpretation of Eastern philosophy for Western audiences.

Aldous Leonard Huxley was a well-known writer, essayist and screenwriter. When he was introduced to meditation, vegetarianism and Vedanta, he became an active member of the Vedanta Society of Southern California.

German scientist Christiane Nusslein-Volhard has been one of the leading researchers in the field of genetics and embryology.

22. A Suitable Boy is a novel by Vikram Seth, published in 1993. At 1,349 pages and 591,552 words, the book is one of the longest novels ever published in a single volume in the English language. A sequel, to be called A Suitable Girl, was due for publication in 2017. As of 2020 the novel was still unpublished.

An Idealist View of Life

S. Radhakrishnan

Beastly tales (Vikram Seth)

23. Courts are meant to judge impartially. So, argument III is vague. The system of local courts shall speed up justice by providing easy approach and simplified procedures, and thus ease the burden of the higher courts. So, I as well as II holds strong.

24. In the final paragraph, the authors tells us that any snow that falls over Antarctica either "remains there permanently, eventually building up into thick ice sheets." or "becomes caught up in the strong winds." This supports options (I) and (II). In the beginning of this paragraph, the author says "the air over Antarctica is too cold to hold water vapor, so there is very little evaporation." This eliminates option (III). Therefore (B) is correct.

25. Clearly, all the three directly follow from the given statement

26. Lichtenstein's success was matched by his focus and energy, and after his initial triumph in the early 1960s, he went on to create an oeuvre of more than 5,000 paintings, prints, drawings, sculptures, murals and other objects celebrated for their wit and invention.

27. Anjolie Ela Menon (born 1940) is one of India's leading contemporary artists. Her paintings are in several major collections. In 2006 her work "Yatra" was acquired by the Asian Art Museum of San Francisco, California. Her preferred medium is oil on masonite, though she has also worked in other media, including glass and water colour. She is a well known muralist. She was awarded the Padma Shree in 2000

28. The Gondi or Gond or Koitur are an Indian ethnic group. They speak the Gondi language which is a Dravidian language. They are one of the largest tribal groups in India. They are spread over the states of Madhya Pradesh, eastern Maharashtra, Chhattisgarh, Uttar Pradesh, Telangana, Andhra Pradesh, Bihar and Odisha.

29. In a) the big triangular shape has been thickened, in b) the big triangular shape has been thinned, and in c) the small triangular shape has been deformed.

30. b) is the only one with the right number of squares; you need only five, because the top is made from the triangles.

31. The question figure is embedded in,

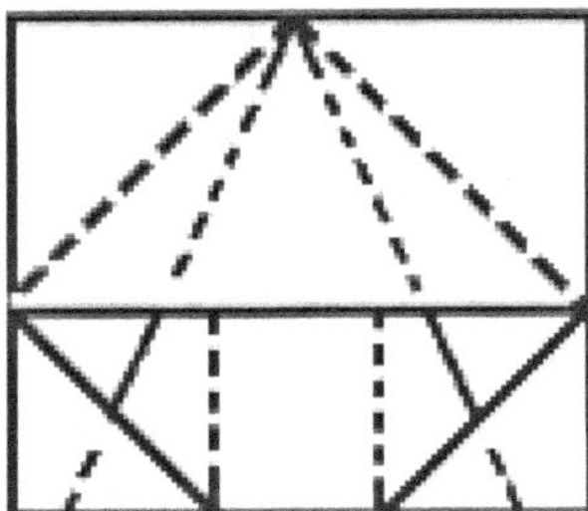

Hence, the correct option is (D).

32. a) is a modified shape, and in b) the central shading has been moved to the rectangle on the right side.

33.

- Elephant
- Human
- Hen/cock

34.

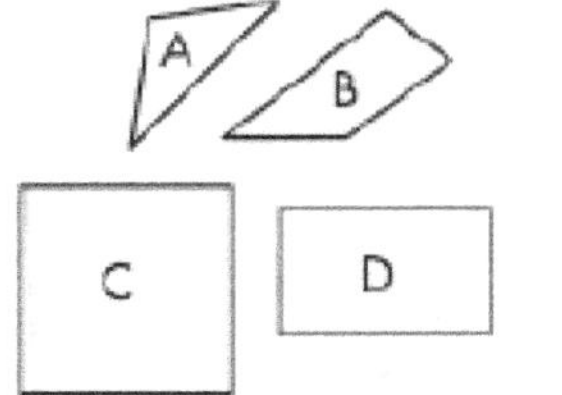

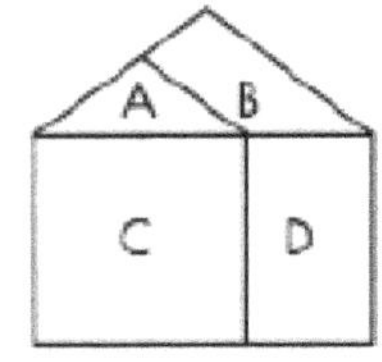

35. options A B D is correct.

36. A histogram is a graphical display of data using bars of different heights. In a histogram, each bar groups numbers into ranges. Taller bars show that more data falls in that range. A histogram displays the shape and spread of continuous sample data.

The Basics: AI Servo AF is a selectable AF mode, for when shooting through the viewfinder in an EOS DSLR. Short for Artificial Intelligence Servo Automatic Focusing, AI Servo is Canon's dedicated focusing mode for moving subjects.

Bokeh is an interactive visualization library for modern web browsers. It provides elegant, concise construction of versatile graphics.

In optics, an aperture is a hole or an opening through which light travels. More specifically, the aperture and focal length of an optical system determine the cone angle of a bundle of rays that come to a focus in the image plane. An optical system typically has many openings or structures that limit the ray bundles.

Hence, the correct options are (A), (B), (C) and (D).

37. option B is correct

38. Oil, Crayon, Pastel, Water Color are used, paintings have been made.

39. To mix a **brown** you mix a primary with its complementary color, so purple and yellow; blue and orange; or red and green. There is a diverse amount of Brown in nature. This color can be mixed with any other color.

40. The logic followed is:

In all the figures except figure (D), the base of the semi-circle is along with the line segment.

But,

In figure D, the semi-circle is inverted and its base is away from the line segment.

Hence, the correct option is (D).

41. In pulley B,

Moment (I) = O

Radius of A = R

Radius of B = $\frac{1}{2}$R

If $M_1 = M_2$

M_2 goes down by 10 cm then distance by,

$M_1 = \frac{R/2}{R} \times distance$

$= \frac{1}{2} \times 10 = 5$ cm

So Mass M_1 goes up by 5cm

42. Dhundiraj Govind Phalke, popularly known as Dadasaheb Phalke (About this soundpronunciation (help·info)) (30 April 1870 – 16 February 1944), was an Indian producer-director-screenwriter, known as the Father of Indian cinema. His debut film, Raja Harishchandra, was the first Indian movie in 1913, and is now known as India's first full-length feature film. He made 95 feature-length films and 27 short films in his career, spanning 19 years, until 1937, including his most noted works: Mohini

Bhasmasur (1913), Satyavan Savitri (1914), Lanka Dahan (1917), Shri Krishna Janma (1918) and Kaliya Mardan (1919).

43. Apart from D, each row contains one figure with one stroke, one with two strokes, one with three strokes, one with four strokes and one with five strokes. In row D there are two figures with four strokes and none with five strokes.

44. The figure is rotating clockwise

45. Stripes go the opposite way when reflected in a mirror.

46. Sometimes it's not possible to clearly see orange because red is the colour that stands out. The colour of the rainbow after orange is yellow. This intense tone is most visible when the rainbow is pronounced, but nevertheless may go unnoticed in a rainbow of lesser intensity. The fourth colour of the rainbow is green.

47. The dots on the shapes follow the sequence of the first six prime numbers: 2, 3, 5, 7, 11, 13 (this is a sequence that you should learn to recognize if you do not already know it).

48. The dots on the pole increase by three each step in the series, from 2 to 5, 8 and 11. The shapes on the top of the pole form the four possible combinations when the bases of the triangles remain horizontal.

49. The shape at the bottom of the previous step moves into the circle, and the shape at the top in the previous shape moves to the bottom.

50. At each step in the sequence the operation alternates from plus to minus and follows the sequence 4 + 1 = 5, – 2 = 3, + 3 = 6, – 4 = 2.

51. At each step the shape is rotating 90 degrees.

52. In all the given figures, the open corner of the partial circle and the longer end of the diagonal strip are facing each other except figure C where the shorter end of the diagonal stripe is facing the open corner of the partial circle.

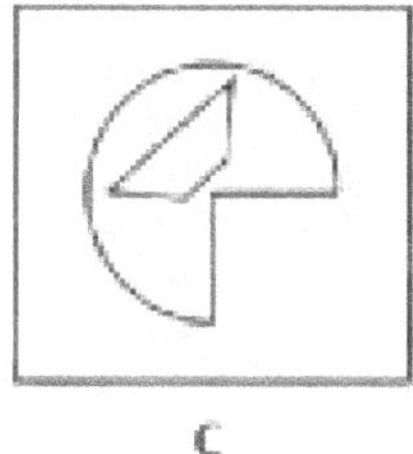

C

Hence, the correct option is (C).

53. option C

54. The figure is tumbling 45° at each stage and alternates white/black/striped

55. it contains a triangle in a circle, a circle in a triangle (with the same orientation of the triangle) and a black dot in a square

56. so that the dot appears in two circles and the square

57. The fig. (X) is similar to Form V. So, when the sheet in fig. (X) is folded to form a cube, then the face bearing a square lies opposite to the face bearing a circle. Therefore, the cubes shown in figures (1) and (2) which have the faces bearing the square and the circle adjacent to each other, cannot be formed. Therefore, only the cubes in figures (3) and (4) can be formed.

Hence, the correct option is (B).

58. only lines that appear three times in the same position in the first three squares are carried forward to the final square

59. looking across and down the triangles turn through 90°

60. each circle is repeated rotated

61.

The number of components in each row either increases or decreases from left to right. In the third row, it increases.

Hence, the correct option is (A)

62. it contains four black dots and three white

63. looking both across and down, only lines that appear in both the first two squares are carried forward to the third square

64. so that it appears in a circle with three secants (lines) passing through it

65. The knee patch of option A is solid black, whereas rest options have a grey knee patch

66. each segment is a mirror image of the segment opposite, but with black/white reversal

67. a,c,d,e

Two basic types of bristles: natural and synthetic, synthetic bristles are made from Polyester Natural bristles are made from hog or badger & synthetic bristles are made from nylon

68. option D is correct , when the transparent sheet is folded at the dotted line.

Mock Test 03

Numerical Answer Type (NAT)

Q.1 How many different types of symbols appear in the figure given below?

⦸	✳	☞	✎	⊗	✤	✥	✎	⊗
✦	▩	⌘	▲	✤	●	✸	⓿	⦸
☞	●	✱	✦	●	✳	▲	●	⌘
✹	▲	✹	✸	✹	✶	✹	☜	☯
☞	✶	✳	✹	✹	▲	✶	✱	☺
▲	∴	⓿	▩	✳	✶	✹	✹	∴
⦸	✤	∴	✦	✱	✸	✤	∴	☹
☺	✸	✕	▩	☜	✕	⦸	☮	☹
☯	✕	☛	✸	✦	✹	✸	▩	✕

Q.2 The given image has thirty-six circles with patterns inside, arranged in a six-by-six matrix. How many different types of circles are there in the image, assuming circles may be rotated ?

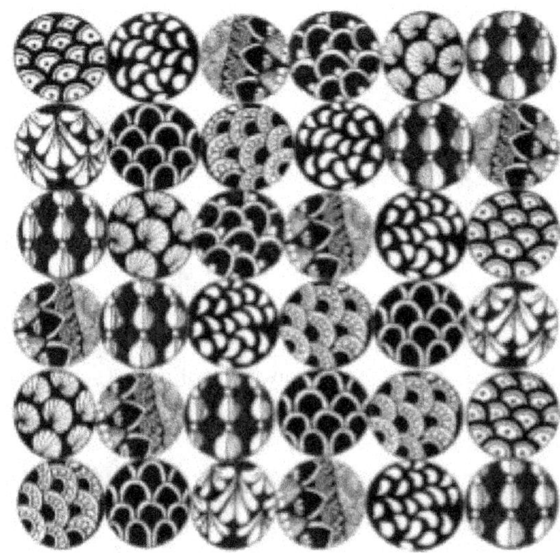

Q.3 Megha walks $10\ km$ towards North. She turns right and walks $15\ km$. She turns right and walks $20\ km$. She turns right and walks $15\ km$. How far (in km) is she from her starting point?

Q.4 Count the different types of caps worn by the group of people in the picture below.

Q.5 Imagine letters are extruded into three-dimensional objects, as shown in the figure on the left (the letter A). If the word QUEUE (shown on the right) were to be extruded, how many surfaces would it have?

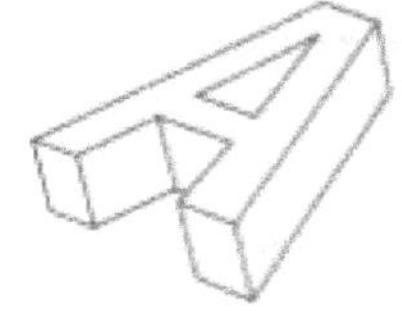

QUEUE

Q.6 All the faces of a cube are painted with red colour. The cube is cut into 64 equal small cubes. How many small cubes have only one face coloured ?

Q.7 How many cases do you need if you have to pack 148 pairs of shoes into cases that each holds 37 shoes?

Q.8 Count the number of cubes in the given figure.

Q.9
Count the number of fonts used in the given set of words.
Design is about progress. It is the conceptualization and creation of new things: ideas, **interactions**, information, objects, typefaces, books, posters, products, places, signs, systems, services, furniture, websites, and more.

Q.10 How many triangles are there in the figure?

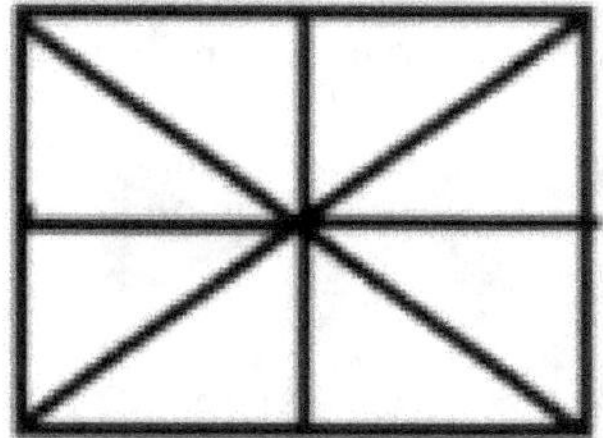

Q.11 What number should replace the question mark?

Q.12 ABCDEFGH

What letter is three to the right of the letter immediately to the left of the letter three to the left of the letter two to the right of letter F?

Q.13 What will come in place of question mark?

$6,11,21,36,56,?$

Q.14 Which point will balance the plank?

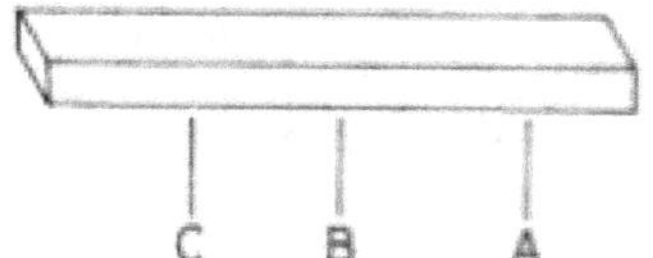

Q.15 If gear B rotates in a particular direction, which direction, in relation to each other, will A and D rotate?

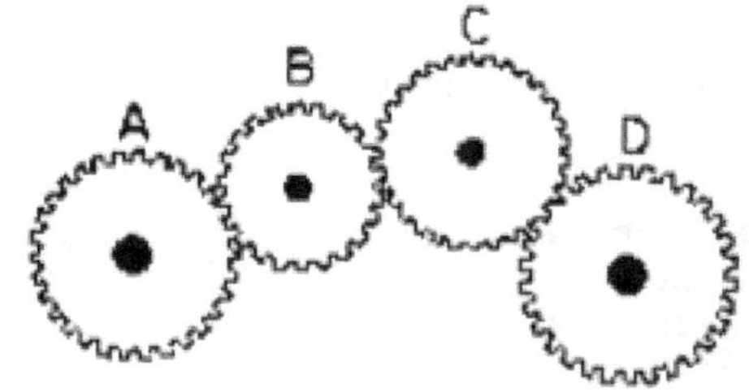

1. In the opposite direction to each other.
2. Same Direction.
3. Wheel can not rotate.

Q.16 A grocer has a sale of $Rs. 6435, Rs. 6927, Rs. 6855, Rs. 7230$ and $Rs. 6562$ for 5 consecutive months. How much sale must he have in the sixth month so that he gets an average sale of $Rs. 6500$?

Q.17 If 21 November 2016 was Monday, what day of the week was 21 November 2015[write the answer in small letters]?

Q.18 What are X and Y in the given series ?

7 8 6 9 5 10 X Y

Multiple Select Questions (MSQ)

Q.19 Select all statements about Indian Indus valley civilization that are true:

A. The Indus valley civilization also known as harappan civilization built around the banks of river indus. It is one of the modern civilizations besides mesopotamia and egypt civilization.

B. This civilization belonged to the Bronze Age. It existed for about 1000 years from 2500 BC to 1500 BC.

C. It was spread to a large area covering about 1,260,000 km^2. This civilization extended from Makran coast of Balochistan in the west to Ghaggar-Hakra River valley in the east, From Afghanistan in the northeastern to Daimabad in Maharashtra in the south.

D. The people of that time had great engineering skills. They discovered tin, lead, copper etc. Their town planning was also exceptional. They used bricks to build their buildings and they had a very efficient drainage system.

Q.20 Which of the following statements is/are true?

A. Kumar Bhattacharyya is an Indian British engineer who founded the Warwick Manufacturing Group (WMG), an academic department at the University of Warwick, which provides research, education and knowledge transfer in engineering, manufacturing and technology.

B. Aruna Roy is an Indian social activist who co-founded the MazdoorKisan Shakti Sangathana (MKSS), a social and grassroots organization for the empowerment of workers and peasants.

C. Manmohan Singh is an eminent Indian economist and politician who served as the Prime Minister of India for three consecutive terms.

D. Carl Edward Sagan was an American astronomer, cosmologist, astrophysicist, astro-biologist and author.

Q.21 From the options below, select the Indian author/s writing in English whose works are represented below:

1. English, August
2. The algebra of infinite justice
3. Hullabaloo in the guava orchard
4. Fairy tales at fifty
5. The God of small things
6. Inheritance of loss

A. Amitav Ghosh
B. Upamanyu Chatterjee
C. Arundhati Roy
D. Kiran Desai

Q.22 Question given below consists of a statement, followed by three arguments numbered I, II and III You have to decide which of the arguments is a 'strong' argument.

Statement:

Should there be a complete ban on manufacture and use of firecrackers?

Arguments:

I. No. This will render thousands of workers jobless.
II. Yes. The firecracker manufacturers use child labour to a large extent.
III. Yes. This will be a concrete step to reduce noise and air pollution. IV. No. Use of firecrackers makes certain special occasions more lively and joyful.

A. Only I and II are strong
B. Only I and III are strong
C. Only III and IV are strong
D. Only I, II and III are strong

Q.23 Question below is given a statement followed by three assumptions numbered I, II and III. You have to consider the statement and the following assumptions and decide which of the assumptions is implicit in the statement.

Statement:

There is big boom in drug business and a number of jhuggi-jhopari dwellers in Delhi can be seen pedalling with small pouches of smack and brown sugar.

Assumptions:

I. Drug addiction is increasing in the country, specially in the capital.
II. All the big dons involved in the smuggling of drugs live in jhuggi-jhopari areas.
III. Most of the jhuggi-jhopari dwellers would do anything for money.

A. Only I is implicit
B. Only II is implicit
C. Only III is implicit
D. Only I and III are implicit

Q.24 The first step is for us to realize that a city need not be a frustrater of life; it can be among other things, a mechanism for enhancing life, for producing possibilities of living which are not to be realized except through cities. But, for that to happen, deliberate and drastic planning is needed. Towns as much as animals, must have their systems of organs-those for transport and circulation are an obvious example. What we need now are organ systems for recreation, leisure, culture, community expression. This means abundance of open space, easy access to unspoilt Nature, beauty in parks and in fine buildings, gymnasia and swimming baths and recreation grounds in planty, central spaces for celebrations and demonstrations, halls for citizens' meetings, concert halls and theatres and cinemas that belong to the city. And the buildings must not be built anyhow or dumped down anywhere; both they and their groupings should mean something important to the people of the place. The author talks about 'Unspoilt Nature'. In what way / ways can Nature remain unspoilt?

A. If Nature is not allowed to interfere with people's day-to-day life.
B. By building cities with the system of organs like those of animals.
C. By allowing free access to parks and open spaces.
D. By allowing Nature to retain its primitive, undomesticated character.

Q.25 Which of the following paintings is from the renaissance painter Botticelli?

A. A **B.** B **C.** C **D.** D

Q.26 Identify the paintings by the south Indian artist Elayaraja from the following.

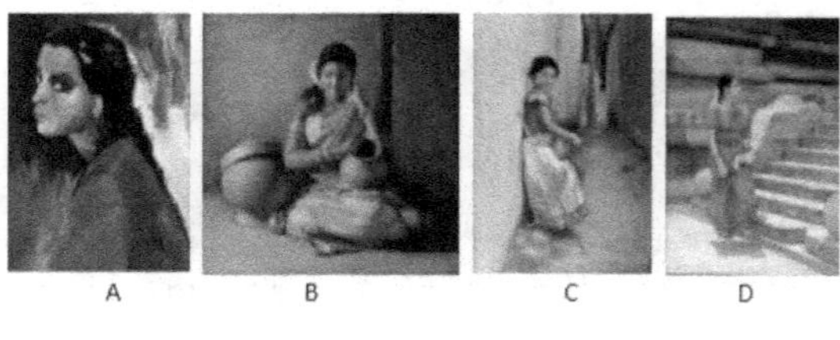

A. A **B.** B **C.** C **D.** D

Q.27 Identify the Indian traditional Art below

A. Kalamkari **B.** Madhubani

C. Mata ni pachedi **D.** None of these

Q.28 In this question identify the new shape that could be constructed if the two example shapes were combined. No other change should be made to the two shapes other than combining them.

A.  **B.** 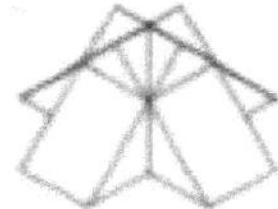

C. 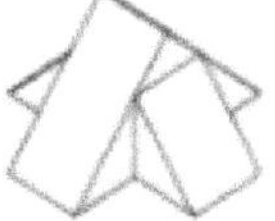 **D.** 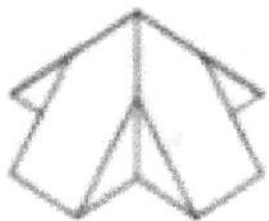

Q.29 Identify the 3D shape's net.

A.  **B.** 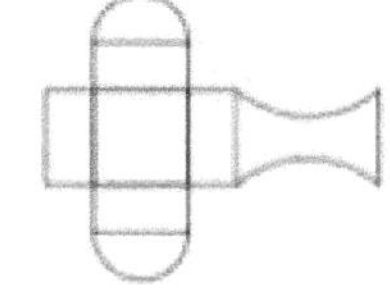

C. 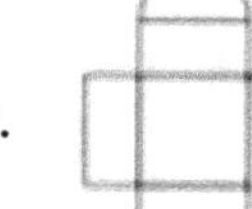 **D.** None of these

Q.30 Identify the answer shape, which has been rotated but is otherwise the same as the question shape.

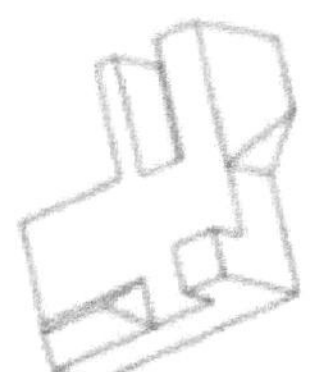

A. 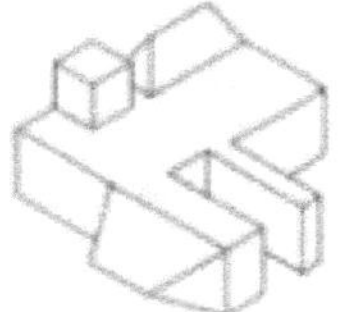 **B.** 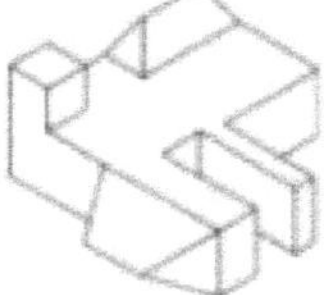

C.  **D.** None of these

Q.31 Identify the mirror image of the question shape.

A. 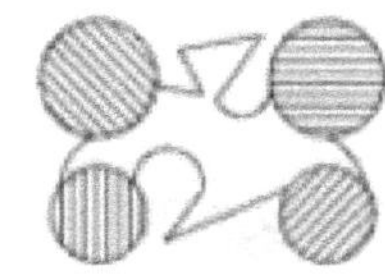 **B.** 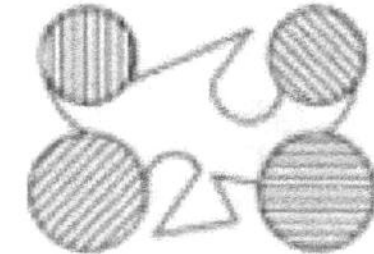

C. 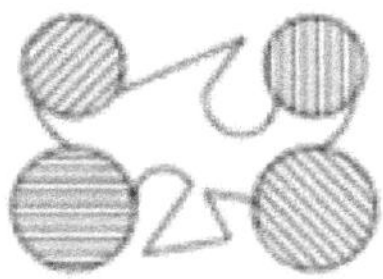 **D.** None of these

Q.32 4–5 pieces are given. Choose the answer choice that represents a figure comprised of ALL pieces. Pieces may be rotated and/or reflected.

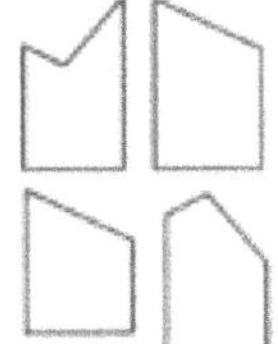

A. 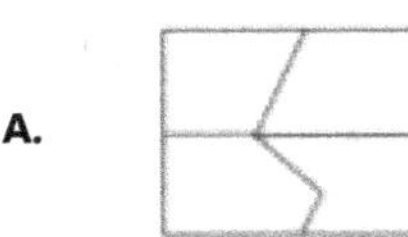

B. 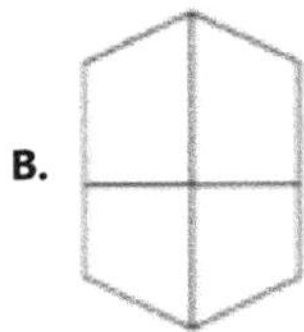

C. 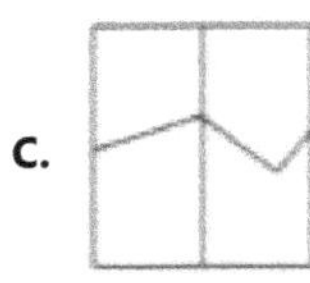

D. 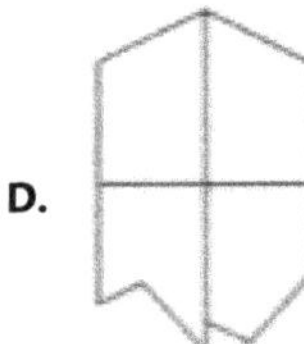

Q.33 Pick the TWO answer choices that will come together to make the figure shown. Pieces may be reflected and or rotated

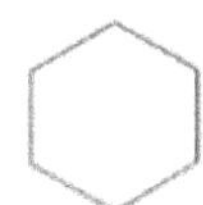

a) 

b) 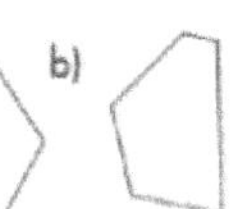

c) 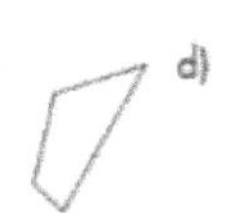

d) 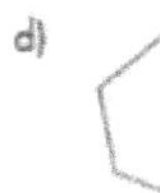

A. a + b **B.** b + c **C.** c + d **D.** a + c

Q.34 A square is cut into 7 pieces as shown on the extreme left of the image. Identify which of the options can be made using all 7 pieces.

A. 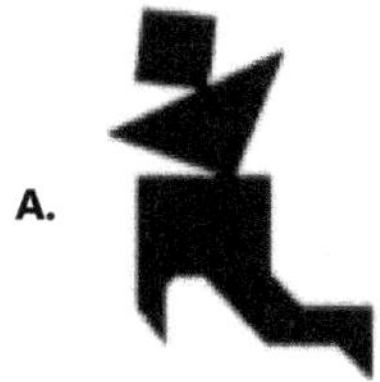

B. 

C. 

D. 

Q.35 Which of the following terms are related to textile design?

A. Batik **B.** Leading **C.** Block **D.** Alpaca

Q.36 Which of the following are the mountain ranges of India?

A. Lushai Hills **B.** Kudremukh ranges

C. Hindu kush **D.** Mount Apo

Multiple Choice Questions (MCQ)

Q.37 Identify the correct art techniques with which the following paintings have been made.

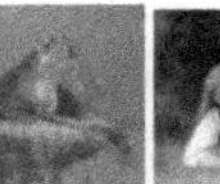

A. Watercolor, Pastel, Oil, Crayons

B. Crayons, Acrylic, Pastel, Oil

C. Watercolor, Oil, Acrylic, Crayon

D. Crayons, Watercolor, Pastel, Acrylic

Q.38

If  becomes 

Then  Will become

A. 

B. 

C. 

D. 

Q.39

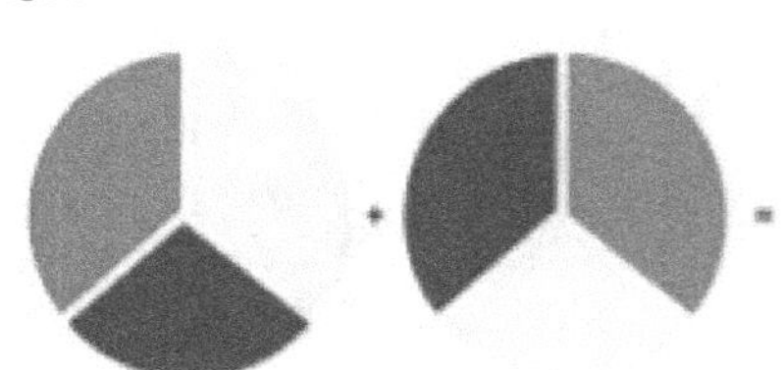

A. 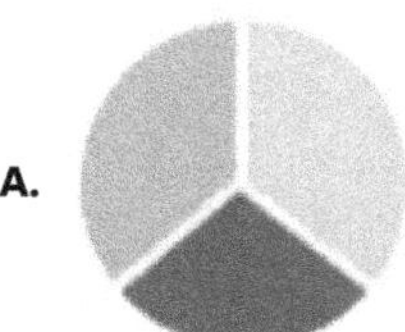

B. 

C. 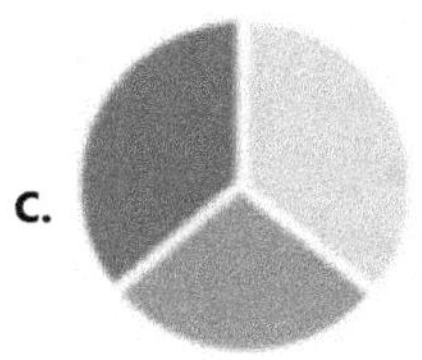

D. 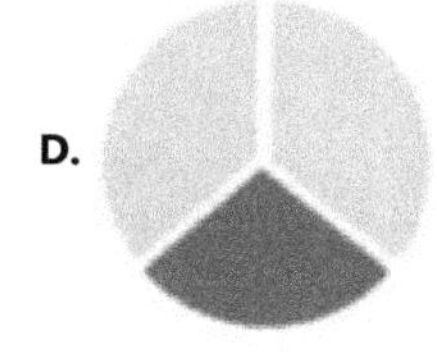

Q.40 Shown are the symbols for different functions. Identify the correct description sequence from the given choices.

A. Phone network, General warning, Rotating parts, Radiation

B. Non ionizing radiation, Rotating parts, General warning, Radiation

C. Phone network, Rotating parts, Radiation, General Warning

D. None of the above

Q.41

Identify the function of the above product

A. Sculpture

B. Fruit juicer

C. NASA Probe

D. Scale model of a Rocket

Q.42 From the given answer figures, select the one in which the question figure is hidden/embedded. (Rotation is not allowed)

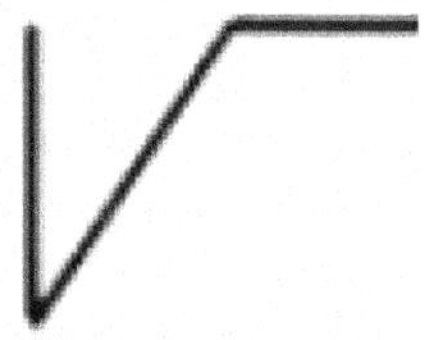

A. 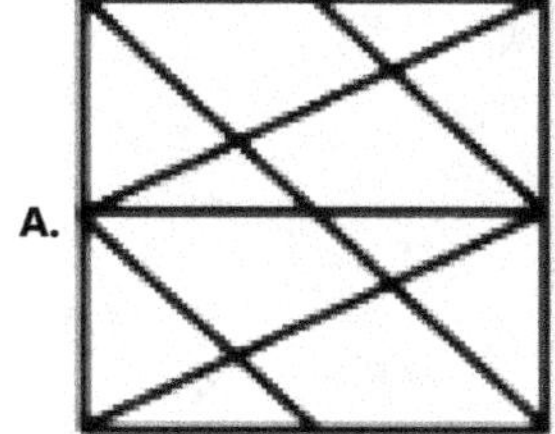

B. 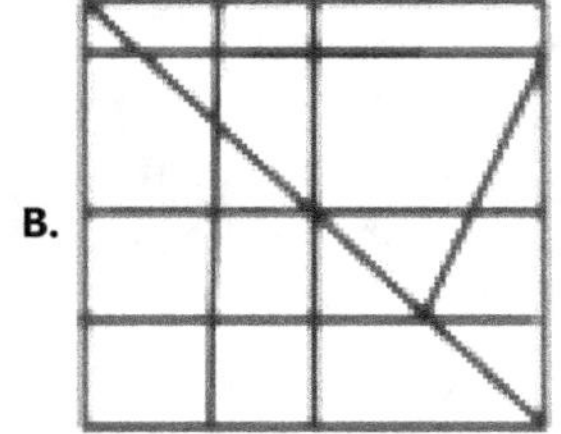

C. 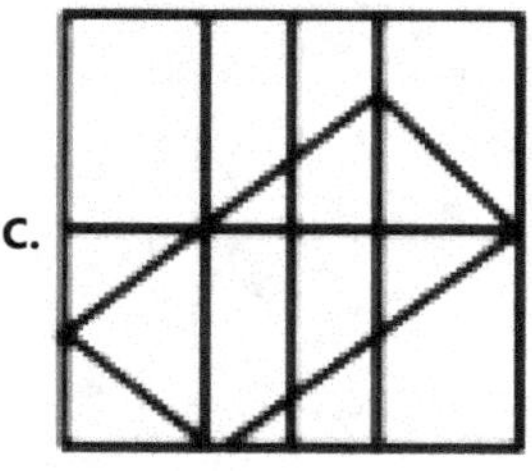

D. 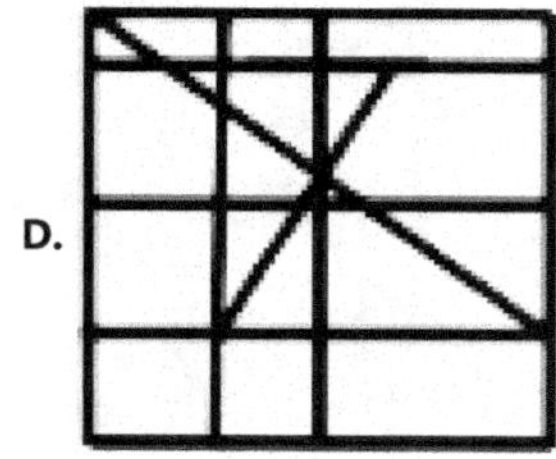

Q.43 Which of the symbols at the bottom should take the place of X?

X

A. B. C. D.

Q.44 Identify the common quality in the given figures.

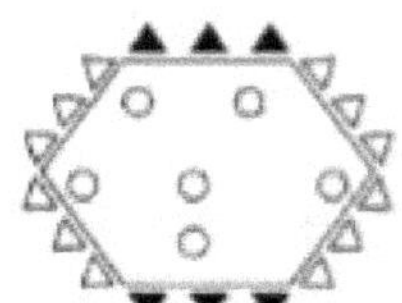 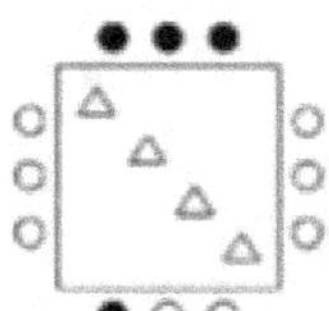

A. 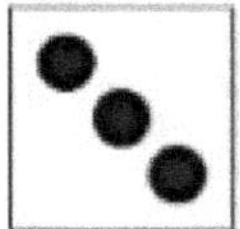

B. 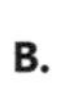 

C.  

D.  

Q.45 Complete the given series.

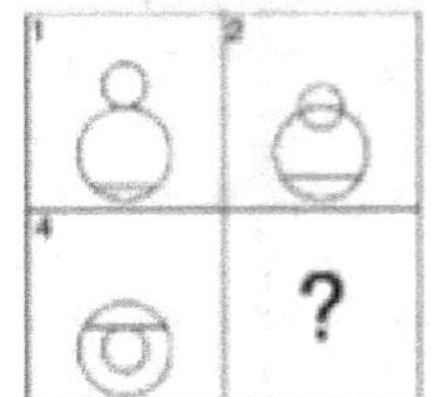

A. 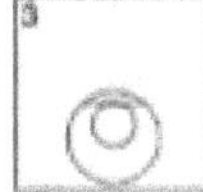

B. 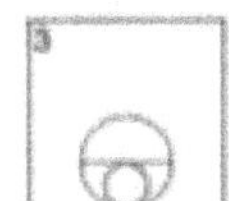

C. 

D. 

Q.46 Complete the series

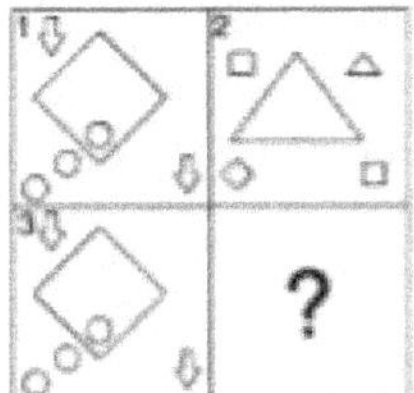

A. 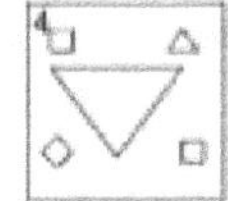

B. 

C. 

D. 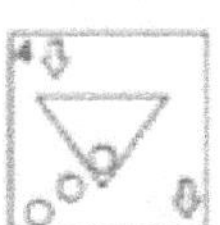

Q.47 Complete the sequence .

?

A. 

B. 

C. 

D. 

Q.48 Identify the figure that completes the pattern.

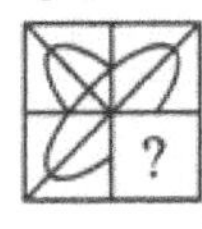

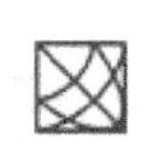

(X) (1) (2) (3) (4)

A. 1 B. 2 C. 3 D. 4

Q.49 Identify the figure that completes the pattern:

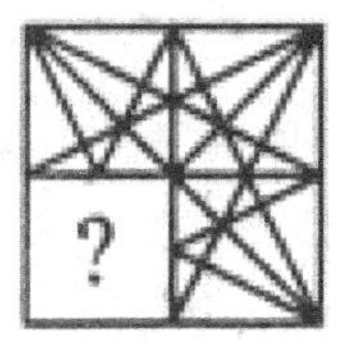

A. 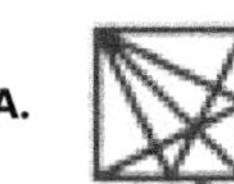 B. 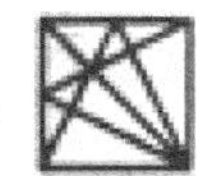 C.  D. 

Q.50

Identify the figure that completes the pattern.

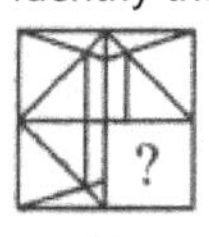
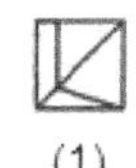
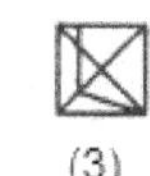

(X) (1) (2) (3) (4)

A. 1 B. 2 C. 3 D. 4

Q.51

Identify the figure that completes the pattern:

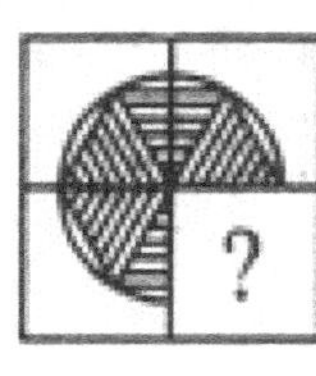

A. 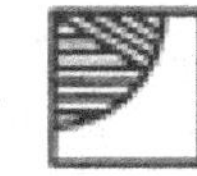 B. 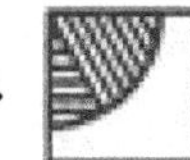 C.  D. 

Q.52

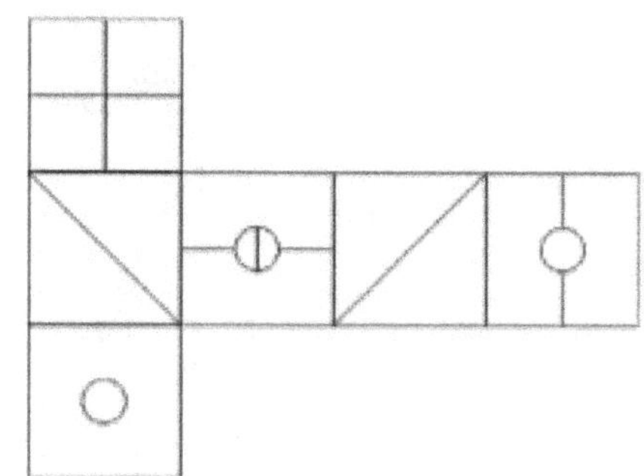

When the above is folded to form a cube, which is the only one of the following that can be produced?

A. 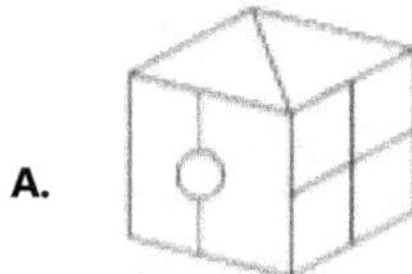

B. 

C. 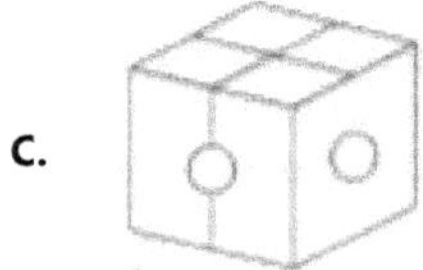

D. 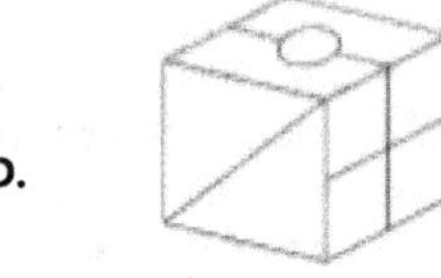

Q.53

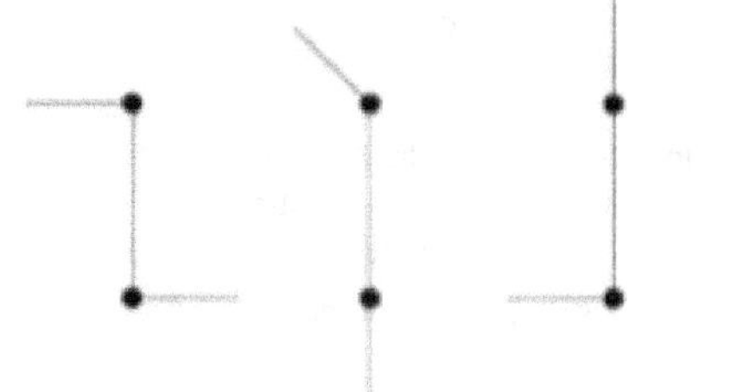

What comes next?

A. 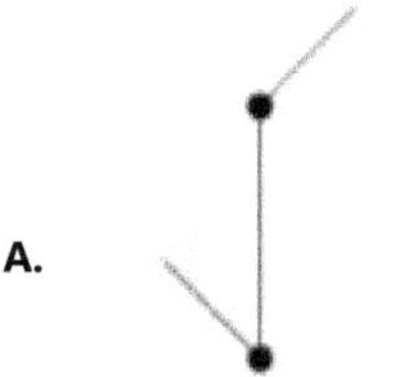

B. 

C. 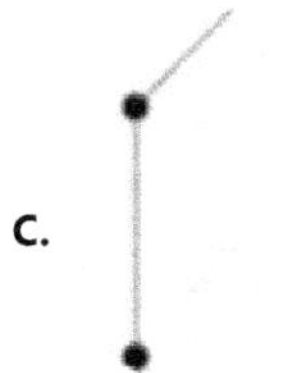

D. 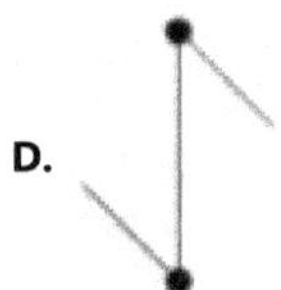

Q.54

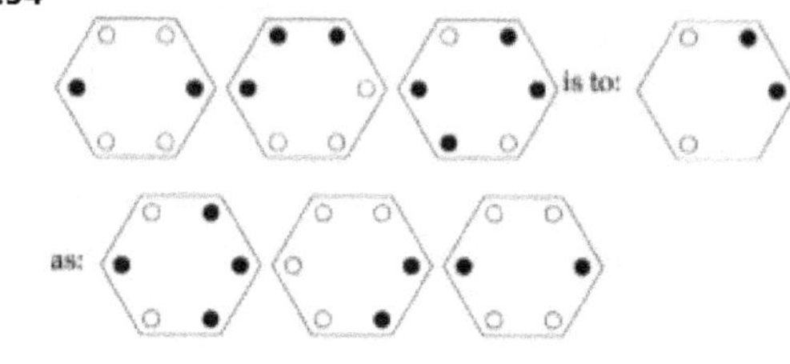

A. 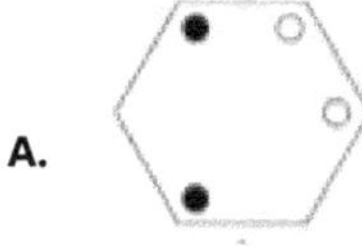

B. 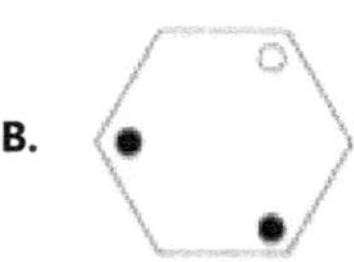

C. 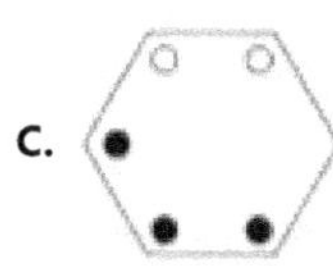

D. 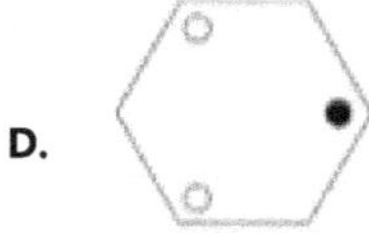

Q.55

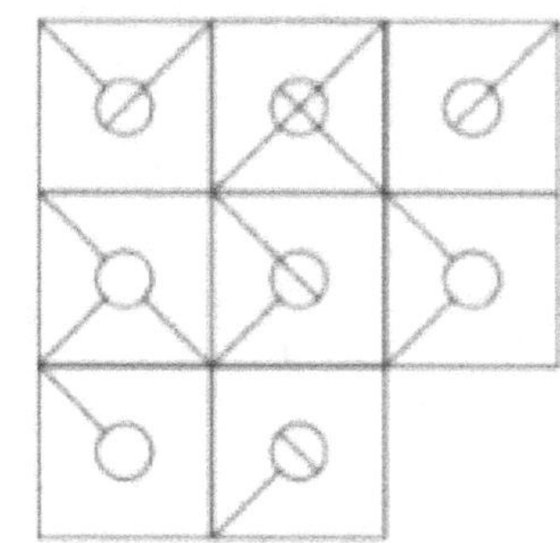

Which is the missing tile?

A. 

B. 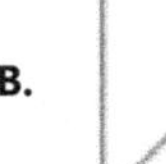 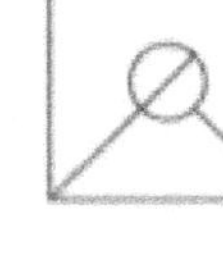

C. 

D. 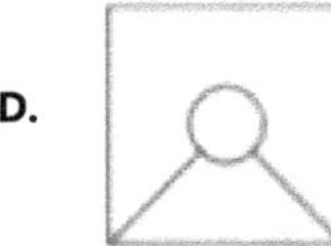

Q.56 Choose the correct water image of the given figure (X) from amongst the four alternatives.

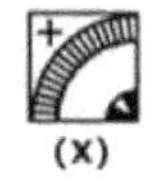
(X)

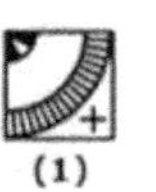
(1)

(2)

(3)

(4)

A. 1 **B.** 2 **C.** 3 **D.** 4

Q.57 Find out from amongst the four alternatives as to how the pattern would appear when the transparent sheet is folded at the dotted line.

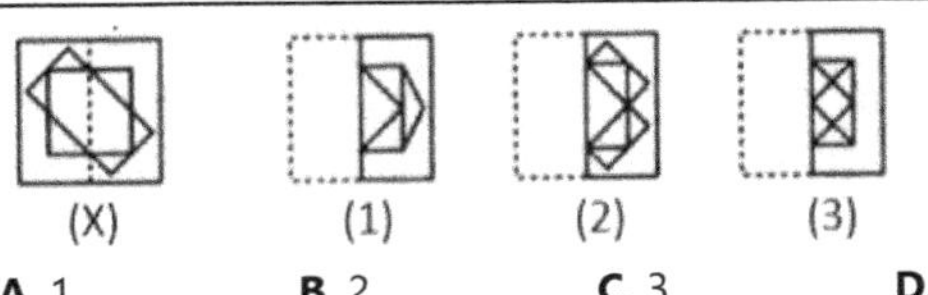

A. 1 **B.** 2 **C.** 3 **D.** 4

Q.58 Choose a figure, which would most closely resemble the unfolded form of Figure (Z).

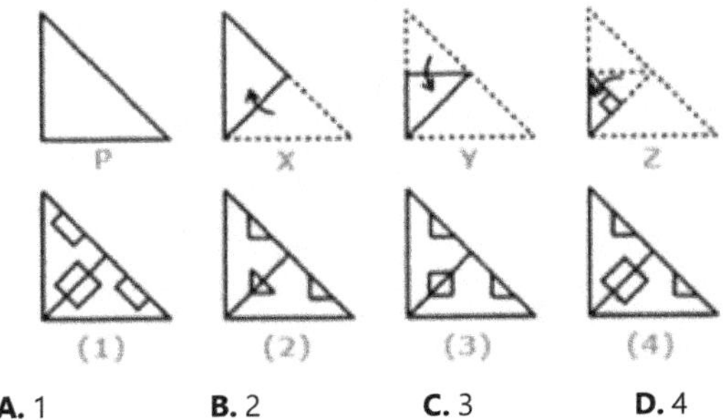

A. 1 **B.** 2 **C.** 3 **D.** 4

Q.59 Choose the alternative, which closely resembles the mirror image of the given combination.

REASONING

(1) ꓤEVƧOИIИG (2) ᘓИIИOƧAƎЯ

(3) ЯƎAƧOИIИG (4) ᘓИIИOSAƎЯ

A. 1 **B.** 2 **C.** 3 **D.** 4

Q.60 Shown below are images that have different visual features. Identify the correct sequence of visual features associated with these images from the given choices.

A B C D

A. Dominance, cropping, figure-ground, pattern
B. Pattern, figure-ground, cropping, dominance
C. Pattern, dominance, cropping, figure-ground
D. Pattern, cropping, dominance, figure-ground

Q.61 What will be the most probable pose at position 5 to complete the sequence below?

C.

D.

Q.62 Rearrange the following five sentences in the proper sequence to form a meaningful paragraph.

A. After Examining him, the doctor smiled at him mischievously and took out a syringe.
B. Thinking that he was really sick, his father summoned the family doctor.
C. That day, Mintu wanted to take a day off from school
D. Immediately, Mintu jumped up from his bed and swore that he was fine
E. Therefore he pretended to be sick and remained in bed.

A. ABCDE **B.** CEABD **C.** CEBAD **D.** CEADB

Q.63 In the following questions four alternatives are given for the idiom/phrase italicized and underlined in the sentence. Choose the alternative which best expresses the meaning of idiom/phrase.

The detective left *no stone unturned* to trace the culprit.

A. took no pains
B. did very irrelevant things
C. resorted to illegitimate practices
D. used all available means

Q.64 What can we infer from the following statement? "Since every child I know likes ice cream, Mike must also like ice cream."

A. The speaker doesn't know many children
B. Mike is a child
C. Mike likes anything sweet
D. The speaker is a good friend of Mike's

Q.65 Spot the difference.

Below are two apparently identical pictures. In fact, there are differences between the two—Spot them.

A. 9 **B.** 10 **C.** 11 **D.** 12

Q.66 Select the correct mirror image of the combination when the mirror is placed at 'PQ' as shown below.

A.

B.

C.

D.

Q.67 In the following questions, four alternatives are given for the idiom/phrase italicized and underlined in the sentence. Choose the alternative which best expresses the meaning of idiom/phrase.

Do no trust a man who *blows his own trumpet.*

A. Flatters **B.** praises others
C. admonishes others **D.** praises himself

Q.68 Rearrange the following five sentences in proper sequence to form a meaningful paragraph, and then answer the questions given below.

a) Indeed, the mutations that the family has undergone in this century have been more challenging than at any time of its evolution.
b) Thus, we have nuclear families, single parent families, surrogate families and global families to name just a few.
c) How these changes have reduced our worldview is an interesting field of study in themselves.
d) What we often forget is that the family as it exists today has expanded its orthodox definition to include several variations.
e) Each of these has brought it own attitudes and priorities.

A. a, b, c, d,e **B.** a, c, d, b, e
C. a, c, b,d, e **D.** c, d, b, e, a

// Smart Answer Sheet //

Correct Indicates percentage of students who answered questions correctly.

Skipped Indicates percentage of students who skipped questions.

Q.	Ans.	Correct	Skipped
1	28	16.4 %	10.21 %
2	9	50.27 %	21.5 %
3	10	44.89 %	25.0 %
4	72	9.14 %	32.53 %
5	47	31.18 %	26.88 %
6	24	44.09 %	27.42 %
7	8	39.78 %	26.08 %
8	46	51.08 %	26.07 %
9	10	12.37 %	33.87 %
10	#	13.44 %	27.96 %
11	8	40.59 %	33.6 %
12	#	29.3 %	29.84 %
13	#	7.8 %	40.05 %
14	#	56.45 %	27.42 %
15	1	61.29 %	28.23 %
16	#	23.39 %	31.45 %
17	#	28.76 %	32.53 %
18	#	10.22 %	31.45 %
19	B, D, C	13.71 %	33.33 %
20	B, A, D	15.05 %	40.33 %
21	B, D, C	20.97 %	38.71 %
22	B	12.37 %	31.18 %
23	D	34.14 %	31.72 %
24	B	9.14 %	38.44 %
25	B, D, C	18.82 %	38.98 %
26	B, D, C	51.08 %	36.55 %
27	B	36.29 %	32.8 %
28	B	26.88 %	32.8 %
29	C	43.82 %	32.52 %
30	B	56.45 %	32.53 %
31	C	52.15 %	31.72 %
32	A	23.39 %	31.72 %
33	D	28.76 %	31.72 %
34	B, D, C	32.53 %	37.9 %
35	A, D, C	35.75 %	35.22 %
36	B, A	11.29 %	37.1 %
37	A	42.47 %	26.62 %
38	A	67.74 %	26.35 %
39	C	47.85 %	28.23 %
40	D	30.65 %	26.88 %
41	B	38.71 %	30.38 %
42	D	52.15 %	31.99 %
43	C	63.98 %	29.03 %
44	C	23.39 %	34.41 %
45	C	29.03 %	28.77 %
46	A	53.23 %	32.79 %
47	C	36.29 %	33.06 %
48	D	45.16 %	32.26 %
49	D	51.88 %	34.41 %
50	B	52.42 %	34.14 %
51	C	50.0 %	32.8 %
52	D	30.91 %	32.26 %
53	C	54.57 %	30.65 %
54	B	36.56 %	35.75 %
55	C	31.72 %	36.83 %
56	D	55.65 %	29.03 %
57	B	60.22 %	29.3 %
58	A	51.34 %	30.65 %
59	B	62.1 %	29.84 %
60	B	29.84 %	29.3 %
61	B	47.31 %	29.84 %
62	C	45.43 %	31.45 %
63	D	56.18 %	31.99 %
64	B	59.95 %	29.3 %
65	B	22.31 %	31.18 %
66	C	49.19 %	33.87 %
67	D	57.26 %	32.79 %
68	B	33.6 %	36.02 %

#

Q.	Answer
10	16
12	G
13	81
14	B
16	4991

17	saturday
18	4, 11

Performance Analysis	
Avg. Score (%)	**40.0%**
Toppers Score (%)	**96.67%**
Your Score	

//Hints and Solutions//

1.

1. ✱	11. ✕	21. ✂
2. ✹	12. ⁂	22. ⌘
3. ✳	13. ⊘	23. ◕
4. ✷	14. ⓿	24. ❉
5. ▴	15. ⊗	25. ☮
6. ✦	16. ꕤ	26. ☺
7. ✹	17. ✠	27. ☹
8. ✴	18. ✎	28. ☹
9. •	19. ✐	
10. ●	20. ✍	

2. There are nine circles formed, when pattern arranged in a six-by-six matrix.

Hence, the correct answer is 9.

3. Let Megha starts from point A and walks $10\ km$ towards the North to reach B. She then turns right and walks $15\ km$ to reach C. She again turns right and walks $20\ km$ southwards. She turns right and walks $15\ km$ to finally stop at point E.

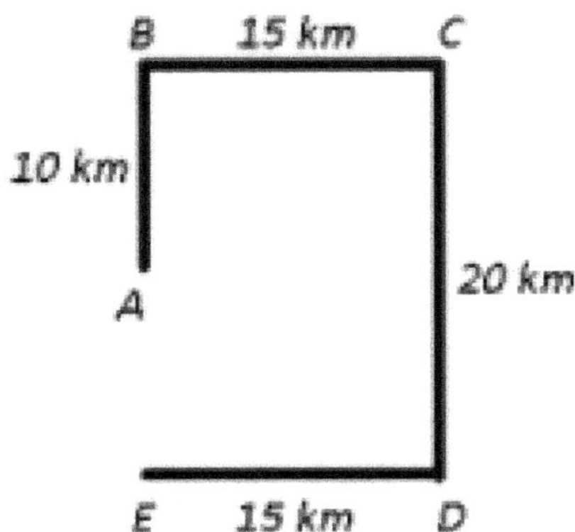

Here, $AB = 10\ km$ i.e., half of $CD = 20\ km$

So, the distance between A and E is $10\ km$.

Therefore, she is $10\ km$ from her starting point.

Hence, the correct answer is 10.

4. There are 72 caps worn by the group of people

5. There are 47 surface required , If the word QUEUE (shown on the right) were to be extruded

6. There are 64 small cubes.

Hence one side of the big cube = $\sqrt[3]{64}$ = 4

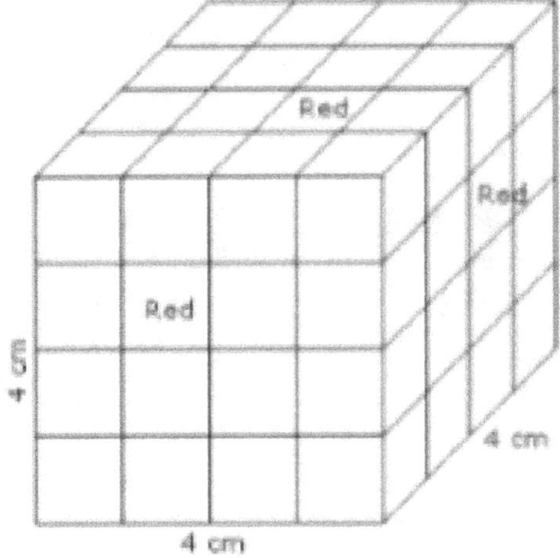

Number of small cubes having only one face coloured

= $6 \times (n-2)^2$

= $6 \times (4-2)^2$

= 6×2^2

= 24

Hence, the correct answer is 24.

7. 8 cases: 148pairs = 296 shoes and 296 + 37 = 8.

8. In this figure there are 21 columns containing 2 cubes each, 4 columns containing 1 cube each,

So, Totalnumberofcubes $= (21 \times 2) + (4 \times 1) = 46$

9. 10 type of font style are used in the given picture.

10. The figure can be labeled as:

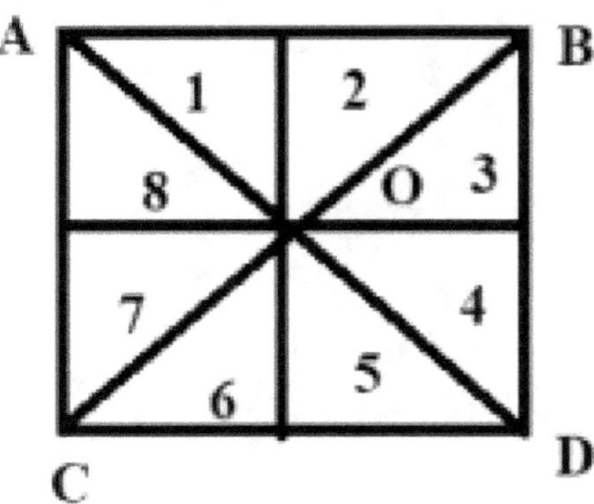

In the figure, the 8 triangles are shown easily and the other triangles are $COD, DOB, BOA, AOC, ACD, BDC, ABC, ABD$.

So that total number of triangles $= 8 + 8 = 16$

Hence, the correct answer is 16.

11. Each number in the segment at the bottom is the sum of the four numbers in the sections either side. Thus: 8+3+4+3=18

12. For ABCDEFGH, let's number the positions as:

12345678

Given position : F = 6

Now, again work out from last instruction.

- Two to right → 6+2 = 8
- Three to left → 8-3 = 5
- Immediately to left → 5-1 = 4
- Three to right → 4+3 = 7 → G

So, our answer becomes G.

As we have to work with numbers here, the thinking process is easier.

13. In the series, consecutive multiples of 5 are added to a term to obtain the next term.

$6(+5) \rightarrow 11(+10) \rightarrow 21(+15) \rightarrow 36(+20) \rightarrow 56(+25) \rightarrow 81$

81 will replace ? in the series.

Hence, the correct answer is 81.

14. B point will balance the plank .

15. If gear B rotates in a particular direction, A and D move in the opposite direction to each other.

16. Total sale for 5 months,

$= \text{Rs. } (6435 + 6927 + 6855 + 7230 + 6562)$

$= \text{Rs. } 34009$

Required sale,

$= Rs.[(6500 \times 6) - 34009]$

$= Rs.(39000 - 34009)$

$= Rs.4991$

Hence, the correct answer is 4991.

17. We know that,

A leap year has 366 days and a non-leap year has 365 days.

Leap year $= 366$ days or 52 weeks and 2 days. So, here the number of odd days is 2.

Non $-$Leap year $= 365$ days or 52 weeks and 1 day. So, here the number of odd days is 1.

The odd days between 2015 to 2016 is 2 odd days (as, 2016 is a leap year).

Code of the day	Day
0	Sunday
1	Monday
2	Tuesday
3	Wednesday
4	Thursday
5	Friday
6	Saturday

Given, 21 November 2016 was Monday.

So, 21 November $2015 =$ Monday $-2 =$ Saturday

Hence, the correct answer is "saturday".

18. There are two alternate series.

One is: 7 6 5 X

In the first series, the numbers are getting decreased by 1, so the value of X is 4.

The other is: 8 9 10 Y

In the second series, the numbers are getting increased by 1, so the value of Y is 11.

Hence, the answer is 4,11.

19. B, C, D are true. "The Indus valley civilization also known as harappan civilization was the ancient civilization built around the banks of river indus. It is one of the ancient civilizations besides mesopotamia and egypt civilization." is wrong.

20. A, B, D are true

Kumar Bhattacharyya is an Indian British engineer who founded the Warwick Manufacturing Group (WMG), an academic department at the University of Warwick, which provides research, education and knowledge transfer in engineering, manufacturing and technology.

Aruna Roy is an Indian social activist who co-founded the MazdoorKisan Shakti Sangathana (MKSS), a social and grassroots organization for the empowerment of workers and peasants.

Carl Edward Sagan was an American astronomer, cosmologist, astrophysicist, astro-biologist and author.

21. Arundhati Roy - The Algebra of Infinite Justice, The God of Small Things.

Upamanyu Chatterjee - English, August, Fairy Tales at Fifty.

Kiran Desai - The Inheritance of Loss, Hullabaloo in the Guava Orchard.

22. Clearly, banning a product would surely render jobless the large number of workers involved in manufacturing it. Besides, firecrackers on burning produce explosive sounds and immense poisonous fumes, which cause both air and noise pollution. So, both arguments I and III hold. However, to stop child labour, it is not necessary to close down the industry but strict laws against child abuse should be enforced and legal actions taken. Similarly, there are many other ways to make parties boisterous and special events enjoyable. Hence, II as well as IV does not hold strong.

23. The statement talks of boom in drug business and cites examples from the capital city. This makes I implicit. Further, it is given that most jhuggi-jhopari dwellers are seen to indulge in transactions of drug pouches. This implies that they give in to their lust for money quite easily and do not hesitate to get involved in illegal activities for the same. So, III is implicit while II is not.

24. By building cities with the system of organs like those of animals.

25. B, C, D

Alessandro di Mariano di Vanni Filipepi, known as Sandro Botticelli, was an Italian painter of the Early Renaissance. Botticelli's posthumous reputation suffered until the late 19th century; since then, his work has been seen to represent the linear grace of Early Renaissance painting.

26. B, C, D

The year 1979 saw the birth of a legend, S Elayaraja, who left the world in amazement witnessing his exquisite artistic skills and his diligence for oil colors. Born in the land rich of culture and tradition, Tamil Nadu, he grasped and explored his artistic skills from Govt. Fine art College, Chennai

27. Madhubani is a town municipality and headquarter of Madhubani district. Madhubani is situated in the Indian state of Bihar. It comes under Darbhanga Division. It lies 26 km northeast of Darbhanga town and was part of the erstwhile 'Bettiah Raj'. The Madhuban Raj in Madhubani was created as a consequence.

28. In a) and c) the right triangular shape has been truncated, and in d) both triangular shapes have had the edges cut off.

29. In a) the long rectangle that covers the volume is in a wrong position, and in b) there is a wrong geometric form.

30. In a) and c) the small cube has been moved.

31. When the mirror is placed vertically in front of the object, the horizontal sides and directions get reversed whereas the vertical sides and directions remain the same.

The mirror image formed looks like -

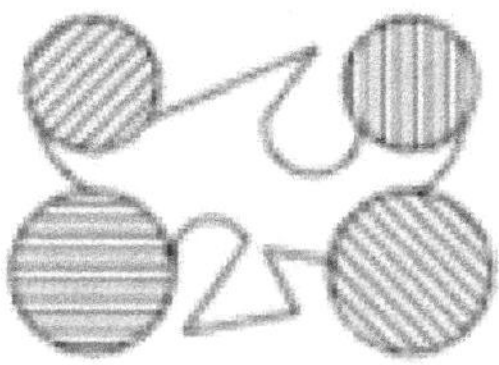

Hence, the correct option is (C).

32.

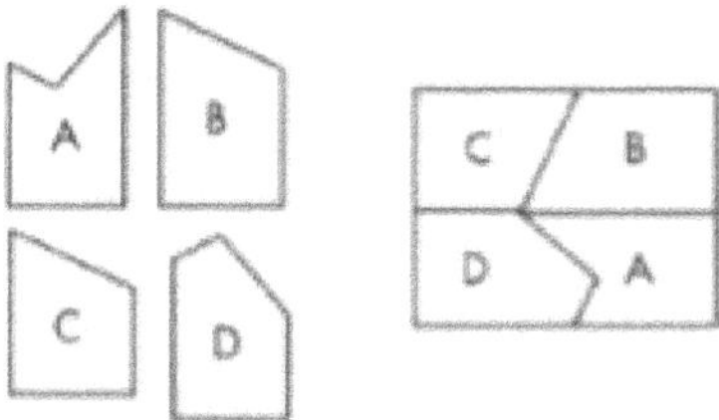

33.

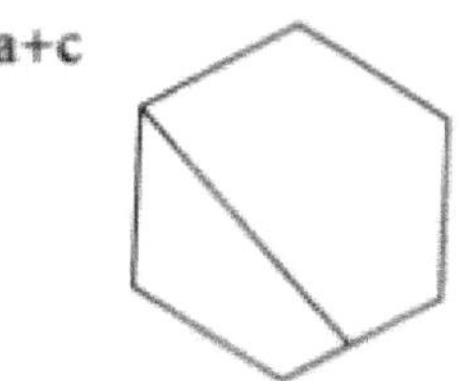

34. BCD Are the correct option when A square is cut into 7 pieces as shown on the extreme left of the image.

35. A C D

Batik is an Indonesian technique of wax-resist dyeing applied to whole cloth. This technique originated from Java, Indonesia. Batik is made either by drawing dots and lines of the resist with a spouted tool called a tjanting, or by printing the resist with a copper stamp called a cap.

The alpaca is a species of South American camelid descended from the vicuña. It is similar to, and often confused with, the llama. However, alpacas are often noticeably smaller than llamas. The two animals are closely related and can successfully cross-breed. Alpacas and llamas are related to the guanaco.

36. Lushai Hills and Kudremukh ranges are the mountain ranges of India.

The Lushai Hills are a mountain range in Mizoram and Tripura, India. The range is part of the Patkai range system and its highest point is 2,157 m high Phawngpui, also known as 'Blue Mountain'.

Kudremukh is a mountain range and name of a peak located in Chikkamagaluru district, in Karnataka, India. It is also the name of a small hill station cum mining town situated near the mountain, about 20 kilometers from Kalasa.

Hence, the correct options are (A) and (B).

37. A

Watercolor, Pastel, Oil, Crayons technique are used paintings have been made.

38. option A

Deep sky blue is an azure-cyan colour associated with deep shade of sky blue. Deep sky blue is a web colour. This colour is the colour on the colour wheel (RGB/HSV colour wheel) halfway between azure and cyan. The traditional name for this colour is Capri.

39. option C

Midnight blue carries the blue symbolism of importance, confidence, power, and authority. Dark blue is associated with intelligence, stability, unity, and conservatism. Because it is very dark, midnight blue can sometimes be a neutral like black, which is also often seen as a conservative and authoritarian color.

The orange is the fruit of various citrus species in the family Rutaceae; it primarily refers to Citrus × sinensis, which is also called sweet orange, to distinguish it from the related Citrus × aurantium, referred to as bitter orange.

In a RGB color space, hex #013220 (also known as Dark green) is composed of 0.4% red, 19.6% green and 12.5% blue. Whereas in a CMYK color space, it is composed of 98% cyan, 0% magenta, 36% yellow and 80.4% black. It has a hue angle of 158 degrees, a saturation of 96.1% and a lightness of 10%.

40. OPTION D

None of the above

41. OPTION B

It increased appetite of our child due to it's handy mechanisms! He likes machines to watch so wants to drink fruit juices to see usage.

42. The question figure is embedded in,

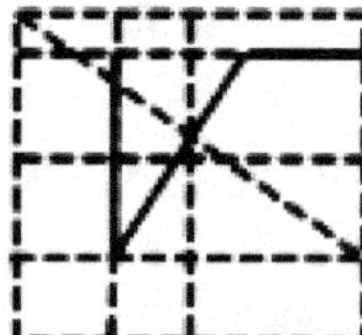

Hence, the correct option is (D).

43. In each row the first symbol is the same as the second in the previous row and the other symbols continue in the same order .

44. Both question shapes have the same number of shapes inside them as they have sides and have the same number of shaded shapes as they have sides. All the suggested answers have only one set of shapes, some of which are shaded, and only suggested answer C has the same number of shapes and shaded shapes as sides.

Hence, the correct option is (C).

45. At each step in the series the small circle is migrating downwards and the line upwards.

Hence, the correct option is (C).

46. Arrows become squares and change back, the three circles become a small triangle and change back, diamonds alternate in size, and the large triangle appears in the second and fourth steps rotated 180 degrees.

47. In the first shape the triangle overlies the circle and then the circle overlies the triangle. In the third step the triangle again overlies the circle; only now it points upwards. In the next step of the sequence you would expect the circle to overlie the triangle and, given its new position, the circle would obscure the triangle. This means that the correct representation of the shape is shown at C.

48. Figure (2) completes the pattern.

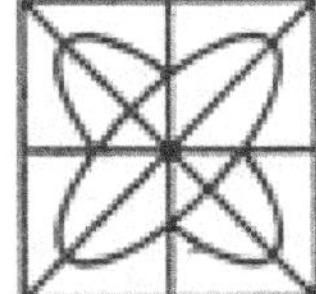

Hence, the correct option is (D).

49. The fourth answer figure -

completes the given figure pattern.

Hence, the correct option is (D).

50. Figure 2 completes the pattern.

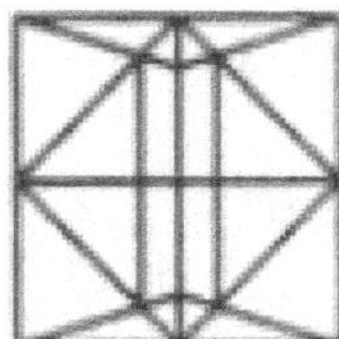

Hence, the correct option is (B).

51. The answer figure given in option (C) completes the question figure.

Hence, the correct option is (C).

52. When the above is folded to form a cube (option D figure) formed.

53. C: the top arm moves 45° clockwise at each stage and the bottom arm moves 90° clockwise

54. B: only dots that appear in the same position just twice in the first three hexagons are carried forward to the final hexagons

55. C: in each row and column only lines that are common to the first two squares are carried forward to the final square

56. water image of the given figure formed in image number 4 which mean option D is correct.

57. the pattern would appear when the transparent sheet is folded at the dotted lin

formed in figure B (2)

58. Option A is correct, it would most closely resemble the unfolded form of Figure

59. Image of REASONING word is formed in figure B (2) .

60.

- A pattern is a regularity in the world, in human-made design, or abstract ideas. As such, the elements of a pattern repeat predictably.
- Figure-ground is the state in which we perceive elements as either the objects of focus or the background. Like closure, figure-ground works through the use of positive and negative space
- Cropping is the removal of unwanted outer areas from a photographic or illustrated image. The process usually consists of the removal of some of the peripheral areas of an image to remove extraneous
- When you create dominance in your work, you create elements that command attention and prevail over

other elements. Every design should have a primary area of interest or focal point that serves to design.

Hence, the correct option is (B).

61. Option B is correct

62. CEBAD

That day, Mintu wanted to take a day off from school.

Therefore he pretended to be sick and remained in bed.

Thinking that he was really sick, his father summoned the family doctor.

After examining him, the doctor smiled at him mischievously and took out a syringe.

Immediately, Mintu jumped up from his bed and swore that he was fine.

63. left no stone unturned: try every possible course of action in order to achieve something.

64. option B

Mike is a child

65.

Hence, the correct option is (B).

66. In a plane mirror, a mirror image is a reflected duplication of an object that appears almost identical, but it is reversed in the direction perpendicular to the mirror surface. As an optical effect, it results from the reflection of substances such as a mirror or water.

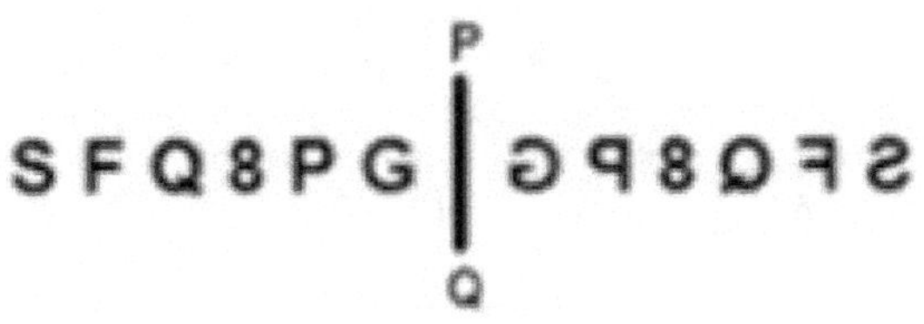

Hence, the correct option is (C).

67. blows his own trumpet: to talk about oneself or one's achievements especially in a way that shows that one is proud or too proud.

68. a, c, d, b, e

Indeed, the mutations that the family has undergone in this century have been more challenging than at any time of its evolution.

How these changes have reduced our worldview is an interesting field of study in themselves.

What we often forget is that the family as it exists today has expanded its orthodox definition to include several variations.

Thus, we have nuclear families, single parent families, surrogate families and global families to name just a few.

Each of these has brought it own attitudes and priorities.

Mock Test 04

Numerical Answer Type (NAT)

Q.1 Shyam walks 5 km towards East and then turns left and walks 6 km. Again he turns right and walks 9 km. Finally he turns to his right and walks 6 km. How far is he from the starting point?

Q.2 Count how many times "!" The sign is used in the picture below.

Q.3

How many triangles are there here?

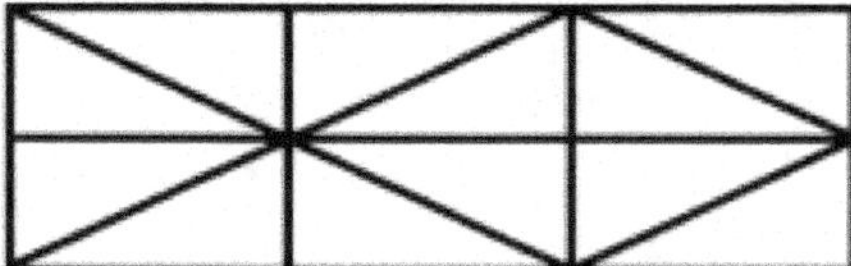

Q.4 Imagine letters are extruded into three-dimensional objects, as shown in the figure on the left (the letter A). If the word EGG (shown on the right) were to be extruded, how many surfaces would it have?

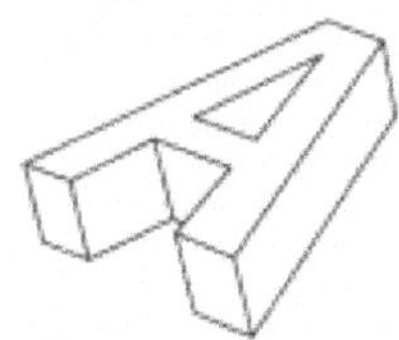

EGG

Q.5 Given below is a series of numbers. Which number will replace the question mark?

1, 1, 2, 3, 5, 8, 13, 21, ?

Q.6 At 11.00am today my watch was showing the correct time, after which it began to lose 14 minutesper hour until three hours ago when it stopped completely. It is now wrongly showing the time as2.50pm. What is the correct time now?

Q.7 Count the number of cubes in the given figure.

Q.8 Count the number of fonts used in the given set of words.

Design is about progress. It is the conceptualization and creation of new things: ideas, INTERACTIONS, information, objects, TYPEFACES, books, posters, products, places, signs, [illegible], services, furniture, websites, and MORE.

Q.9 The given image has sixty-four squares with patterns inside, arranged in an eight-by-eight matrix.How many different types of squares are there in the image, assuming squares may be rotated?

Q.10 How many faces can you see in this tree?

Q.11 What is one-third of one-quarter of one-fifth of one-half of 120?

Q.12 Which number should replace the question mark?

9	17	16
5	4	8
5	4	?
9	17	8

Q.13

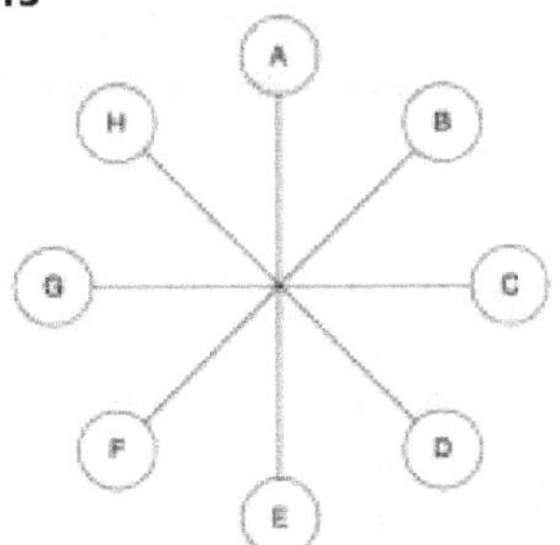

What letter is two letters away clockwise from the letter that is directly opposite the letter threeletters away anticlockwise from the letter C?

Q.14 How many triangles in the figure?

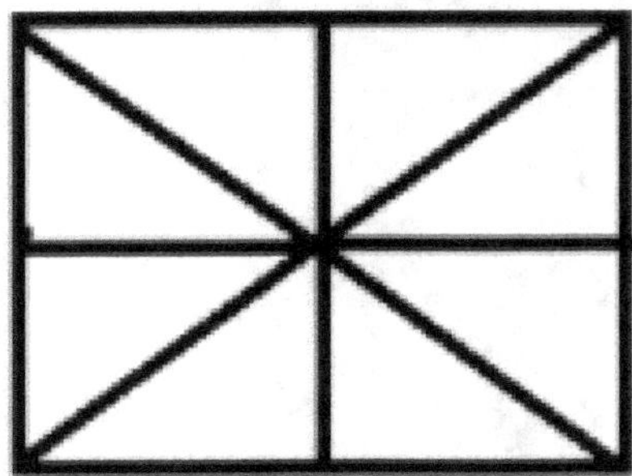

Q.15 A rotates in the opposite direction to C; B rotates anti-clockwise. In which way will D turn?

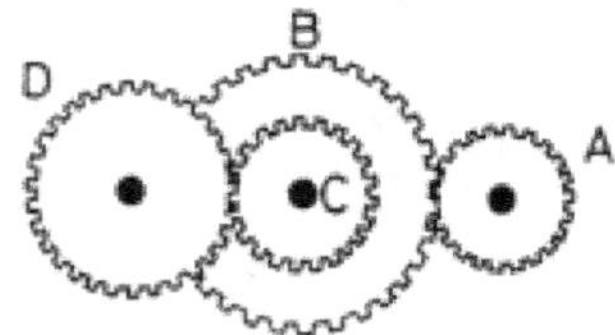

1. clockwise Direction.
2. anticlockwise Direction.
3. Wheel can not rotate.

Q.16 Assume that you can print 400 words on a sheet of A4-size paper. How many A4-size sheets ofpaper would you need to print 6,000 words?

Q.17 What two terms complete this series?

A 1 D 4 H 8 M 13 _ _

Q.18 2/3 of the number is thirty less than the original number. The number is ;-

Multiple Select Questions (MSQ)

Q.19 Select all statements about Revolt of 1857 India that are true:

A. One of the important events of Indian history is the Revolt of 1857. It was the second rebellion against the East India Company, which took the massive form.

B. The main persons behind this rebellion were the soldiers [sepoy]. That is why it is also called sepoy Mutiny. But the revolt did not remain limited to the soldiers, later it spread and took a massive form. Some people also called this- 'India's first war of Independence'.

The revolt was started on 10th May of 1857 in the town of Meerut. Though in some places, fractional clashes began before that. It ended on 20 June 1858. The first martyr of 1857 revolt was MangalPandey. He attacked his British

C. sergeant on 29 March 1857 at Barrackpore. Some of the leaders of the rebellion were- Rani Lakshmibai [Jhansi],Kunwar Singh [Bihar], Bahadur Shah [Delhi], Nana Saheb [Kanpur], Tatia Tope [Kanpur], Begum HazratMahal [Lucknow]. There was a deficiency of central leadership

D. The revolt was started due to the induction of enfield riffles in the army. It was believed that the cartridges used in the riffles were made of pig fat and cow fat which were restricted for the Muslims and Hindus respectively. They protested against these.

Q.20 Which of the following statements is/are true?

A. Guy de Chauliac was a popular surgeon of the Early Medieval Period.

B. David Baltimore is an American biologist who won a share of the 1975 Nobel Prize in Physiology or Medicine. As a researcher, he has made tremendous contributions to immunology, virology, cancer research, biotechnology, and recombinant DNA research.

C. Nikola Tesla was a Serbian-American inventor, best known for his development of alternating current electrical systems. He also made extraordinary contributions to the fields of electromagnetism and wireless radio communications.

D. RaghuramRajan is an American economist and the former Governor of the Reserve Bank of India, who is currently the Vice-Chairman of the Bank for International Settlements.

Q.21 From the options below, select the Indian author/s writing in English whose works are represented

below:

1. The argumentative Indian
2. The shadow lines
3. Inequality reexamined
4. Flood of fire
5. That long silence
6. Roots and Shadows

A. Amartya Sen **B.** Amitav Ghosh

C. Shashi Deshpande **D.** Ruskin Bond

Q.22 Question given below consists of a statement, followed by three arguments numbered I , II and III. You have to decide which of the arguments is a 'strong' argument.

Statement: Should "literacy" be the minimum criterion for becoming a voter in India?

Arguments:

I. No. Mere literacy is no guarantee of political maturity of an individual.

II. Yes. Illiterate people are less likely to make politically wiser decisions of voting for a right candidate or party.

III. No.Voting is the constitutional right of every citizen.

A. Only I and II are strong

B. Only II and III are strong

C. All are strong

D. None is strong

Q.23 Question below is given a statement followed by three assumptions numbered I, II and III. You have to consider the statement and the following assumptions and decide which of the assumptions is implicit in the statement.

Statement: "Fly with us and experience the pleasure of flying."- An advertisement by an airline.

Assumptions:

I. More passengers may be attracted to travel by the airline after reading the advertisement.

II. People generally may prefer an enjoyable flight.

III. Other airlines may not be offering the same facilities.

A. None is implicit **B.** Only I is implicit

C. Only II is implicit **D.** None of these

Q.24 A recent report in News Week says that in American colleges, students of Asian origin outperform not only the minority group students but the majority whites as well. Many of these students must be of Indian origin, and their achievement is something we can be proud of. It is unlikely that these talented youngsters will come back to India, and that is the familiar brain drain problem. However recent statements by the nation's policy-makers indicate that the perception of this issue is changing. 'Brain bank' and not 'brain drain' is the more appropriate idea, they suggest since the expertise of Indians abroad is only deposited in other places and not lost. This may be so, but this brain bank, like most other banks, is one that primarily serves customers in its neighbourhood. The skills of the Asians now excelling in America's colleges will mainly help the U.S.A.. No matter how significant, what non-resident Indians do for India and what their counterparts do for other Asian lands is only a by-product. But it is also necessary to ask, or be reminded, why Indians study fruitfully when abroad. The Asians whose accomplishments News Week records would have probably had a very different tale if they had studied in India. In America they found elbowroom, books and facilities not available and not likely to be available here. The need to prove themselves in their new country and the competition of an international standard they faced there must have cured mental and physical laziness. But other things helping them in America can be obtained here if we achieve a change in social attitudes, especially towards youth. We need to learn to value individuals and their unique qualities more than conformity and respectability. We need to learn the language of encouragement to add to our skill in flattery. We might also learn to be less liberal with blame and less tightfisted with appreciation, especially.

Which statement or statements are true?

In general, the talented young Indians studying in America:

A. have a reputation for being hard working.

B. have the opportunity to contribute to India's development.

C. can solve the brain drain problem because of recent changes in policy.

D. will not return to pursue their careers in India.

Q.25 Which of these paintings is / are by Pablo Picasso

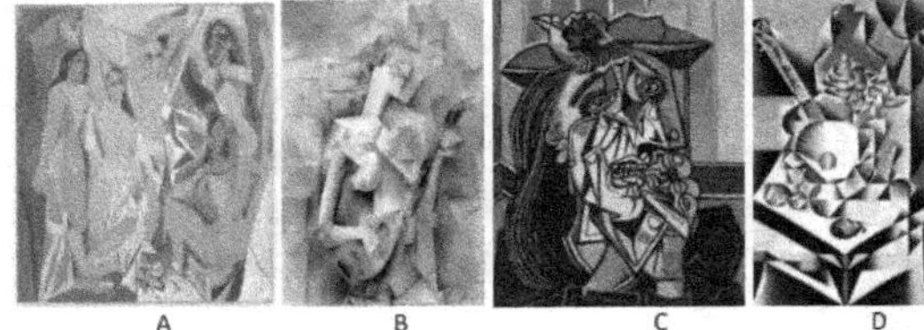

A. A **B.** B **C.** C **D.** D

Q.26 Which of the following are the paintings by the artist Gajendranath Tagore?

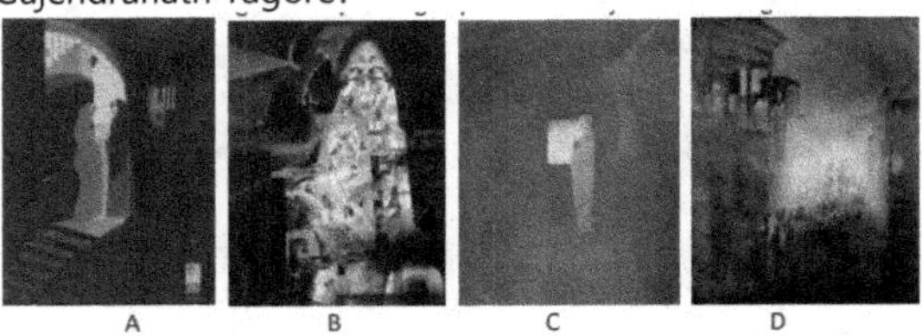

A. A **B.** B **C.** C **D.** D

Q.27 Identify the Indian traditional Art below

A. Kalamkari
B. Madhubani
C. Mysore painting
D. None of these

Q.28 In this question identify the new shape that could be constructed if the two example shapes werecombined. No other change should be made to the two shapes other than combining them.

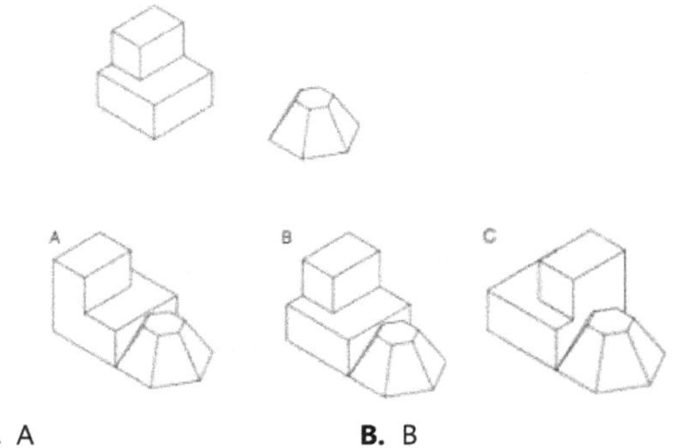

A. A
B. B
C. C
D. None of these

Q.29 Identify the 3D shape's net.

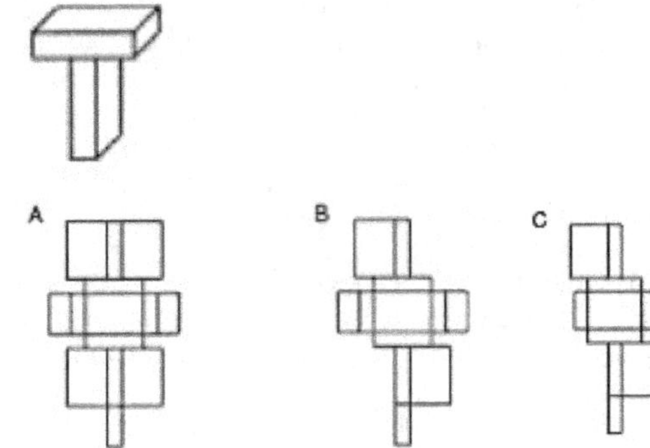

A. A
B. B
C. C
D. None of these

Q.30 Identify the answer shape, which has been rotated but is otherwise the same as the questionshape.

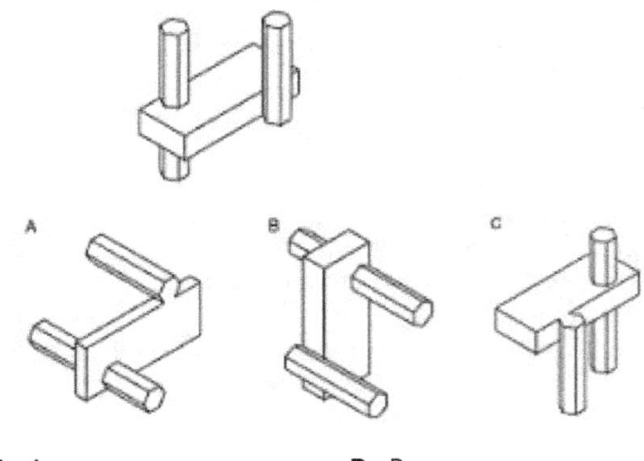

A. A
B. B
C. C
D. None of these

Q.31 Identify the mirror image of the question shape.

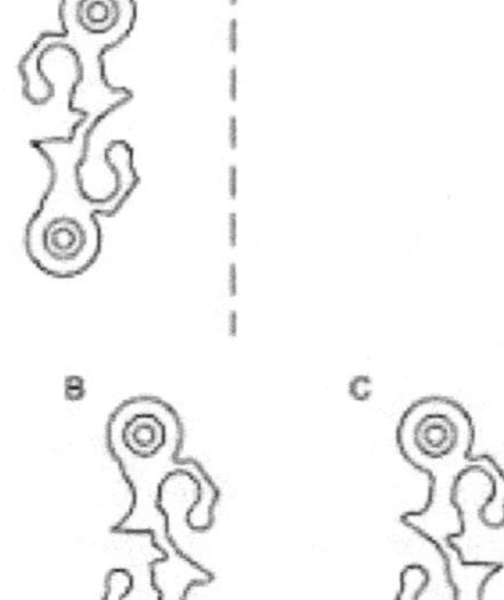

A. A
B. B
C. C
D. None of these

Q.32 Select the figure that does not belong to the following group.

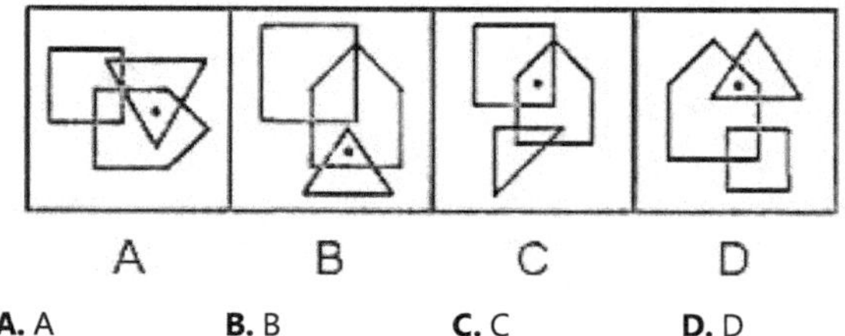

A. A **B.** B **C.** C **D.** D

Q.33 From the given answer figures, select the one in which the question figure is hidden/embedded.

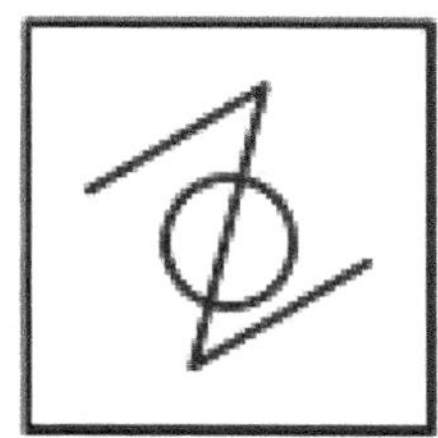

A. 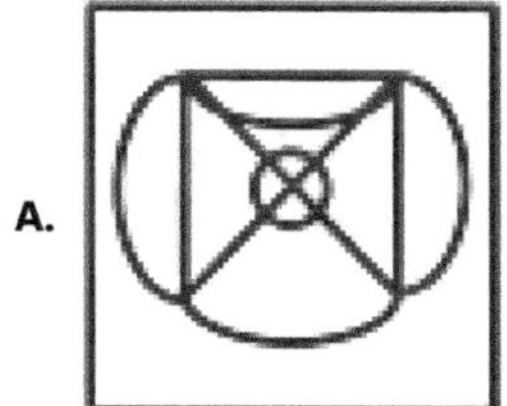

B. 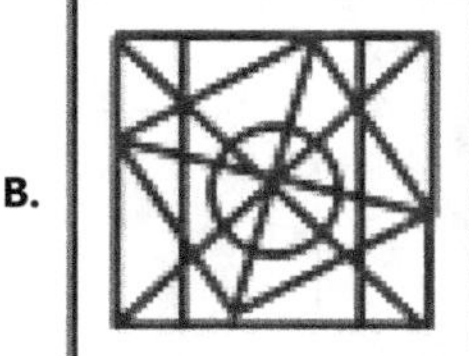

C. 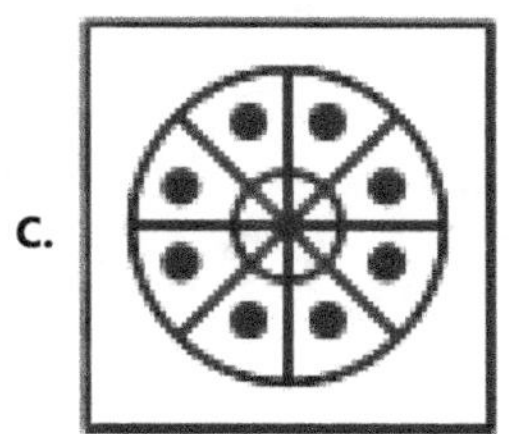

D. 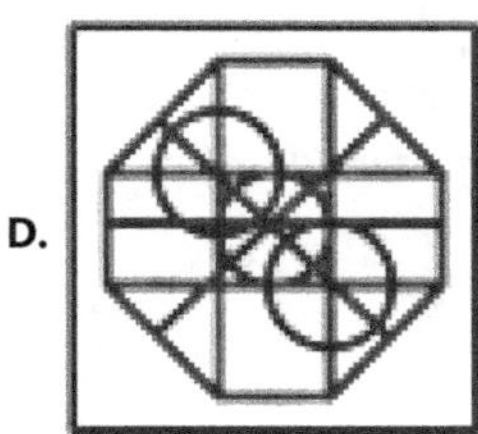

Q.34 A square is cut into 7 pieces as shown on the extreme left of the image. Identify which of theoptions can be made using all 7 pieces.

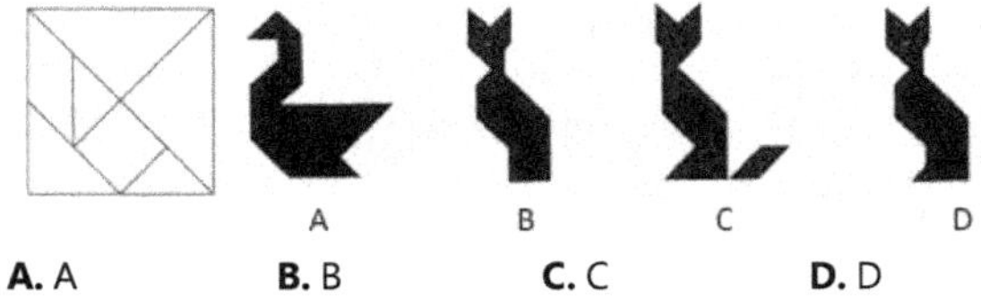

A. A **B.** B **C.** C **D.** D

Q.35 Which of the following terms are related to Industrial design?

A. Gestaltung **B.** CAD
C. Ergonomics **D.** Grafting

Q.36 Shown are logos of different companies/organizations. Select the option(s) that identifies thedesigner of the logo.

A. Benoy Sarkar
B. Arun Kolatkar
C. Devashish Bhattacharya
D. Yeshwant Chaudhary

Multiple Choice Questions (MCQ)

Q.37 From the following options, choose the set of colors that is present in the painting below.

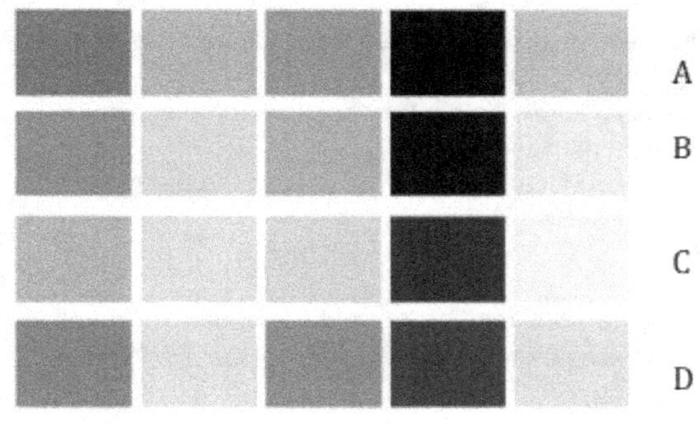

A. A **B.** B **C.** C **D.** D

Q.38 Identify the correct art techniques with which the following paintings have been made.

A. Crayons, Pastel, Oil, Watercolor
B. Pastel, Oil, Acrylic, Crayons
C. Water color, Oil, Pastel, Crayons
D. Crayon, oil, Pastel, Water color

Q.39

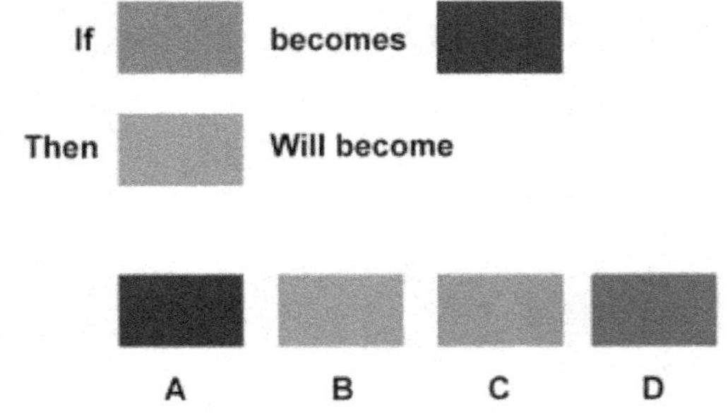

A. A **B.** B **C.** C **D.** D

Q.40

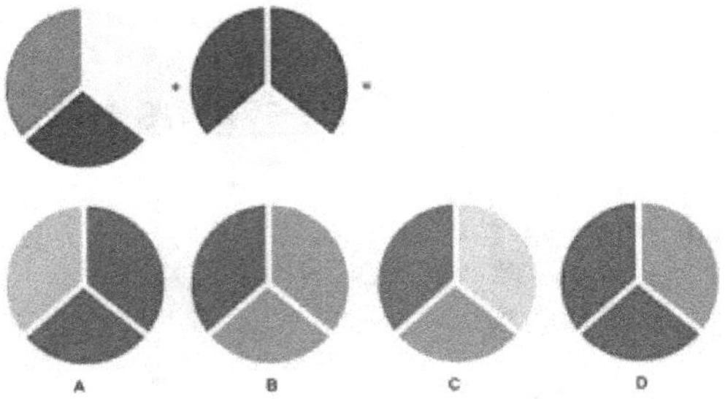

A B C D

A. A **B.** B **C.** C **D.** D

Q.41 Shown are the symbols for different functions. Identify the correct description sequence from thegiven choices

A. Low temperature, Slippery surface, Overhead loads, Rotating parts

B. Overhead loads, Slippery surface, Rotating parts, Low temperature

C. Overhead loads, Slippery surface, Low temperature, Rotating parts

D. Slippery surface, Overhead loads, Rotating parts, Low temperature.

Q.42

Select a figure from amongst the Answer Figures which will continue the same series as established by the five Problem Figures.

Problem Figures: Answer Figures:

(A) (B) (C) (D) (E) (1) (2) (3) (4)

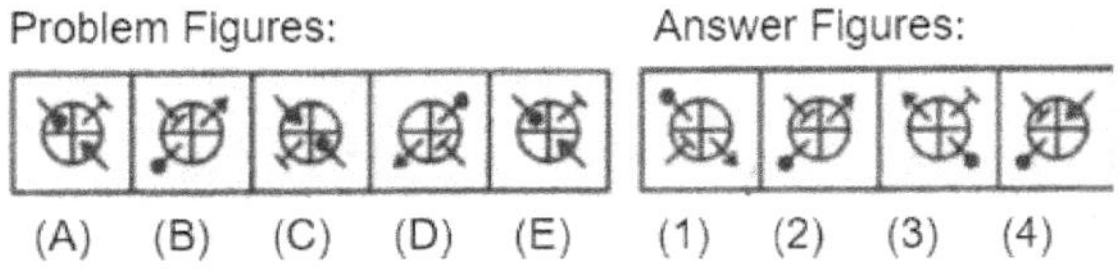

A. 1 **B.** 2 **C.** 3 **D.** 4

Q.43 Select a figure from amongst the Answer Figures which will continue the same series as established by the five.

Problem Figures: **Answer Figures:**

(A) (B) (C) (D) (E) (1) (2) (3) (4)

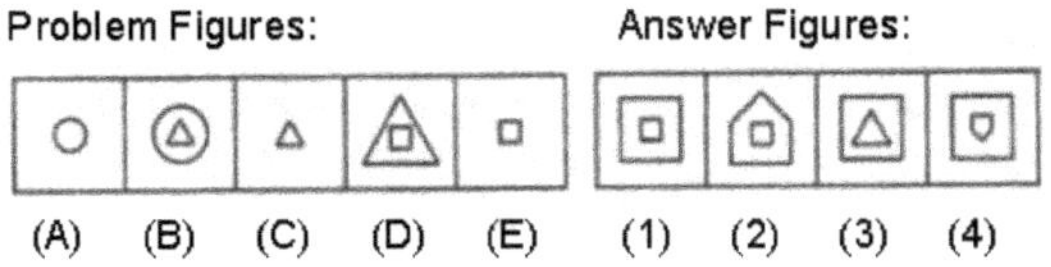

A. 1 **B.** 2 **C.** 3 **D.** 4

Q.44 Which among A,B, C, D will complete the figure series given:

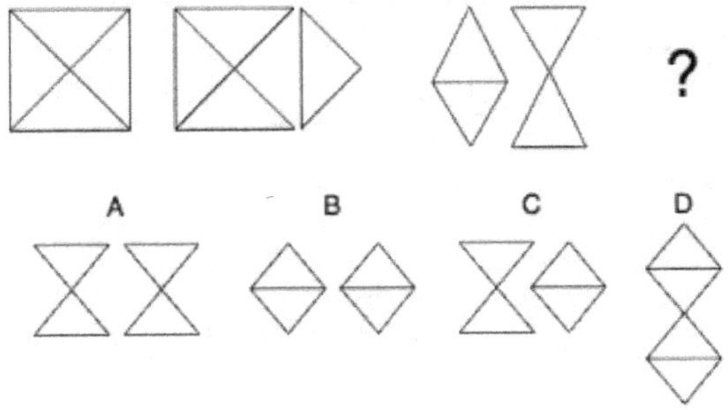

?

A B C D

A. A **B.** B **C.** C **D.** D

Q.45 Complete the series

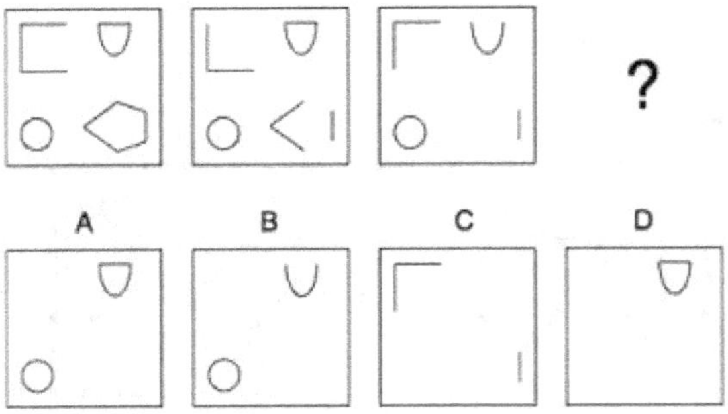

?

A B C D

A. A **B.** B **C.** C **D.** D

Q.46 Complete the series

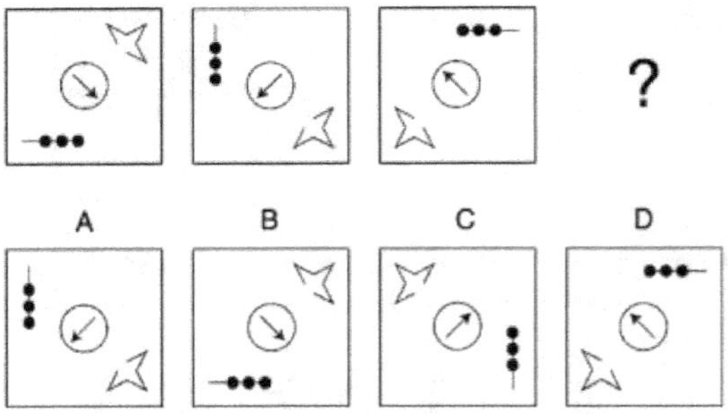

?

A B C D

A. A **B.** B **C.** C **D.** D

Q.47 Identify the quality in common.

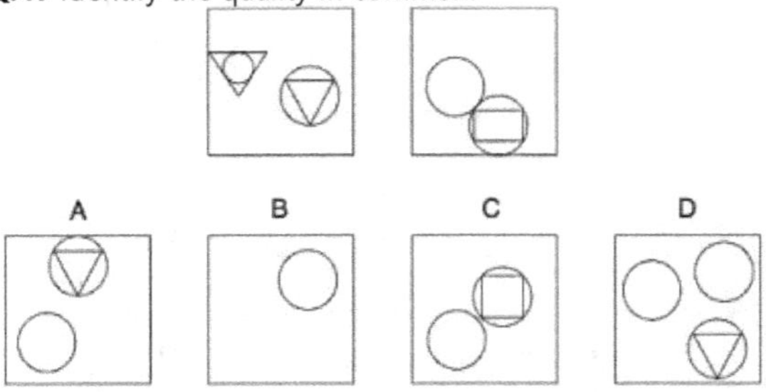

A B C D

A. A **B.** B **C.** C **D.** D

Q.48 Identifv the aualitv in common.

A. A **B.** B **C.** C **D.** D

Q.49 There are eight rules which when applied to the sequence will transform it to one of the fouroptions shown below. Identify the correct option.

AB Delete the last character

BC Replace the third character with the next in the alphabet

CD Insert the letter P between the third and fourth characters

DE Exchange the first and last characters

EF Replace the second character with the previous letter in the alphabet

FG Replace the fifth character with the next in the alphabet

GH Reverse the whole sequence of letters

HI Delete the third character

PBSATTS = HI + CD + FG =

A. PBSPATTS **B.** PBAPUTS

C. PBPATTS **D.** PBSAPTT

Q.50 There are eight rules which when applied to the sequence will transform it to one of the fouroptions shown below. Identify the correct option.

- ■ Cancel all shading
- ○ Shade the second and last shapes
- ● Exchange the second and fourth shapes
- □ Reverse the sequence of shapes
- ⬇ Change all circles to shaded squares
- ⇩ Replace all shaded shapes with unshaded triangles (with the apex at the top)
- ▲ Replace the first shape with a shaded triangle with its apex pointing downwards
- △ Change the middle shape to an unshaded circle

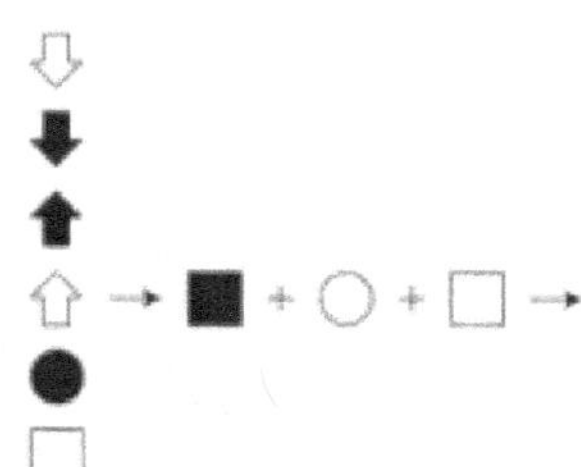

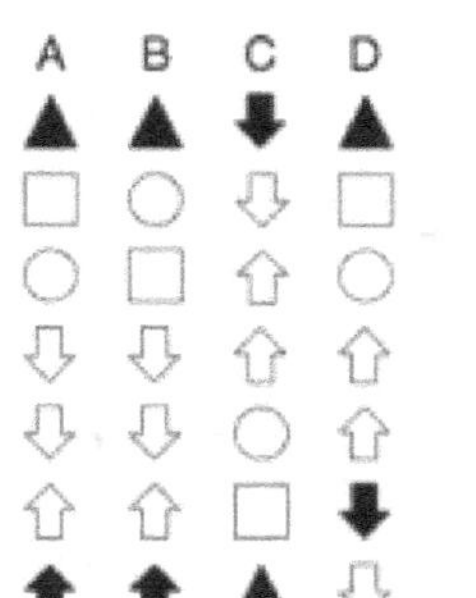

A. A **B.** B **C.** C **D.** D

Q.51

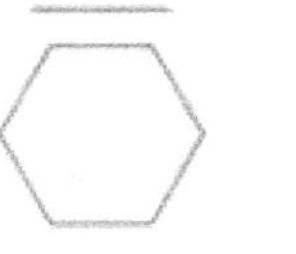  

A. 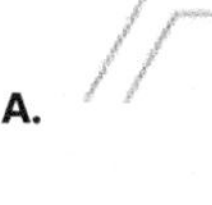 

B. 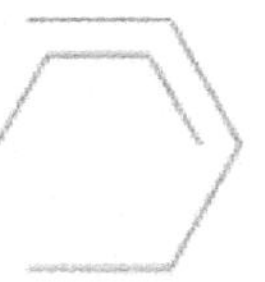

C. **D.** 

Q.52

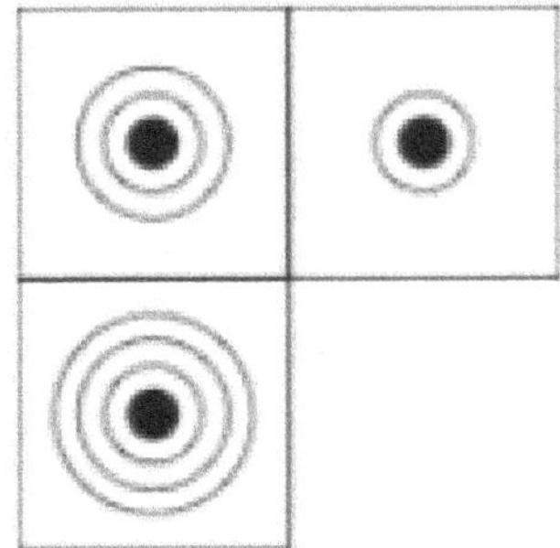

Which is the missing figure?

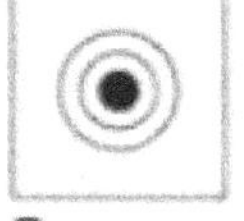

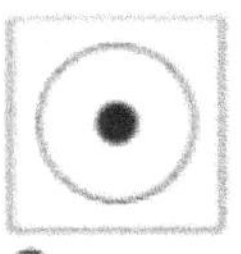

A. A **B.** B **C.** C **D.** D

Q.53

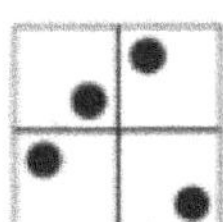
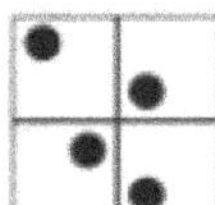
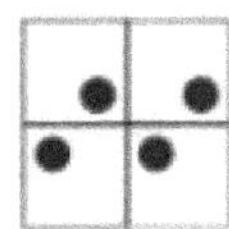

What comes next in the above sequence?

A. 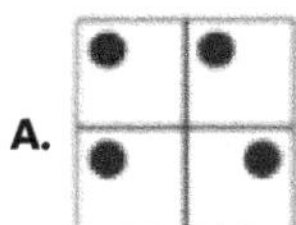

B. 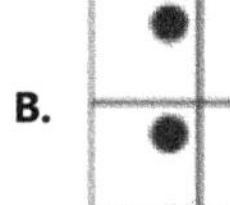

C. 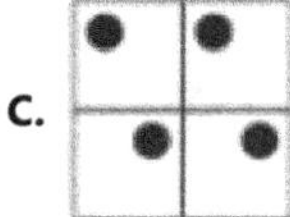

D. 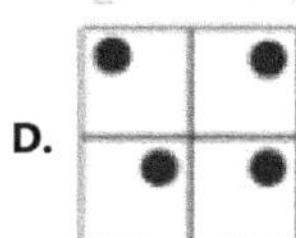

Q.54 The contents of which shield below are most like the contents of the shield above?

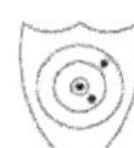

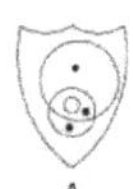

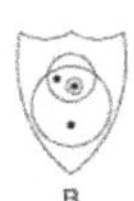

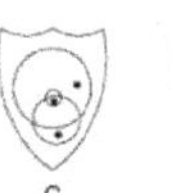

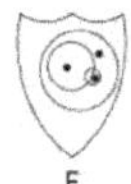

A. A **B.** C
C. B **D.** none of these

Q.55 Which is the missing section?

A. 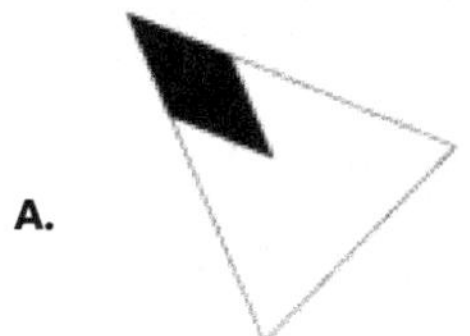

B. 

C. 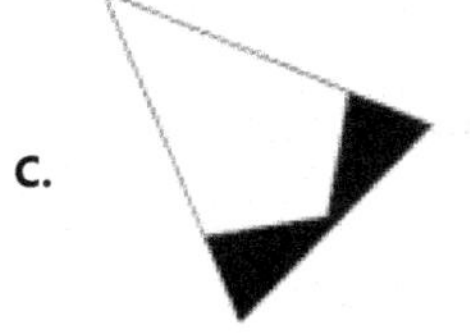

D. 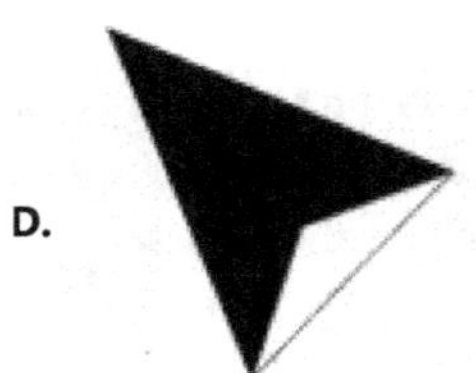

Q.56 What number should replace the question mark?

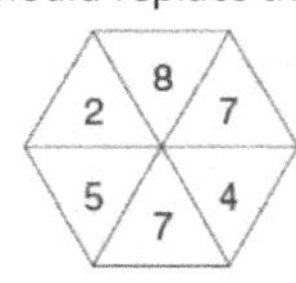

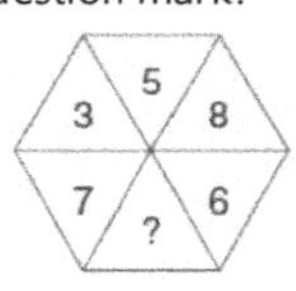

A. 1 **B.** 2 **C.** 4 **D.** 9

Q.57

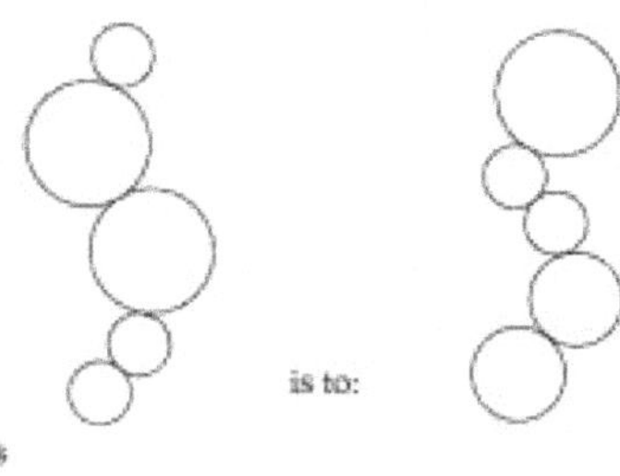

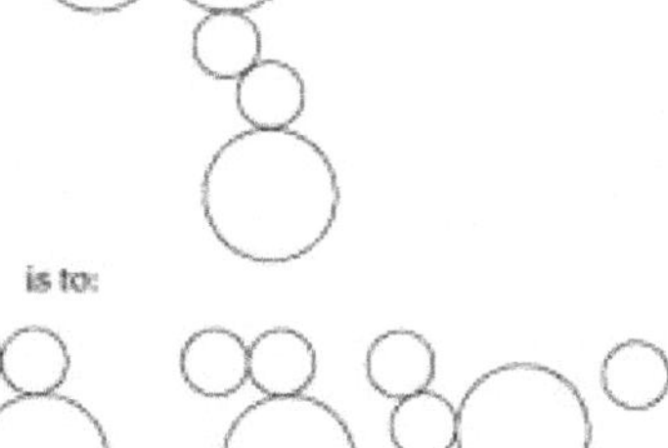

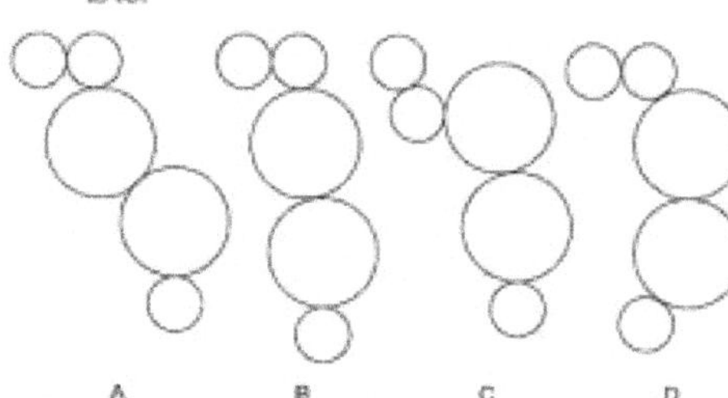

A. A **B.** B **C.** C **D.** D

Q.58 Choose the correct water image of the given figure (X) from amongst the four alternatives.

(X) (1) (2) (3) (4)

A. 1 **B.** 2 **C.** 3 **D.** 4

Q.59 Find out from amongst the four alternatives as to how the pattern would appear when thetransparent sheet is folded at the dotted line.

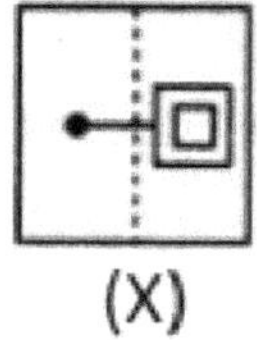

(X)

A. 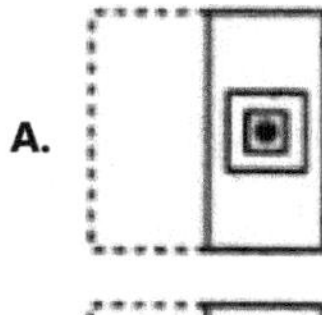

B. 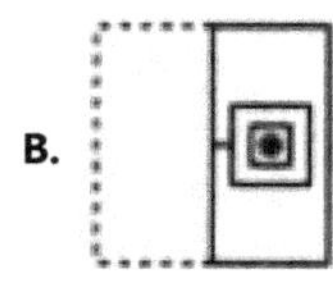

C. 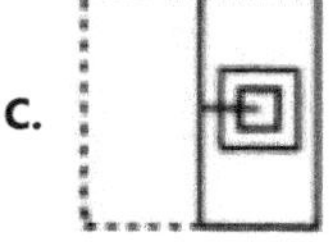

D. 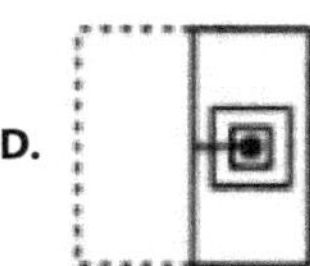

Q.60
Choose a figure, which would most closely resemble the unfolded form of Figure (Z).

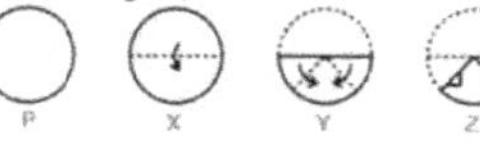

A. 

B. 

C. 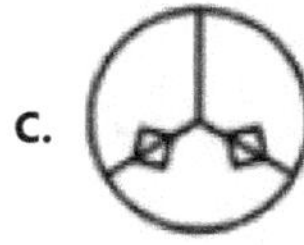

D. none of above

Q.61 Choose the alternative which is closely resembles the mirror image of the given combination

247596

(1) 695742 (2) 247569 (mirrored)

(3) 247569 (mirrored) (4) 247596 (mirrored)

A. 1 **B.** 2 **C.** 3 **D.** 4

Q.62 Shown below are images that have different visual features. Identify the correct sequence of visualfeatures associated with these images from the given choices.

A

B

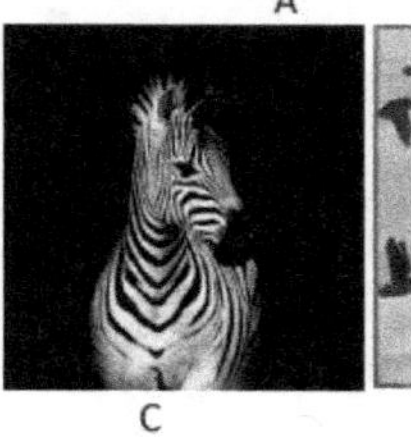

C

D

A. Scale, balance, contrast, harmony
B. Balance, scale, contrast, harmony
C. Scale, balance, harmony, contrast
D. Harmony, scale, balance, contrast

Q.63 What will be the most probable pose at position 3 to complete the sequence below?

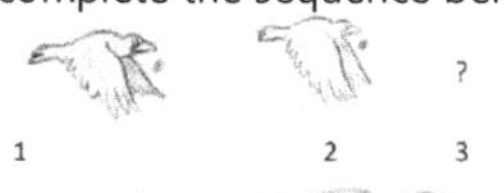

A. 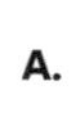

B. 

C. 

D. 

Q.64 Rearrange the following five sentences in proper sequence to form a meaningful paragraph, and then answer the questions given below.

1. But by then it was too late to correct things.
2. It is impossible to steer such a large project to success without planning.
3. He had to standby and watch helplessly.
4. The whole scheme was destined, to fail from the beginning.
5. Bhaskar started realizing this only towards the end.

A. 42513 **B.** 42135 **C.** 42531 **D.** 24513

Q.65 Read the following sentences and try to choose the best definition for the italicized word by searching for context clues in the sentence.

The doctors were pleased that their theory had been *fortified* by the new research.

A. reinforced **B.** altered
C. disputed **D.** developed

Q.66 The angle between the minute hand and the hour hand of a clock when the time is 4:20, is:

A. 0° **B.** 10° **C.** 5° **D.** 20°

Q.67 Identify the product.

A. Riveting tool **B.** Punching tool
C. Scissor translator **D.** Metal clamping tool

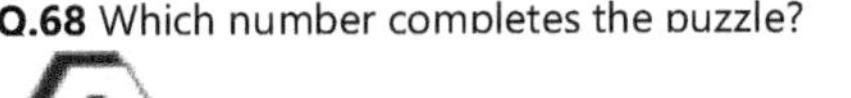
Q.68 Which number completes the puzzle?

A. 19 **B.** 23 **C.** 25 **D.** 29

// Smart Answer Sheet //

Correct — Indicates percentage of students who answered questions correctly.

Skipped — Indicates percentage of students who skipped questions.

Q.	Ans.	Correct	Skipped
1	14	74.01 %	6.13 %
2	25	49.46 %	15.52 %
3	23	28.88 %	15.16 %
4	32	22.38 %	15.53 %
5	34	70.76 %	18.05 %
6	7	21.66 %	21.3 %
7	48	55.23 %	15.89 %
8	11	16.61 %	23.82 %
9	9	47.29 %	18.05 %
10	10	67.87 %	16.97 %
11	1	66.79 %	19.49 %
12	16	48.38 %	23.1 %
13	#	49.82 %	19.13 %
14	16	49.46 %	21.66 %

Q.	Ans.	Correct	Skipped
15	1	72.92 %	17.33 %
16	15	75.81 %	17.33 %
17	#	37.55 %	17.68 %
18	#	53.79 %	19.86 %
19	B, D, C	27.44 %	29.24 %
20	B, A, C	22.02 %	32.85 %
21	B, A, C	26.71 %	33.58 %
22	C	33.21 %	22.75 %
23	D	10.83 %	22.74 %
24	D	13.72 %	28.88 %
25	B, A, C	44.77 %	23.1 %
26	B, A, D, C	58.84 %	28.16 %
27	C	50.54 %	22.75 %
28	B	44.77 %	20.21 %

Q.	Ans.	Correct	Skipped
29	B	30.69 %	26.71 %
30	B	28.16 %	21.3 %
31	C	74.37 %	20.21 %
32	C	58.12 %	21.66 %
33	B	36.46 %	20.22 %
34	A, D, C	45.13 %	27.79 %
35	B, A, C	28.16 %	29.24 %
36	A, C	35.74 %	27.44 %
37	B	63.9 %	18.41 %
38	D	49.82 %	18.05 %
39	D	40.79 %	17.69 %
40	B	69.31 %	18.78 %
41	B	75.81 %	18.05 %
42	B	56.32 %	20.21 %

Q.	Ans.	Correct	Skipped
43	D	58.84 %	18.78 %
44	B	25.99 %	28.52 %
45	B	60.65 %	21.66 %
46	C	76.17 %	18.41 %
47	A	22.74 %	27.08 %
48	B	51.99 %	25.63 %
49	B	61.01 %	22.38 %
50	D	59.21 %	24.18 %
51	B	70.76 %	18.41 %
52	B	33.21 %	18.78 %
53	D	62.45 %	21.67 %
54	C	61.73 %	20.94 %
55	D	73.29 %	19.13 %
56	A	26.71 %	27.44 %

Q.	Ans.	Correct	Skipped
57	A	63.9 %	23.1 %
58	C	67.51 %	18.41 %
59	D	75.09 %	19.49 %
60	D	55.23 %	21.67 %
61	D	72.92 %	19.5 %
62	A	62.09 %	19.14 %
63	A	53.79 %	19.5 %
64	A	47.29 %	20.22 %
65	A	44.77 %	24.91 %
66	B	37.55 %	19.85 %
67	A	35.38 %	26.35 %
68	A	75.45 %	19.13 %

#

Q.	Answer
13	F
17	S 19
18	90

Performance Analysis	
Avg. Score (%)	47.5%
Toppers Score (%)	96.67%
Your Score	

//Hints and Solutions//

1.

C — 9km. — D
6 km. — 6 km.
A — 5 km. — B — E

Required distance = AE

5+9=14 KM

2. There are 25 times ! sign used in given figure.

3. There are 23 triangles are formed in given figure.

4. There are 32 surfaces required ,If the word EGG (shown on the right) were to be extruded,

5. The pattern is the next number = sum of two previous number

∴ Missing number =13+21=34

So the missing number is 34.

6. At 11.00am it was showing 11.00am, at 12 noon it showed 11.46am, at 1.00pm it showed12.32pm, at 2.00pm it showed 1.18pm, at 3.00pm it showed 2.04pm and at 4.00pm it showed2.50pm. Plus 3 hours means that the time is now 7.00pm.

7. There are 48 cubes are formed in given figure.

8. There are 11 types of fond style used in given figure

9. When there are 9 pattern formed , arranged in an eight-by-eight matrix.

10.

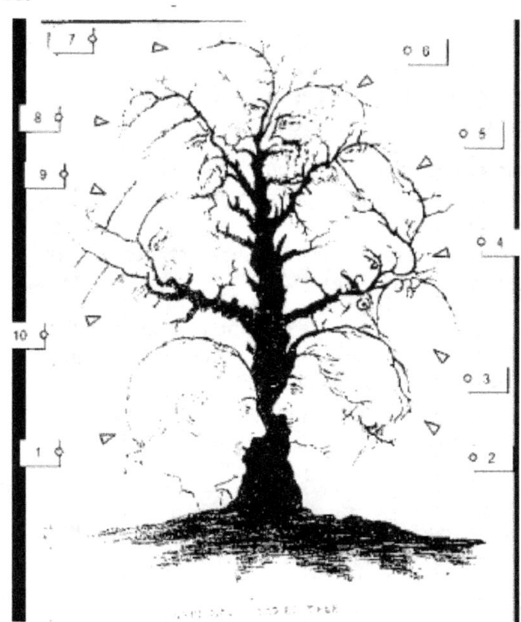

11. work backwards from 120; that is, 120–60–12–3–1

12. From column I: (9 $\times$ 5) $\div$ 5 = 9

From column II: (17 $\times$ 4) $\div$ 4 = 17

From column III: (16 $\times$ 8) $\div$? = 8

$\Rightarrow \frac{16\times8}{8} = ?$

$\Rightarrow ? = 16$

Hence, the correct answer is 16.

13. Three letters clockwise from C is H.

Opposite to H is D.

Two letters away from D is F

14.

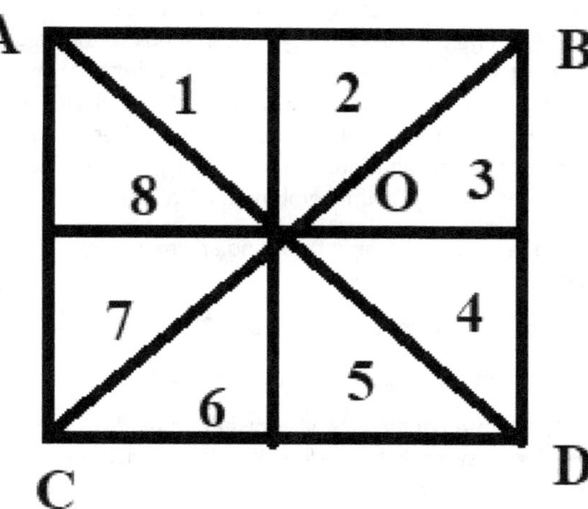

In the figure, the 8 triangle is shown easily and another is COD , DOB, BOA, AOC, ACD, BDC,ABC, ABD so that total no. of triangle is 8+8=16

Hence, the correct answer is 16.

15. A rotates in the opposite direction to C; B rotates anti-clockwise , D will turn clockwise Direction.

16. 6000/400

15 A4-size sheets of paper would you need to print 6,000 words

17. There are two separate series. The letters advance missing the first two (A to D), then three (D to H) and so on. After M there must be five missing letters, bringing us to S. The numbers advance in the same way. Hence the answer is S 19.

18. Let the original number is x. Then

$$\frac{2}{3}x = x - 30$$

$$\Rightarrow x\left(1 - \frac{2}{3}\right) = 30 \Rightarrow x = 90$$

19. The main persons behind this rebellion were the soldiers [sepoy]. That is why it is also called sepoy Mutiny. But the revolt did not remain limited to the soldiers, later it spread and took a massive form. Some people also called this-'India's first war of Independence'.

The revolt was started due to the induction of enfield riffles in the army. It was believed that the cartridges used in the riffles were made of pig fat and cow fat which were restricted for the Muslims and Hindus respectively. They protested against these.

The revolt was started on 10th May of 1857 in the town of Meerut. Though in some places, fractional clashes began before that. It ended on 20 June 1858. The first martyr of 1857 revolt was MangalPandey. He attacked his British sergeant on 29 March 1857 at Barrackpore. Some of the leaders of the rebellion were-Rani Lakshmibai [Jhansi],Kunwar Singh [Bihar], Bahadur Shah [Delhi], Nana Saheb [Kanpur], Tatia Tope [Kanpur], Begum HazratMahal [Lucknow]. There was a deficiency of central leadership

20. A, B, C are true

Guy de Chauliac was a popular surgeon of the Early Medieval Period. Nikola Tesla was a Serbian-American inventor, best known for his development of alternating current electrical systems. He also made extraordinary contributions to the fields of electromagnetism and wireless radio communications. David Baltimore is an American biologist who won a share of the 1975 Nobel Prize in Physiology or Medicine. As a researcher, he has made tremendous contributions to immunology, virology, cancer research, biotechnology, and recombinant DNA research.

21. Amartya Sen - The Argumentative Indian, Inequality Reexamined

Amitav Ghosh - The Shadow Lines, Flood of Fire

Shashi Deshpande - That Long Silence, Roots and Shadows

22. Clearly, illiterate people lack will power and maturity in thoughts. They may easily be misled intofalse convictions or lured into temptations to vote for a particular group. So, argument II holds.However, a person is literate does not mean that he is conscious of all political movements, whichrequires practical awareness of everyday events. Thus, I also holds strong. Besides, Constitution hasextended the right to vote equally to all its citizens. Hence, III also holds.

23. Clearly, the advertisement is meant to lure the passengers into travelling by the airline. So, I isimplicit. Also, the advertisement promises an enjoyable flight. So, II is also implicit. The facilitiesoffered by other airlines cannot be ascertained from the statement. So, III is not implicit.

24. will not return to pursue their careers in India.

option D is correct

25. Pablo Ruiz Picasso was a Spanish painter, sculptor, printmaker, ceramicist and theatre designer who spent most of his adult life in France.

A B C are painting of Pablo Picasso

26. Gaganendranath Tagore was an Indian painter and cartoonist of the Bengal school. Along with his brother Abanindranath Tagore, he was counted as one of the earliest modern artists in India.

A B C D are all painting of Tagore.

27. Mysore painting (Kannada: ಮೈಸೂರು ಚಿತ್ರಕಲೆ) is an important form of classical South Indian painting that originated in and around the town of Mysore in Karnataka encouraged and nurtured by the Mysore rulers

28. In A and C the small box has been moved.

29. In A the sides of the 'T' are double, and in C the closure on the top of theshape is missing.

30. option B is correct .

31. A is the same shape, and B has been reflected vertically

32.

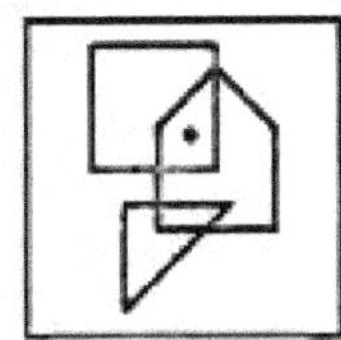

In all the given images except image C, the dot appears in the region common to pentagon and triangle.

Thus, figure C is the odd one among the given options.

Hence, the correct option is (C).

33.

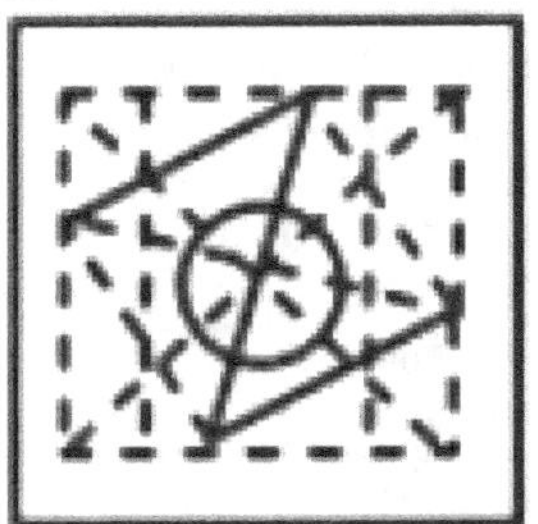

Therefore, the figure given in option (B) is the correct one.

Hence, the correct option is (B).

34. A square is cut into 7 pieces as shown on the extreme left of the image, A C D figure are formed by using all 7 pieces.

35. The word ergonomics comes from the Greek word "ergon" which means work and "nomos" which means laws. It's essentially the "laws of work" or "science of work". ... Ergonomics draws on many disciplines to optimize the interaction between the work environment and the worker.

Computer-aided design is the use of computers to aid in the creation, modification, analysis, or optimization of a design. CAD software is used to increase the productivity of the designer, improve the quality of design, improve communications through documentation, and to create a database for manufacturing.

Gestaltung - It means Layout in German.

36. Benoy Sarkar designed the logo of Trade Fair Authority of India.

The old logo, also called the DD eye, was designed by Devashis Bhattacharyya, an alumnus of the National Institute of Design

(NID) along with his friends. The logo had been chosen by the then prime minister Indira Gandhi.

37.

option B is correct

38. Option D is correct (paintings have been made by Crayon, oil, Pastel, Watercolor.)

39. Option D

In a RGB color space, hex #013220 (also known as Dark green) is composed of 0.4% red, 19.6% green and 12.5% blue. Whereas in a CMYK color space, it is composed of 98% cyan, 0% magenta, 36% yellow and 80.4% black. It has a hue angle of 158 degrees, a saturation of 96.1% and a lightness of 10%

40. Option B

Olive Green - Mehndi (Mehndi is the Hindi word for Henna. Further words like Sukhi (dry) and Geeli (wet) are prefixed, as Henna changes color when it becomes wet.)

Purple combines the calm stability of blue and the fierce energy of red.

41. option B

Overhead loads, Slippery surface, Rotating parts, Low temperature

42. All the elements move one space ACW (each space is equal to a quadrant of the circle) and get inverted in each step.

(2)

Hence, the correct option is (B).

43. In one step, the existing element enlarges and a new element appears inside this element. In the next step, the outer element is lost.

Hence, the correct option is (D).

44. In the first step of the series four triangles point towards each other. In the secondstep, three triangles point towards each other and one points away. In the third step, two trianglespoint towards each other. So suggested answer B correctly completes the series, as all four-pointaway from each other.

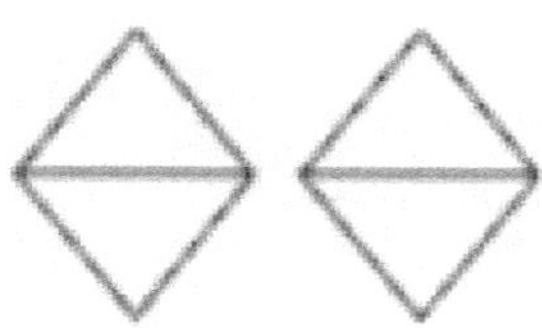

Hence, the correct option is (B).

45. The number of flat surfaces in the shape is decreasing by three each step in the series,beginning with nine. The final shape in the series would have no flat surfaces.

46. At each step in the series the shape is rotated clockwise by 90 degrees.

47. Both question shapes contain two circles, as do suggested answers A and C, but onlysuggested answer A also shares the quality with the question shapes that one of its shapes touchesthe outer edge of the square containing the shapes.

48. The sum of the shapes making up both question shapes is a multiple of 3, and onlysuggested answer B is also made up of a sum of shapes that is a multiple of 3.

49. First the S is deleted, then a P is inserted between the A and the first T and finally wereplace the first T with a U.

50. Option D

51. the inner hexagon is being dismantled one side at a time working anti- clockwise, while the outerhexagon is being constructed one side at a time working clockwise.

52. The pattern here is:

Looking up an outer circle is removed and looking down an outer circle is added.

Hence, the correct option is (B).

53. looking across, the dot in the top left-hand quarter moves to the opposite corner, the dot in thetop right-hand quarter moves one corner anticlockwise at each stage, the dot in the bottom lefthand quarter moves between the top two corners, and the dot in the bottom right-hand quartermoves one corner clockwise at each stage.

54. it contains one dot in one circle, one dot in two circles and one dot in three circles

55. each segment is a mirror image of the segment opposite

56. The number formed at the top is half of the number formed at the bottom i.e., 358 x 2 = 716

Hence, the correct option is (B).

57. large circles turn to small, and vice versa

58. figure (3) is the correct image of water.

so, option c is correct.

59. option D

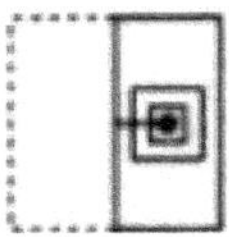

60. Option D

61. Option D

the mirror image of the given number (247596) is Figure D(4).

62. Harmony® Balance is a combination of 4 vital herbs, plus Vitamins D3 and B6, which are traditionally used to relieve the symptoms of premenstrual syndrome, menstrual cramps and to help regulate the menstrual cycle. ... The nature of Harmony PMS is balancing and calming.

Contrast is the difference in luminance or colour that makes an object distinguishable. In visual perception of the real world, contrast is determined by the difference in the colour and brightness of the object and other objects within the same field of view.

Scale, balance, contrast, harmony (Option A) is correct

63. option A

64. 4 2 5 1 3

The whole scheme was destined, to fail from the beginning.

It is impossible to steer such a large project to success without planning.

Bhaskar started realizing this only towards the end.

But by then it was too late to correct things.

He had to standby and watch helplessly.

65. To be *fortified* is to be strengthened or *reinforced.*

66. Angle traced by hour hand in $\frac{13}{3}hrs = \left(\frac{360}{12} \times \frac{13}{3}\right)^2 =$ $130°$

Angle traced by min. hand in $20\text{min.} = \left(\frac{360}{60} \times 20\right)^2 =$ $120°$

∴ Required angle $= (130 - 120)° = 10°$

Hence, the correct option is (B).

67. A rivet gun, also known as a rivet hammer or a pneumatic hammer, is a type of tool used to drive rivets. ... The energy from the hammer in the rivet gun drives the work and the rivet against the bucking bar. As a result, the tail of the rivet is compressed and work-hardened.

68. The answer is **19**.

all are prime numbers in ascending order.

Mock Test 05

Numerical Answer Type (NAT)

Q.1 Except for one number, all the four-digit numbers given below are written using a single font. Identify the number that does not use the same font as the other numbers.

5985
3697 5574 1767 6367
7514 3270
1676 3683
8431 3584 2018
1450 1070
4208 1190
3601 1847 8504 8075
6063 2044
7070 4338 3015
1502
6049 1342 8075 4852

Q.2 Rohit walked 25 m towards south. Then he turned to his left and walked 20 m. He then turned to his left and walked 25 m. He again turned to his right and walked 15 m. At what distance is he from the starting point in East direction?

Q.3 Count the number of parallelograms in the given figure.

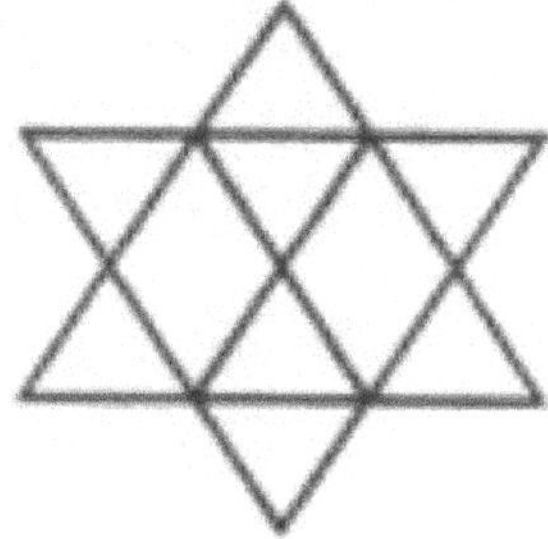

Q.4 Imagine letters are extruded into three-dimensional objects, as shown in the figure on the left (the letter A). If the word GOLD (shown on the right) were to be extruded, how many surfaces would it have?

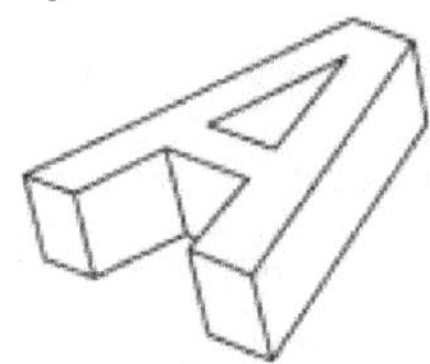

GOLD

Q.5 All the six faces of a cube of a cube are coloured with six different colours - black, brown, green, red, white and blue. Red face is opposite to the black face. Green face is between red and black faces. Blue face is adjacent to white face. Brown face is adjacent to blue face. Red face is in the bottom. The face opposite to brown is ________

Q.6 When I was 8 years old my brother's age was half of my age. Then calculate the age of my brother when I was 80 years old.

Q.7 Find the number of quadrilaterals in the given figure.

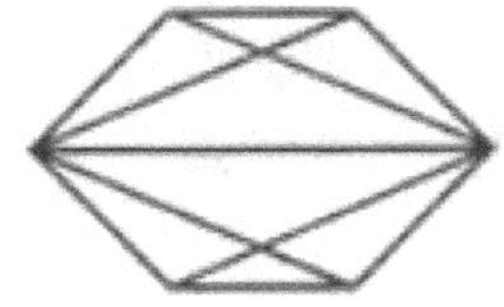

Q.8 Which group of shapes can be assembled to make the shape shown below?

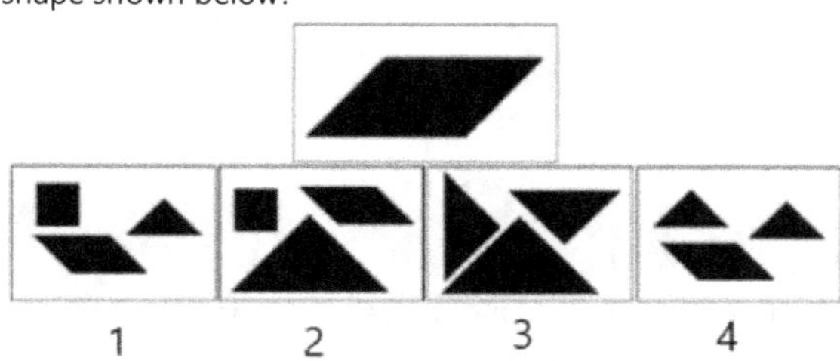

Q.9 In the illustration, three flat cube-like shapes are shown. Their patterns are drawn with bold black lines. Which of them can you draw without taking your pencil off the paper or going along the same line twice? Which of them can't be drawn in this way?

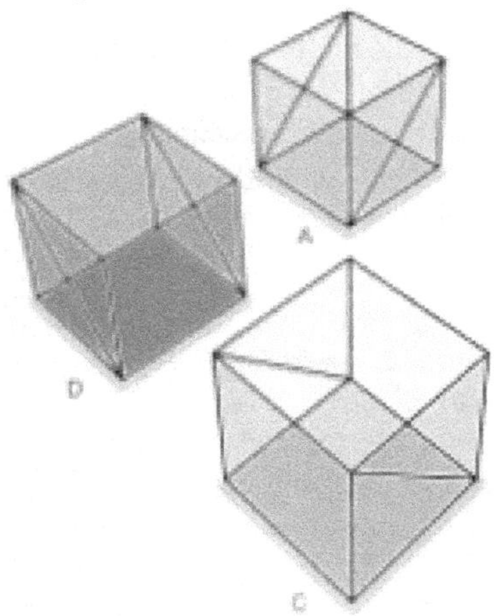

Q.10 The given image has sixty -four circles with patterns inside, arranged in an eight-by-eight matrix. How many different types of circles are there in the image, assuming circles may be rotated?

Q.11 What value should come in place of the question mark?

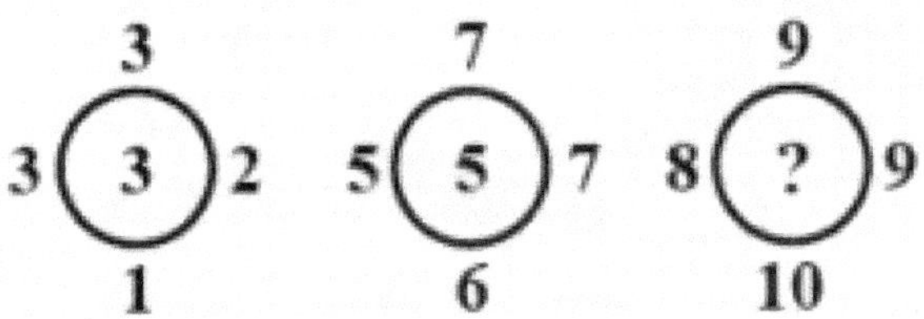

Q.12 AB C D E F G H

Which letter is two to the left of the letter that is four to the right of the letter immediately to the right of the letter A?

Q.13 A statue is being carved by a sculptor. The original piece of marble weighed 250 kg. In the first week 30 per cent is cut away. In the second week 20 per cent of the remainder is cut away. In the third week the statue is completed when 25 per cent of the remainder is cut away. What is the weight of the final statue?

Q.14 Sunday MondayTuesdayWednesdayThursdayFridaySaturday

What day is two days before the day immediately following the day three days before the day two days after the day immediately before Friday?

Q.15 By starting at the Q in the centre and moving from letter to adjacent letter to an outside Z, how many different ways can the word QUIZ be spelt out?

```
      Z
    Z I Z
  Z I U I Z
Z I U Q U I Z
  Z I U I Z
    Z I Z
      Z
```

Q.16 Which letter replaces the question mark to complete this circle?

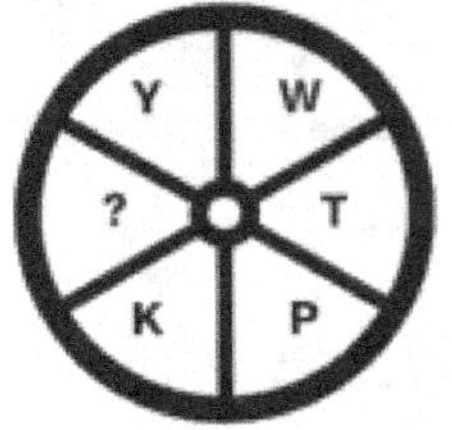

Q.17 Which is the odd number out ?

1, 8, 512, 1331, 6859, 277, 1000

Q.18 Which number replaces the question mark and completes the puzzle?

?
9 25
4 36
1 81 64 49

Multiple Select Questions (MSQ)

Q.19 Which of the following statements is/ are true?

A. India's Kumbh Mela is the world's largest human gathering. The Kumbh Mela is a Hindu pilgrimage that keeps getting bigger.

B. It's held every three years and rotates between Allahabad, Haridwar, Nashik, and Ujjain,

C. Allahabad KumbhMelas — held every 10 years — are the largest and holiest.

D. The main festival site is located on the banks of a river: the Ganges (Ganga) at Haridwar; the confluence (Sangam) of the Ganges and the Yamuna and the invisible Sarasvati at Allahabad; the Godavari at Nashik; and the Shipra at Ujjain. Bathing in these rivers is thought to cleanse a person of all sins

Q.20 Which of the following statements is/are true?

A. Garry Kasparov is a Ukrainian chess Grandmaster considered by many to be the greatest chess player of all time.

B. Larry Page, is an American entrepreneur and computer scientist who, along with Sergey Brin, cofounded Google Inc.

C. Anton Chekhov was one of the most illustrious and celebrated short-story writers in the history of literature.

D. Shiva Ayyadurai is an American inventor of Indian origin credited by some sources to be the inventor of email

Q.21 From the options below, select the Indian author/s writing in English whose works are represented below:

i. The great Indian Novel

ii. Interpreter of maladiesiii. PaxIndicaiv. The Namesakev. Bookless in Baghdadvi. Unaccustomed earth

A. JhumpaLahari **B.** Shashi Tharoor

C. R . L. Singh **D.** Jawaharlal Nehru

Q.22 Question given below consists of a statement, followed by three arguments numbered I , II and III. You

have to decide which of the arguments is a 'strong' argument.

Statement: Should the parliamentary elections in India be held every three years as against five years at present?

Arguments:

I. No. This will enhance wastage of money and resources.

II. Yes. This will help the voters to change non-performing representatives without much delay.

III. No. The elected representatives will not have enough time to settle and concentrate on

developmental activities

A. None is strong
B. Only I and II are strong
C. Only II and III are strong
D. Only I and III are strong

Q.23 Question below is given a statement followed by three assumptions numbered I, II and III. You have to consider the statement and the following assumptions and decide which of the assumptions is implicit in the statement.

Statement: Bombay people were spellbound, mesmerized and got mad when they saw the famous pop-singer Michael Jackson's hi-tech pulsating megawatt performance.

Assumptions:

I. When a show is accompanied with latest technology, it has a magical effect.

II. Bombay people were never impressed with performances by Indian musicians.

III. Michael Jackson is a super singer.

A. Only I is implicit
B. Only II is implicit
C. Only I and III are implicit
D. Either II or III is implicit

Q.24 Which of these paintings is / are by Piet Mondrian

A. 

B. 

C. 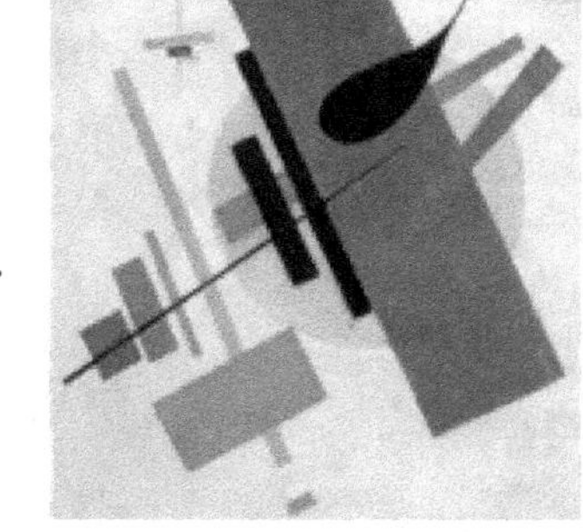

D. 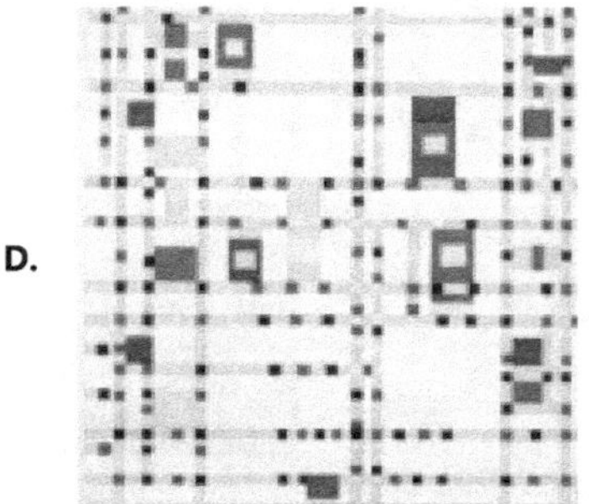

Q.25 Identify the paintings by Nandalal bose from the following

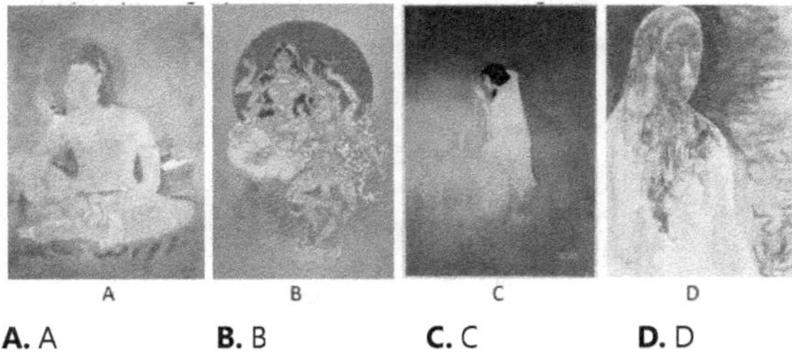
A B C D

A. A **B.** B **C.** C **D.** D

Q.26 Name the states of the folk art forms below in their respective order

Tanjore Mysore

A. Tamil Nadu and Karnataka
B. Bihar and Maharasht

C. Orissa and Karnataka

D. Kerala and Karnataka

Q.27 In this question identify the new shape that could be constructed if the two example shapes were combined. No other change should be made to the two shapes other than combining them.

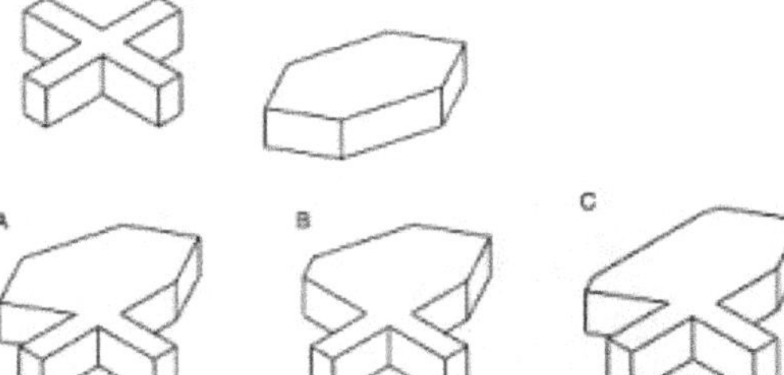

A. A  **B.** B 

C. C **D.** None of these

Q.28 Identify the 3D shape's net.

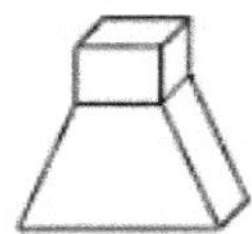

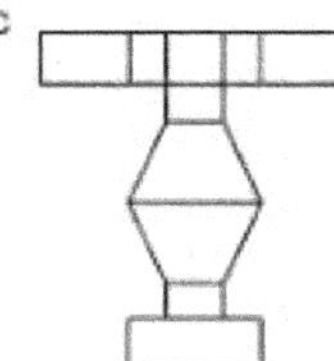

A. A **B.** B

C. C **D.** None of these

Q.29 Identify the answer shape, which has been rotated but is otherwise the same as the question shape.

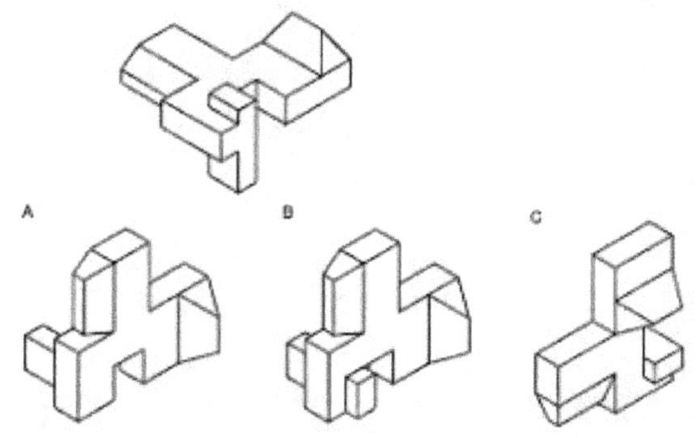

A. A **B.** B

C. C **D.** None of these

Q.30 Identify the mirror image of the question shape.

A. A **B.** B

C. C **D.** None of these

Q.31 Pick the TWO answer choices that will come together to make the figure shown. Pieces may be reflected and or rotated

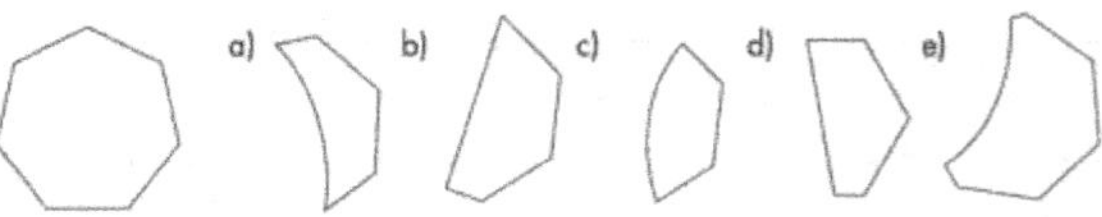

A. A + B **B.** C + E **C.** D + E **D.** A + E

Q.32 4–5 pieces are given. Choose the answer choice that represents a figure comprised of ALL pieces. Pieces may be rotated and/or reflected.

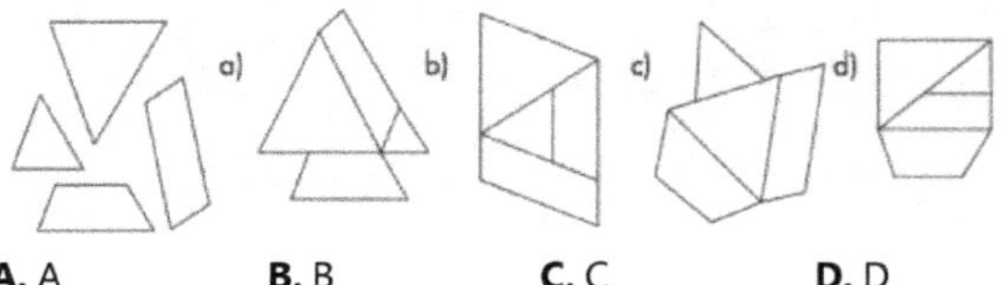

A. A **B.** B **C.** C **D.** D

Q.33 A square is cut into 7 pieces as shown on the extreme left of the image. Identify which of the options can be made using all 7 pieces

A. 

B. 

C. 

D. 

Q.34 Which of the following terms are related to graphic design?

A. Pantone (PMS) **B.** Tracking

C. ISO **D.** Leading

Q.35 Given below are logos of different companies or organizations. Select the options that identify the designers of the logos given:

A. R. K. Joshi **B.** Shekhar Kammat
C. Arun Kolatkar **D.** Sudarshan Dheer

Q.36 Which of the given figures can be drawn without either lifting the pen or retracing any line?

A. 

B. 

C. 

D. 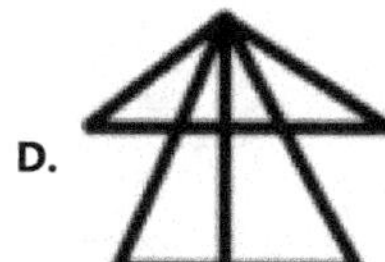

Multiple Choice Questions (MCQ)

Q.37 Identify the logo given below:

A. Toyota **B.** BMW **C.** LIC **D.** LG

Q.38 Identify the correct art techniques with which the following paintings have been made.

A

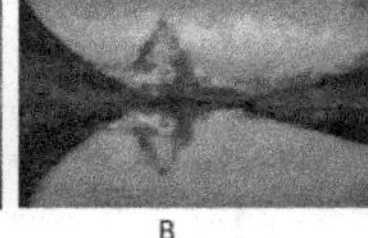
B

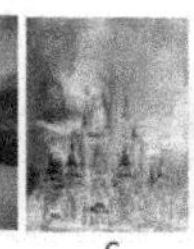
C

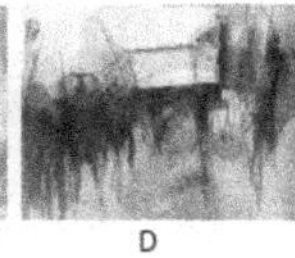
D

A. Oil, Water color, Pastel, Crayons
B. Oil, Pastel, Water Color, Crayons
C. Oil, Crayons, Acrylic, Pastel
D. Pastel, Oil, Watercolor, Crayons

Q.39

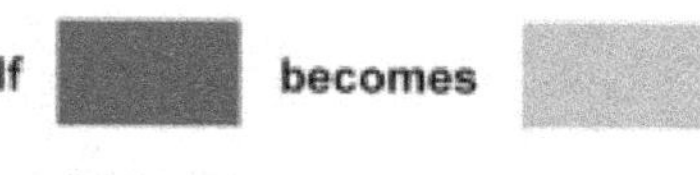

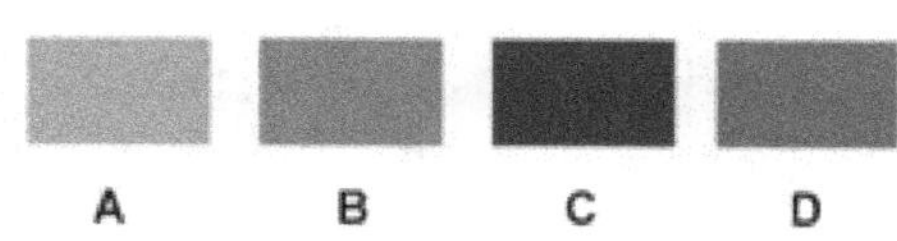

A. A **B.** B **C.** C **D.** D

Q.40

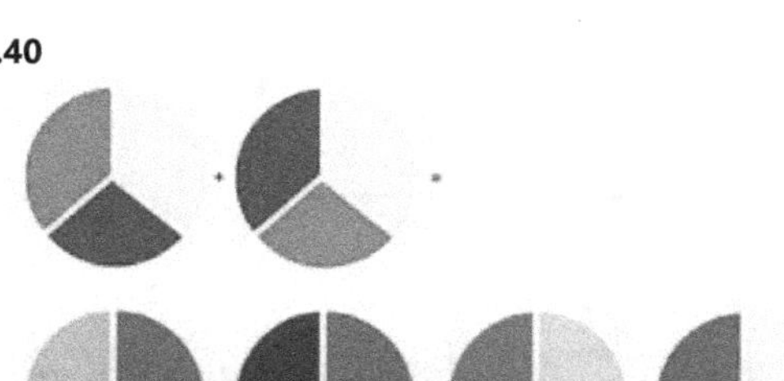

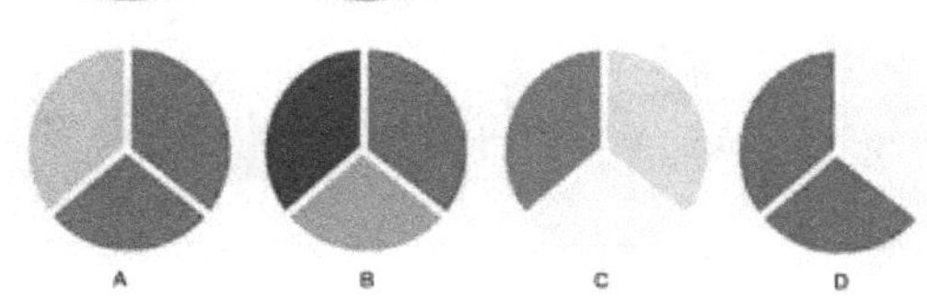

A. A **B.** B **C.** C **D.** D

Q.41 Shown are the symbols for different functions. Identify the correct description sequence from the given choices.

A. Bio Hazard, Ultraviolet Radiation, Watch your step, Suffocation hazard
B. Biohazard, Suffocation hazard, Ultraviolet radiation, Watch your step
C. Ultraviolet Radiation, Biohazard, Watch your step, Suffocation Hazard
D. Biohazard, Suffocation hazard, Ultraviolet radiation, Watch your step

Q.42 Identify the function of the given product.

A. Metal detector **B.** Fan
C. Insect repellent **D.** Water ionizer

Q.43 Complete the series

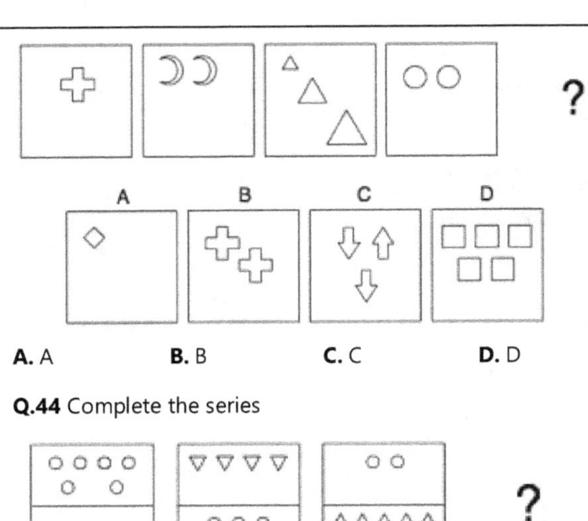

A. A **B.** B **C.** C **D.** D

Q.44 Complete the series

A. A **B.** B **C.** C **D.** D

Q.45 There are eight rules which when applied to the sequence will transform it to one of the four options shown below. Identify the correct option.

AB Delete the last character

BC Replace the third character with the next in the alphabet

CD Insert the letter P between the third and fourth characters

DE Exchange the first and last characters

EF Replace the second character with the previous letter in the alphabet

FG Replace the fifth character with the next in the alphabet

GH Reverse the whole sequence of letters

HI Delete the third character

NOITIDE – AB + FG + GH

A. DITTON **B.** DITION

C. DJTION **D.** EDITION

Q.46 There are eight rules which when applied to the sequence will transform it to one of the four options shown below. Identify the correct option.

■ Cancel all shading

○ Shade the second and last shapes

● Exchange the second and fourth shapes

□ Reverse the sequence of shapes

⬇ Change all circles to shaded squares

⇩ Replace all shaded shapes with unshaded triangles (with the apex at the top)

▲ Replace the first shape with a shaded triangle with its apex pointing downwards

△ Change the middle shape to an unshaded circle

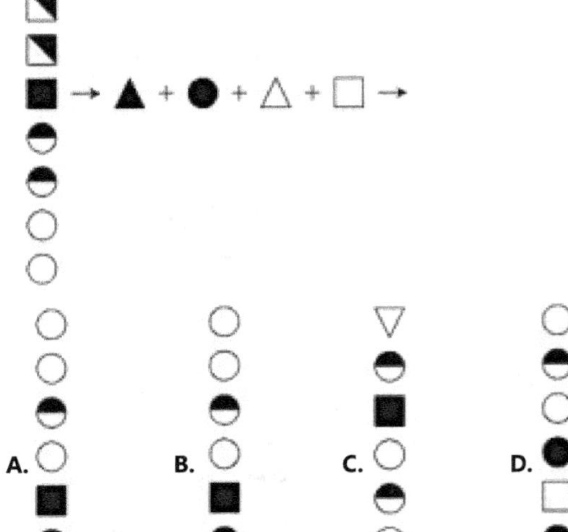

Q.47

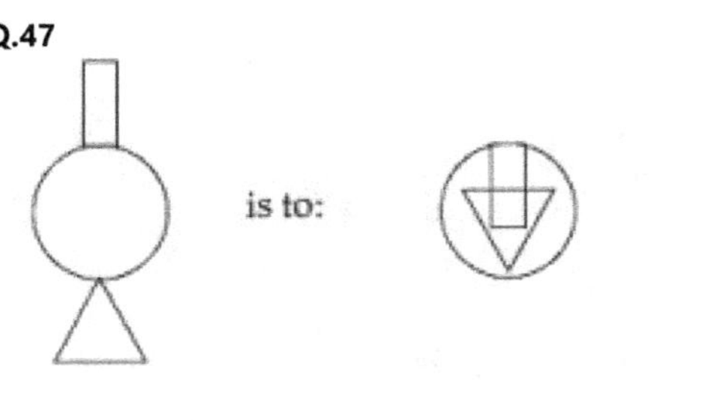

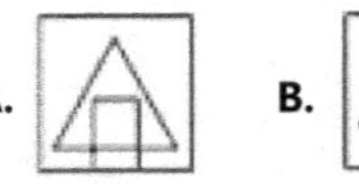

Q.48 Each line and symbol that appears in the four outer circles, above, is transferred to the centre circle according to these rules. If a line or symbol occurs in the outer circles:

Once: it is transferred

Twice: it is possibly transferred

3 times: it is transferred

4 times: it is not transferred

Which of the circles A, B, C, D or E, shown below, should appear at the centre of the diagram, above?

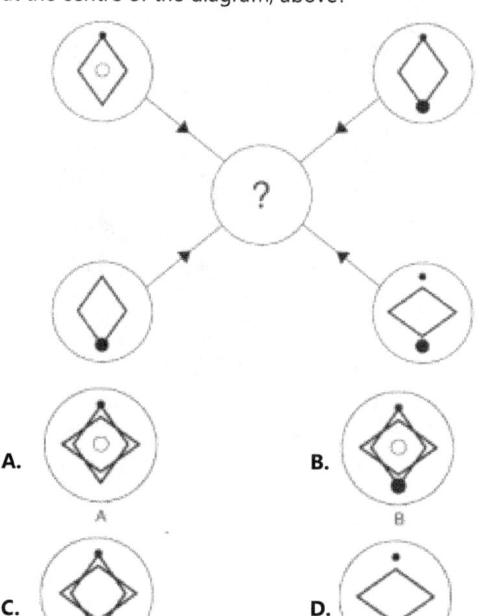

A.

B.

C.

D.

Q.49

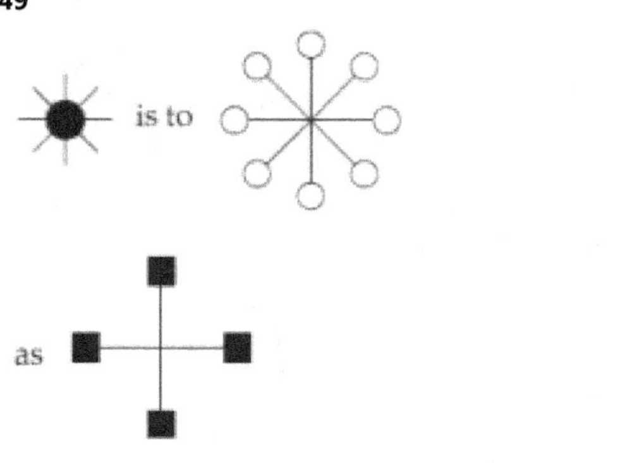

is to

A. 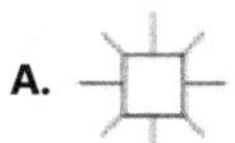 **B.** **C.** 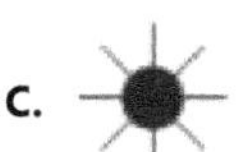 **D.** 

Q.50 Which square below has most in common with the square above?

A. A **B.** B **C.** C **D.** D

Q.51 What comes next in the above sequence?

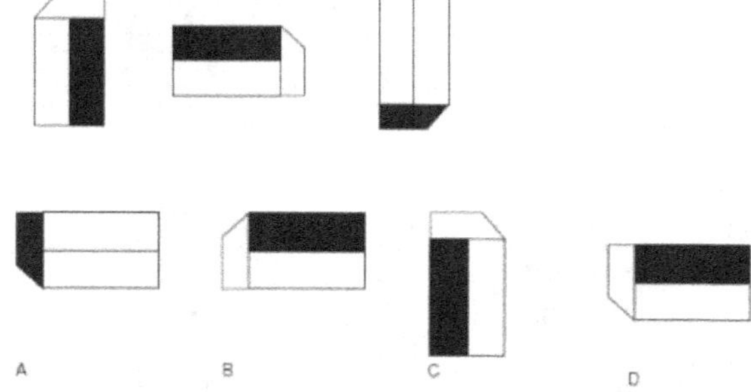

A. A **B.** B **C.** C **D.** D

Q.52 Which option continues the above sequence?

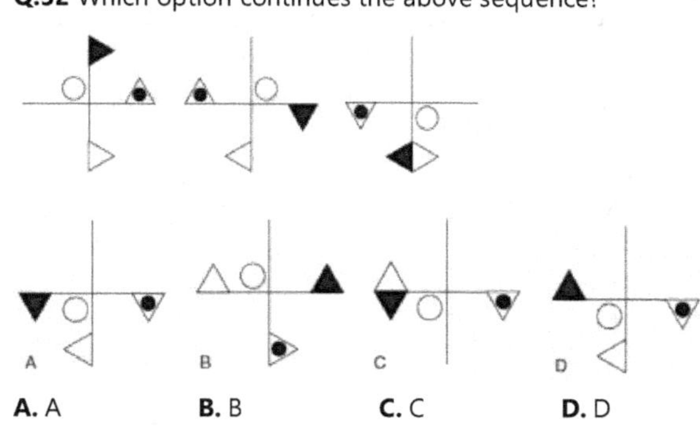

A. A **B.** B **C.** C **D.** D

Q.53 Direction: Select the Answer figure that will complete the series of question figures.

Question figures:

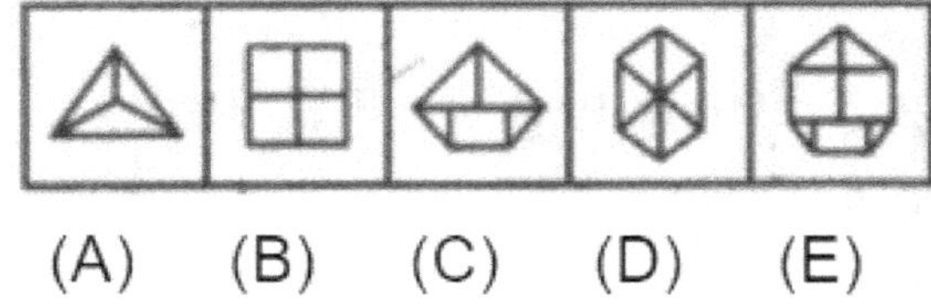

(A) (B) (C) (D) (E)

Answer figures:

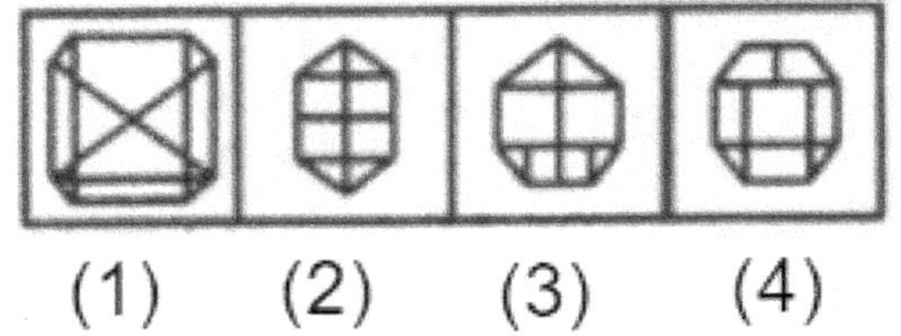

A. (1) **B.** (2) **C.** (3) **D.** (4)

Q.54 What comes next in the above sequence?

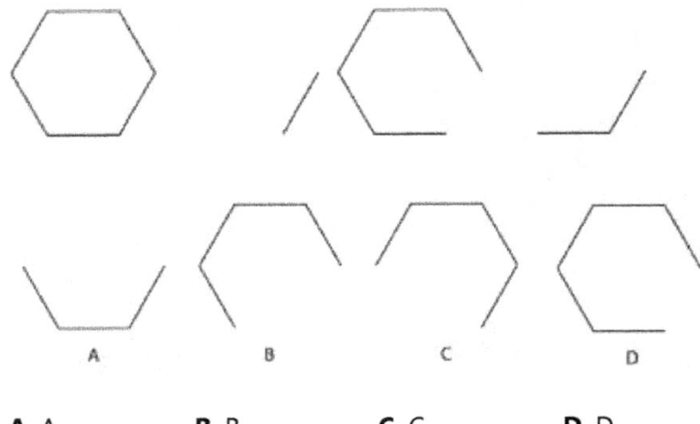

A. A **B.** B **C.** C **D.** D

Q.55 Which symbol should replace the question mark?

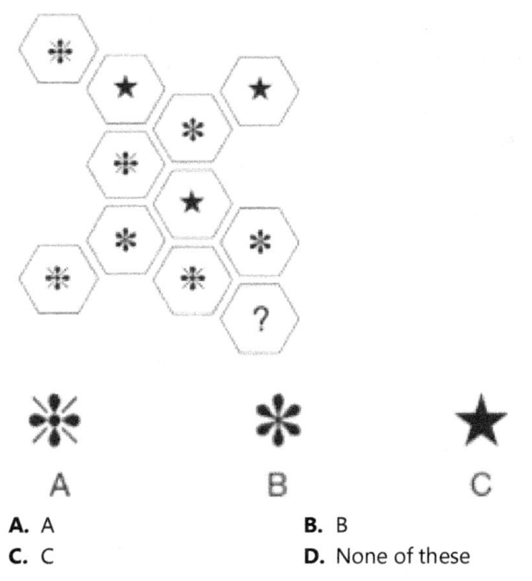

A. A **B.** B
C. C **D.** None of these

Q.56 Which is the missing segment?

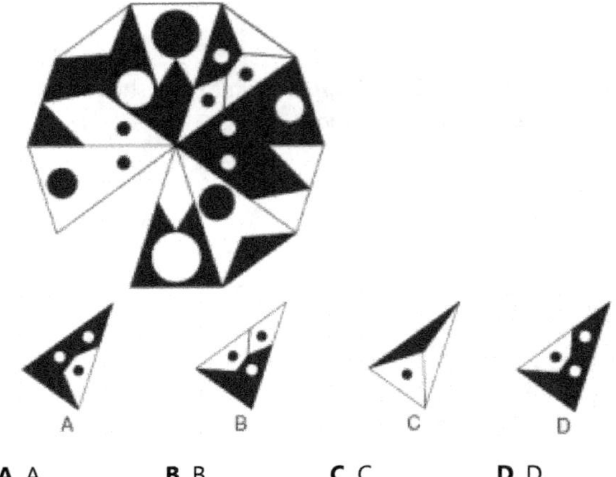

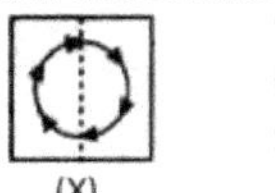

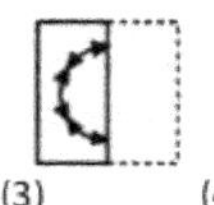

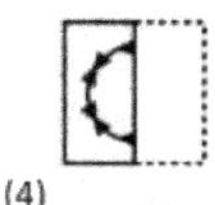

A. A **B.** B **C.** C **D.** D

Q.57 Choose the alternative which is closely resembles the water-image of the given combination.

FAMILY

(1) ƎAMILY (2) FAMIꓶY

(3) FAMIꓶY (4) FAMILY

A. 1 **B.** 2 **C.** 3 **D.** 4

Q.58 Find out from amongst the four alternatives as to how the pattern would appear when the transparent sheet is folded at the dotted line.

(X) (1) (2) (3) (4)

A. 1 **B.** 2 **C.** 3 **D.** 4

Q.59 Choose a figure, which would most closely resemble the unfolded form of Figure (Z)

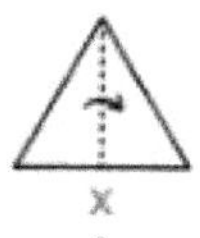

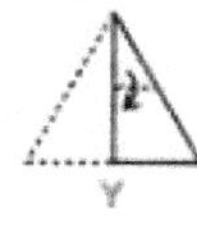

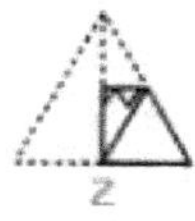

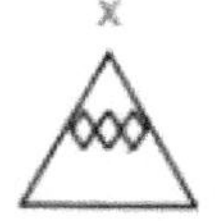

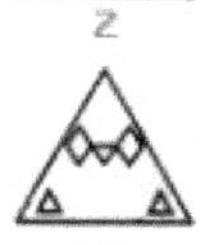

A. 1 **B.** 2 **C.** 3 **D.** 4

Q.60 Choose the alternative which closely resembles the mirror image of the given combination

PAINTED

(1) DƎTNIAꟼ (2) DƎTИIAꟼ

(3) DƎꓕИIAꟼ (4) DETИIAꟼ

A. 1 **B.** 2 **C.** 3 **D.** 4

Q.61 Shown below are images that have different visual features. Identify the correct sequence of visual features associated with these images from the given choices.

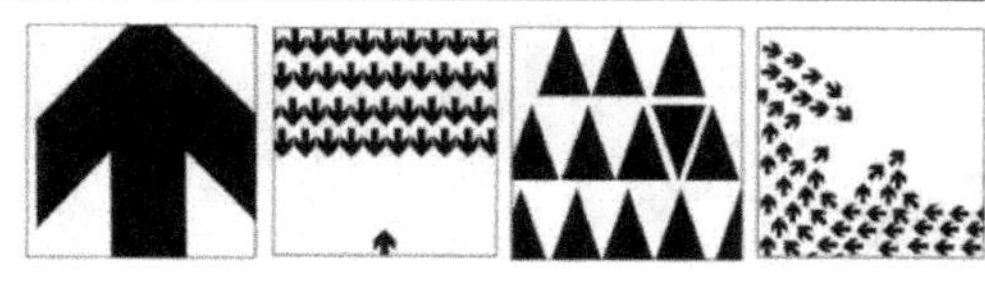

A. Bold, isolation, placement, direction
B. Direction, bold, isolation, placement
C. Placement, bold, isolation, direction
D. Bold, placement, direction, placement

Q.62 What will be the most probable pose at position 5 to complete the sequence below?

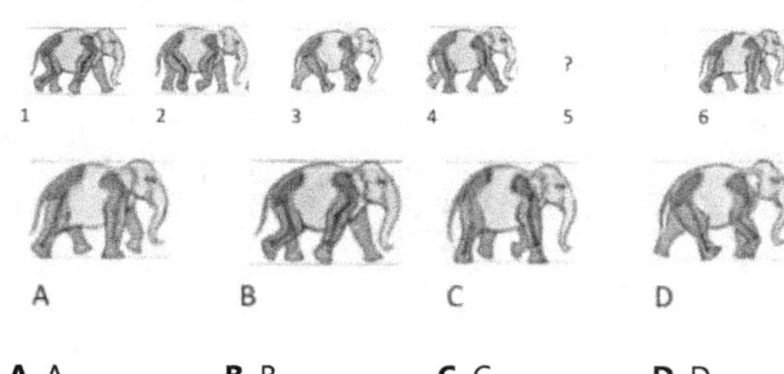

A. A **B.** B **C.** C **D.** D

Q.63 USB stands for –

A. Universal Serial Bus
B. Universe series Barrier
C. Unplug able Serial blower
D. Uranium Series Bus

Q.64 Identify the texture.

A. Coconut tree **B.** Palm tree
C. Neem tree **D.** Banyan tree

Q.65 Identify the logo

A. Punjab Tourism
B. Indian Tourism Development Corporation
C. National human resource development Corporation
D. Literacy promotion center.

Q.66 Identify the Architecture style

A. Rock cut architecture
B. Indo Islamic Architecture
C. Persian architecture
D. Cave architecture

Q.67 The tool shown above would most likely be used to

A. Drive nails. **B.** Weld meta
C. Tighten bolts **D.** Carve wood.

Q.68 Identify the material used for the sculpture.

A. Wood **B.** Wax
C. Newspaper **D.** Sandstone

// Smart Answer Sheet //

Correct Indicates percentage of students who answered questions correctly.

Skipped Indicates percentage of students who skipped questions.

Q.	Ans.	Correct	Skipped
1	1190	44.49 %	20.76 %
2	35	70.76 %	15.26 %
3	15	34.75 %	17.37 %
4	28	43.22 %	17.37 %
5	#	21.19 %	19.49 %
6	76	43.64 %	20.34 %
7	11	30.93 %	20.76 %
8	3	26.69 %	23.73 %
9	#	3.39 %	25.85 %
10	11	24.15 %	22.04 %
11	6	64.83 %	18.64 %
12	#	52.12 %	21.61 %
13	105	41.1 %	21.61 %
14	#	25.0 %	22.03 %
15	28	17.8 %	20.76 %
16	#	33.05 %	21.61 %
17	277	28.81 %	27.97 %
18	16	61.86 %	25.0 %
19	B, A, D	40.68 %	23.3 %
20	B, D, C	20.34 %	30.51 %
21	B, A	20.34 %	31.35 %
22	D	30.08 %	22.46 %
23	C	45.76 %	23.73 %
24	A, D	33.47 %	28.39 %
25	B, A, C	44.07 %	28.39 %
26	A	56.78 %	22.88 %
27	A	53.81 %	22.04 %
28	B	62.29 %	22.46 %
29	B	63.98 %	22.46 %
30	A	70.34 %	21.61 %
31	B	67.37 %	22.46 %
32	B	30.51 %	23.3 %
33	D	7.2 %	26.27 %
34	B, A, D	33.9 %	27.96 %
35	A, D	27.54 %	28.39 %
36	B, A, D, C	61.86 %	22.46 %
37	A	61.86 %	20.77 %
38	B	54.66 %	20.34 %
39	A	61.86 %	19.92 %
40	D	76.27 %	20.34 %
41	A	77.54 %	20.34 %
42	B	29.66 %	21.61 %
43	D	27.97 %	24.15 %
44	D	58.9 %	22.03 %
45	C	60.59 %	25.0 %
46	A	46.19 %	26.27 %
47	C	62.71 %	21.19 %
48	B	54.24 %	28.81 %
49	B	40.25 %	21.19 %
50	B	25.42 %	25.0 %
51	D	51.69 %	22.46 %
52	D	65.68 %	22.03 %
53	D	44.07 %	21.18 %
54	B	72.88 %	20.34 %
55	C	65.25 %	23.73 %
56	D	58.47 %	20.77 %
57	D	73.31 %	21.18 %
58	C	62.29 %	21.18 %
59	A	65.68 %	22.88 %
60	B	69.49 %	20.76 %
61	A	65.68 %	21.61 %
62	C	63.56 %	21.19 %
63	A	62.71 %	21.19 %
64	B	50.42 %	20.77 %
65	B	28.81 %	23.31 %
66	A	50.42 %	24.16 %
67	C	75.0 %	21.61 %
68	B	37.71 %	21.19 %

#

Q.	Answer
5	White
9	C
12	D
14	Tuesday
16	E

Performance Analysis	
Avg. Score (%)	45.0%
Toppers Score (%)	100.0%
Your Score	

//Hints and Solutions//

3697 5574 1767 5985 6367
7514 3270
1676 3683
8431 3584 2018
1450 1070
4208 1190
3601 1847 8504 8075
6063 2044
7070 4338 3015
1502
6049 1342 8075 4852

1.

Tabular just means the numbers are monospaced — every number occupies the same horizontal space, instead of varying space according to their own shape (which is called "proportional" in typography terms), therefore 1190 is in lining form.

2.

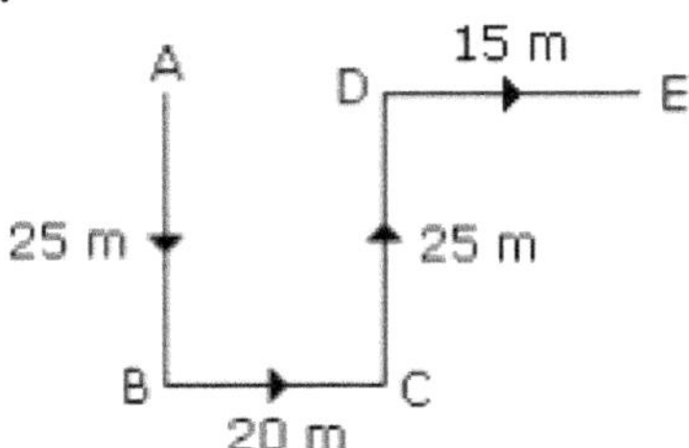

Distance required=20+15

=35 km

3. The figure may be labeled as shown.

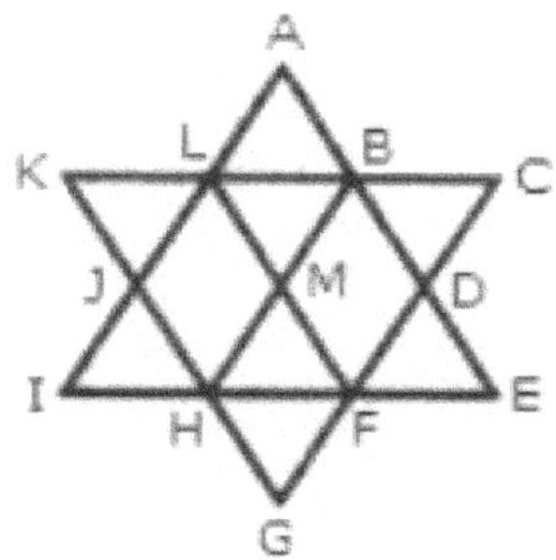

The simplest parallelograms are $LMHJ$ and $BDFM$ i.e. 2 in number. The parallelograms are composed of two components each is $ABML$ and $MFGH$ i.e. 2 in number.

The parallelograms are composed of three components each is $LBHI, LBEF, BDGH, DFLA, BCFH, KLFH, ABHJ$, and $LFGJ$ i.e. 8 in number.

The parallelograms are composed of six components each are $LCFI, KBEH,$ and $ADGJ$ i.e. 3 in number.

Total number of parallelograms in the figure $= 2 + 2 + 8 + 3 = 15$.

Hence, the correct answer is 15.

4. There are 28 surfaces required, If the word GOLD (shown on the right) were to be extruded,

5.

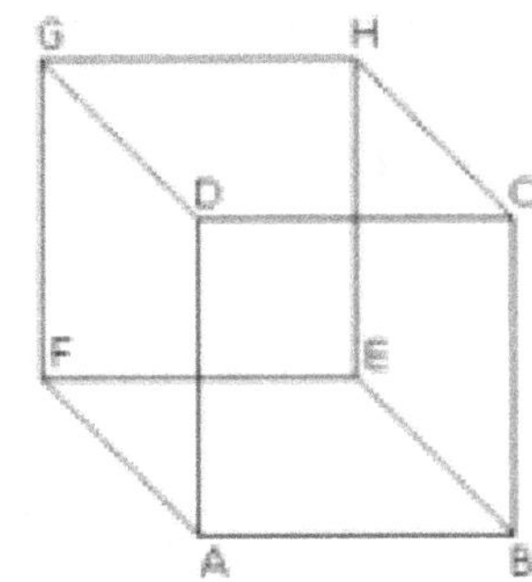

$\triangle BEF \rightarrow Red$

$DCHO \rightarrow Black$

$ABCD \rightarrow$ Oreen

EFGH → Blue

$APO \rightarrow$ White

BCHE → Brown

6. Given:

I was 8 years and my brother's age was half of my age.

My brother's age $= \frac{8}{2} = 4$

The Age gap of my and my brothers $= 8 - 4 = 4$

Then my age $= 80$

My brother's age $= 80 - 4 = 76$ years

∴ When my age is 80 years at that time My brother's age is 76 years.

Hence, the correct answer is 76.

7. The figure may be labeled as shown.

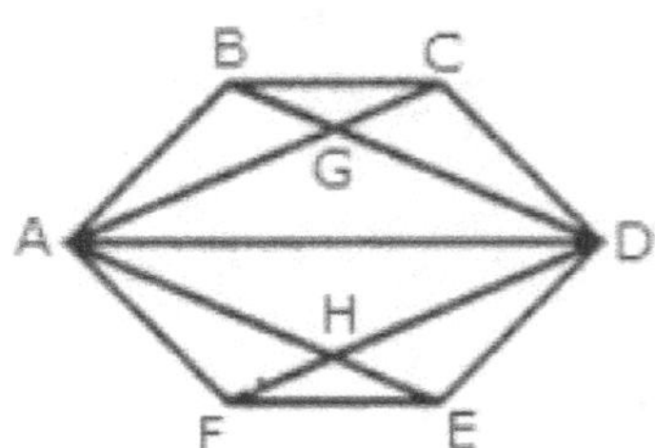

The quadrilaterals in the figure are $ABCD, ABDE, ABDF, ABDH, CDHA, CDEA, CDFA, DEAG, DEFA, FAGD$, and $AGDH$.

The number of quadrilaterals in the figure is 11.

Hence, the correct answer is 11.

8. The group of shapes shown in diagram 3 can be assembled to make the shape shown as a question figure.

Hence, the correct answer is 3.

9. Shapes A and D can be drawn without taking your pencil off the paper or going along the same line twice. Shape C can't be drawn in this way.

Hence, the correct answer is shape C.

10. There are 11 circles formed when arranged in an eight-by-eight matrix.

11. In the first figure

3+3+2+1=9.

The number in the circle is the square root of the total numbers outside the circle.

Therefore,

8+9+9+10=36

The square root of 36 is 6.

Hence, the correct answer is 6.

12. Four to the right of B is F.

Two to the left of F is D.

13. 105 kg; 250 × 0.7 × 0.8 × 0.75

14. The answer is Tuesday. This is how I got this answer: The day that comes immediately after Thursday is Friday.

15. There are 28 ways can the word QUIZ be spelt out.

16. E

Starting with Y and moving clockwise, letters move backwards through the alphabet in steps of 2 letters, then 3 then 4 etc.

17. 277 is the odd one out as all the other numbers are perfect cube numbers.

Hence, the correct answer is 277.

18. Starting bottom left and moving clockwise around the triangle, numbers follow the sequence of Square Numbers.

19. Allahabad Kumbh Melas — held every 12 years — are the largest and holiest

A B D are all correct statement.

20. B, C, D are true

Shiva Ayyadurai is an American inventor of Indian origin credited by some sources to be the inventor of email , Anton Chekhov was one of the most illustrious and celebrated short-story writers in the history of literature. Larry Page, is an American entrepreneur and computer scientist who, along with Sergey Brin, cofounded Google Inc.

21. The Great Indian Novel is a satirical novel by Shashi Tharoor, first published by Viking Press in 1989. It is a fictional work that takes the story of the Mahabharata, the Indian epic, and recasts and resets it in the context of the Indian Independence Movement and the first three decades post-independence

Interpreter of Maladies. Interpreter of Maladies is a book collection of nine short stories by American author of Indian origin Jhumpa Lahiri published in 1999. ... The stories are about the lives of Indians and Indian Americans who are caught between their roots and the "New World".

Pax Indica: India and the World in the Twenty-first Century is a 2012 non-fiction book written by Shashi Tharoor, about India's foreign policy.

The Namesake is a 2006 English-language drama film directed by Mira Nair and written by Sooni Taraporevala based on the novel The Namesake by Jhumpa Lahiri. It stars Tabu, Irrfan Khan, Kal Penn and Sahira Nair. The film was produced by Indian, American and Japanese studios.

Bookless in Baghdad is a 2005 book by author Shashi Tharoor that consists of a collection of previously published articles, book reviews and columns on writers, books and literary musings.

Unaccustomed Earth is a collection of short stories from American author Jhumpa Lahiri. It is her second collection of stories, following Interpreter of Maladies (which won the Pulitzer Prize for Fiction).

22. Only I and III are strong

The election process entails exorbitant expenditure. So, holding elections very often will surely lead to wastage of money and resources. Thus, I holds strong. Also, the elected representatives need a considerable period of time to implement their policies and also convince the voters of their working. So, III holds strong while II does not.

23. The use of the words 'hi-tech pulsating mega-watt performance' in the statement makes I implicit. Nothing is mentioned ab out the performances of Indian musicians. So, II is not implicit. The facts that Michael Jackson is a pop-singer and his performance left people spellbound make III implicit.

24. A, D

Pieter Cornelis Mondriaan, after 1906 Piet Mondrian, was a Dutch painter and theoretician who is regarded as one of the greatest artists of the 20th century.

25. A, B, C

Nandalal Bose was one of the pioneers of modern Indian art and a key figure of Contextual Modernism. A pupil of Abanindranath Tagore, Bose was known for his "Indian style" of painting. He became the principal of Kala Bhavan, Santiniketan in 1922.

26. Tamil Nadu and Karnataka

option A is correct .

27. In b) and c) the hexagonal shape has been deformed.

28. In a) the right side is double, and in c) the depth of the figure is missing.

29. In a) the parallelepiped has been moved towards the opposite side of the 'roof' shape, and in c) the 'roof' shape has been moved.

30. The other shapes are only partially reflected (some bits of the mirror image are represented in the original form

31.

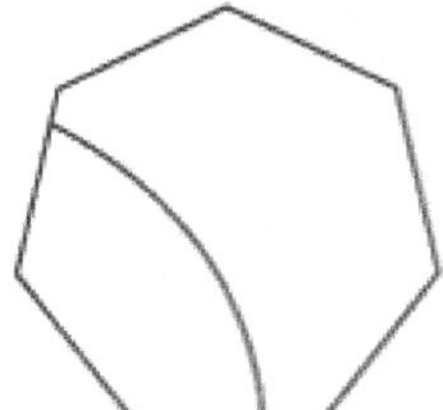

32.

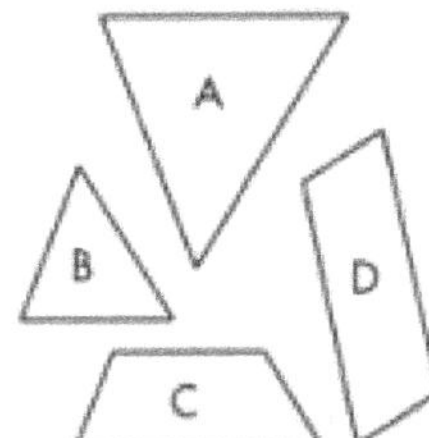

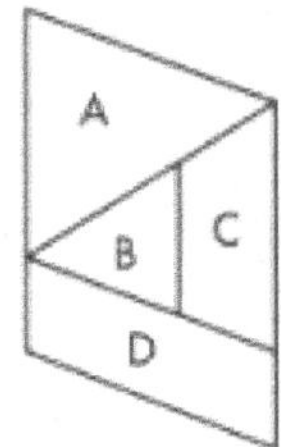

33.

34. A- Pantone (PMS)

B- Tracking

D- Leading

Pantone Color Finder tool - identify or convert Pantone Colors, then find matching products to buy online. Partner with Pantone for your color inspiration.

Tracking and kerning are essential elements of design that can have a great impact on the readability and visual appeal of your documents. Tracking refers to loosening or tightening a selected block of text, while kerning is the process of adding or subtracting space between specific pairs of characters.

35. Professor R.K. Joshi was an academic type designer and calligrapher. He designed the core Indian fonts used in Microsoft Windows.

Sudarshan Dheer designed the TITAN logo in 1987 with the joint venture of Tata Group and Tamil Nadu Industrial Development Corporation (TIDCO) to form TITAN Industries.

Hence, the correct options are (A), (D).

36. A, B, C, D are correct option.

37. The logo given in the question is of Toyota.

Toyota went through several incarnations of logo designs over the course of its history. The emblem on the model AA, Toyota's first passenger car, featured a hood ornament with wings to convey speed. This logo included the word Toyoda (the original name of the company) on a red and blue background.

Hence, the correct option is (A).

38. Oil, Pastel, Water Color, Crayons are used by paintings have been made.

39. Azure is a bright, cyan-blue color named after the mineral Lapis lazuli. It is often described as the color of the sky on a clear day. On the RGB color wheel, "azure" (hexadecimal #007FFF) is defined as the color at 210 degrees, i.e., the hue halfway between blue and cyan.

option A

40. option D

41. Option A is correct.

Bio Hazard, Ultraviolet Radiation, Watch your step, Suffocation hazard

42. option B

Fan

43. Explanation: The series follows the sequence 1, 2, 3, 2. You can make sense of this as 1 + 2 = 3 + 2 =

5, so the correct answer is suggested answer D with five shapes

44. At each step the number of circles decreases by two (from 6 to 0), and the number of triangles increases by four from 0 to 12. The direction of the triangles alternates, and the shapes alternate top and bottom.

45. The first rule deletes the E, then the second I is replaced with a J and finally the sequence is reversed to read DJTION.

46.

As per the given instructions, Option (1) is going to be the answer

47. C: the top bit folds down into the square, and the bottom bit folds up into it.

48.

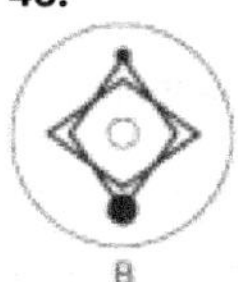

option B is correct .

49. reversing the first analogy, the four black squares become one white square in the center with four arms attached to it

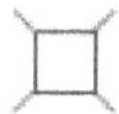

50. It has lateral symmetry, in other words if the square was cut from top to bottom down the middle, the two halves (left and right) would be identical

51. D the figure rotates 90° at each stage and a different portion is shaded in

52. the black triangle affixes itself to each arm in turn, the white triangle moves backwards and forwards between two positions, the triangle with the dot moves to each end of the middle arm (above then below) in turn, and the circle moves clockwise to each internal corner in tur

53. The number of parts increases by one along with the number of sides in the figure. Thus, the answer figure is,

Hence, the correct option is (D).

54. There are two alternate sequences. In the first, the hexagon is losing one side at a time, in the other the hexagon is being constructed one line at a time

55. C

so that each straight line of three hexagons contains one each of the three different symbols

56. Opposite segments are mirror images of each other, but with black/ white reversal

57. Image water of the Word Family - option 4 (D) is correct.

58. option C

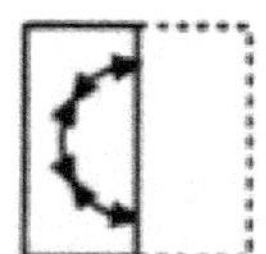

59. option A

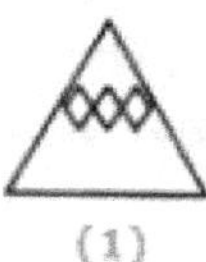

(1)

60. option B is correct,.

the mirror image of the PAINTED word is figure 2.

61. option A

Bold, isolation, placement, direction

62. Pose C will be the most probable pose at position 5 to complete the sequence.

C

Hence, the correct option is (C).

63. A Universal Serial Bus (USB) is a common interface that enables communication between devices and a host controller such as a personal computer (PC). It connects peripheral devices such as digital cameras, mice, keyboards, printers, scanners, media devices, external hard drives and flash drives.

64. The Arecaceae are a botanical family of perennial flowering plants in the monocot order Arecales. Their growth form can be climbers, shrubs, tree-like and stemless plants, all commonly known as palms. Those having a tree-like form are colloquially called palm trees.

65. The India Tourism Development Corporation is a hospitality, retail and education company owned by Government of India, under Ministry of Tourism. Established in 1966, it owns over 17 properties under the Ashok Group of Hotels brand, across India.

66. Rock cut architecture

Indian rock-cut architecture is more various and found in greater abundance in that country than any other form of rock-cut architecture around the world.

67. Try to pick a wrench that is the closest size to the bolt and try different combinations of coins to get a snug fit. If the wrench is too small you can take a long nut and a bolt, screw the nut onto the bolt and tighten the bolt around the nut you want to tighten or loosen.

option C Tighten bolts

68. Waxes are widely used throughout the world for a range of applications, including packaging, coatings, cosmetics, foods, adhesives, inks, castings, crayons, chewing gum, polishes and – of course – candles.

Mock Test 06

Numerical Answer Type (NAT)

Q.1 Radha moves towards Southeast a distance of 7 km, and then she moves towards West and travels a distance of 14 km. From here she moves towards Northwest a distance of 7 km and finally she moves a distance of 4 km towards east. How far is she now from the starting point?

Q.2 How many triangles are there in this figure?

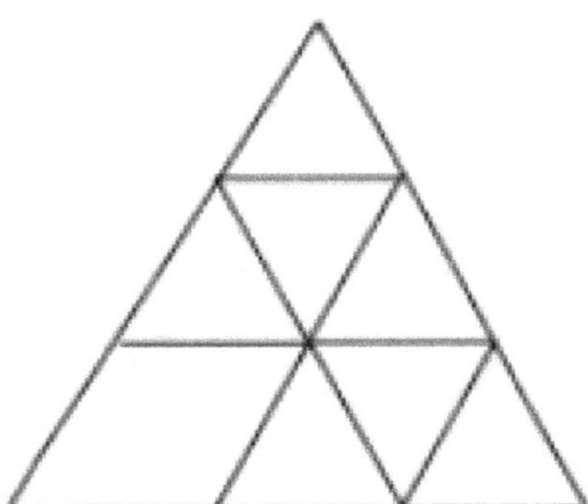

Q.3 The maximum number of squares in the given figure is:

Q.4 All the six faces of a cube are colored with six different colors - black, brown, green, red, white and blue. The red face is opposite to the black face. The green face is between red and black faces. A blue face is adjacent to a white face. Brown face is adjacent to blue face. The red face is at the bottom. The upper face is ________

Q.5 The five rings of the Olympic Flag are Blue, Black, Red, Yellow and Green in that order. In how many different ways could the five rings have been arranged in addition to the order shown above?

Q.6 Count the number of cubes in the given figure.

Q.7 In the question find the number of triangles:

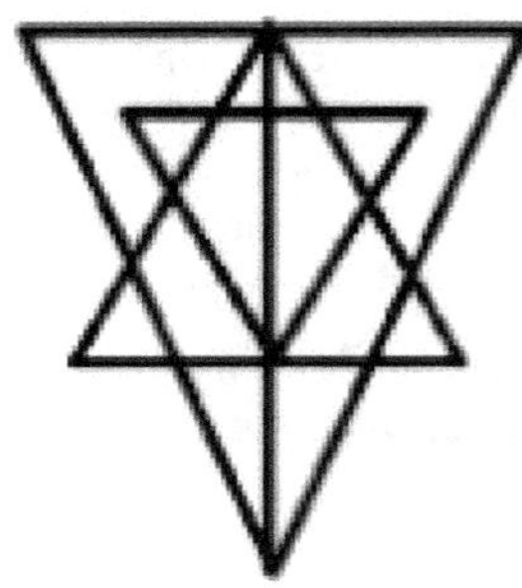

Q.8 Count the number of parallelograms in the given figure.

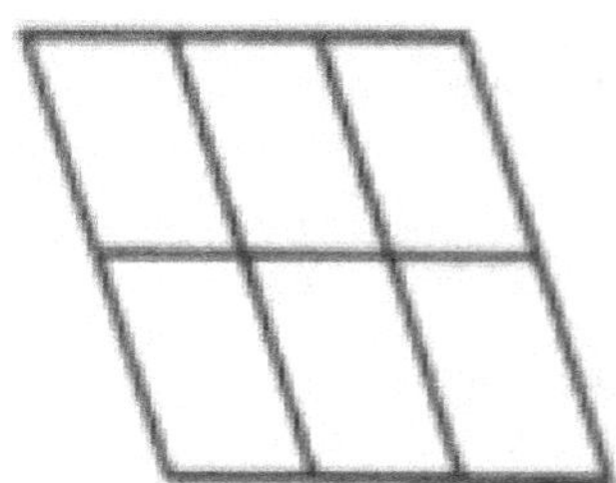

A. 20 **B.** 18 **C.** 16 **D.** 12

Q.9 Select the missing number from the given responses.

4	10	?
1	7	8
4	5	9

Q.10 The given image has sixty -four circles with patterns inside, arranged in an eight -by-eight matrix. How many different types of circles are there in the image, assuming circles may be rotated?

Q.11 A, C, F, J, O,? What letter comes next?

Q.12 Direction: Write the next term that will come.

$2, A, 9, B, 6, C, 13, D, ?$

Q.13 What number should replace the question mark?

7	4	5	2
5	1	9	3
2	9	1	6
?	4	3	7

Q.14 Enumerate the number of spelling mistakes in the following paragraph:

My visit to an slum area after a rainy season is a sad affair. The pit were still full of rain water. Their was mud all around. The poluted water had causing various diseases. Their was no home without a sick persons. Small childran suffered from stomach troubles. The governent should imediately rush to the help of the suferers in the slum area.

Q.15 How many lines appear below?

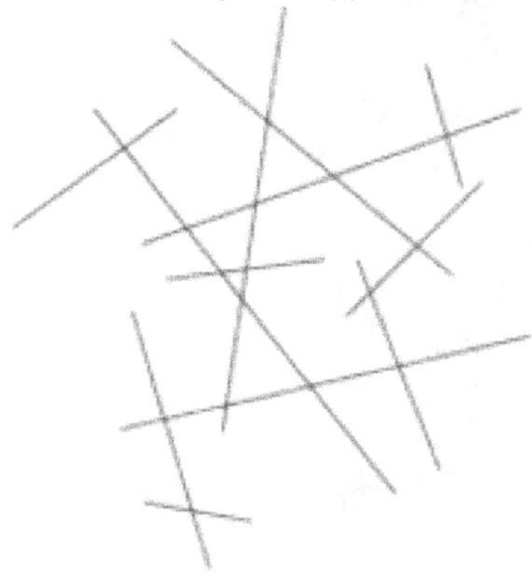

Q.16 What comes next?

208 CIV 52 XXVI –

Q.17 In the following figure, the black ball moves one position at a time clockwise. The white ball moves two positions at a time counterclockwise, In how many moves will they meet again?

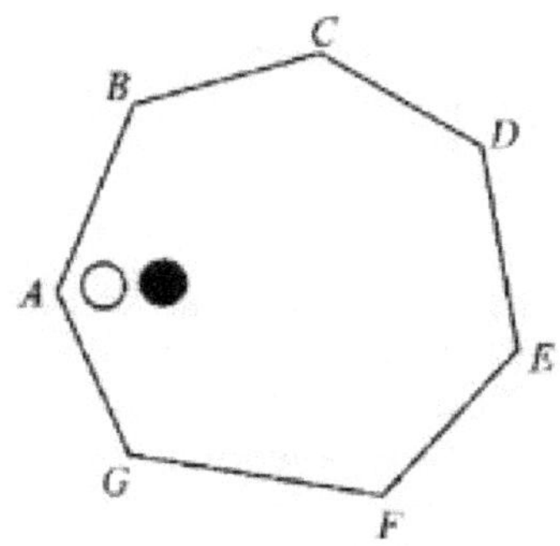

Q.18 Which four of the five pieces below can be fitted together to form a perfect square?

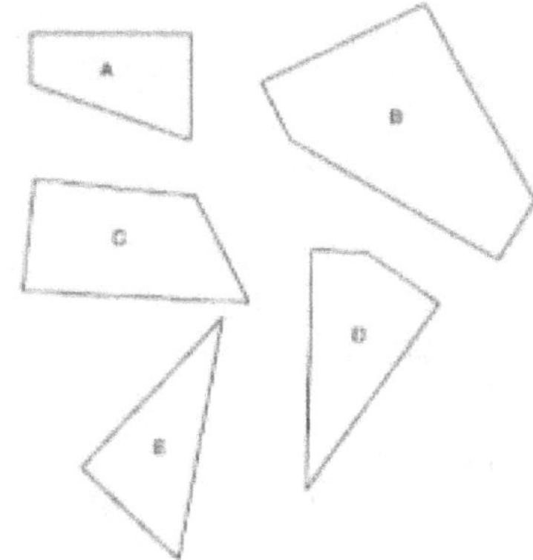

Multiple Select Questions (MSQ)

Q.19 Which of the following statements is/ are true?

A. Gupta Empire was one of the greatest empires, which had ruled India. During this time India made a huge progress in science, arts and literature. Thus, this period is sometime referred as "Silver Age of India".

B. Maharaja Sri Gupta was the founder of the Gupta Empire and Shashakgupta was the last emperor of this empire. Gupta Empire was existed about 230 years from 320 CE to 550 CE.

C. The great Mathematician Aryabhata was lived during this age. He discovered the number "1" and value of Pi. He wrote "Aryabhatiya" and "Suryasiddhanta".

D. The great Physician Dhanvantari was also born in this era. The Ajanta Paintings were also created during this age.

Q.20 Who was the first Muslim President of India?

A. Dr. APJ Abdul Kalam

B. Gyani Zail Singh

C. Dr. Zakir Hussain

D. Fakhruddin Ali Ahmed

Q.21 From the options below, select the Indian author/s writing in English whose works are represented below:

1. India after Gandhi
2. A suitable boy
3. Beastly Tales
4. Arion and the Dolphin
5. Chronicle of a Corpse bearer
6. The radiance of ashes

A. Salman Rushdie **B.** Vikram Seth

C. Cyrus Mistry **D.** Ramchandra Guha

Q.22 Question given below consists of a statement, followed by three arguments numbered I , II and III. You have to decide which of the arguments is a 'strong' argument. Statement: Should class IV children have Board examination?

Arguments:

I. Yes. This will motivate the children to study and get higher marks, and thus more knowledge can be imbibed at a younger age.

II. No. The children will be forced to study and won't enjoy the process.

III. Yes. In today's competitive world the children need to be prepared right from the beginning to face such difficult examinations.

IV. No. This will add pressure on tender aged children and leave very little time for them to play.

A. All are strong

B. Only I, II and IV are strong

C. Only II, III and IV are strong

D. Only I and III are strong

Q.23 Question below is given a statement followed by three assumptions numbered I, II and III. You have to consider the statement and the following assumptions and decide which of the assumptions is implicit in the statement.

Statement:

The residents of the locality wrote a letter to the Corporation requesting to restore normalcy in the supply of drinking water immediately as the supply at present is just not adequate.

Assumptions:

I. The Corporation may not take any action on the letter.

II. The municipality has enough water to meet the demand.

III. The water supply to the area was adequate in the past.

A. Only I and III are implicit

B. Only II is implicit

C. Only II and III are implicit

D. Only III is implicit

Q.24 An ecosystem is a group of animals and plants living in a specific region and interacting with one another and with their physical environment. Ecosystems include physical and chemical components, such as soils, water, and nutrients. These components support the organisms living in the ecosystem. Ecosystems can also be thought of as the interactions among all organisms in a given habitat. These organ- isms may range from large animals to microscopic bacteria and work together in various ways. For example, one species may serve as food for another. People are part of the ecosystems where they live and work. Human activities, such as housing developments and trash disposal, can greatly harm or even destroy local ecosystems. Proper ecosystem management is crucial for the overall health and diversity of our planet. We must find ways to protect local ecosystems without stifling economic development.

Which sentence best expresses the main idea of this passage?

A. Our actions can have a great impact on our ecosystems.

B. Ecosystems have been badly managed in the past.

C. Humans must clean up their trash.

D. Ecosystems interact with one another.

Q.25 Which of these paintings is / are by M C Escher.

A. 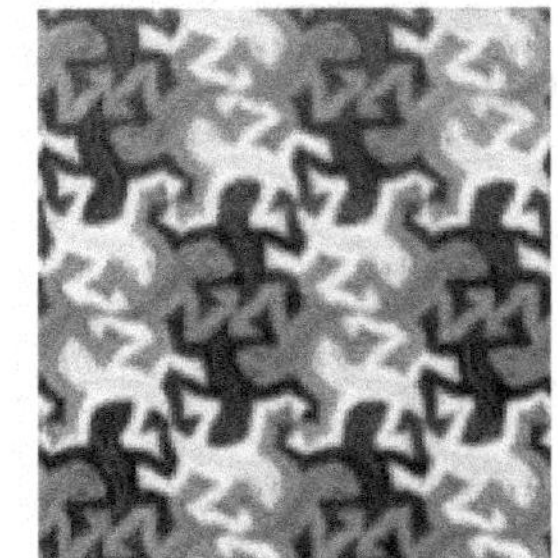

B. 

C. 

D. 

Q.26 Identify the paintings by the famous Indian artist Raja Ravi Varma from the following.

A. 

B. 

C. 

D. 

Q.27 Name the states of the folk art forms below in their respective order.

Pattachitra

Kalamkari

A. Orissa and Andhra pradesh
B. Bihar and Maharashtra
C. Orissa and Karnataka
D. Kerala and Karnataka

Q.28 In this question identify the new shape that could be constructed if the two example shapes were combined. No other change should be made to the two shapes other than combining them.

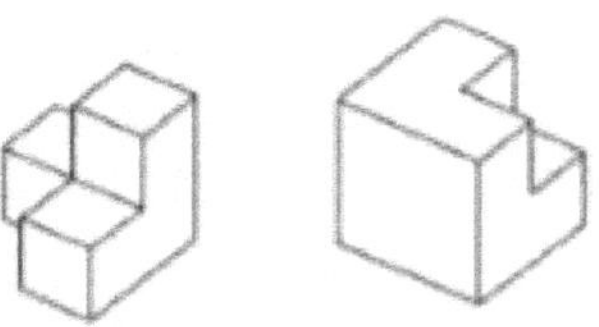

A. 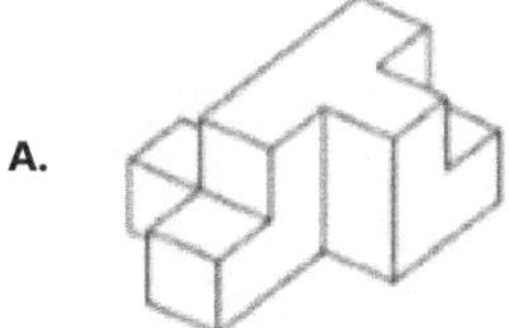

B. 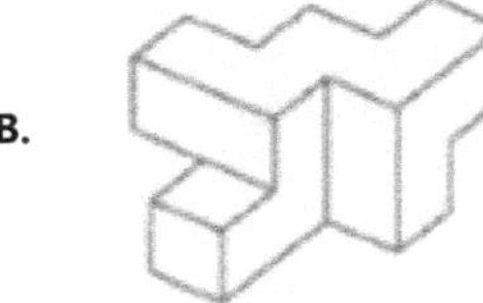

C. 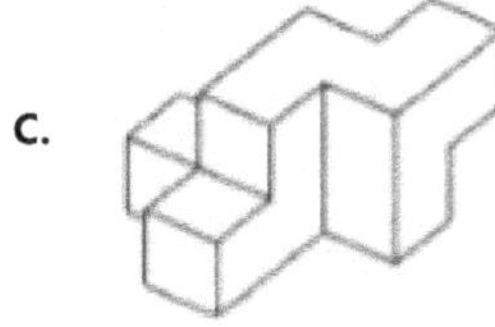

D. None of these

Q.29 Identify the 3D shape's net.

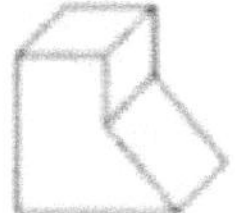

A. 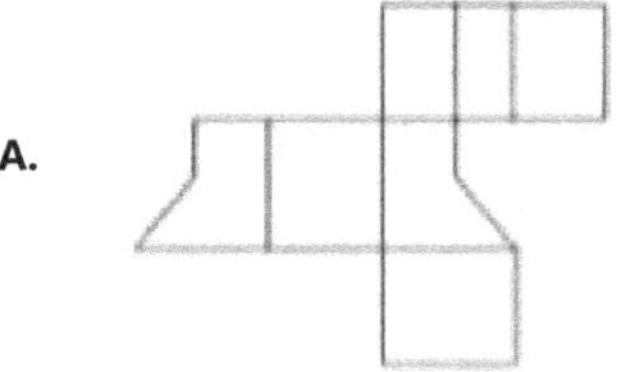

B. 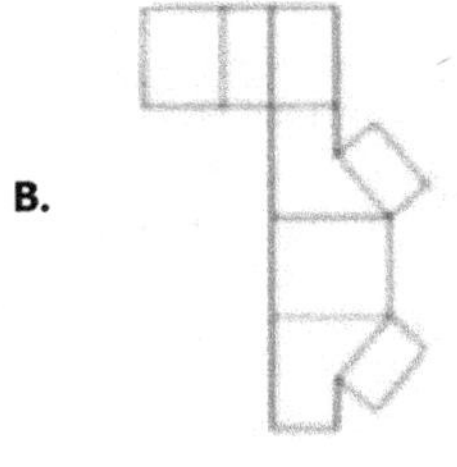

C. 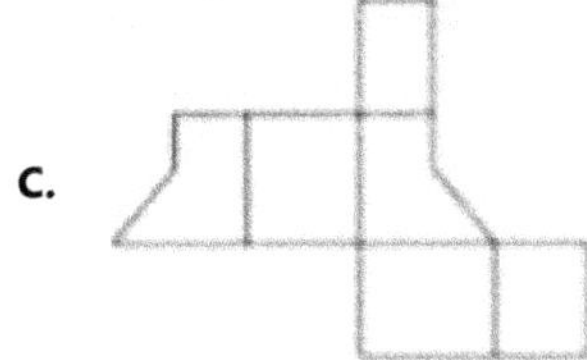

D. None of these

Q.30 Identify the answer shape, which has been rotated but is otherwise the same as the question shape.

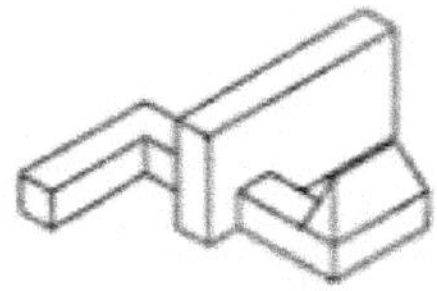

A. 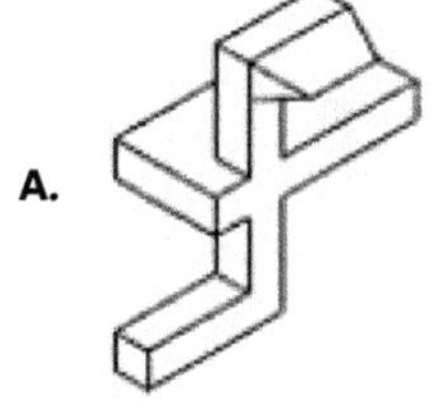

B. 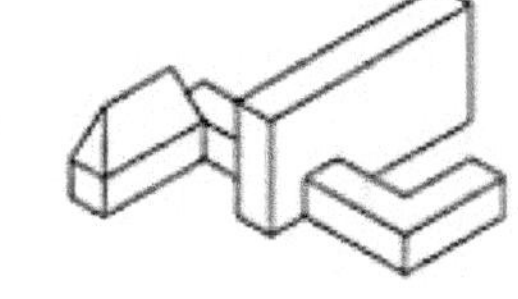

C. 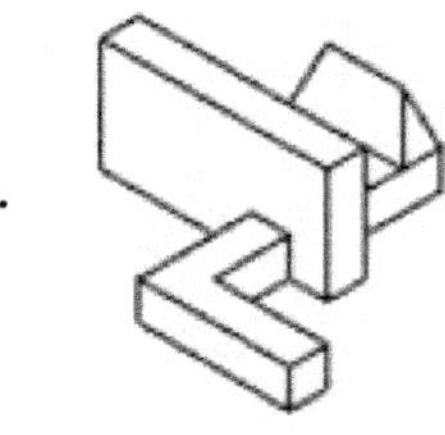

D. None of these

Q.31 Identify the mirror image of the question shape (reject any suggested answer in which any change other than reflection has occurred).

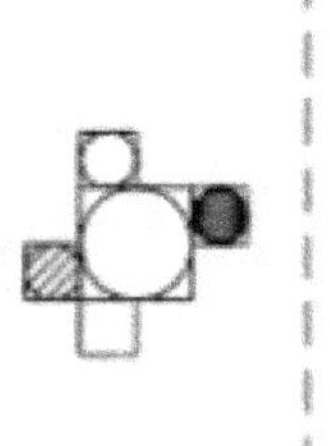

A. 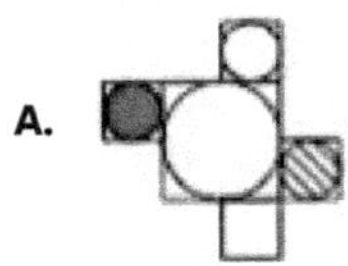

B. 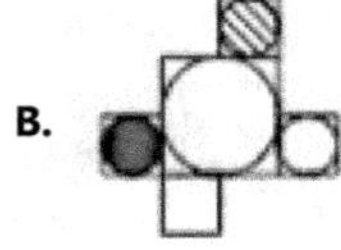

C. 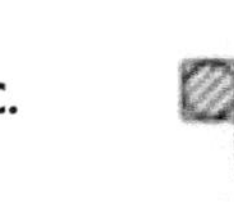 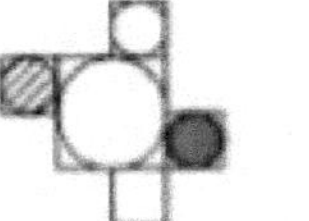

D. None of these

Q.32 Pick the TWO answer choices that will come together to make the figure shown. Pieces may be reflected and or rotated

A. 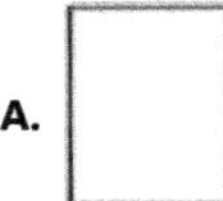

B. 

C. 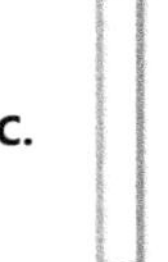

D. 

Q.33 4–5 pieces are given. Choose the answer choice that represents a figure comprised of ALL pieces. Pieces may be rotated and/or reflected.

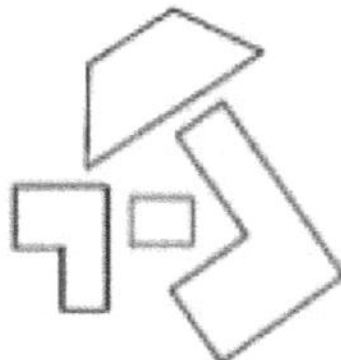

A. 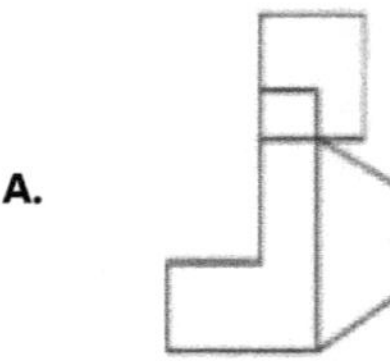

B. 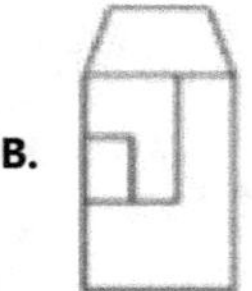

C. 

D. 

Q.34 A square is cut into 7 pieces as shown on the extreme left of the image. Identify which of the options can be made using all 7 pieces.

A. 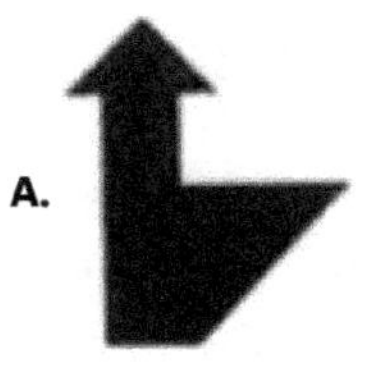 **B.** 

C.  **D.** 

Q.35 Which of the following terms are related to photography?

A. Bracketing **B.** Metering
C. Noise **D.** Burst mode

Q.36 Select the appropriate word(s) which can be made from the word given below:

UNDERGROUND

A. ROUND **B.** GROUND
C. UNMATCHED **D.** GROWL

Multiple Choice Questions (MCQ)

Q.37 Identify the correct art techniques with which the following paintings have been made.

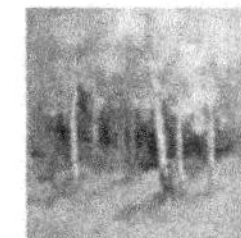   

A. Pastel, Oil, Watercolor, Crayon
B. Crayons, Pastel, Oil, Watercolor
C. Pastel, Watercolor, Oil, Acrylic
D. Acrylic, Oil, Pastel, Watercolor

Q.38 What three colors would you mix to make grey?

A. Yellow, Blue, Red **B.** Red, Green, Yellow
C. Green, blue, red **D.** Blue, yellow, green

Q.39 Which of these mixtures would create a tertiary color?

A. Red and Yellow **B.** Yellow and Blue
C. Red and Orange **D.** Blue and Red

Q.40 Shown are the symbols for different functions. Identify the correct description sequence from the given choices.

A. Mind your step, Danger of harming hands, Entrapment hazard, Sharp surface
B. Entrapment hazard, Danger of harming hands, Mind your step, Sharp surface
C. Danger of harming hands, Mind your step, Entrapment hazard, Sharp surfaces
D. Sharp surface, Mind your step, Entrapment hazard, Danger of harming hands.

Q.41 Complete the series

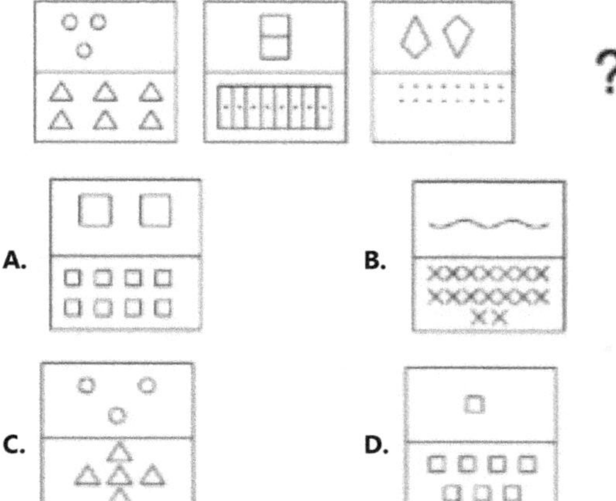

Q.42 Complete the series

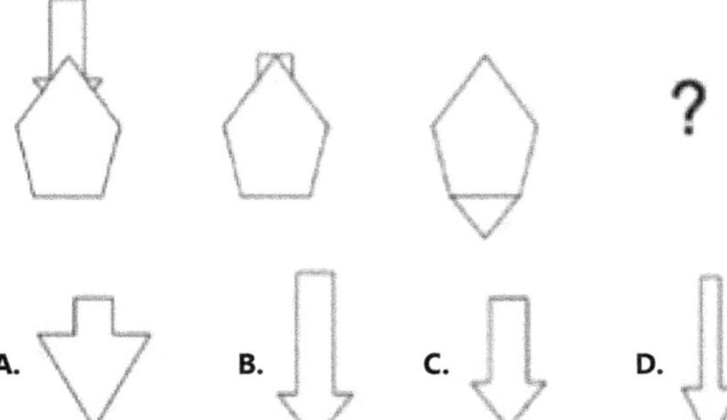

Q.43 There are eight rules which when applied to the sequence will transform it to one of the four options shown below. Identify the correct option.

AB Delete the last character

BC Replace the third character with the next in the alphabet

CD Insert the letter P between the third and fourth characters

EF Replace the second character with the previous letter in the alphabet

FG Replace the fifth character with the next in the alphabet

GH Reverse the whole sequence of letters

HI Delete the third character

Please find the next term in GNISSAP –>HI + GH + BC + FG.

A. PATSOG **B.** PASSNG
C. PANTGO **D.** PASSGNI

Q.44 Each line and symbol that appears in the four outer circles, above, is transferred to the centre circle according to these rules. If a line or symbol occurs in the outer circles:

Once: it is transferred

Twice: it is possibly transferred

3 times: it is transferred

4 times: it is not transferred

Which of the circles A, B, C, D or E, shown below, should appear at the centre of the diagram, above?

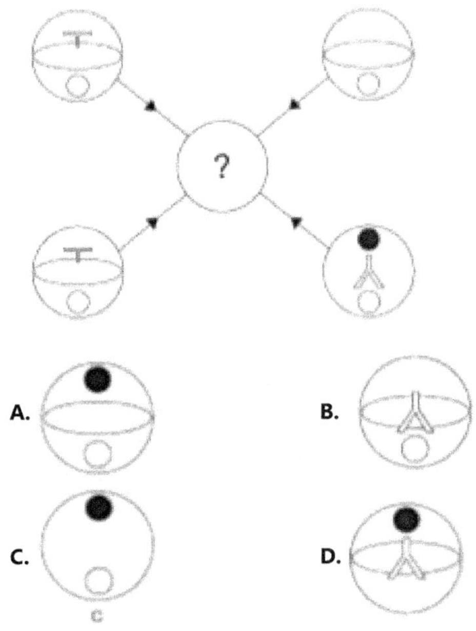

Q.45 Choose the alternative, which is closely, resembles the water-image of the given combination.

rise

A. ɹısǝ **B.** esir **C.** ꓶısǝ **D.** ǝsıɹ

Q.46 Find out from amongst the four alternatives as to how the pattern would appear when the transparent sheet is folded at the dotted line.

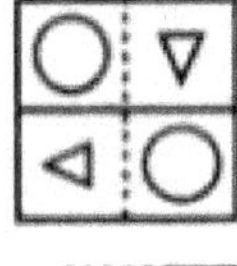

A. 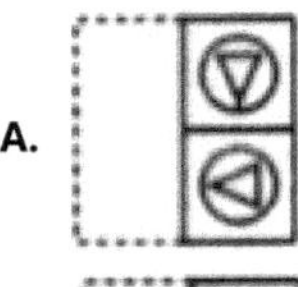 **B.** 

C. 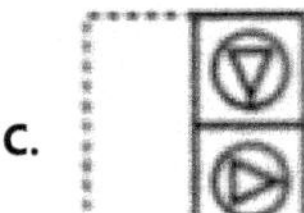 **D.** 

Q.47 Choose a figure, which would most closely resemble the unfolded form of Figure (Z).

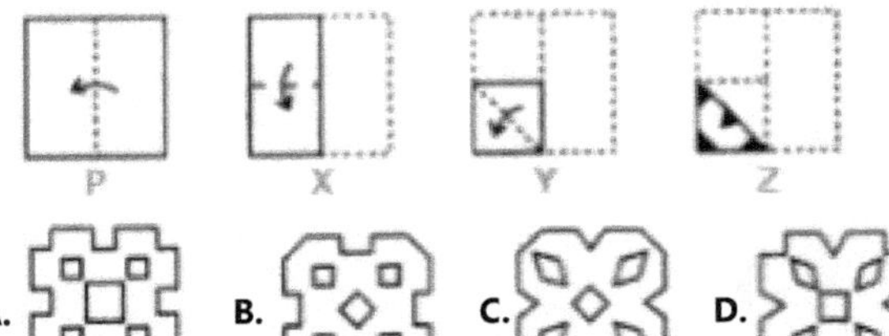

Q.48 Choose the alternative which is closely resembles the mirror image of the given combination.

Nu56p7uR

A. ИuƧ6qΓuЯ **B.** ЯnΓq6ƧnИ
C. ЯuΓq6ƧuИ **D.** ЯuΓd9ƧuИ

Q.49 What will be the most probable pose at position 4 to complete the sequence below?

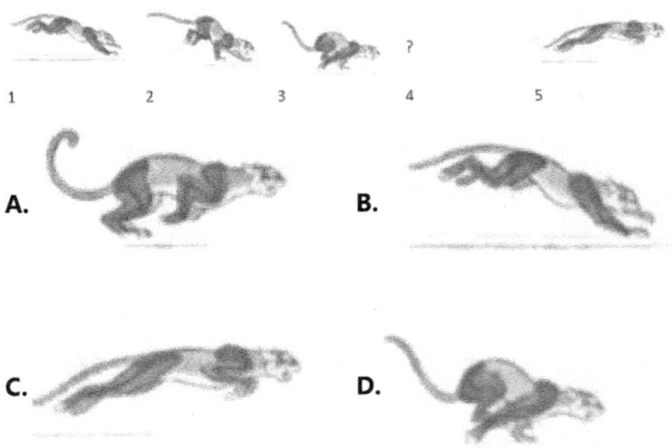

Q.50 The friction experienced by a body, when in motion, is known as

A. Rolling friction **B.** Dynamic friction
C. Limiting friction **D.** Static friction

Q.51 Identify the function of the tool below:

A. Scribe on surface
B. Draw arcs on metal and wood.
C. Measure accurately
D. All of the above.

Q.52 Correct the wrong sentence "You need not come unless you want to. "

A. You don't need to come unless you want to
B. You come only when you want to
C. You come unless you don't want to

D. You needn't come until you don't want to

Q.53 Identify the material used for the following artwork.

A. Plaster of Paris **B.** Cement
C. Marble **D.** Paper

Q.54 The technique to capture clearly the moving object with a blurred background is called:

A. Aperture controlling
B. Exposure controlling
C. Chirography
D. Panning

Q.55 Car modelling is done by which type of clay?

A. Polymer clay **B.** Wax
C. Ceramic clay **D.** Paper clay

Q.56 An early sample, model of a product built to test a concept or process or to act as a thing to be replicated or learned from is called?

A. Product **B.** concept
C. prototype **D.** mold

Q.57 Identify the Indian traditional art

A. Inlay art **B.** Marble engraving
C. Glass painting **D.** Fresco work

Q.58 Lacquer paints

A. Are generally applied on structural steel
B. Are less durable as compared to enamel paints
C. Contain alcohol as thinner
D. All of the above

Q.59

What flightless bird leaves footprints like this?

A. Emu **B.** Kiwi **C.** Rhea **D.** Ostrich

Q.60 Ergonomics is the study of:

A. Effects of work on humans
B. People in their working environment
C. Freeing oneself from constraints
D. Cultures

Q.61 Below given image is captured with which lens

A. Macro Lens **B.** Fish eye lens
C. Wide angle lens **D.** Telephoto lens

Q.62 What type of lens is a Magnifying Glass?

A. Convex **B.** Concave
C. Parabolic **D.** Plane

Q.63 Which of the following is/are feature of the Dravida style of temple architecture?

1. Curvilinear shikara
2. Recessed sculptures
3. Gopuram

Select the correct answer using the codes given below.

A. 1 and 2 only **B.** 2 and 3 only
C. 3 only **D.** 1, 2 and 3

Q.64 With reference to phad paintings, consider the following statements:

1. They are the folk paintings of Maharashtra.
2. Their themes include rural life, animals, and narratives of folk deities.

Which of the statements given above is/are correct?

A. 1 only **B.** 2 only
C. Both 1 and 2 **D.** Neither 1 nor 2

Q.65 Which is the missing tile?

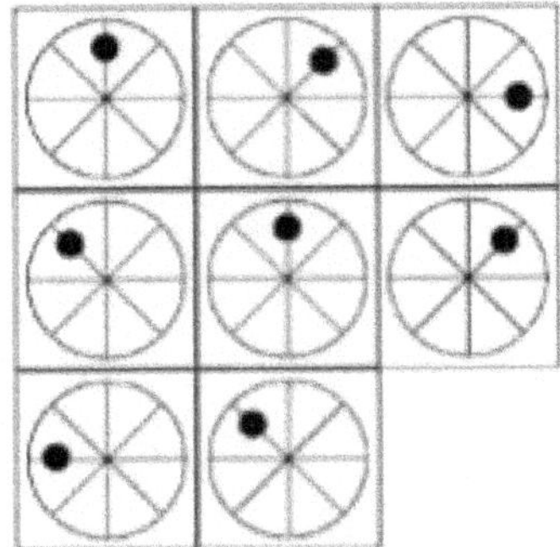

A. 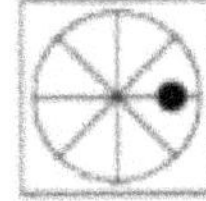

B. 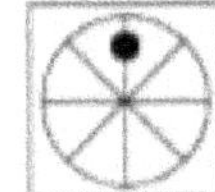

C. 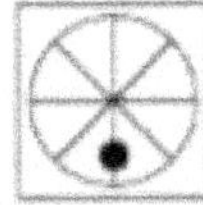

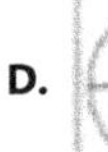

D.

Q.66 In questions below, each passage consists of six sentences. The first and sixth sentences are given in the beginning. The middle four sentences in each have been removed and jumbled up. These are labeled as P, Q, R and S. Find out the proper order for the four sentences.

S1: Your letter was big relief.

P : How did you exams go?

Q : After your result, you must come here for a week.

R : You hadn't written for over a month.

S : I am sure you will come out with flying colors.

S6: But don't forget to bring chocolate for Geetha.

The Proper sequence should be:

A. PSRQ **B.** QRPS **C.** RPSQ **D.** RSPQ

Q.67 Proverb/idiom is given below together with their meanings. Choose the correct meaning of proverb/idiom,

To hit the nail right on the head Proverb/idiom is given below together with their meanings. Choose the correct meaning of proverb/idiom,

To hit the nail right on the head

A. To do the right thing

B. To destroy one's reputation

C. To announce one's fixed views

D. To teach someone a lesson

Q.68 Proverb/idiom is given below together with their meanings. Choose the correct meaning of proverb/idiom,

To leave someone in the lurch

A. To come to compromise with someone

B. Constant source of annoyance to someone

C. To put someone at ease

D. To desert someone in his difficulties

// Smart Answer Sheet //

Correct — Indicates percentage of students who answered questions correctly.

Skipped — Indicates percentage of students who skipped questions.

Q.	Ans.	Correct	Skipped
1	10	62.56 %	5.21 %
2	14	15.64 %	19.43 %
3	55	13.74 %	20.38 %
4	#	33.65 %	21.8 %
5	119	11.37 %	26.07 %
6	132	36.97 %	21.32 %
7	27	11.85 %	22.75 %
8	B	18.01 %	21.8 %
9	#	21.8 %	26.54 %
10	12	38.86 %	23.7 %
11	#	60.66 %	22.75 %
12	10	22.75 %	32.23 %
13	4	49.29 %	25.12 %
14	5	10.9 %	23.7 %
15	12	59.24 %	23.22 %
16	13	42.18 %	29.38 %
17	#	30.81 %	23.69 %
18	#	2.84 %	29.39 %
19	B, D	9.95 %	30.81 %
20	C	31.28 %	30.81 %
21	B, D, C	27.96 %	33.18 %
22	C	27.49 %	27.01 %
23	D	31.75 %	28.44 %
24	A	19.91 %	29.38 %
25	B, A, D	50.71 %	30.33 %
26	A, D, C	42.65 %	27.02 %
27	A	41.71 %	27.48 %
28	A	62.09 %	26.06 %
29	A	47.39 %	27.49 %
30	C	54.03 %	26.06 %
31	A	69.19 %	25.12 %
32	D, C	52.13 %	25.12 %
33	D	25.59 %	25.59 %
34	B, D, C	36.49 %	31.76 %
35	B, A, D, C	66.82 %	27.02 %
36	B, A	28.91 %	26.54 %
37	A	56.4 %	23.69 %
38	A	34.6 %	26.06 %
39	C	50.24 %	25.12 %
40	A	63.51 %	23.22 %
41	B	36.49 %	31.28 %
42	C	54.98 %	25.59 %
43	A	47.87 %	30.8 %
44	D	42.18 %	31.28 %
45	A	67.3 %	23.7 %
46	C	63.98 %	24.17 %
47	C	59.72 %	24.17 %
48	C	66.35 %	23.22 %
49	A	69.67 %	23.22 %
50	B	45.5 %	24.64 %
51	D	52.61 %	23.69 %
52	A	55.45 %	24.17 %
53	D	23.7 %	23.22 %
54	D	35.07 %	25.59 %
55	D	10.9 %	27.49 %
56	C	45.97 %	25.12 %
57	A	25.59 %	27.02 %
58	D	43.13 %	29.86 %
59	D	33.65 %	29.86 %
60	B	27.49 %	27.96 %
61	A	54.03 %	26.06 %
62	A	43.13 %	25.12 %
63	B	17.06 %	34.6 %
64	B	27.49 %	28.43 %
65	B	70.62 %	24.64 %
66	C	55.92 %	26.07 %
67	A	41.23 %	25.59 %
68	D	49.29 %	27.49 %

#

Q.	Answer
4	Black
9	14
11	U
17	7
18	BCDE

Performance Analysis	
Avg. Score (%)	40.42%
Toppers Score (%)	102.92%
Your Score	

//Hints and Solutions//

1.

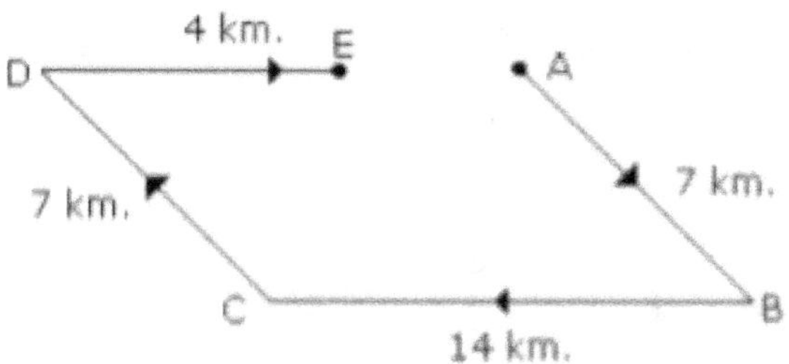

Required distance $= AE$

$= 14 - 4$

$= 10km$

2. Small triangles $= 8$

Triangles formed by 2 triangles $= 2$

Triangles formed by 2 triangles and one trapezium $= 2$

Larger triangles $= 2$

Thus, total triangles $= 8 + 2 + 2 + 2 = 14$

Hence, the correct answer is 14.

3. $n \times n$ type

$n = 1$ to 5

$1^2 + 2^2 + 3^2 + 4^2 + 5^2$

$1 + 4 + 9 + 16 + 25 = 55$

Hence, the answer is 55.

4.

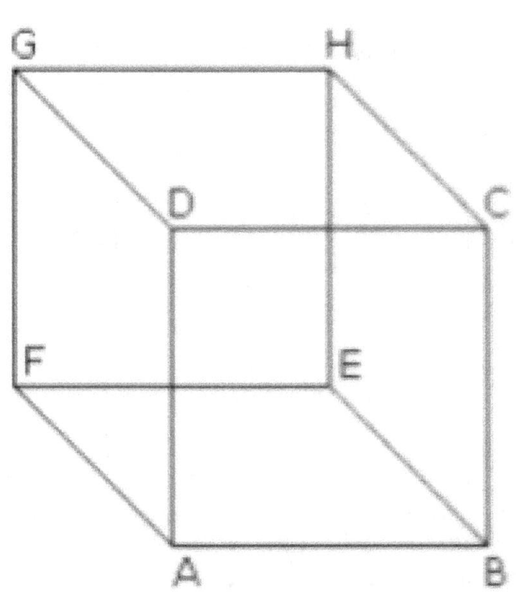

$ABEF \rightarrow Brown$

$DCHG \rightarrow Red$

$ABCD \rightarrow Green$

$EFGH \rightarrow Blue$

$AFGD \rightarrow White$

$BCHE \rightarrow Brown$

Hence, the answer is Black.

5. 119 different ways apart from the one shown above (the calculation is 5 x 4 x 3 x 2 x 1 = 120).

6. There are total of 132 cubes.

7.

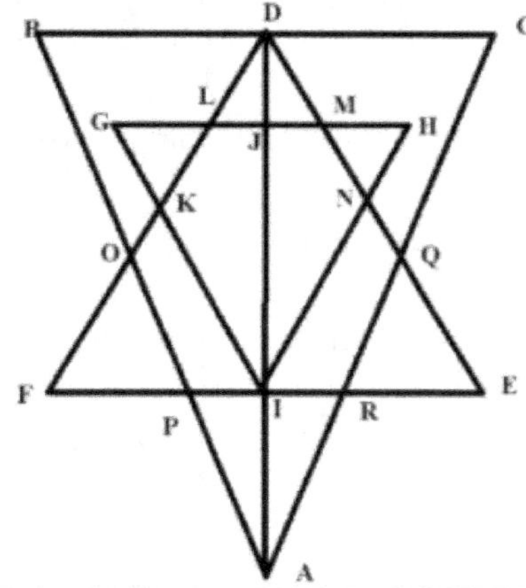

In the figure the simplest triangles are GLK, DLJ, DJM, HMN, QRE, IRA, IPA and FPO which makes a total of 8 triangles.

Then we have BDO, CDQ, DLM, PRA, KFI, NEI, HJI, GJI, DKI and DNI which makes a total of 10 triangles.

We also have DIE, DFI, DOA, DQA and GHI which makes a total of 5 triangles.

We have DCA, DBA, DEF and ABC that is 4 triangles.

Sum total = 8+10+5+4

= 27

Hence, the correct answer is 27.

8. The figure may be labeled as shown.

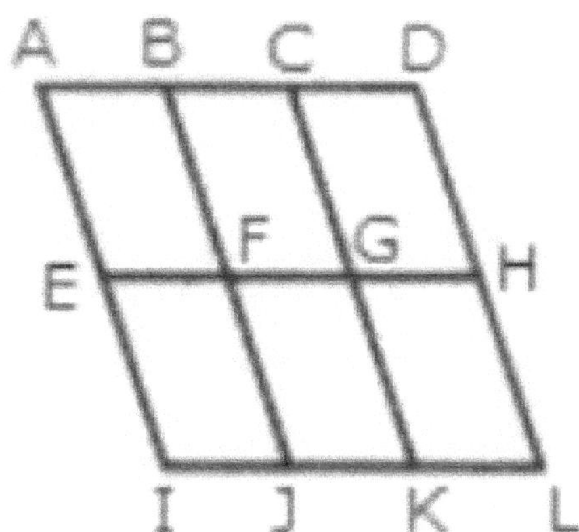

The simplest parallelograms are ABFE, BCGF, CDHG, EFJI, FGKJ and GHLK. These are 6 in number.

The parallelograms are composed of two components each are ACGE, BDHF, EGKI, FHLJ, ABJI, BCKJ and CDLK. Thus, there are 7 such parallelograms.

The parallelograms are composed of three components each are ADHE and EHLI i.e. 2 in number.

The parallelograms composed of four components each are ACKI and BDLJ i.e. 2 in number

There is only one parallelogram composed of six components, namely ADLI.

Thus, there are 6 + 7 + 2 + 2 + 1 = 18 parallelograms in the figure.

Hence, the correct option is (B).

9. The pattern here is,

First column $+$ Second column $=$ Third column

$1+7=8$

$4+5=9$

Similarly,

$4+10=14$

Hence, the correct answer is 14.

10. There are 12 types of circle.

11. The next letter will be U.

A

A+1=C

C+2=F

F+3=J

J+4=O

O+5=U

12. The given sequence is a combination of two series:

I. $2,9,6,13,?$ and II. A,B,C,D

The pattern in I is $:2 \overset{+7}{\rightarrow} 9 \overset{-3}{\rightarrow} 6 \overset{+7}{\rightarrow} 13 \overset{-3}{\rightarrow} 10$

So, the missing term is 10.

Hence, the correct answer is 10.

13. all lines and columns total 18

Therefore, 7+5+2+? = 18

=> 14+? = 18

=> ? = 18-14 = 4

14. The correct passage is:

My visit to a slum area after the rainy season was a sad affair. The pits were still full of rainwater. There was mud all around. The polluted water had caused various diseases. There was no home without a sick person. Small children suffered from stomach troubles. The government should immediately rush to the help of the sufferers in the slum area.

Hence, the correct answer is 5.

15. Total number of lines : 12

16. The answer is 13.

17. The balls will meet again in 7 moves.

Jot down the location of the balls for every movement:

(Black, White)
(B,F)
(C,D)
(D,B)
(E,G)
(F,E)
(G,C)
(A,A)

Hence, the correct answer is 7.

18.

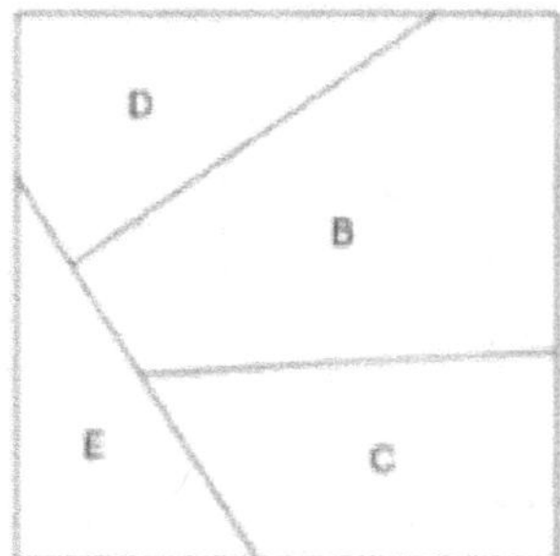

19. Gupta Empire was one of the greatest empires, which had ruled India. During this time India made a huge progress in science, arts and literature. Thus, this period is sometime referred as "Golden Age of India".

The great Mathematician Aryabhata was lived during this age. He discovered the number "0" and value of Pi. He wrote "Aryabhatiya" and "Suryasiddhanta".

20. Zakir Husain, (born Feb. 8, 1897, Hyderabad, India - died May 3, 1969, New Delhi), Indian statesman, **the first Muslim to hold the largely ceremonial position of president of India**. His fostering of secularism was criticized by some Muslim activists.

Hence, the correct option is (C).

21. Vikram Seth - A Suitable Boy, Beastly Tales, Arion and the Dolphin

Cyrus Mistry - Chronicle of a Corpse Bearer, The Radiance of Ashes

Ramchandra Guha - India After Gandhi

22. Young children of class IV ought to be taught the basic fundamentals of subjects in a gradual process via practical examples and practice in a playful manner. They need not be made to study through compulsion and their age is not such as to bear the tension and burden of examinations. So, both II and IV hold strong. However, facing examinations at this stage shall prepare them to tackle the competitions in later life. So, III also holds. However, holding examinations cannot motivate such young and immature students, neither is it a way to make them learn more. So, I does not hold strong.

23. The Corporation's response to the letter cannot be deduced from the statement. So, I is not implicit. The municipality's position in regard to water supply is also not mentioned. So, II is also not implicit. Since the residents talk of 'restoring' normalcy, it means that water supply was adequate in the past. So, III is implicit.

24. "Our actions can have a great impact on our ecosystems." best describes the above passage.

25. option A, B and D are correct.

Maurits Cornelis Escher was a Dutch graphic artist who made mathematically inspired woodcuts, lithographs, and mezzotints. Despite wide popular interest, Escher was for long somewhat neglected in the art world, even in his native Netherlands. He was 70 before a retrospective exhibition was held.

26. option A, C and D are correct.

Raja Ravi Varma was a celebrated Indian painter and artist. He is considered among the greatest painters in the history of Indian art for a number of aesthetic and broader social reasons. Firstly, his works are held to be among the best examples of the fusion of European techniques with a purely Indian sensibility.

27. Pattachitra is a traditional painting of Odisha, India. These paintings are based on Hindu mythology and specially inspired by Jagannath and Vaishnava sect. All colours used in the Paintings are natural and paintings are made fully old traditional way by Chitrakaras that is Odiya Painter.

Kalamkari is a type of hand-painted or block-printed cotton textile, produced in Isfahan and Indian states of Andhra Pradesh and Telangana. Only natural dyes are used in Kalamkari and it involves twenty-three steps.

28. In b) both shapes are different, and in c) the right shape has been modified.

29. In b) the cover of the sloped side is double, and c) has not enough surfaces

30. a) has the roof upside down, and in b) the 'L' shape with the 'roof' has been reflected.

31. b) has the little squares and the shadings in different positions, and c) is the same as a) but the shadings have been inverted

32.

33.

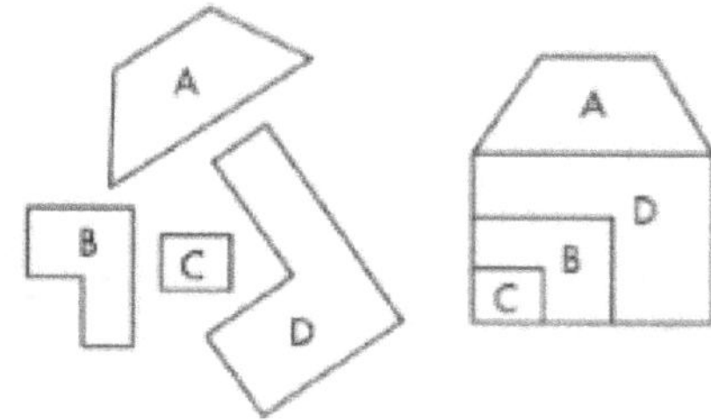

34. option B, C and D is correct.

35. Bracketing: In photography, bracketing is the general technique of taking several shots of the same subject using different camera settings.

Metering: Metering is how your camera determines what the correct shutter speed and aperture should be, depending on the amount of light that goes into the camera and the ISO. Back in the old days of photography, cameras were not equipped with a light "meter", which is a sensor that measures the amount and intensity of light.

Noise: In digital photographs, "noise" is the commonly-used term to describe visual distortion. It looks similar to grain found in film photographs, but can also look like splotches of discoloration when it's really bad, and can ruin a photograph. Noise tends to get worse when you're shooting in low light.

Burst mode: Burst mode, also called continuous shooting mode, sports mode or continuous high speed mode, is a shooting mode in still cameras.

36. The word given in the question is - **UNDERGROUND**.

Only two words - **ROUND** and **GROUND** can be made from the given word.

Hence, the correct options are (A), (B).

37. Pastel, Oil, Watercolor, Crayon

38. Yellow, Blue, Red

39. Red and Orange

40. Mind your step, Danger of harming hands, Entrapment hazard, Sharp surface

41. Each step represents a fraction (for example, 3 circles over 6 triangles = 3/6). If you cancel the fractions down you get the sequence 1/2, 1/4, 1/8, and the next step is 1/16.

42. The shapes portray a pentagon overlying an arrow that is moving downwards. In the last step of the series the hexagon has been removed, and by studying previous diagrams you are able to estimate the dimensions of the arrow correctly as in suggested answer C.

43. The correct answer is PATSOG.

First the I is deleted, then the sequence is reversed to read PASSNG, next the first S becomes a T and finally the N is replaced with an O.

Hence, the correct option is (A).

44.

45. option A is correct.

L!86

46.

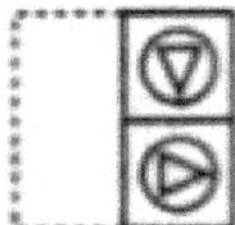

47.

48.

ЯuTqə6uИ

49.

50. Dynamic friction: The friction experienced by a body, when in motion, is known as dynamic friction.

option B is correct.

51. option D is correct.

52. Correct form is - "You don't need to come unless you want to."

53. The material used is paper.

Hence option D is correct.

54. **Panning** is a popular professional photography technique that involves tracking a moving subject with your camera before, during and after taking the photo. Any moving subject can be photographed using the panning technique, but the faster the subject is moving the easier it is to get a more blurry background.

Hence, the correct option is (D).

55. Car modelling is done by **Paper clay**.

Hence option D is correct.

56. An early sample, model of a product built to test a concept or process or to act as a thing to be replicated or learned from is called **prototype**.

57. Inlay covers a range of techniques in sculpture and the decorative arts for inserting pieces of contrasting, often coloured materials into depressions in a base object to form ornament or pictures that normally are flush with the matrix.

58. All of the above

Hence option D is correct.

59. The common ostrich (Struthio camelus) or simply ostrich, is a species of large flightless bird native to certain large areas of Africa. It is one of two extant species of ostriches, the only living members of the genus Struthio in the ratite order of birds. The other is the Somali ostrich (Struthio molybdophanes), which was recognized as a distinct species by BirdLife International in 2014 having been previously considered a very distinctive subspecies of ostrich.

60. Ergonomics is the study of people in their working environment. More specifically, an ergonomist (pronounced like an economist) designs or modifies the work to fit the worker, not the other way around. The goal is to eliminate discomfort and risk of injury due to work. In other words, the employee is our first priority in analyzing a workstation.

Hence, the correct option is (B).

61. Given image is captured with Macro Lens.

62. A magnifying glass (called a hand lens in laboratory contexts) is a convex lens that is used to produce a magnified image of an object. The lens is usually mounted in a frame with a handle. A magnifying glass can be used to focus light, such as to concentrate the sun's radiation to create a hot spot at the focus for fire starting.

Hence, the correct option is (A).

63. 2 and 3 only. Curvilinear shikara is a feature of the Nagara style. The other two features – recessed sculptures and gopuram are feature of Dravida style.

64. 2 only. Phad paintings are folk paintings of Rajasthan. Their themes includes rural life, animals, and narratives of folk deities, like Pabuji and Dev Narayan. The ancient tradition of scroll painting survives in Rajasthan as Phad. A Phad is a long rectangular cloth painting that tells of the adventures and travails of Pabuji, a local hero or other epic heroes. The Hindu has covered phad paintings regularly in last few months.

65. looking across, the dot moves 45° clockwise at each stage, but looking down it moves 45° anticlockwise.

66. S1: Your letter was big relief.

R : You hadn't written for over a month.

P : How did you exams go?

S : I am sure you will come out with flying colors.

Q : After your result, you must come here for a week.

S6: But don't forget to bring chocolate for Geetha.

67. To do exactly the right thing; to do something in the most effective and efficient way.

68. To leave someone in the lurch: To desert someone in his difficulties.

Mock Test 07

Numerical Answer Type (NAT)

Q.1 How many different types of symbols appear in the figure given below?

□	○	◉	©	❖	ǃ	❖	©	❖
●	◆	+	◈	●	●	ǃ	◈	ǃ
©	◇	◈	•	○	□	♣	●	❖
⊙	◆	◈	◇	▦	◘	●	+	○
ǃ	+	●	◆	□	○	■	●	❖
◉	▣	●	■	▦	▣	⊙	■	◘
©	●	©	●	▣	•	◈	♣	◆
●	❖	●	♣	▣	●	●	❖	●
+	•	◈	■	○	◈	⊙	•	◆

Q.2 Sundar runs 20 m towards East and turns to right and runs 10 m. Then he turns to the right and runs 9 m. Again he turns to right and runs 5 m. After this he turns to left and runs 12 m and finally he turns to right and 6 m. Now to which direction is Sundar facing?

Q.3 How many lines appear below?

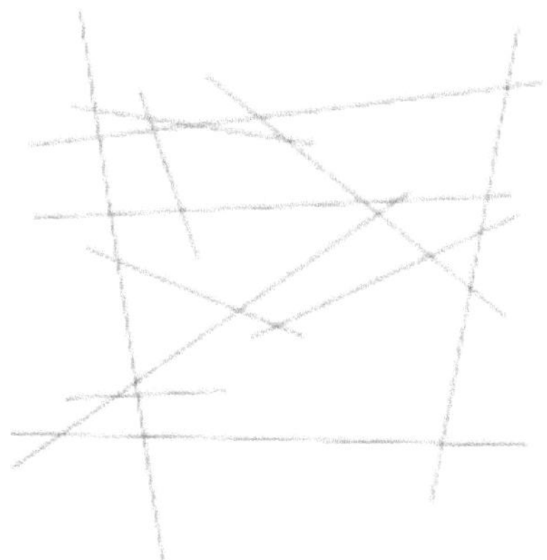

Q.4 Imagine letters are extruded into three-dimensional objects, as shown in the figure on the left (the letter A). If the word FISH (shown on the right) were to be extruded, how many surfaces would it have?

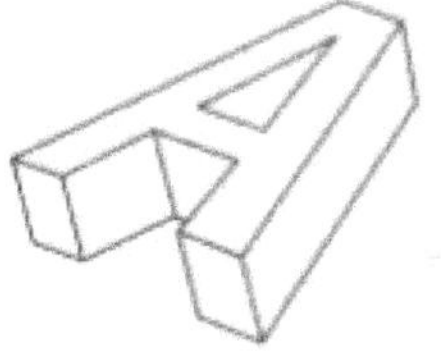

FISH

Q.5 A rectangular field $50\ m$ long and $40\ m$ broad contains a rectangular lawn inside is surrounded by a gravel path of uniform width of $6\ m$. Then the area of the path (in m^2) is:

Q.6 The combined age of Harry and Sally is 25. Two years ago, Harry was twice as old as Sally. How old will Harry be when Sally is 10?

Q.7 Count the number of cubes in the given figure.

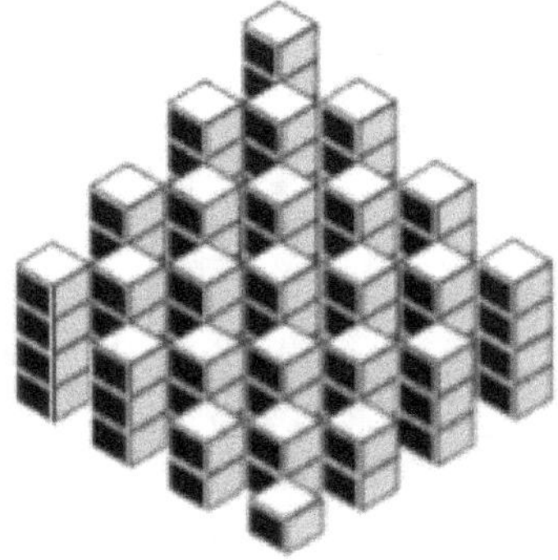

Q.8 Count the number of squares in the given figure:

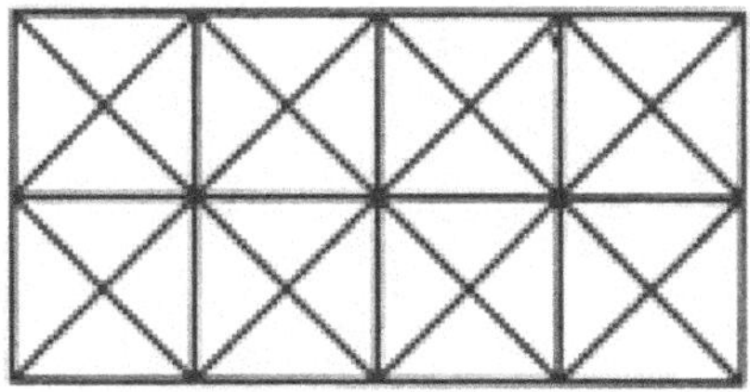

Q.9 Count the number of different types of fruits in the picture below

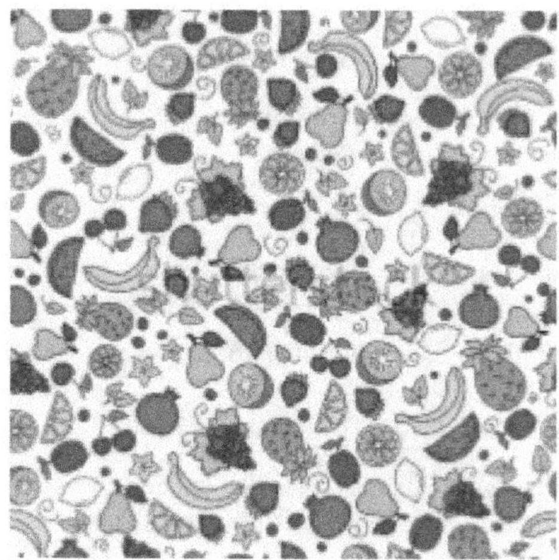

Q.10 In the adjoining figure, if the centres of all the circles are joined by horizontal and vertical lines, then find the number of squares that can be formed.

Q.11 Count the number of triangles in the given figure.

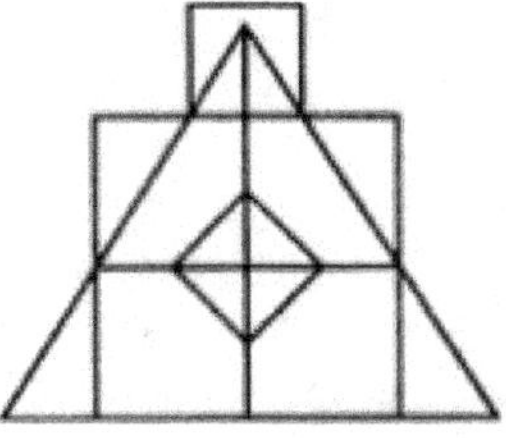

Q.12 What letter is two letters to the right of the letter two letters above the letter four letters to the left of the letter Z?

A	B	C	D	E	
F	G	H	I	J	
K	L	M	N	O	
P	Q	R	S	T	
U	V	W	X	Y	Z

Q.13 What number should replace the question mark?

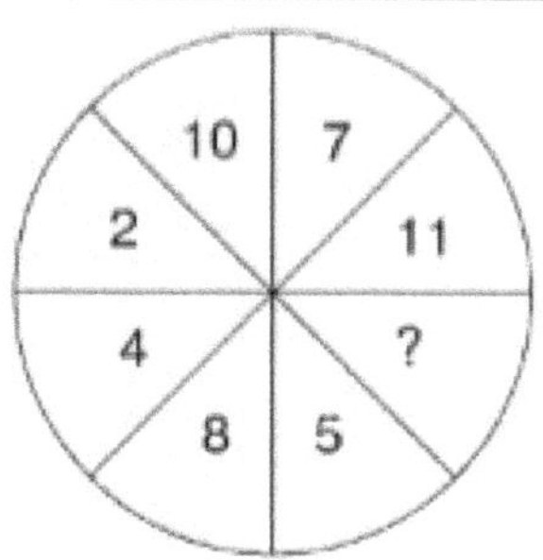

Q.14 Find out the total number of surfaces of the object, given below in the problem figure. Problem figure

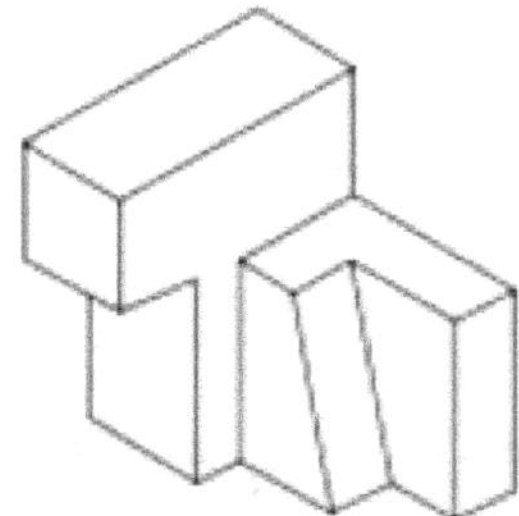

Q.15 How many different sized circles appear below?

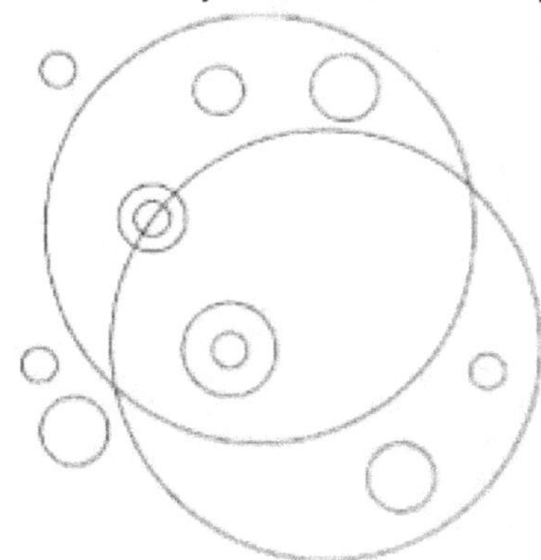

Q.16 5 6 3 2 9 7 1 4 2 6 8 3 7 5 9 7 1

Delete all the numbers that appear more than once in the above list; then multiply the remaining numbers together. What is the answer?

Q.17 100 aliens attended the intergalactic meeting on Earth:

78 had two heads

28 had three eyes

21 had four arms

12 had two heads and three eyes

9 had three eyes and four arms

8 had two heads and four arms

3 had all three unusual features

How many had none of these unusual features?

Q.18 How many revolutions of 1 will take place in order to bring the black teeth into mesh with the other:

A If 1 rotates clockwise

B If 1 rotates anti clockwise?

Multiple Select Questions (MSQ)

Q.19 Which of the following statement is/ are true?

A. Wright Brothers were aviation pioneers.

B. Karl Marx was the foremost Socialist intellectual.

C. Henry Ford pioneered the use of Mass production for motorcars, helping to reduce the price and make cars affordable for the average American consumer.

D. Malala Yousafzai, a Pakistani schoolgirl who defied threats of the Taliban to campaign for the right to education.

Q.20 Select the statements below that are TRUE.

A. Gautama Buddha taught his disciples at Benares in India about the same time that Isaiah was prophesying among the Jews in Babylon and Heraclitus was carrying on his speculative enquiries into the nature of things at Ephesus. All these men were in the world at the same time, in the sixth century B.C

B. About 2000 B.C., Aryan-speaking people came down from the north-west into India either in one invasion or in a series of invasions; and were able to spread its language and traditions over most of north India. Its peculiar variety of Aryan speech was the Sanskrit.

C. Siddhattha Gautama was the son of an aristocratic family which ruled a small district on the aaravali slopes.

D. News was brought to him that his wife had been delivered of his first-born son. He returned to the village amidst the rejoicings of his fellow clansmen. He resolved to leave his happy aimless life forthwith and went out into the bright Indian moonshine, mounted his horse and rode off into the world.

Q.21 From the options below, select the Indian author/s writing in English whose works are represented below:

1) Cuckold
2) God's little soldier
3) The blue umbrella
4) Bombay lost and found
5) The flight of pigeons
6) Maximum city

A. Ruskin Bond **B.** Suketu Mehta
C. Kiran Nagarka **D.** Manu Joseph

Q.22 Each problem consists of three statements. Based on the first two statements, the third statement

may be true, false, or uncertain.

Class A has a higher enrollment than Class B.

Class C has a lower enrollment than Class B.

Class A has a lower enrollment than Class C.

If the first two statements are true, the third statement is

A. True **B.** False
C. Uncertain **D.** Certain

Q.23 Many people who are looking to get a pet dog get a puppy. There are many reasons why people get puppies. After all, puppies are cute, friendly, and playful. But even though puppies make good pets, there are good reasons why you should consider getting an adult dog instead.

When you get a puppy, you have to teach it how to behave. You have to make sure that the puppy is housebroken so that it does not go to the bathroom inside the house. You have to teach the puppy not to jump up on your guests or chew on your shoes. You have to train the puppy to walk on a leash. This is a lot of work.

On the other hand, when you get an adult dog, there is a good chance that it will already know how to do all of the previously mentioned things. Many adult dogs have already been housebroken. Many adult dogs will not jump on or chew things that you do not want them to jump on or chew. Many adult dogs will be able to walk on a leash without pulling you to the other side of the street. Puppies also have a lot of energy and want to play all of the time. This can be fun, but you might not want to play as much as your puppy does. Puppies will not always sleep through the night or let you relax as you watch television.

On the other hand, most adult dogs will wait on you to play. What is more, they will sleep when you are sleeping and are happy to watch television on the couch right beside you.

There is one last reason why you should get an adult dog instead of a puppy. When most people go to the pound to get a dog, they get a puppy. This means that many adult dogs spend a lot of time in the pound, and some never find good homes. So if you are looking to get a dog for a pet, you should think about getting an adult dog. They are good pets who need good homes.

Based on information in the passage, which of the following statements is TRUE?

A. Puppies have a lot of energy.

B. Puppies need a lot of attention.

C. Adult dogs do not like to play.

D. Adult dogs do not need eat very much.

Q.24 Question given below consists of a statement, followed by three arguments numbered I , II and III. You have to decide which of the arguments is a 'strong' argument. Statement: Should the rule of wearing helmet for both driver and pillion rider while driving a motor bike be enforced strictly?

Arguments:

I. Yes. It is a rule and rules should be followed strictly by all.

II. No. Each individual knows how to protect his own life and it should be left to his discretion.

III. No. It does not ensure safety as only the head is protected and rest of the body is not.

IV. Yes. It is a necessity as head, being the most sensitive organ, is protected by the helmet.

A. None is strong

B. Only I and III are strong

C. Only I and IV are strong

D. Only II and IV are strong

Q.25 Question below is given a statement followed by three assumptions numbered I, II and III. You have to consider the statement and the following assumptions and decide which of the assumptions is implicit in the statement.

Statement: "We have the distinction of being the only company in India as well as the second in the world to have won an ISO 9002 certification in our line of business." - Statement of Company X's Chairman.

Assumptions:

I. There were not many companies in the line of business of Company X.

II. Getting ISO 9002 in the line of business of Company X is not easy.

III. The Company X desires to expand its business.

A. Only I is implicit

B. Only II is implicit

C. Only III is implicit

D. Only II and III are implicit

Q.26 Identify which of the following paintings are from Leonardo daVinci.

A. 

B. 

C. 

D. 

Q.27 From the following, which are the paintings by Rabindranath Tagore?

A. 

B. 

C. 

D. 

Q.28 Name the states of the folk art forms below in their respective order

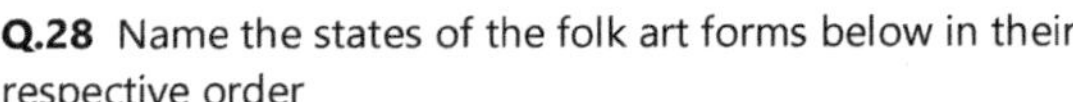

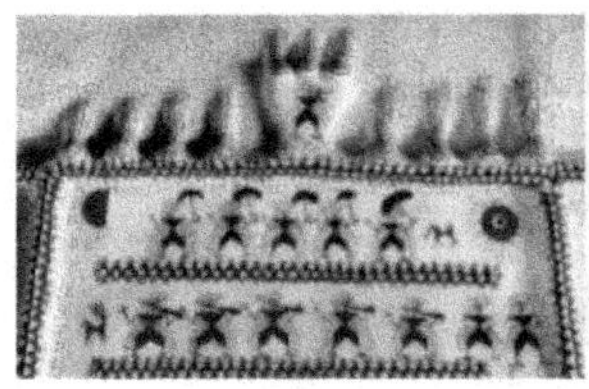 

A. Uttarakhand and Maharashtra
B. Bihar and Maharashtra
C. issa and Karnataka
D. Kerala and Karnataka

Q.29 In this question identify the new shape that could be constructed if the two example shapes were combined. No other change should be made to the two shapes other than combining them.

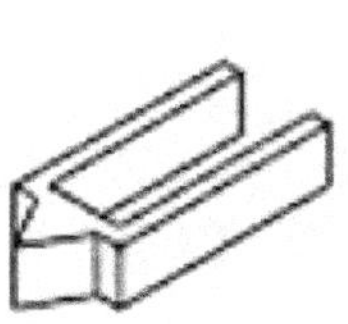 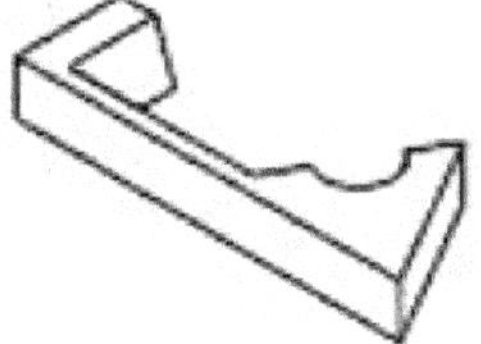

A. 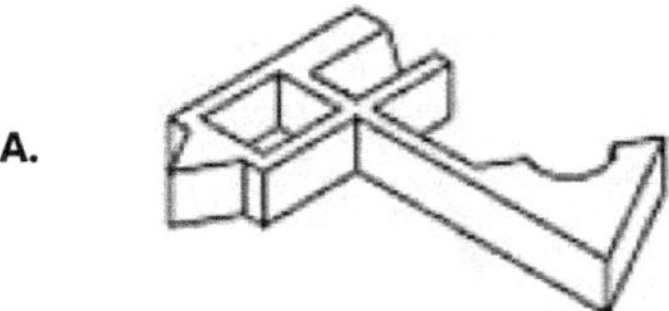

B. 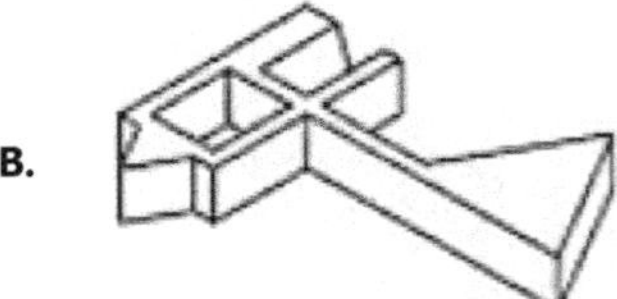

C. 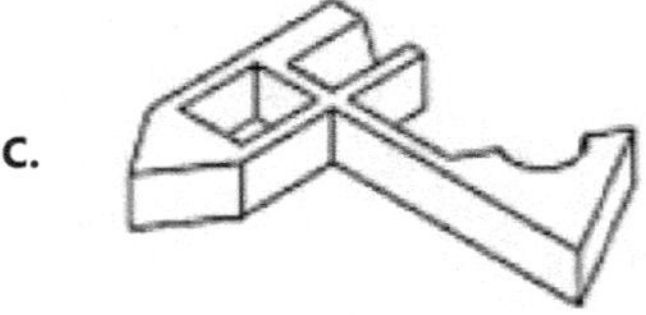

D. None of these

Q.30 Identify the 3D shape's net.

A. 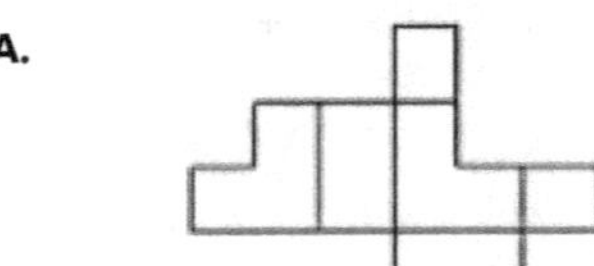

B. 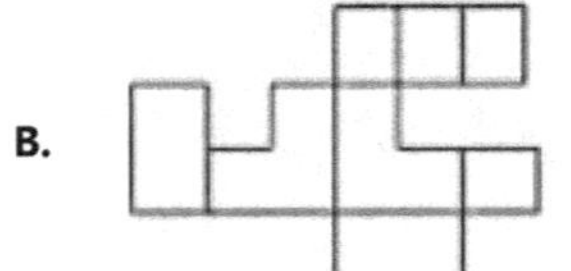

C. 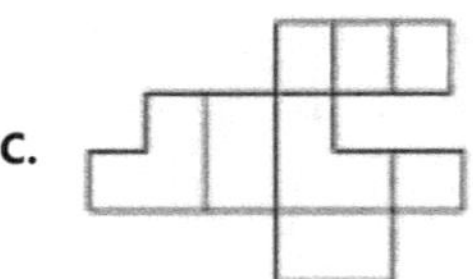

D. None of these

Q.31 Identify the answer shape, which has been rotated but is otherwise the same as the question shape.

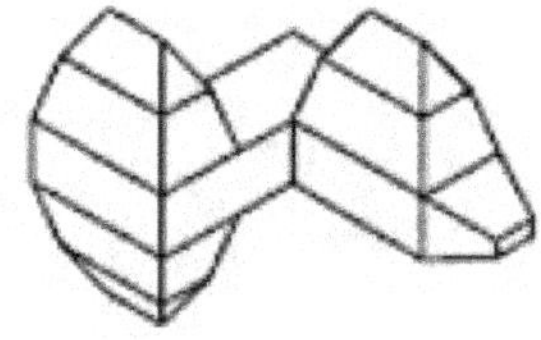

A. 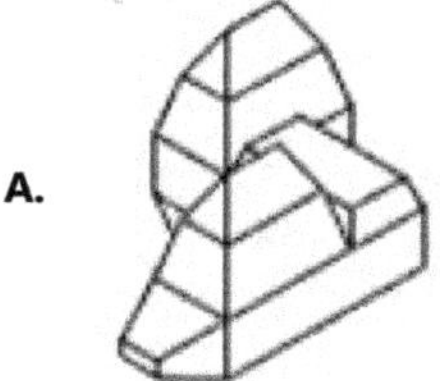

B. 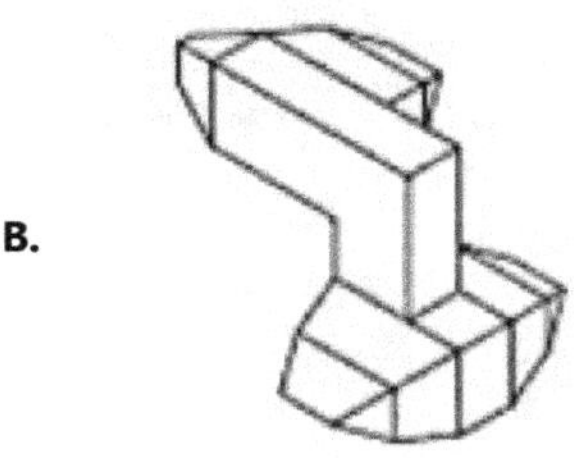

C. 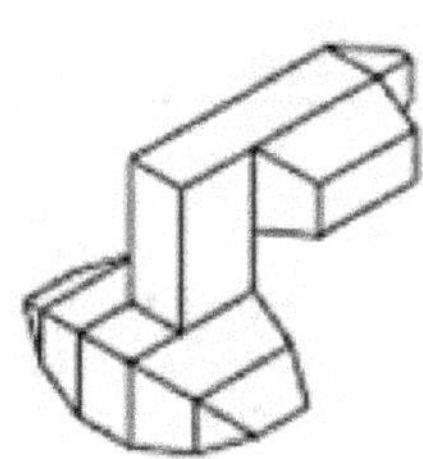

D. none of these

Q.32 Identify the mirror image of the question shape (reject any suggested answer in which any change other than reflection has occurred).

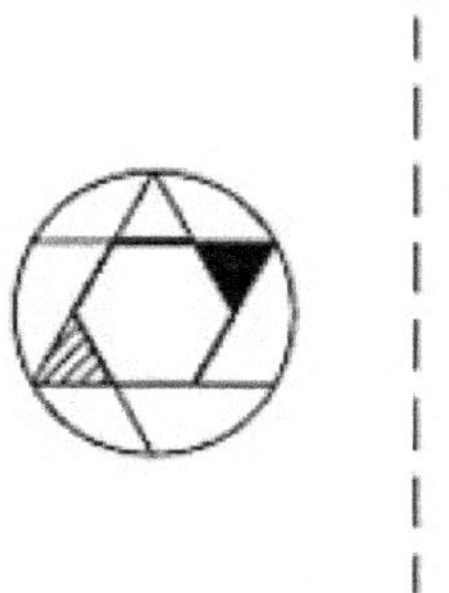

A. 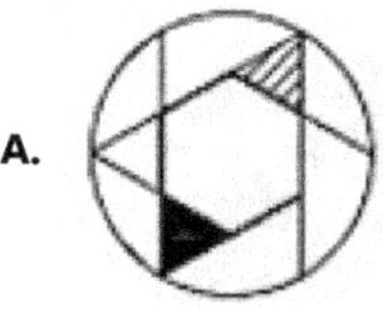

B. 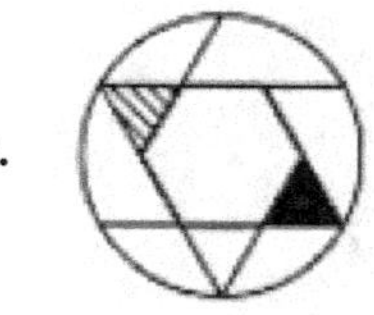

C. 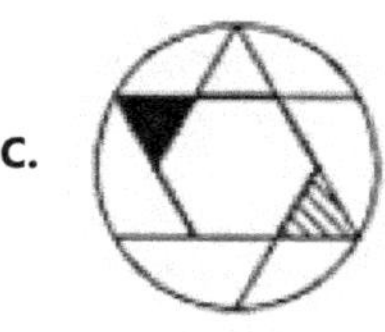

D. none of these

Q.33 Pick the TWO answer choices that will come together to make the figure shown. Pieces may be reflected and or rotated

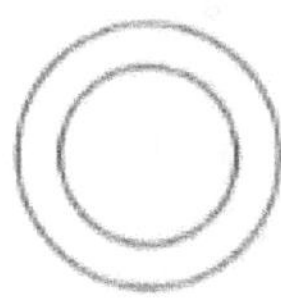

A. 

B. 

C. 

D. 

Q.34 A square is cut into 7 pieces as shown on the extreme left of the image. Identify which of the options can be made using all 7 pieces.

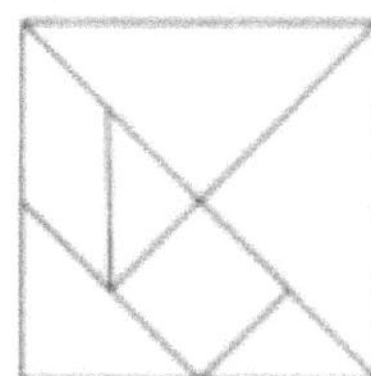

A. 

B. 

C. 

D. 

Q.35 Which of the following terms are related to textile design?

A. Tessellation
B. Absorbency
C. Gauge
D. Clustering

Q.36 Which of the given figures can be drawn without either lifting the pen or retracing any line?

A. 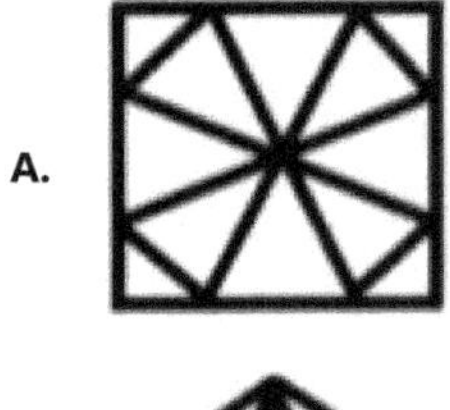

B. 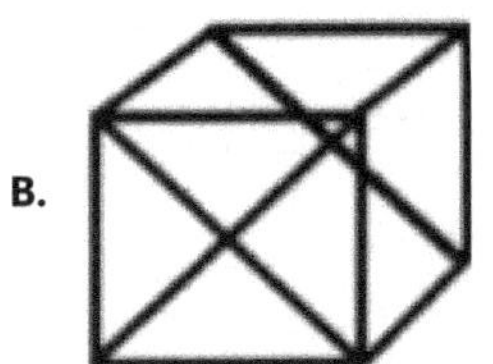

C. 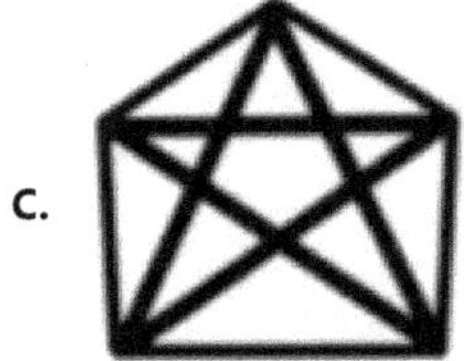

D. 

Multiple Choice Questions (MCQ)

Q.37

The above can was designed by Andy Warhole inspired by what art movement?

A. Renaissance
B. Cubism
C. De still
D. Pop art

Q.38 The above is an icon for what camera feature?

A. Shutter
B. ISO
C. Aperture
D. Focal Point

Q.39

 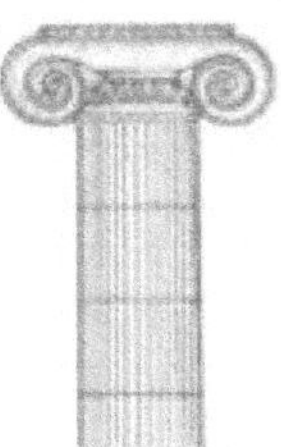 

Identify the correct sequence of the above type of columns

A. Ionic, Corinthian, Doric
B. Doric, Ionic, Corinthian
C. Corinthian, Doric, Ionic
D. Doric, Corinthian, Ionic

Q.40 Direction: In the question figures below, a piece of paper is folded and cut as shown below. Find out from the answer figures how it will appear when opened.

Question figure:

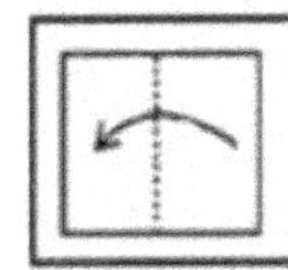  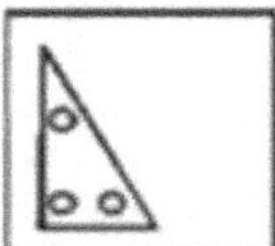

Answer Figure:

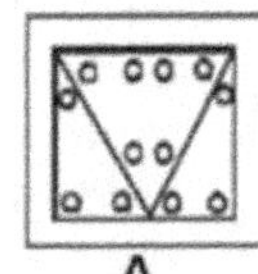 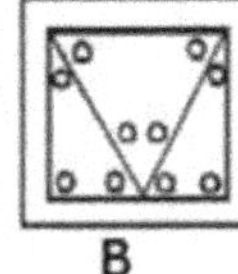 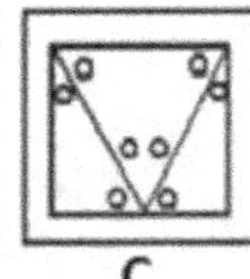 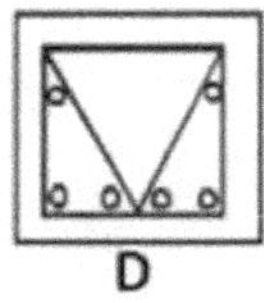

A B C D

A. A
B. B
C. C
D. D

Q.41 Shown are the symbols for different functions. Identify the correct description sequence from the given choices.

A. Level difference, General warning, Hot surface, Irritant
B. Irritant, Hot surface, Level difference, General warning
C. Level difference, hot surface, General warning, Irritant
D. Irritant, General warning, Level difference, hot surface

Q.42 Which of these shapes is the hardest to turn over?

A. 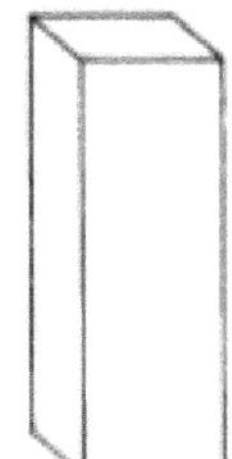

B.

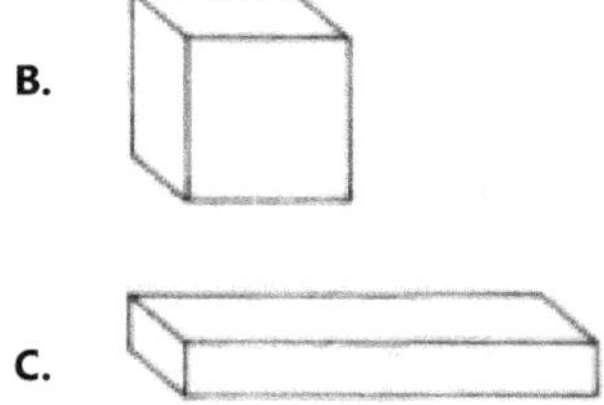

C.

D. None of these

Q.43 What is a Hue?

A. A mixture of two primary colors
B. One of the colors of the spectrum
C. A mixture of any color with white
D. A mixture of two of the colors of the spectrum

Q.44 The following diagrams show the combination of different colors of light.

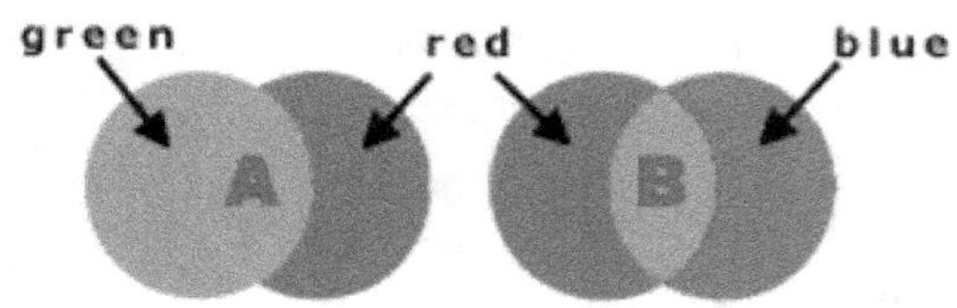

Considering the colors of light that are being combined, what colors should appear in positions A and B in the diagram?

A. A - yellow, B - magenta
B. A - cyan, B - magenta
C. A - magenta, B - yellow
D. A - magenta, B - cyan

Q.45 Which figure must replace the question mark?

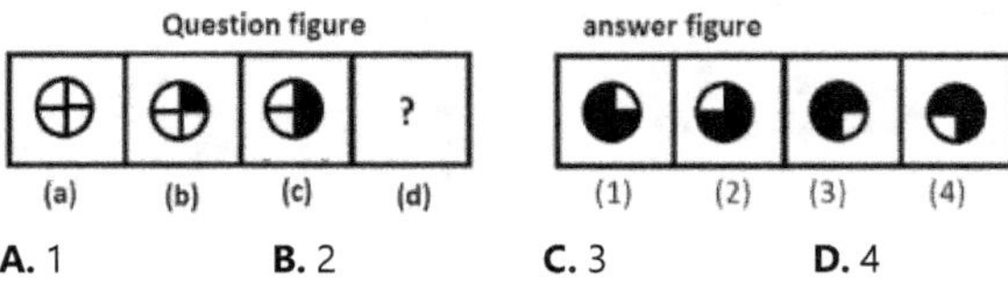

A. 1 **B.** 2 **C.** 3 **D.** 4

Q.46 Complete the series

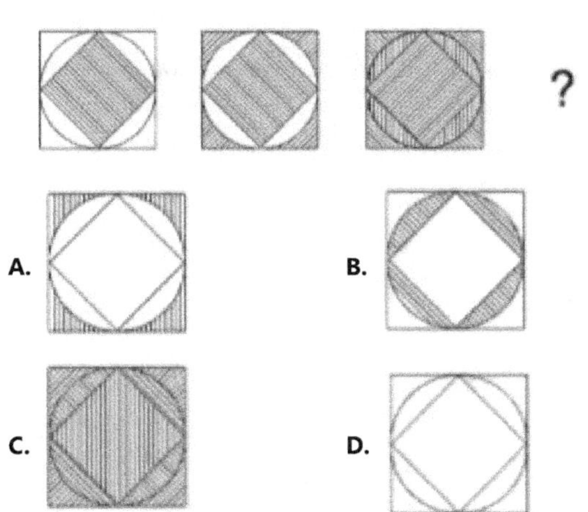

Q.47 Complete the series

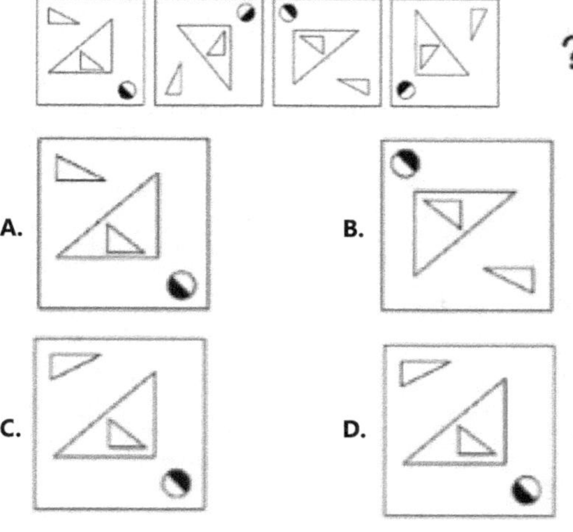

Q.48 Complete the series

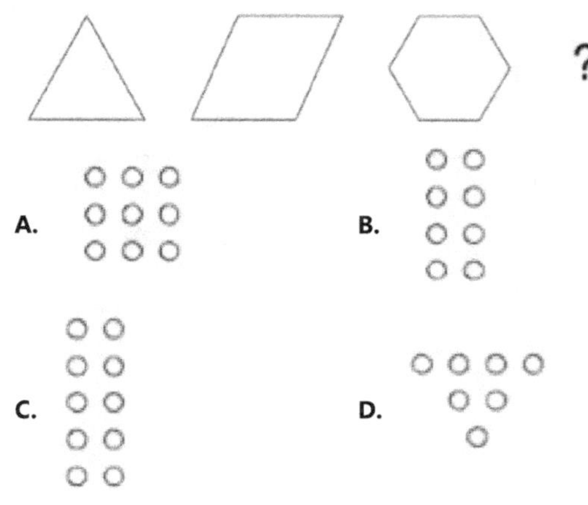

Q.49 Complete the series

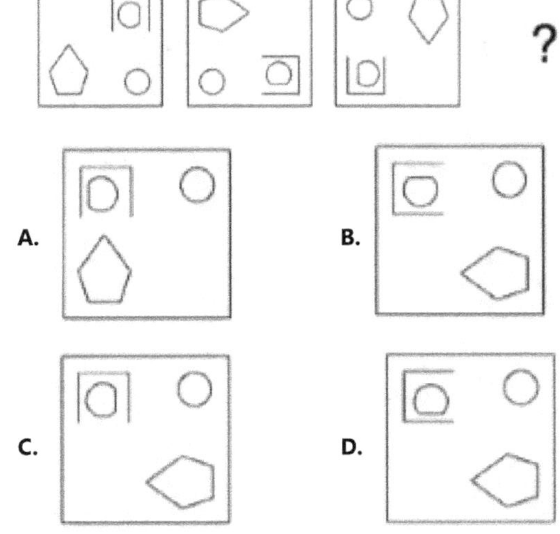

Q.50 There are eight rules which when applied to the sequence will transform it to one of the four options shown below. Identify the correct option.

AB Delete the last character

BC Replace the third character with the next in the alphabet
CD Insert the letter P between the third and fourth characters
DE Exchange the first and last characters
EF Replace the second character with the previous letter in the alphabet
FG Replace the fifth character with the next in the alphabet
GH Reverse the whole sequence of letters
HI Delete the third character
EQGTHST –DE + CD + BC + AB

A. TQHPTHS **B.** EQHPTHS
C. TQHPTHSE **D.** TQGPTHS

Q.51 Choose the Water image of the following figure along the AB axis.

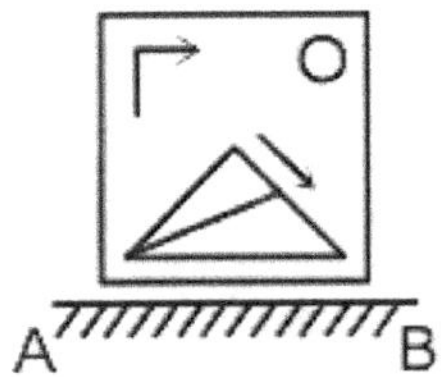

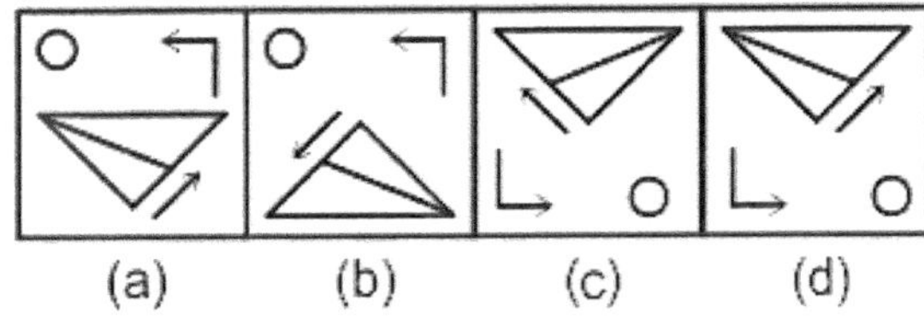

A. a **B.** b **C.** c **D.** d

Q.52 Choose the alternative which is closely resembles the water-image of the given combination.

FROG

A. FROG B. GORF
C. GORF D. FROG

Q.53 Find out from amongst the four alternatives as to how the pattern would appear when the transparent sheet is folded at the dotted line.

A. 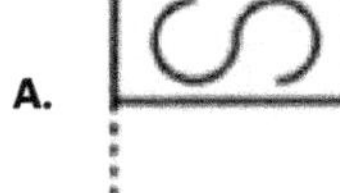 **B.** 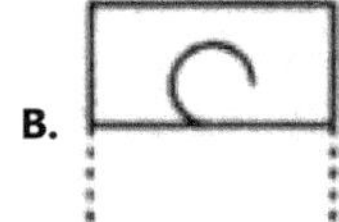

C. 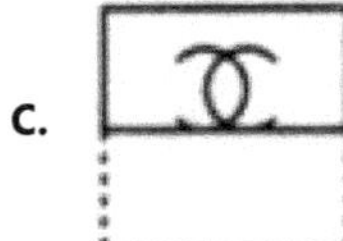 **D.** 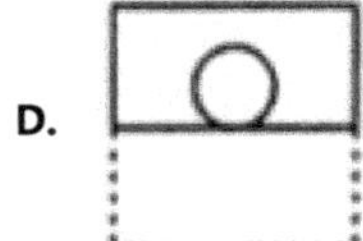

Q.54 Choose a figure which would most closely resemble the unfolded form of Figure (Z).

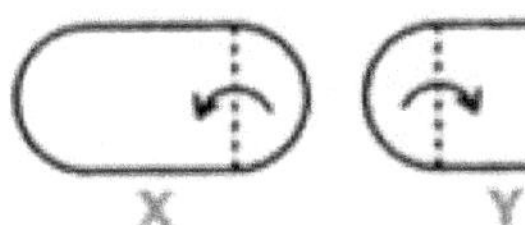

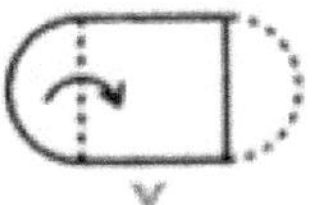

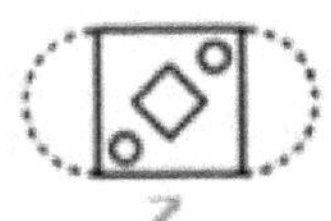

A. 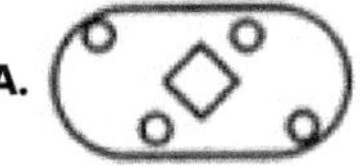 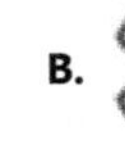 **B.** 

C.  **D.** 

Q.55 Choose the correct mirror image of the given figure (X) from amongst the four alternatives.

A. 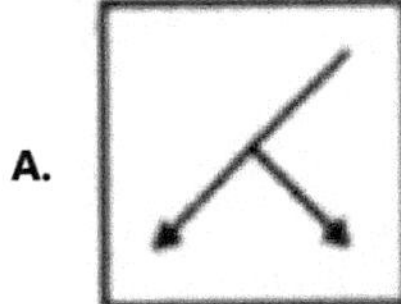 **B.** 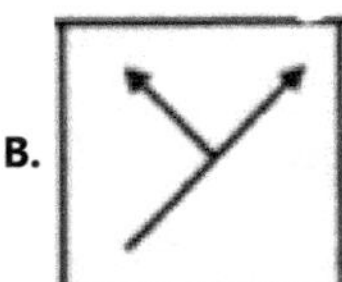

C. 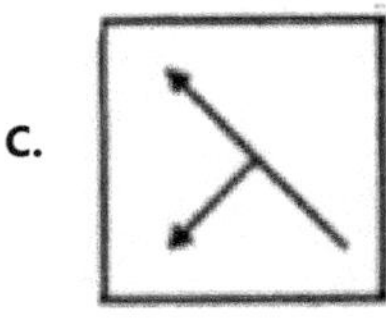 **D.** 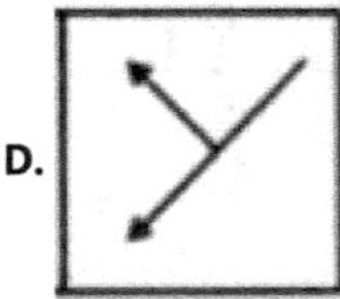

Q.56 What will be the most probable pose at position 5 to complete the sequence below?

    ?

A. 

B. 

C. 

D. 

Q.57 Identify the function of the tool below.

A. Riveting
B. Push Drilling
C. Scribing
D. Voltage testing

Q.58 Which of the following pairs of Indian embroidery is correctly matched with their state?

1. Kashida : Karnataka
2. Phulkari: Punjab
3. Kasuti : West Bengal

Select the correct answer using the codes given below.

A. 1 and 2 only
B. 2 and 3 only
C. 2 only
D. None

Q.59 Many new elements were added in Indian architecture during the Muslims rule. These include

1. Use of shapes instead of natural forms.
2. Use of calligraphy as inscriptional art.
3. Use of trabeated roof.

Select the correct answer using the codes given below.

A. 1 and 2 only
B. 1 and 3 only
C. 2 only
D. 1, 2 and 3

Q.60 In questions below, each passage consists of six sentences. The first and sixth sentences are given in the beginning. The middle four sentences in each have been removed and jumbled up. These are labeled as P, Q, R and S. Find out the proper order for the four sentences.

S1: The heart is pump of life.

P: They have even succeeded in heart transplants.

Q: Nowadays surgeons are able to stop a patients heart and carry out complicated operations.

R: A few years ago it was impossible to operate on a patient whose heart was not working properly.

S: If heart stops we die in about five minutes.

S6: All this was made possible by the invention of heart-lung machine.

The Proper sequence should be:

A. SRQP
B. SPRQ
C. SQPR
D. SRPQ

Q.61 Proverb /idiom is given below together with their meanings. Choose the correct meaning of proverb/idiom,

To beg the question

A. To refer to
B. To take for granted
C. To raise objections
D. To be discussed

Q.62 In the questions below the sentences have been given in Direct/Indirect speech. From the given alternatives, choose the one which best expresses the given sentence in Indirect/Direct speech.

He said to his father, "Please increase my pocket-money."

A. He told his father, "Please increase the pocket-money"
B. He pleaded his father to please increase my pocket money.
C. He requested his father to increase his pocket money.
D. He asked his father to increase his pocket money.

Q.63 Identify the function of the tool below.

A. Soft hammering.
B. Inscribing on surfaces
C. Nailing
D. Rust removal

Q.64 Identify the texture.

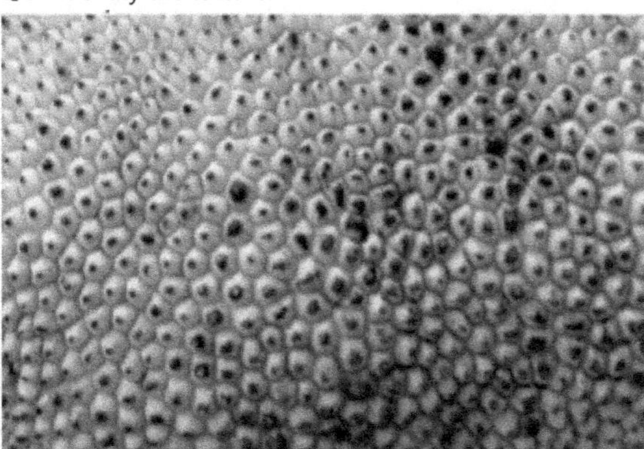

A. Jackfruit
B. Strawberry
C. Pineapple
D. Custard apple

Q.65 Why is "AMBULANCE" spelled backwards on the front of this ambulance?

A. So that the ambulance driver can see it clearly

B. So it can be read properly in a car rear-view mirror

C. So that it can be read by oncoming vehicles

D. So it can be read from a plane or helicopter.

Q.66 Which common bird makes tracks like this?

A. Sparrow **B.** Robin

C. Blackbird **D.** Red Kite

Q.67 Pran Kumar sharma is known for creator of which cartoon character

A. Shrimatiji **B.** ChachaChaudhary

C. Billoo **D.** All of the above

Q.68

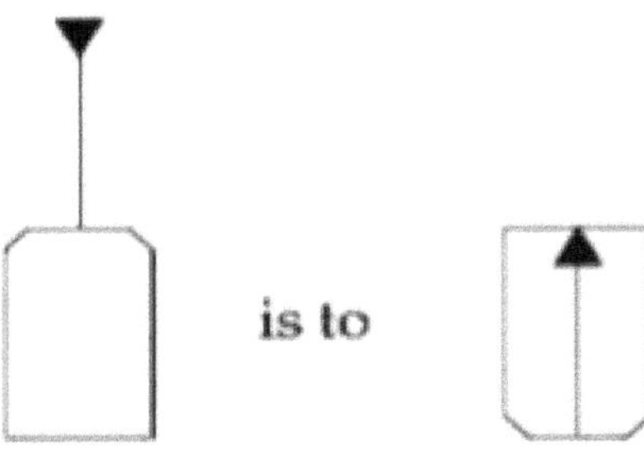

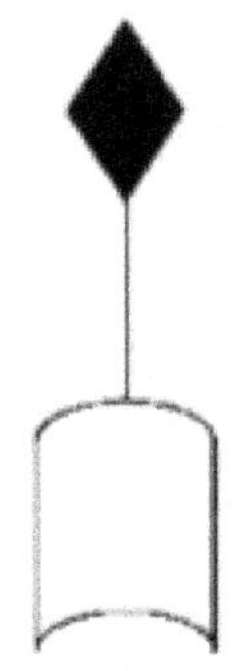

is to

A. 

B. 

C.  

D. 

// Smart Answer Sheet //

Correct — Indicates percentage of students who answered questions correctly.

Skipped — Indicates percentage of students who skipped questions.

Q.	Ans.	Correct	Skipped
1	25	16.87 %	5.42 %
2	#	46.39 %	14.45 %
3	12	66.87 %	14.46 %
4	38	59.04 %	15.66 %
5	936	33.73 %	21.69 %
6	17	41.57 %	19.88 %
7	100	59.04 %	16.86 %
8	24	21.69 %	19.27 %
9	13	22.29 %	18.67 %
10	8	58.43 %	15.06 %
11	21	39.16 %	16.26 %
12	#	48.19 %	16.87 %
13	13	44.58 %	19.88 %
14	13	47.59 %	15.66 %
15	5	42.17 %	16.26 %
16	32	57.83 %	17.47 %
17	4	10.84 %	22.89 %
18	106	5.42 %	20.48 %
19	B, A, D, C	62.05 %	22.29 %
20	B, A, D	19.88 %	27.71 %
21	B, A, C	30.72 %	27.71 %
22	B	65.66 %	19.28 %
23	B, A, D	62.05 %	22.29 %
24	C	59.64 %	18.67 %
25	D	19.28 %	20.48 %
26	B, A, D, C	74.7 %	19.88 %
27	B, A, C	43.98 %	22.89 %
28	A	37.95 %	19.88 %
29	A	70.48 %	20.48 %
30	C	59.04 %	20.48 %
31	B	35.54 %	22.89 %
32	C	74.1 %	19.88 %
33	A, D	54.22 %	21.08 %
34	B, A	16.87 %	28.31 %
35	B, A, C	24.7 %	25.9 %
36	A, D, C	64.46 %	21.08 %
37	D	43.37 %	18.08 %
38	C	47.59 %	16.87 %
39	B	40.96 %	24.1 %
40	A	28.92 %	25.3 %
41	A	79.52 %	17.47 %
42	C	60.84 %	19.88 %
43	B	47.59 %	18.07 %
44	A	45.78 %	18.08 %
45	B	27.11 %	25.3 %
46	D	39.76 %	20.48 %
47	A	64.46 %	18.67 %
48	A	35.54 %	21.09 %
49	B	66.87 %	16.86 %
50	A	66.27 %	21.68 %
51	D	56.02 %	22.29 %
52	A	75.3 %	18.07 %
53	D	72.89 %	17.47 %
54	C	68.67 %	19.28 %
55	C	75.9 %	18.68 %
56	A	69.28 %	18.07 %
57	B	39.16 %	21.68 %
58	C	38.55 %	20.49 %
59	A	30.12 %	22.29 %
60	A	62.65 %	19.28 %
61	B	16.27 %	19.87 %
62	C	66.27 %	19.27 %
63	B	69.88 %	20.48 %
64	A	75.9 %	18.08 %
65	B	71.08 %	18.08 %
66	A	50.0 %	22.29 %
67	D	43.37 %	21.09 %
68	A	63.25 %	19.28 %

#

Q.	Answer
2	North
12	N

Performance Analysis	
Avg. Score (%)	46.25%
Toppers Score (%)	108.75%
Your Score	

//Hints and Solutions//

1.

1. •
2. ●
3. ○
4. **o**
5. ⊙
6. ◉
7. ■
8. □
9. ◘
10. ⊡
11. ▣
12. ▩
13. ◇
14. ◈
15. ◈
16. ⬨
17. ◆
18. ⬟
19. ●
20. ●
21. +
22. ♠
23. ❖
24. ⁑
25. ©

2.

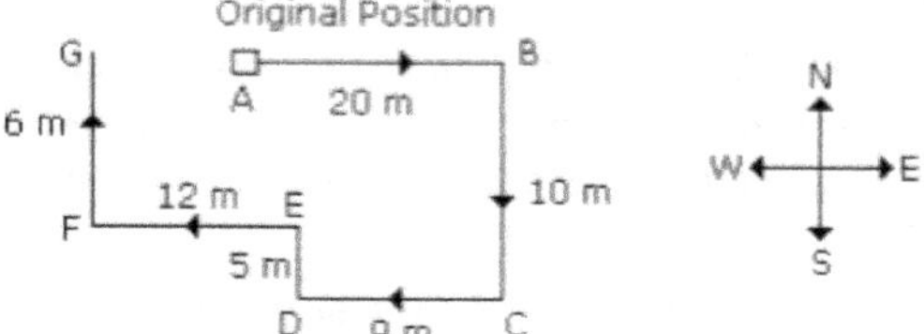

3. There are 12 lines.

4. FISH will have 38 surfaces.

5. Given:

Length of rectangle $= 50\ m$

Breadth of rectangle $= 40\ m$

Width of path $= 6\ m$

We know that,

Area of rectangle $=$ Length $\times$ breadth

Now,

Length of outer rectangle $= 50\ m$

Breadth of outer rectangle $= 40\ m$

Area of outer rectangle $= 50 \times 40 = 2000\ m^2$

Length of inner rectangle $= 50 - 6 - 6 = 38\ m$

Breadth of inner rectangle $= 40 - 6 - 6 = 28\ m$

Area of inner rectangle $= 38 \times 28 = 1064\ m^2$

Area of path $=$ Area of outer rectangle $-$ Area of inner rectangle

$= 2000 - 1064$

$= 936\ m^2$

Hence, the correct answer is $936\ m^2$.

6. Harry is now 16 and Sally is 9. Two years ago Harry was 14 and Sally 7, and in one year's time Harry will be 17 and Sally 10.

7. There are 100 cubes in given image.

8. The figure can be labelled as:

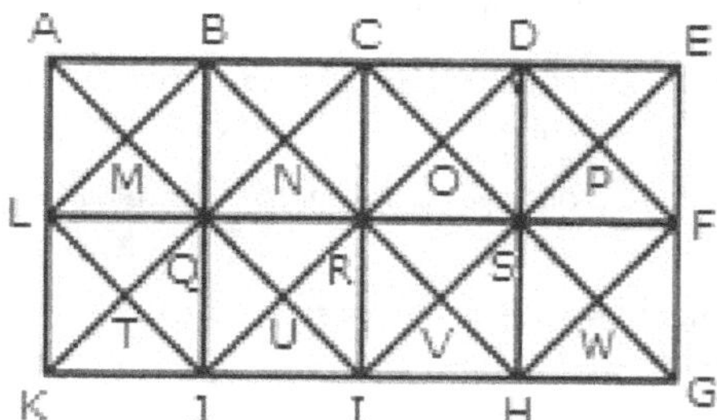

The squares composed of two components each are BNQM, CORN, DPSO, MQTL, NRUQ, OSVR, PFWS, QUJT, RVIU and SWHV i.e. 10 in number.

The squares composed of four components each are ABQL, BCRQ, CDSR, DEFS, LQJK, QRIJ, RSHI and SFGH i.e. 8 in number.

The squares composed of eight components each are BRJL, CSIQ and DFHR i.e. 3 in number.

The squares composed of sixteen components each are ACIK, BDHJ and CEGI i.e. 3 in number.

Thus, there are 10 + 8 + 3 + 3 = 24 squares in the figure.

Hence, the correct answer is 24.

9. 13 different types of fruits

10. The figure may be labeled as shown.

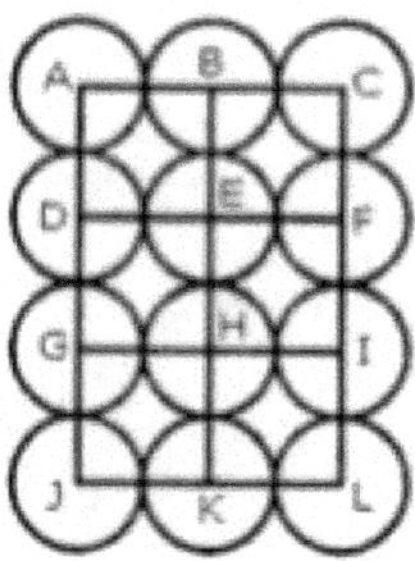

We shall join the centres of all the circles by horizontal and vertical lines and then label the resulting figure as shown. The simplest squares are ABED, BCFE, DEHG, EFIH, GHKJ and HILK i.e. 6 in number. The squares composed of four simple squares are ACIG and DFLJ i.e. 2 in number. Thus, 6 + 2 = 8 squares will be formed

11. The figure may be labelled as shown.

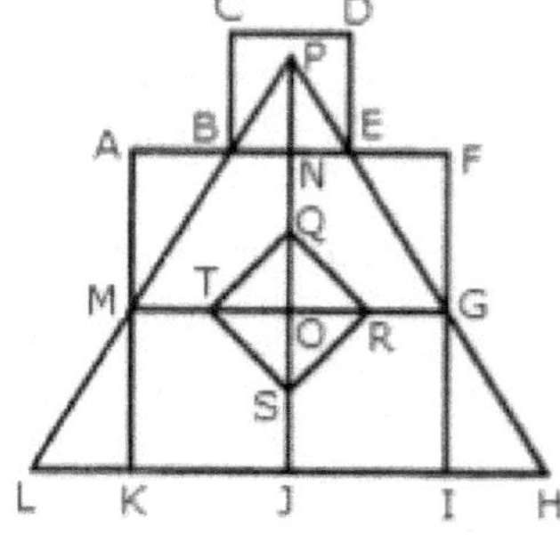

The simplest triangles are BPN, PNE, ABM, EFG, MLK, GHI, QRO, RSO, STO and QTO i.e. 10 in number.

The triangles composed of two components each are BPE, TQR, QRS, RST and STQ i.e. 5 in number.

The triangles composed of three components each are MPO and GPO i.e. 2 in number.

The triangles composed of six components each are LPJ, HPJ and MPG i.e. 3 in number.

There is only one triangle LPH composed of twelve components.

Total number of triangles in the figure = 10 + 5 - 2 + 3 + l = 21.

12. Four letter left of Z: V

Two letters above V: L

Two letters right of L: N

Hence N is correct.

13. 13: opposite numbers total 15

14. There are total 13 surfaces of given figure.

15. There are 5 different sized circles in the above image.

16. After deleting all the repeating numbers, the only numbers left are: 3 2

17. A = 1 head, 2 eyes, 2 arms

B = 1 head, 2 eyes, 4 arms

C = 1 head, 3 eyes, 2 arms

D = 1 head, 3 eyes, 4 arms

E = 2 heads, 2 eyes, 2 arms

F = 2 heads, 2 eyes, 4 arms

G = 2 heads, 3 eyes, 2 arms

H = 2 heads, 3 eyes, 4 arms

100 = A+B+C+D+E+F+G+H

73 = E+F+G+H

28 = C+D+G+H

21 = B+D+F+H

12 = G+H

9 = D+H

8 = F+H

3 = H

A = ?

D = 9-3 = 6

F = 8-3 = 5

G = 12-3 = 9

C = 28-6-9-3 = 10

B = 21-6-5-3 = 7

E = 73-5-9-3 = 56

A = 100-7-10-6-56-5-9-3 = 4

So the requested number of aliens is four.

18. $106A/revolution$

B 2 % revolutions.

19. The Wright brothers—Orville (August 19, 1871 – January 30, 1948) and Wilbur (April 16, 1867 – May 30, 1912)—were two American aviation pioneers generally credited with inventing, building, and flying the world's the first successful motor-operated airplane.

Karl Heinrich Marx (5 May 1818 – 14 March 1883) was a German philosopher, economist, historian, sociologist, political theorist, journalist and socialist revolutionary. He was the foremost Socialist intellectual.

Henry Ford (July 30, 1863 – April 7, 1947) was an American industrialist and business magnate, founder of the Ford Motor Company, and chief developer of the assembly line technique of mass production. By creating the first automobile that middle-class Americans could afford, he converted the automobile from an expensive curiosity into an accessible conveyance that profoundly impacted the landscape of the 20th century.

Malala Yousafzai often referred to mononymously as Malala, is a Pakistani activist for female education and the youngest Nobel Prize laureate. She is known for human rights advocacy, especially the education of women and children in her native Swat Valley in Khyber Pakhtunkhwa, northwest Pakistan, where the local Pakistani Taliban had at times banned girls from attending school.

Hence, all of the above statements are correct.

20. option A, B and D are correct.

21. Ruskin Bond - The Blue Umbrella, A Flight of Pigeons

Suketu Mehta - Bombay Lost and Found, Maximum City

Kiran Nagarka - Cuckold, God's little soldier

22. From the first two statements, we know that of the three classes, Class A has the highest enrollment, so the third statement must be false.

23. C is false.

The author says ' most adult dogs will wait on you to play' This is not meant to say that adult dogs don not like to play. The author says this simply to contrast adult dogs with puppies.

24. Clearly, the rule has been devised for the safety of two-wheeler riders, as majority of two wheeler accidents result in direct fall of the rider, leading to head injury and finally death. And the objective of a rule cannot be fulfilled until it is followed by all and this requires strict enforcement. Thus, both I and IV hold strong, while III does not. Besides, it is the basic duty of the Government to look after the safety of the citizens and it ought not leave it to the discretion of the individuals. So, argument II does not hold strong.

25. The statement mentions that there are only two companies in this line of business which are ISO 9002 certified. But nothing about the total number of companies in this line can be deduced. So, I is not implicit. Also, had it been easy to get ISO 9002 certification, there would have been a large number of ISO 9002 companies. So, II is implicit. Also, the company must have reached up to such high international standards to make its mark in its line of business. So, III is also implicit.

26. All the above paintings are from Leonardo DaVinci.

27. The paintings shown in option A, B and C are from Rabindranath Tagore.

28. Uttarakhand and Maharashtra.

Hence option A is correct.

29. In b) the semicircular shape is missing, and in c) the small triangular shape has been enlarged.

30. a) has not enough surfaces, and in b) the rectangle that gives the depth to the form is in a wrong position.

31. In a) a truncated 'roof' shape has been added to the central part of the figure, and in c) a small 'roof' shape has been removed.

32. a) has been mirrored but also rotated, and b) is the same as c) but the shadings have been inverted.

33. $a + d$

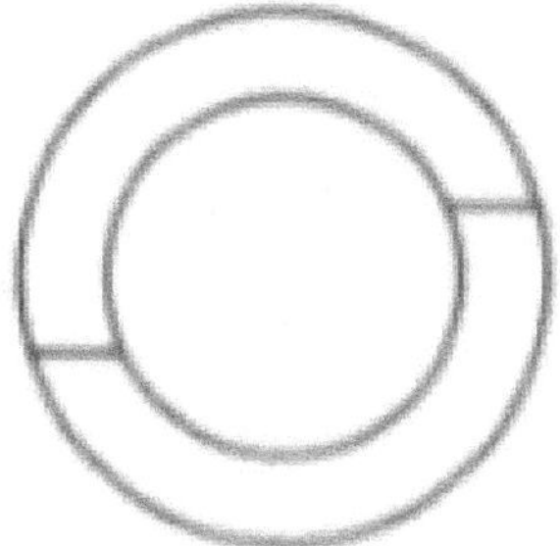

34. option A and B are correct.

35. option A, B and C are correct.

36. option A, C and D are correct.

37. Pop art

Hence option D is correct.

38. Aperture

Hence option C is correct.

39. Doric, Ionic, Corinthian

Hence option B is correct.

40. After unfolding, we will get the following image:

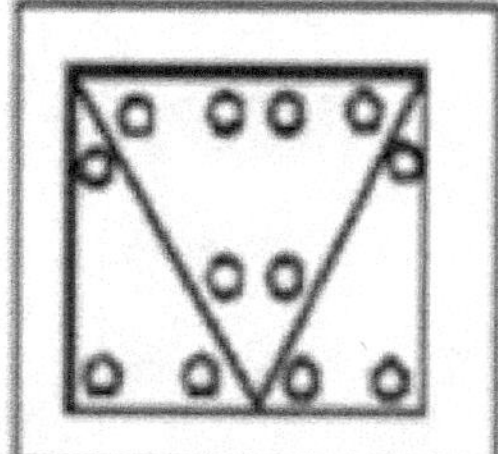

Hence, the correct option is (A).

41. Level difference, General warning, Hot surface, Irritant

Hence option A is correct.

42. It is hard to turn over the block shown in option C.

43. Hue is one of the colors of the spectrum.

44. A - yellow, B - magenta

45. In each step, one-quarter of the figure is shaded in the clockwise direction.

Hence, the correct option is (B).

46. The direction of the shading is irrelevant to the question. The series starts with an unshaded square overlaid by an unshaded circle and shaded square; then there is a shaded square overlaid by an unshaded circle and shaded square, and then a shaded square, circle and square. The only combination not included in the series is all three shapes unshaded, which is found in suggested answer D.

47. The shape is rotating anticlockwise 90 degrees each step in the series.

48. The number of sides to the shapes follows the sequence 3 + 1 = 4 + 2 = 6. The next step in the sequence is 6 + 3 = 9, which is represented as 9 circles in suggested answer A.

49. The shape is rotated 90 degrees clockwise each step in the series.

50. First exchange the E with the last letter T, then insert a P between the G and the second T, next change the G into an H and finally delete the E.

51. The image will be flipped vertically.

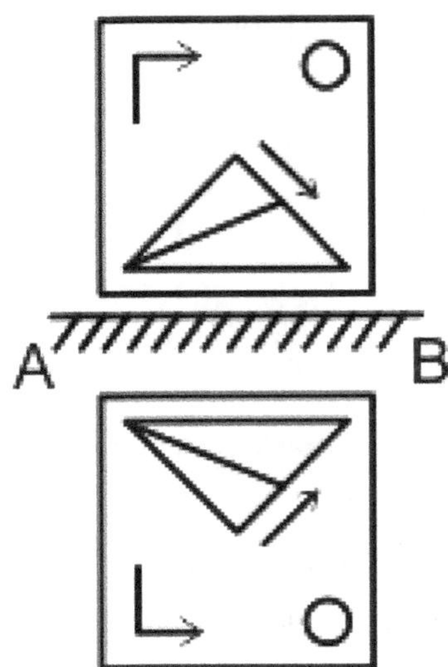

Hence, the correct option is (D).

52. option A is the water image of FROG.

53. option D is correct.

54. the unfolded form of Z will be option C.

55. The mirror image of X will be option C.

56. option A will be correct for position 5.

57. Push Drilling

Hence option B is correct.

58. 2 only. Kashida is of Jammu Kashmir, while Kasuti is of Karnataka. Phulkari is of Punjab.

59. 1 and 2 only. Trabeated roof was used before the Muslims came. The Muslims added the feature of arcuate roof as reflected in the dome and double dome in their buildings. Indian architecture took new shape with the advent of Islamic rule in India towards the end of the twelfth century AD. Islam introduced new elements into the Indian architecture including: use of shapes (instead of natural forms); inscriptional art using decorative lettering or calligraphy; inlay decoration and use of colored marble, painted plaster and brightly colored glazed tiles.

60. SRQP

Hence option A is correct.

61. To beg the question: To take for granted

62. He requested his father to increase his pocket money.

Hence option C is correct.

63. Inscribing on surfaces

Hence option B is correct.

64. Jackfruit

Hence option A is correct.

65. So it can be read properly in a car rear-view mirror

66. Sparrow

Hence option A is correct.

67. All of the above

Hence option D is correct.

68. the top and bottom figures fold down and up onto the line respectively

Mock Test 08

Numerical Answer Type (NAT)

Q.1 The given image has sixty -four grids with patterns inside, arranged in an eight -by-eight matrix. How many different types of patterns are there in the image?

Q.2 Sachin walks 20 km towards North. He turns left and walks 40 km. He again turns left and walks 20 km. Finally he moves 20 km after turning to the left. How far is he from his starting position

Q.3 How many different sized circles appear below?

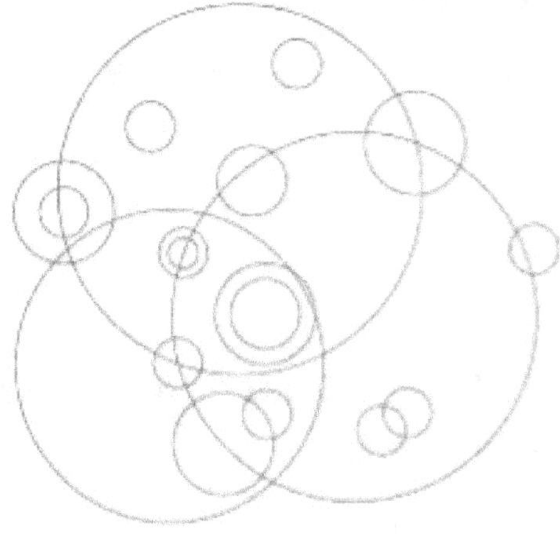

Q.4 Find the value of the missing number:

13	54	?
7	45	32
27	144	68

Q.5 A cube is cut in two equal parts along a plane parallel to one of its faces. One piece is then colored red on the two larger faces and green on the remaining, while the other is colored green on two smaller adjacent faces and red on the remaining. Each is then cut into 32 cubes of same size and mixed up. What is the number of cubes with at least one green face each?

Q.6 A market trader took delivery of a box of eggs and was disgruntled to find that 56 were cracked, which was eight per cent of the total quantity of eggs in the box. How many eggs were in the box?

Q.7 Count the number of cubes in the given figure.

Q.8 Select the option figure that will come next in the following figure series.

$EB, HC, KD, NE, QF, ?$

Q.9 Count the number of squares in the given figure.

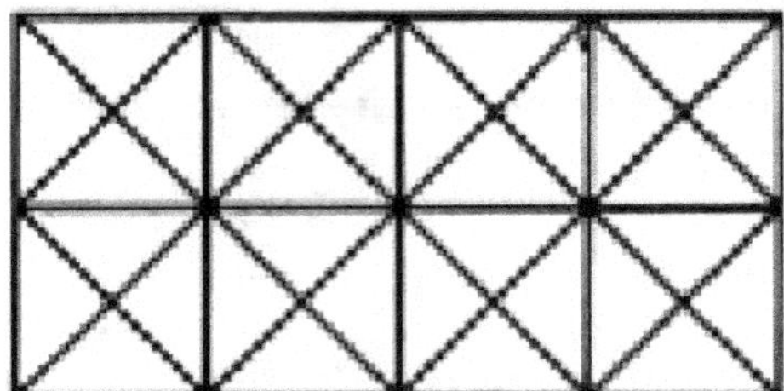

Q.10 The average of three numbers is 48. The average of two of these numbers is 56. What is the third number?

Q.11 What letter is directly opposite the letter that is two letters away clockwise from the letter that is directly opposite the letter that is three letters away anticlockwise from the letter E?

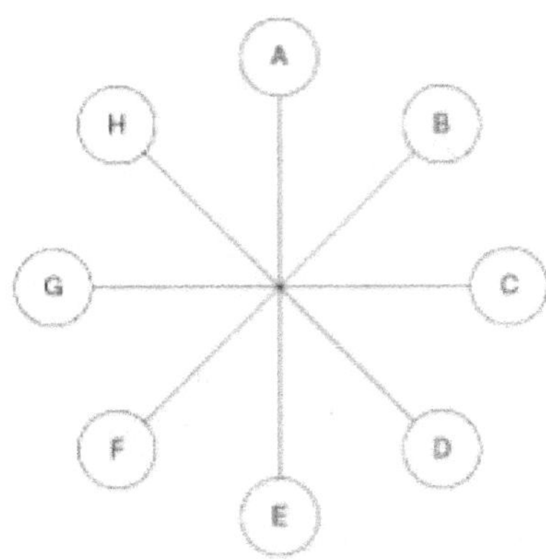

Q.12 A man walks $1\ km$ to the East and then he turns to the South and walks $5\ km$. Again he turns to East and walks $2\ km$. After this, he turns to North and walks $9\ km$. Now, how far (in km) is he from his starting point?

Q.13 Multiply the highest even number in the grid by the lowest odd number.

171	23	18
17	19	29
78	56	27
28	71	82

Q.14 AB C D E F G H What letter is two letters to the right of the letter immediately to the left of the letter four letters to the right of the letter two letters to the left of the letter E?

Q.15 Find out the total number of surfaces of the object, given below in the problem figure. Problem figure

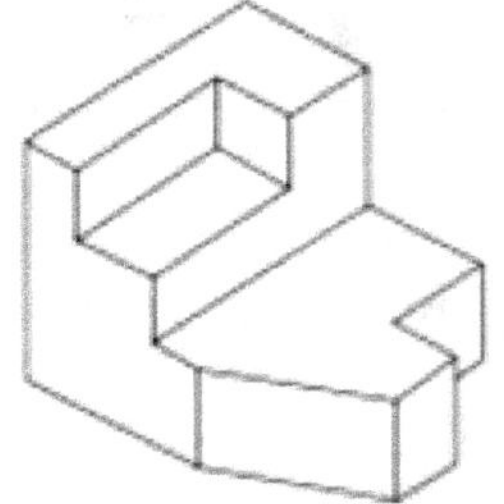

Q.16 Enumerate the number of spelling mistakes in the following paragraph: Dowry consist of thing given by parent to there daughters at the time of there marriage. Onesthese was done to start life well. But the greedy parents of bridegroms demand more money and material. Some girls have to loose therelifes for bringing fewer dowries. Burning brides is daily news these days. Both the, Goverment and the public should discourage the dowry seekers.

Q.17 How many different types of symbols appear in the figure given below?

Q.18 Which number will replace the question mark?

9	17	16
5	4	8
5	4	?
9	17	8

Multiple Select Questions (MSQ)

Q.19 From the options at bottom, select the Indian author/s writing in English whose works are represented below:

i. The Ministry of Utmost Happiness
ii. The God of Small things
iii. Ignited Minds
iv. Wings of Fire,
v. Guiding souls vi. No time to pause-book

A. Arundhati Roy
B. Dr. A.P. J Abdul Kalam
C. Pavithra Ramesh

D. PramodKapoor

Q.20 Which of the following statements is/are true?

A. Friedrich Nietzsche was a famous German philosopher and philologist known for his critical texts on religion, morality, contemporary culture, philosophy and science, widely known for his ideas like death of God, perspectivism and the Übermensch.

B. Carl Gustav Jung was a famous psychiatrist and psychotherapist who founded the school of analytical psychology. He made immense contributions like analytical psychology, personality profiling, collective unconscious, and the complex.

C. Guy de Chauliac was a popular surgeon of the modern medicine.

D. Aleksandr Prokhorov was one of the frontrunners of Russian physics who earned a Nobel Prize in 1964 for developing the maser-laser principle.

Q.21 Select the statements below that are TRUE.

A. Naturalists divide the class Mammalia into a number of orders. At the head of these is the order Primates, which includes the lemurs, the monkeys, apes and man. Their classification was based originally upon anatomical resemblances and took complete account of any mental qualities.

B. By the middle Cainozoic period there have appeared various apes with many quasi–human attributes of the jaws and leg bones, but it is only as we approach these Glacial Ages that we find traces of creatures that we can speak of as "almost human."

C. At Trinil in Java, in accumulations of this age, a piece of a skull and various teeth and bones have been found of a sort of ape man, with a brain case bigger than that of any living apes, which seems to have walked erect. This creature is called Pithecanthropus erectus, the walking ape man.

D. It is not until we come to sands that are almost a quarter of a million years old that we find any other particle of a sub–human being. They are no longer clumsy Eoliths; they are now shapely instruments made with considerable skill. And they are much bigger than the similar implements afterwards made by true man.

Q.22 Coral reefs are among the most diverse and pro- ductive ecosystems on Earth. Consisting of both living and non-living components, this type of ecosystem is found in the warm, clear, shallow waters of tropical oceans worldwide. The func- tionality of the reefs ranges from providing food and shelter to fish and other forms of marine life to protecting the shore from the ill effects of ero- sion and putrefaction. In fact, reefs actually cre- ate land in tropical areas by formulating islands and contributing mass to continental shorelines.Although coral looks like a plant, it is mainly comprised of the limestone skeleton of a tiny ani- mal called a coral polyp. While corals are the main components of reef structure, they are not the only living participants. Coralline algae cement the myriad corals, and other miniature organisms such as tubeworms and mollusks con- tribute skeletons to this dense and diverse struc- ture. Together, these living creatures construct many different types of tropical reefs.

According to the passage, which of the following statements is true?

A. Coral reefs are beneficial for fish.

B. Coral reefs are good for shorelines in tropical areas.

C. Coral reefs are composed exclusively of coral.

D. Coral reefs contain living and non-living components.

Q.23 Question given below consists of a statement, followed by three arguments numbered I , II and III. You have to decide which of the arguments is a 'strong' argument. Statement: Should coal engines be replaced by electric engines in trains? Arguments:

I. Yes. Coal engines cause a lot of pollution.

II. Yes. Electric engines are good on performance, easy to operate and low on maintenance.

III. No. India does not produce enough electricity to fulfil its domestic needs also.

A. All are strong

B. Only I and II are strong

C. Only II and III are strong

D. Only I is strong

Q.24 For two months, I have been trying to decide who makes the best ice cream. I have narrowed it down to my four favorite manufacturers: Randolph Farms, Goodies, Disco, and Twinkle. Let's start with Randolph Farms. Randolph Farms makes very good ice cream. They have lots of different flavors, but this doesn't really matter to me. That's because I always get coffee flavor. They make the best coffee ice cream in the world. I've never had hot coffee (the drink) but people tell me that Randolph Farms coffee ice cream tastes just like the real thing. Also, Randolph Farms uses all natural ingredients to make their ice cream. This is a good idea, I think. Second, we have Goodies. Goodies makes ice cream. Like Randolph Farms, Goodies uses all natural ingredients. They only make three different —strawberry, vanilla, and chocolate— but they make them very well. The strawberry is amazing. Every bite of it reminds me of the strawberries that I used to pick behind my old house. The vanilla is wonderful. It is very smooth and has a refreshing, creamy taste. The chocolate is outstanding. It is made with real cocoa beans from Bolivia. I didn't know where Bolivia is so I decided to look for it on a map. After hunting awhile, I discovered that it is in South America! That's a long way to go to get cocoa, so it must be good. I would say that the only drawback to Goodies ice cream is that they only make three different flavors. Third, we have Disco. Disco ice cream is okay. They don't have many good flavors. Actually, the only Disco flavor I like is Bubblegum. It is vanilla ice cream with little chunks of bubblegum in it. After you eat the ice cream, you can blow bubbles with the gum. That's pretty fun. Finally, there is Twinkle. Twinkle ice cream is mediocre. The only good thing about Twinkle is that it is relatively inexpensive. You can buy a whole carton of twinkle ice cream for $4.50. That's only two weeks' allowance for me. According to the passage, the author likes Randolph Farms ice cream because it

I. is all natural

II. is made in Bolivia

III. comes in many flavors

A. I only

B. I and II only

C. II and III only

D. I, II, and III

Q.25 Question below is given a statement followed by three assumptions numbered I, II and III. You have to consider the statement and the following assumptions and decide which of the assumptions is implicit in the statement. Statement: "I want to present a book on techniques of yoga to Ajay on his birthday."- A tells Assumptions:
I. A will be invited by Ajay on his birthday.
II. The person, to whom the book is to be presented, is not keeping good health.
III. Book is an acceptable gift for birthday.

A. Only I and II are implicit
B. Only II and III are implicit
C. Only I and III are implicit
D. None is implicit

Q.26 Identify the paintings by Michelangelo from the following.

A. A **B.** B **C.** C **D.** D

Q.27 Identify the paintings by S.H.Raza from the following.

A. 

B. 

C. 

D. 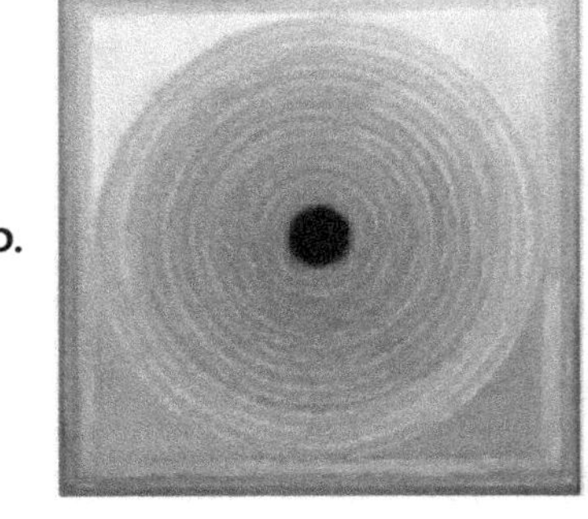

Q.28 Identify the Indian traditional Art below

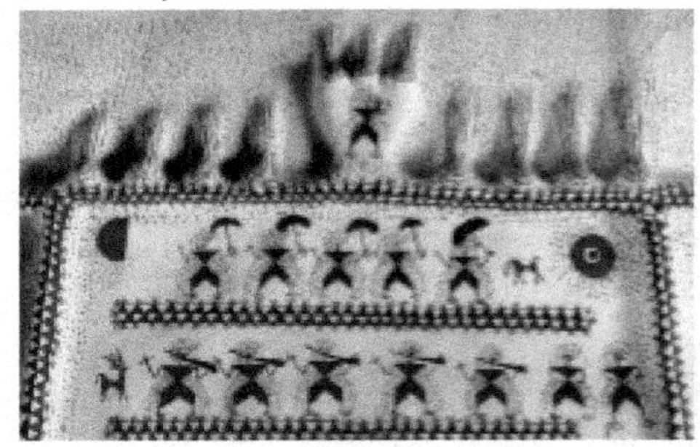

A. Kalamkari **B.** Madhubani
C. Tharu **D.** None of these

Q.29 Shown on the left is a socket with four holes in it. Which of the plugs will fit perfectly in this socket?

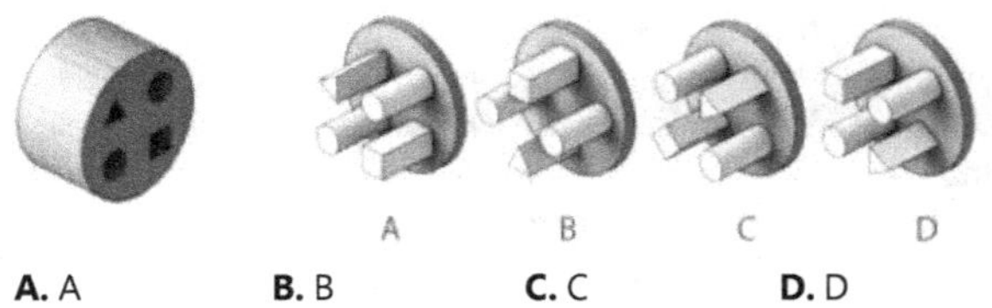

A. A **B.** B **C.** C **D.** D

Q.30 Identify the 3D shape's net.

A. 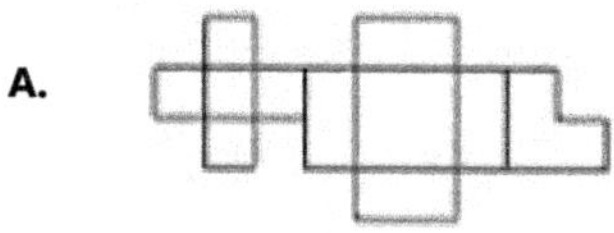

B. 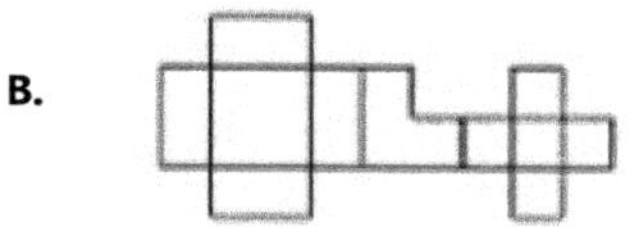

C. 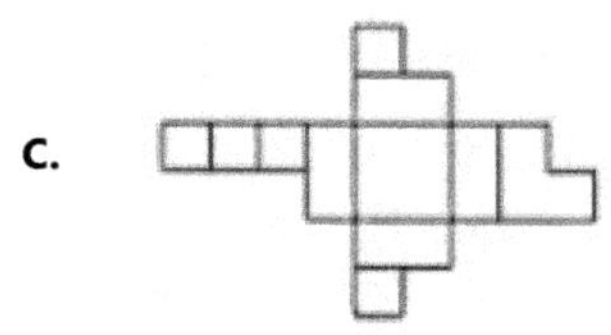

D. None of these

Q.31 Identify the answer shape, which has been rotated but is otherwise the same as the question shape.

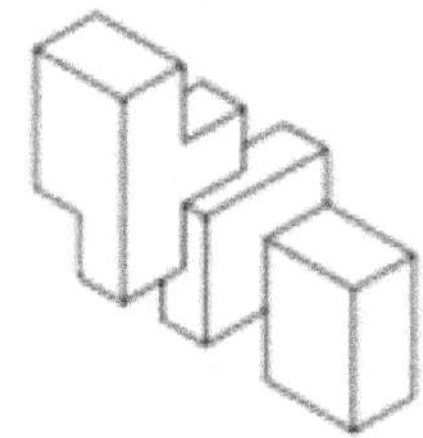

A. 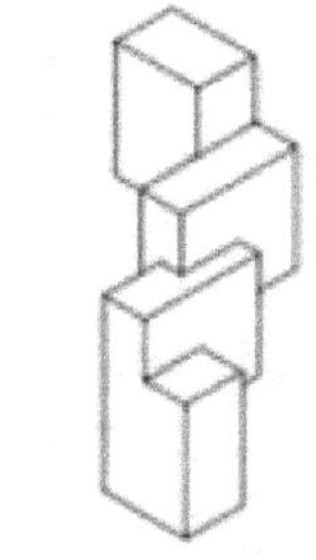

B. 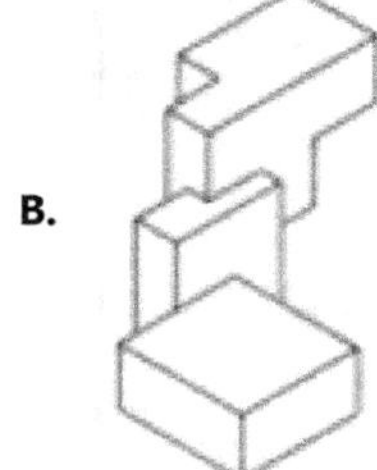

C. 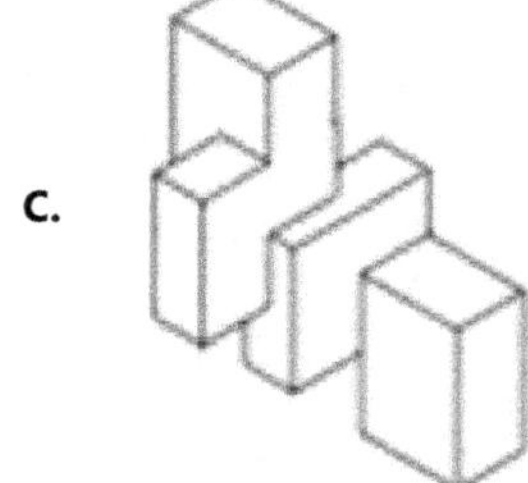

D. None of these

Q.32 Identify the mirror image of the question shape (reject any suggested answer in which any change other than reflection has occurred).

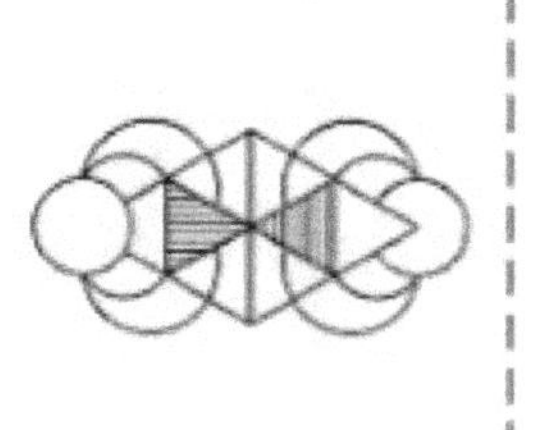

A. 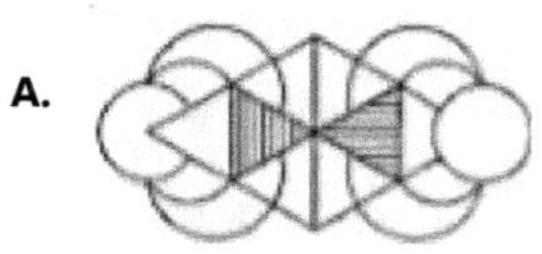

B. 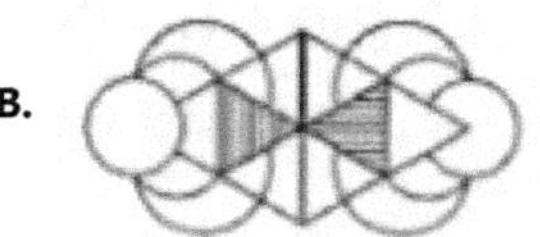

C. 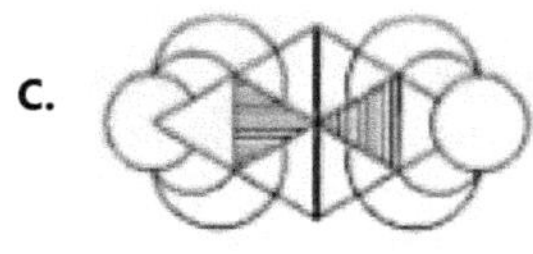

D. None of these

Q.33 Pick the TWO answer choices that will come together to make the figure shown. Pieces may be reflected and or rotated

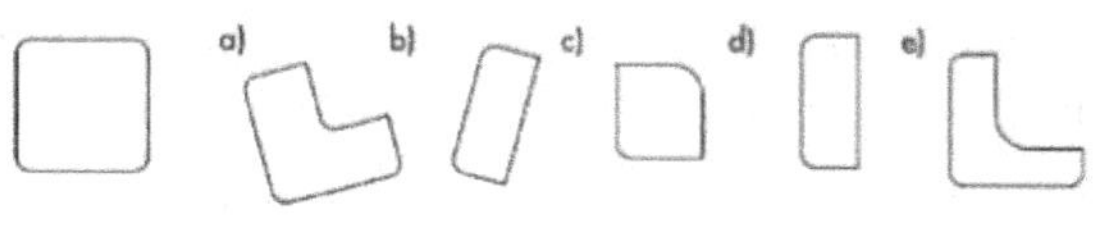

A. a + c **B.** b + d **C.** c +d **D.** c + e

Q.34 4–5 pieces are given. Choose the answer choice that represents a figure comprised of ALL pieces. Pieces may be rotated and/or reflected.

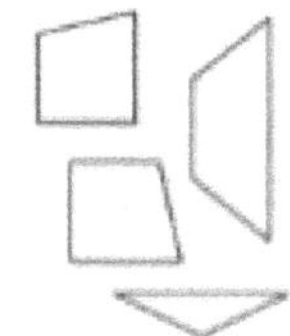

A. 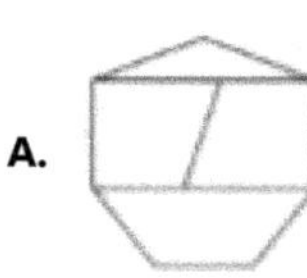

B. 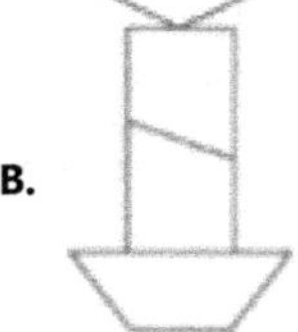

C. 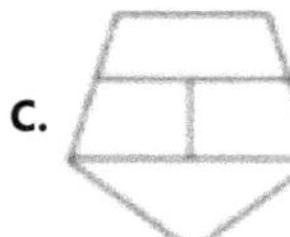

D. 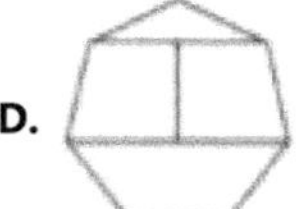

Q.35 A square is cut into 7 pieces as shown on the extreme left of the image. Identify which of the options can be made using all 7 pieces.

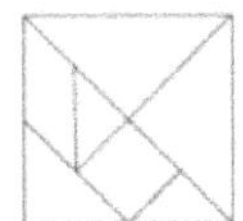

A B C D

A. A **B.** B **C.** C **D.** D

Q.36 The ratio of width of our National flag to its length is

A. 3:5 **B.** 2:3 **C.** 1:2 **D.** 3:4

Multiple Choice Questions (MCQ)

Q.37 Identify the correct art techniques with which the following paintings have been made.

A. Oil, Pastel, Crayon, Watercolor
B. Oil, Watercolor, pastel, acrylic
C. Oil, Pastel, Acrylic, Watercolor
D. Oil, Watercolor, Acrylic, Pastel

Q.38 Purple can be used as a symbol of ....?

A. Peace **B.** Anger **C.** Luxury **D.** Danger

Q.39 Objects that cannot be seen through are called-

A. translucent **B.** transparent
C. opaque **D.** refracting

Q.40 Shown are the symbols for different functions. Identify the correct description sequence from the given choices.

A. Radiation, Mind your step, Inflammable, Danger
B. Danger, Mind your step, Radiation, Inflammable
C. Radiation, Mind your Step, Danger, Flammable
D. Inflammable, Mind your step, Danger, Radiation

Q.41 In the following question, select the related word from the given alternatives.

Lion : Cub :: Kangaroo : ?

A. Fawn **B.** Joey **C.** Kitten **D.** Calf

Q.42 Complete the series

?

A.  

B. 

C. 

D. 

Q.43 There are eight rules which when applied to the sequence will transform it to one of the four options shown below. Identify the correct option.

AB Delete the last character
BC Replace the third character with the next in the alphabet
CD Insert the letter P between the third and fourth characters.
DE Exchange the first and last characters
EF Replace the second character with the previous letter in the alphabet
FG Replace the fifth character with the next in the alphabet
GH Reverse the whole sequence of letters
HI Delete the third character

ANIHCS = GH + EF + CD + AB =

A. AMIPHC **B.** SBHPIN
C. SDHPINA **D.** CHINAS

Q.44 In the following question, select the odd image from the given alternatives.

A. 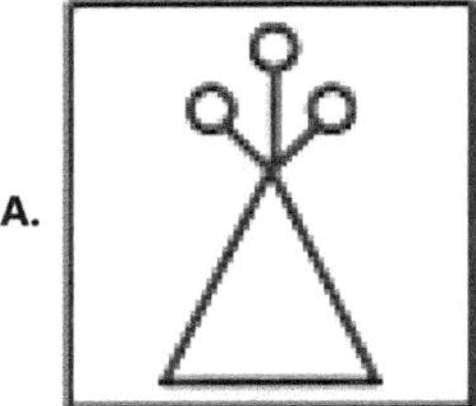

B. 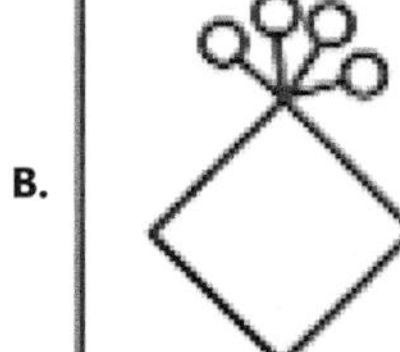

C. 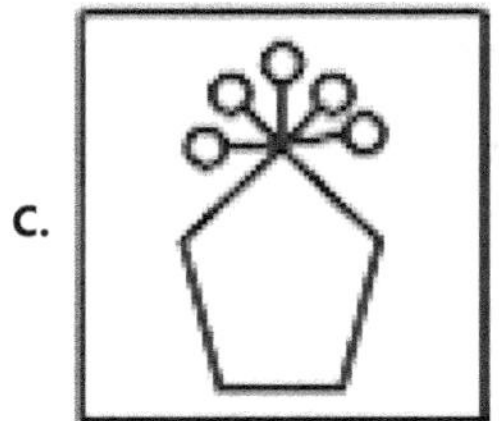

D. 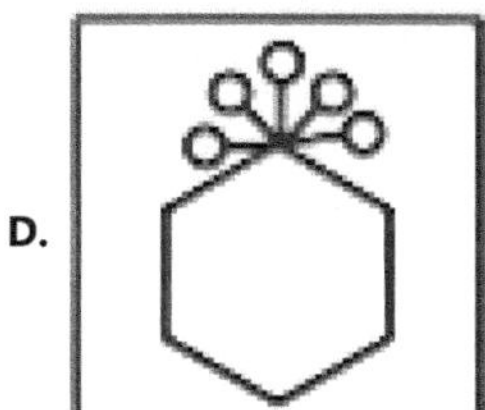

Q.45 Choose the alternative which is closely resembles the water-image of the given combination.

RAJ589D8

(1) ꓤ∀1Ƨ89D8 (2) ꓤ∀1Ƨ89D8
(3) ꓤ∀ſƧ89D8 (4) ꓤ∀ſƧ89D8

A. 1 **B.** 2 **C.** 3 **D.** 4

Q.46 Find out from amongst the four alternatives as to how the pattern would appear when the transparent sheet is folded at the dotted line.

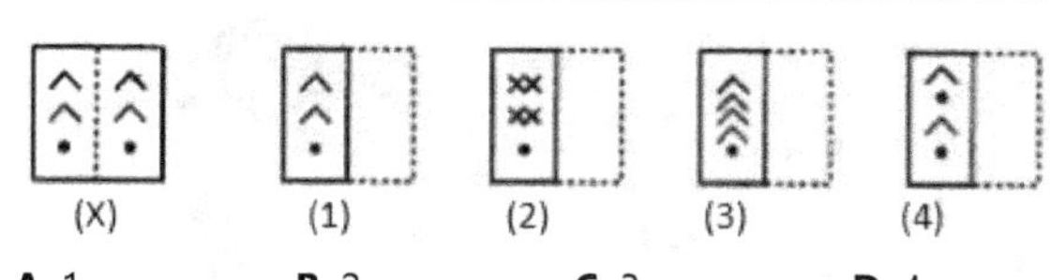

A. 1 **B.** 2 **C.** 3 **D.** 4

Q.47 Choose a figure which would most closely resemble the unfolded form of Figure (Z).

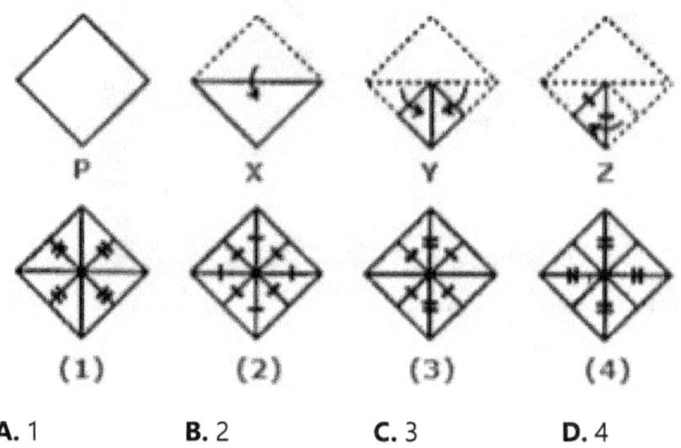

A. 1 **B.** 2 **C.** 3 **D.** 4

Q.48 Choose the correct mirror image of the given figure (X) from amongst the four alternatives.

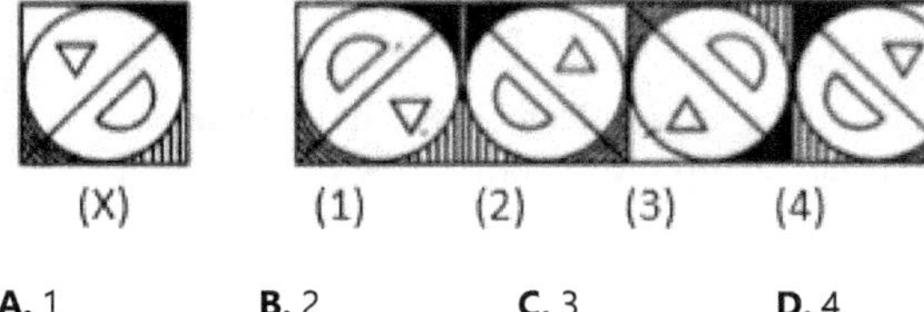

A. 1 **B.** 2 **C.** 3 **D.** 4

Q.49 What will be the most probable pose at position 5 to complete the sequence below?

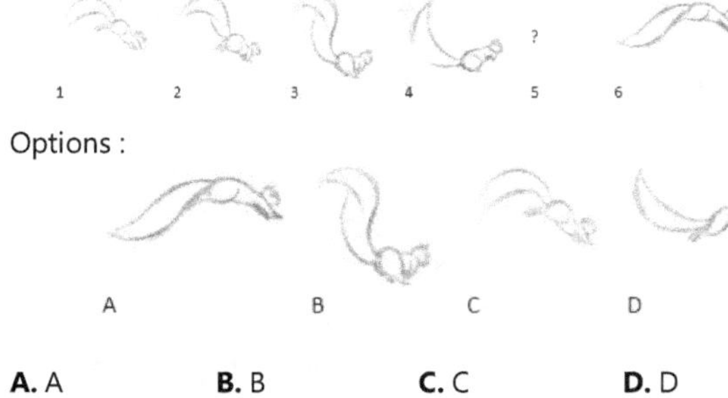

A. A **B.** B **C.** C **D.** D

Q.50 Which element was NOT important in Cubist painting?

A. Multiple viewpoints
B. Relativity
C. Perspective drawing
D. Drawing from memory

Q.51 Spot the difference. Below are two apparently identical pictures. In fact, there are differences between the two - Spot them.

A. 5 **B.** 6 **C.** 7 **D.** 8

Q.52 Identify the function of the tool below.

A. Drilling
B. Inscribing
C. Nailing
D. None of the above.

Q.53 In each question, an incomplete statement (Stem) followed by fillers is given. Pick out the best one which can complete incomplete stem correctly and meaningfully.

His appearance is unsmiling but ......

A. his heart is full of compassion for others
B. he looks very serious on most occasions
C. people are afraid of him
D. he is uncompromising on matters of task performance

Q.54 In each question, an incomplete statement (Stem) followed by fillers is given. Pick out the best one which can complete incomplete stem correctly and meaningfully.

I felt somewhat more relaxed ......

A. but tense as compared to earlier
B. and tense as compared to earlier
C. as there was already no tension at all
D. and tension-free as compared to earlier

Q.55 Rearrange the following five sentences in proper sequence to form a meaningful paragraph, then answer the questions given below.

1. A Study to this effect suggests that the average white-collar worker demonstrates only about 25% listening efficiency.
2. However for trained and good listeners it is not unusual to use all the three approaches during a setting, thus improving listening efficiency.
3. There are three approaches to listening: Listening for comprehension, Listening for empathy and Listening for evaluation.
4. Although we spend nearly half of each communication interaction listening, we do not listen well. 5. Each approach has a particular emphasis that may help us to receive and process information in different settings.

A. 35241 **B.** 35421 **C.** 35214 **D.** 32541

Q.56 Pick up the one which is most nearly the same in meaning as the word printed in bold and can replaces it without altering the meaning of the sentence.

She has an **insatiable** love for music.

A. unsatisfiable **B.** Unchanging
C. Irreconcilable **D.** Undesirable

Q.57 Pick up the one which is most nearly the same in meaning as the word printed in bold and can replaces it without altering the meaning of the sentence.

The great dancer impressed the appreciative crowd by his **nimble** movements.

A. Unrhythmic **B.** lively
C. quickening **D.** clear

Q.58 Identify the type of Photography.

A. Motion Blur Photography
B. Panoramic Photography
C. Black & White Photography
D. Tilt-Shift Photography

Q.59 Which kind of Photography is this?

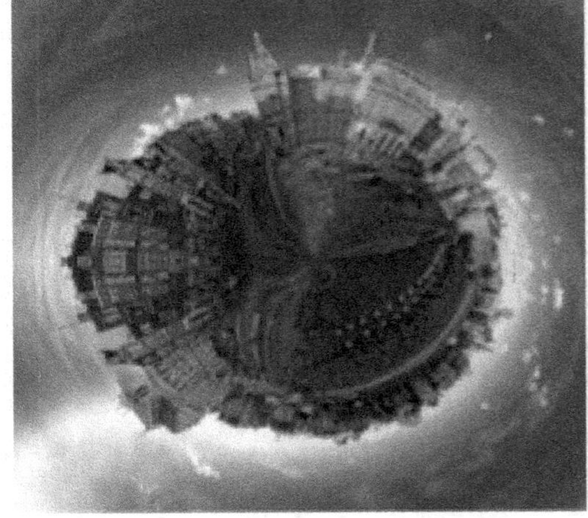

A. Panoramic Photography
B. RAW Processing
C. Special Issues
D. HDR

Q.60 Choose the word opposite in meaning to the given word:

Relinquish

A. Convert **B.** Condense
C. Longest **D.** Possess

Q.61 In the following questions choose the word, which is the exact OPPOSITE of the given words.

EXPAND

A. Convert **B.** Condense
C. Congest **D.** Conclude

Q.62 In the questions below the sentences have been given in Direct/Indirect speech. From the given alternatives, choose the one which best expresses the given sentence in Indirect/Direct speech.

She said that her brother was getting married.

A. She said, "Her brother is getting married."
B. She told, "Her brother is getting married."
C. She said, "My brother is getting married."
D. She said, "My brother was getting married."

Q.63 In the questions below the sentences have been given in Direct/Indirect speech. From the given alternatives, choose the one which best expresses the given sentence in Indirect/Direct speech.

The boy said, "Who dare call you a thief?"

A. The boy enquired who dared call him a thief.
B. The boy asked who called him a thief.
C. The boy told that who dared call him a thief.
D. The boy wondered who dared call a thief.

Q.64 Direction: The sentence has been given in the Active/Passive voice. From the given options, choose the one which best expresses the given sentence in the Passive/Active voice.

Darjeeling grows tea.

A. Tea grows in Darjeeling.
B. Tea is grown in Darjeeling.

C. Let the tea be grown in Darjeeling.
D. Tea is being grown in Darjeeling.

Q.65 In the questions below the sentences have been given in Active/Passive voice. From the given alternatives, choose the one which best expresses the given sentence in Passive/Active voice.

They have built a perfect dam across the river.

A. Across the river a perfect dam was built.
B. A perfect dam has been built by them across the river.
C. A perfect dam should have been built by them.
D. Across the river was a perfect dam.

Q.66 The first two words are related in a particular manner. Select the word from given choices, which is related to the third one in the same manner:

Light : Blind :: Speech :

A. Tongue **B.** Dumb **C.** Sound **D.** Chat

Q.67 Each question consist of two words which have a certain relationship to each other followed by four pairs of related words, Select the pair which has the same relationship

WAN:COLOUR

A. corpulent:weight **B.** insipid:flavour
C. pallid:complexion **D.** enigmatic:puzzle

Q.68 Identify the name of this Statue

A. Martin Luther King **B.** Anthony Wayne
C. Andrew Johnson **D.** Abraham Lincoln

// Smart Answer Sheet //

Correct Indicates percentage of students who answered questions correctly.

Skipped Indicates percentage of students who skipped questions.

Q.	Ans.	Correct	Skipped
1	24	25.79 %	3.14 %
2	20	62.26 %	17.61 %
3	6	35.85 %	20.75 %
4	4	13.84 %	20.12 %
5	38	18.87 %	27.04 %
6	700	64.78 %	22.64 %
7	52	50.94 %	20.13 %
8	#	22.01 %	25.79 %
9	24	57.23 %	18.87 %
10	32	55.97 %	18.87 %
11	#	35.85 %	20.75 %
12	5	16.98 %	26.42 %
13	1394	61.01 %	19.49 %
14	#	54.72 %	22.64 %
15	14	59.75 %	20.12 %
16	10	8.81 %	22.01 %
17	15	55.97 %	21.39 %
18	4	8.18 %	23.27 %
19	B, A, C	45.28 %	25.79 %
20	B, A, D	16.35 %	32.08 %
21	B, D, C	6.29 %	33.96 %
22	B, A, D	49.69 %	23.89 %
23	B	49.06 %	23.27 %
24	A	43.4 %	24.52 %
25	C	42.14 %	23.9 %
26	A, D	46.54 %	19.5 %
27	B, A, D, C	64.78 %	24.53 %
28	C	44.65 %	20.13 %
29	A, D	67.92 %	20.76 %
30	A	43.4 %	21.38 %
31	A	25.16 %	22.64 %
32	A	53.46 %	19.5 %
33	D	23.9 %	20.13 %
34	D	23.27 %	20.13 %
35	A, C	19.5 %	27.04 %
36	B	54.72 %	21.38 %
37	A	38.99 %	16.98 %
38	C	74.21 %	17.61 %
39	C	56.6 %	17.61 %
40	C	77.36 %	17.61 %
41	B	55.97 %	20.13 %
42	B	40.25 %	25.16 %
43	B	64.15 %	22.64 %
44	D	60.38 %	25.15 %
45	A	75.47 %	19.5 %
46	A	74.21 %	19.5 %
47	B	69.81 %	19.5 %
48	D	74.84 %	20.13 %
49	D	72.33 %	20.12 %
50	C	27.04 %	24.53 %
51	C	12.58 %	27.04 %
52	C	37.11 %	20.12 %
53	A	67.92 %	22.65 %
54	D	65.41 %	22.64 %
55	A	35.85 %	25.16 %
56	A	40.88 %	22.01 %
57	C	34.59 %	23.27 %
58	D	37.11 %	22.01 %
59	A	56.6 %	23.9 %
60	D	23.27 %	24.53 %
61	B	47.17 %	23.9 %
62	C	54.09 %	22.64 %
63	A	42.77 %	23.9 %
64	B	44.65 %	21.39 %
65	B	63.52 %	23.27 %
66	B	47.8 %	21.38 %
67	B	22.64 %	32.08 %
68	D	61.01 %	20.75 %

#

Q.	Answer
8	TG
11	D
14	H

Performance Analysis	
Avg. Score (%)	45.0%
Toppers Score (%)	106.25%
Your Score	

//Hints and Solutions//

1. 24 patterns

2.

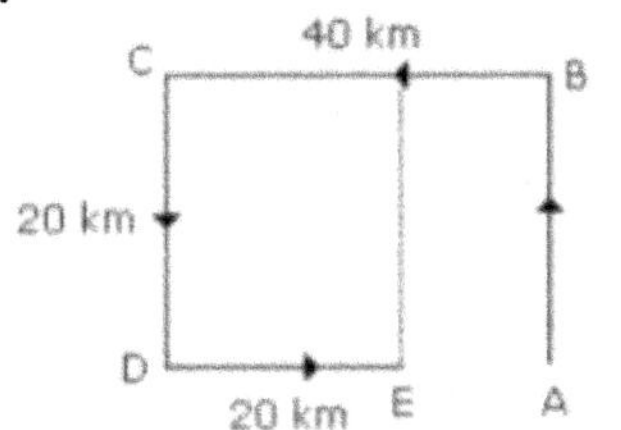

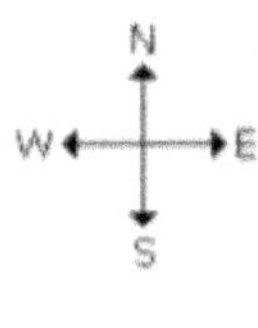

Required distance $= 40 - 20 = 20km$

3. There are six different sized circles.

4. In the first column,

$$27 - (7 \times 2) = 13$$

In the second column,

$$144 - (45 \times 2) = 54$$

Likewise,

In the third column,

$$68 - (32 \times 2) = 4$$

The value of the missing number is 4.

Hence, the correct answer is 4.

5.

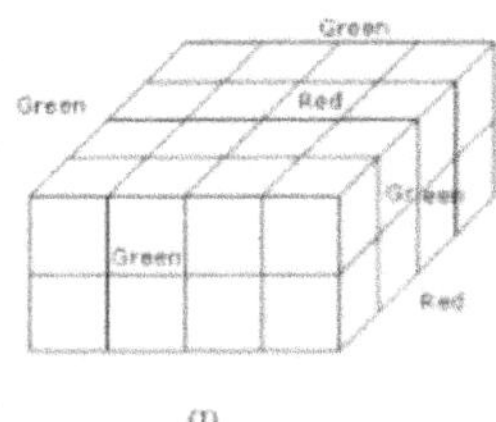

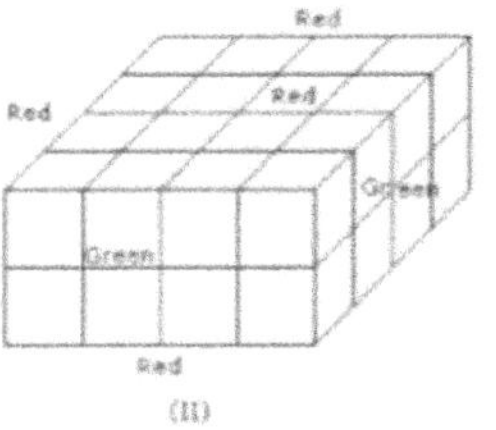

24 from (I) and 14 from (II)

6. (56 ÷ 8) x 100.

7. There are 52 cubes.

8. The given series:

$$EB, HC, KD, NE, QF, ?$$

$$E \xrightarrow{+3} H \xrightarrow{+3} K \xrightarrow{+3} N \xrightarrow{+3} Q \xrightarrow{+3} T$$

$$B \xrightarrow{+1} C \xrightarrow{+1} D \xrightarrow{+1} E \xrightarrow{+1} F \xrightarrow{+1} G$$

Hence, the correct answer is TG.

9.

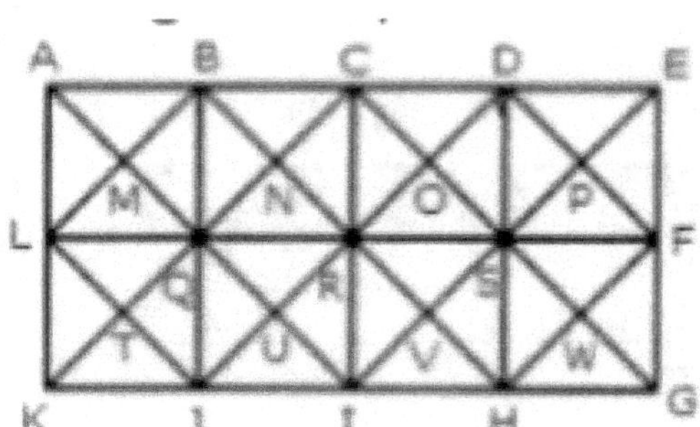

The squares composed of two components each are BNQM, CORN, DPSO, MQTL, NRUQ, OSVR, PFWS, QUJT, RVIU and SWHV i.e. 10 in number. The squares composed of four components each are

$ABQL, BCRQ, CDSR, DEFS, LOJK, QRIJ, RSHI$ and SFGH i.e. 8 in number.

The squares composed of eight components each are BRJL, CSIQ and DFHR i.e. 3 in number. The squares composed of sixteen components each are ACIK, BDHJ and CEGI i.e. 3 in number. Thus, there are $10 + 8 + 3 + 3 = 24$ squares in the figure.

10. The total of three numbers must be 48 × 3 = 144. The total of two numbers must be 56 × 2 = 112. Therefore, 144 – 112 = 32

11. Three letters anti-clockwise of E = B

Opposite of B = F

Two letters clockwise of F = H

Opposite of H=D

Hence, the correct answer is D.

12. The motion of the man can be shown through the diagram given below:

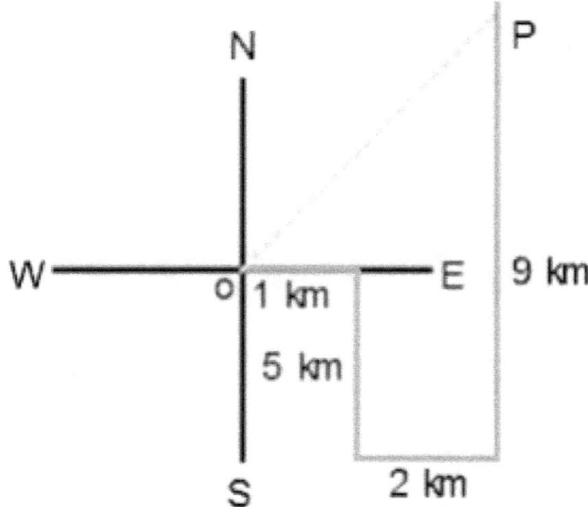

The last position of the man is P and OEP is a right-angled triangle in which $EP = 3\ km$ and $OE = 4\ km$

Now,

$OP = \sqrt{(3^2 + 4^2)}$

$\Rightarrow OP = \sqrt{25}$

$\Rightarrow OP = 5\ km$

So, he is $5\ km$ far from his starting point.

13. (82 × 17)

14. Two letters to the left of E - C

Four letters to the right of C - G

Immediate left of G - F

Two letters right of F - H.

15. There are 14 surfaces to the object.

16. Dowry **consist** of **thing** given by **parent** to **there** daughters at the time of **there** marriage. **Onesthese** was done to start life well. But the greedy parents of **bridegroms** demand more money and material. Some girls have to **loose therelifes** for bringing fewer dowries. Burning brides is daily news these days. Both the, **Goverment** and the public should discourage the dowry seekers.

Correction Dowry consists of things given by parents to their daughters at the time of their marriage. Once this was done to start life well. But the greedy parents of bridegrooms demand more money and material. Some girls have to lose their lives for bringing fewer dowries. Burning brides is daily news these days. Both the, Government and the public should discourage the dowry seekers.

17. There are 15 different types of symbols.

18. From column I: $(9 \times 5)/5 = 9$

From column II: $(17 \times 4)/4 = 17$

From column III: $(16 \times ?)/8 = 8$

$16 \times ? = 64$

$\Rightarrow ? = 4$

Hence, the correct answer is 4.

19. A, B, C

20. A, B, D are true.

21. B, C, D are true

22. A, B, D C- is not true. The second sentence of the second paragraph states that, while corals are the main components of reef structure, they are not the only living participants.

23. Clearly, electric engines shall be smoke-free and thus not cause pollution as the coal engines. They also run at higher speeds and perform better. Thus, both I and II hold strong. Argument III does not provide a convincing reason and hence does not hold strong.

24. The author writes, "Randolph Farms uses all natural ingredients to make their ice cream. This is a good idea, I think." We can understand from this information that one of the things the author likes about Randolph Farms ice cream is that it is made using all natural ingredients. This supports option (I). In paragraph 3 the author tells us that Goodies' chocolate ice cream is "is made with real cocoa beans from Bolivia." Nothing in the passage supports the idea that Randolph Farms makes their ice cream in Bolivia. This eliminates option (II). The author writes that Randolph Farms has "lots of different flavors, but this doesn't really matter to me." This eliminates option (III). Therefore (A) is correct.

25. Since A has decided to gift a book to Ajay on his birthday, it is quite evident that he will be invited by Ajay and that a book is an acceptable gift. So, both I and III are implicit. Nothing about the state of health of the person can be deduced from the statement. So, II is not implicit.

26. A and D are the paintings of Michelangelo.
Hence, the correct options are (A) and (D).

27. ABCD- All of the above

28. C-Tharu

29. Plugs A and D will fit perfectly in this socket.

Hence, the correct options are (A) and (D).

30. In b) the little squares that form the cube are in the wrong position, and c) has one of the little squares in a wrong position.

31. In b) the small rectangular shape has been lengthened, and in c) the irregular shape has changed.

32. In b) only the triangles with stripes have been reflected, and in c) the triangles with stripes have not been reflected.

33.

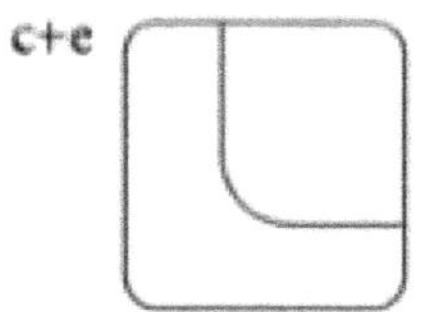

34.

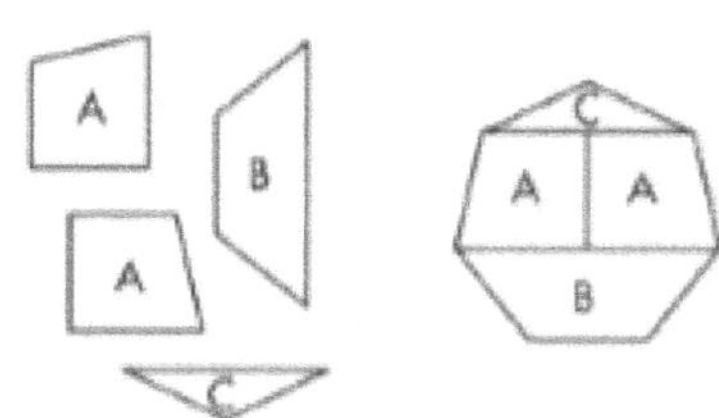

35. A, C

36. B. 2:3

37. Oil, Pastel, Crayon, Watercolor

38. C- Luxury

39. Opaque objects block light from travelling through them. Most of the light is either reflected by the object or absorbed and converted to thermal energy. Materials such as wood, stone and metals are opaque to visible light.

Hence, the correct option is (C).

40. Radiation, Mind your Step, Danger, Flammable

41. The baby of the Lion is called Cub. Similarly, the baby of Kangaroo is called Joey.

Hence, the correct option is (B).

42. The outer shapes of the first two steps are a semi- complete and a complete square – a four-sided shape. The next two steps are a semi-complete and a complete three-sided shape. The next shape in the series therefore would be a semi-complete two-sided shape. The inner shapes alternate complete and incomplete, and in the next step of the series it is the turn of the complete shape.

43. First reverse the sequence to read SCHINA, then change the C into a B, then insert a P between the H and the I and finally delete the A.

44. The pattern followed here is:

In each of the above figures except figure D, the number of vertices/sides/lines of the given shape is equal to the number of lines and circles drawn above them.

Therefore, the figure given in option D is the odd one.

Hence, the correct option is (D).

45. 1 is water image of RAJ589D8

46. 1

Hence option A is correct.

47. 2 is unfolded form of Z.

48. 4 is mirror image of X.

49.

D

D will come at position 5.

Hence, the correct option is (D).

50. Perspective drawing

Hence option C is correct.

51. There are 7 differences between the pictures.

C-7 differences

Hence, the correct option is (C).

52. Nailing

Hence option C is correct.

53. his heart is full of compassion for others

54. and tension-free as compared to earlier

55. 35241

Hence option A is correct.

56. unsatisfiable is meaning of insatiable.

57. quickening is meaning of nimble.

58. Tilt-Shift Photography

59. Panoramic Photography

60. 'Relinquish' means 'voluntarily cease to claim or own'. For example, 'to relinquish one's assets'.

Option (D): 'Possess' means 'to own something'. It means the exact opposite of the given word. Therefore, (D) is correct.

Option (A): 'Convert' means 'to change the form or character'.

Option (B): 'Condense' means 'to make something denser or more concentrated'.

Option (C): 'Longest' is a superlative adjective that speaks of length.

These words do not express the opposite meaning of the given word. Therefore (A), (B), and (C) are incorrect.

Hence, the correct option is (D).

61. Condense is opposite of Expand.

62. She said, "My brother is getting married."

63. In the questions below the sentences have been given in Active/Passive voice. From the given alternatives, choose the one which best expresses the given sentence in Passive/Active voice.

64. The correct answer is "Tea is grown in Darjeeling."

An action in a sentence can be represented in two ways, namely active and passive voice. The passive voice always uses the past participle form of the main verb irrespective of any tense. Only the auxiliary verbs depend upon the sentence given in the active voice.

Option (B) is correct as the given sentence is in the active voice and to transform it into the passive voice the subject of the given sentence (Darjeeling) comes in the place of the object(tea) and vice versa. Also, the given sentence is in the simple present tense.

Options (A), (C), and (D) are wrong as it is in the active voice, 'let' changes the meaning of the given sentence, and the sentence is not in the present continuous tense respectively,

Hence, the correct option is (B).

65. A perfect dam has been built by them across the river.

66. The word 'Light' means something that makes vision possible. The word 'Blind' means sightless or visionless. Therefore, we can say that the words "Light and Blind" are opposite to each other.

The word 'Speech' means the communication or expression of thoughts in spoken words thus we now have to find its opposite word from the given options.

Now let us explore the given options:

- Tongue means manner or quality of utterance with respect to tone or sound or the intention of the speaker.
- Dumb means lacking the power of speech.
- Sound means the impression conveyed.
- Chat means to talk in an informal or familiar manner.

Therefore, the word related to 'Speech' in the same manner as the "Light: Blind" is 'Dumb'.

Hence, the correct option is (B).

67. insipid : flavour

68. Abraham Lincoln

Mock Test 09

Numerical Answer Type (NAT)

Q.1 How many different types of symbols appear in the figure given below?

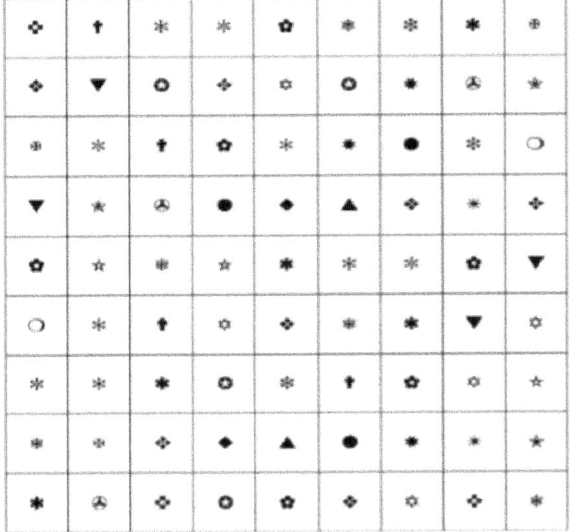

Q.2 From his house, Lokesh went 15 km to the North. Then he turned west and covered 10 km. Then he turned south and covered 5 km. Finally turning to the east, he covered 10 km. In which direction is he from his house?

Q.3 How many lines appear below?

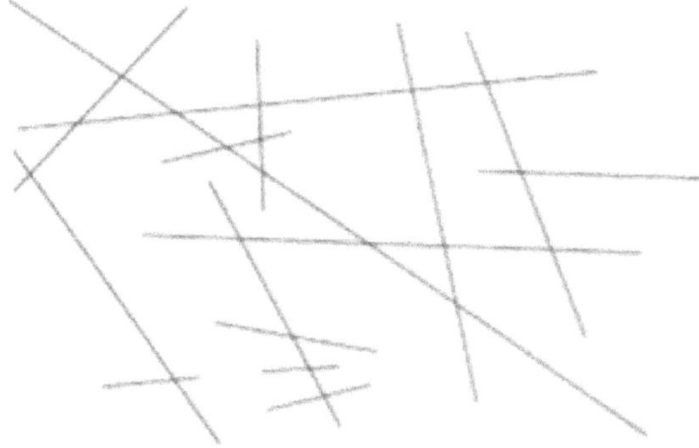

Q.4 The given image has thirty six circles with patterns inside, arranged in an six-by-six matrix. How many different types of circles are there in the image, assuming circles may be rotated?

Q.5 Imagine letters are extruded into three-dimensional objects, as shown in the figure on the left (the letter A). If the word TUB (shown on the right) were to be extruded, how many surfaces would it have?

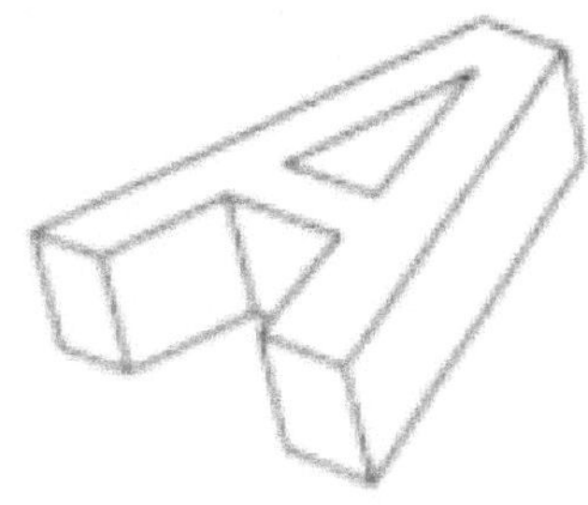

TUB

Q.6 All the faces of a cube are painted with blue color. Then it is cut into 125 small equal cubes. How many small cubes will be formed having only one face coloured ?

Q.7 If five men can build a house in 21 days, how long will it take seven men to build the house, assuming all men work at the same rate?

Q.8 Count the number of cubes in the given figure.

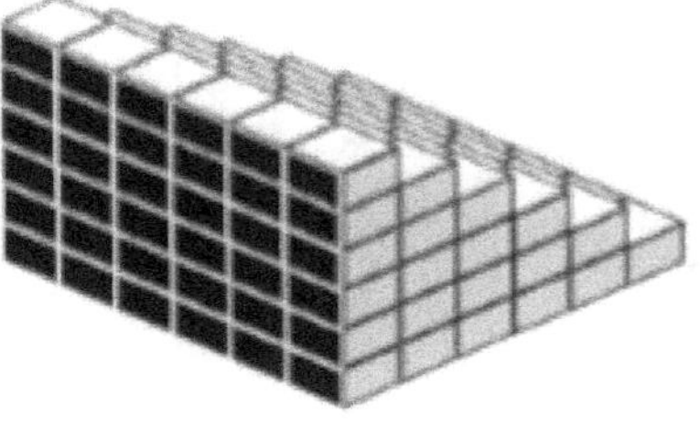

Q.9 In the following question, the number of triangles are:

Q.10 Count the number of squares in the given figure.

Q.11 What is the minimum number of different colours required to paint the given figure such that no two adjacent regions have the same colour?

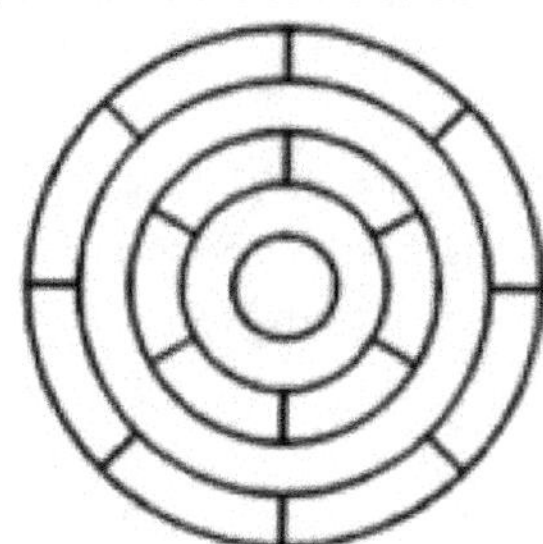

Q.12 Jack is twice as old as Jill, but in five years time he will only be one and a half times as old. How old are Jack?

Q.13 What letter is directly opposite the letter two places anticlockwise away from the letter directly opposite the letter H?

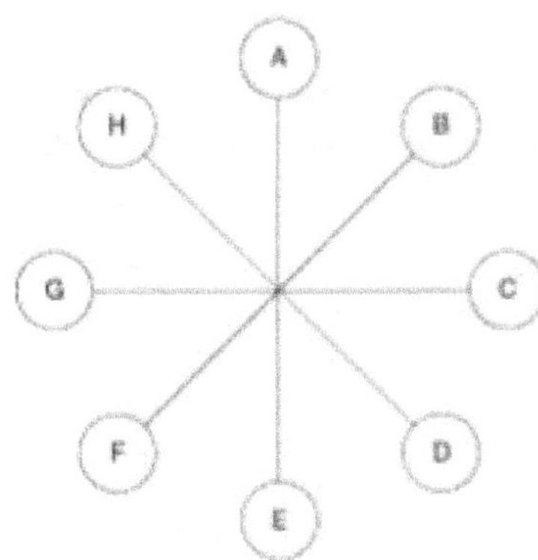

Q.14 What number should replace the question mark?

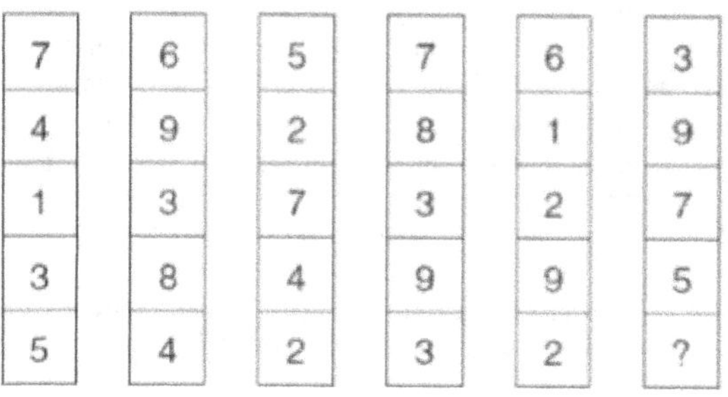

7	6	5	7	6	3
4	9	2	8	1	9
1	3	7	3	2	7
3	8	4	9	9	5
5	4	2	3	2	?

Q.15 Find out the total number of surfaces of the object, given below in the problem figure.

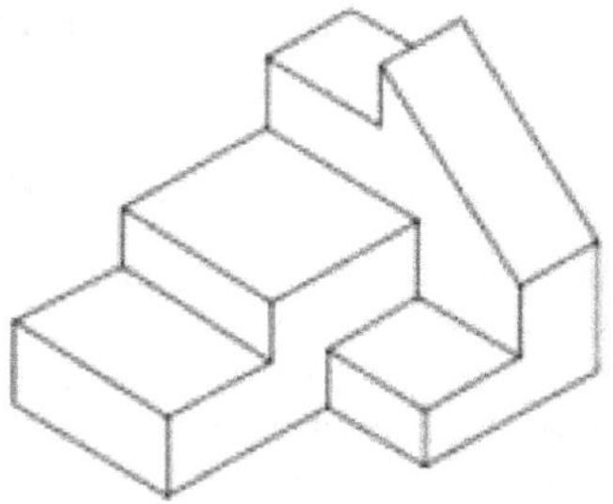

Q.16 What number should replace the question mark?

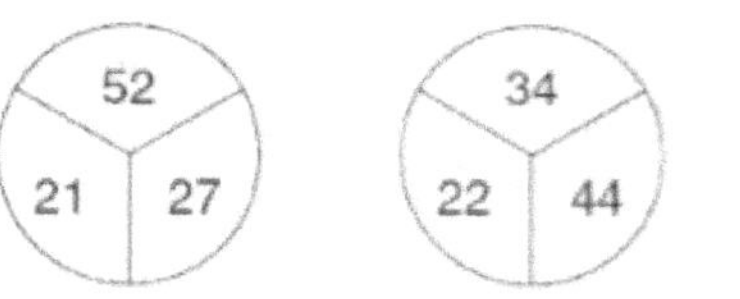

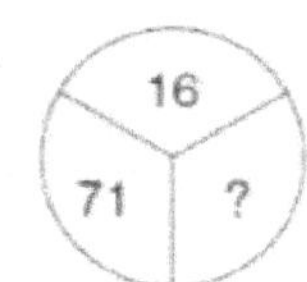

Q.17 What number should replace the question mark?

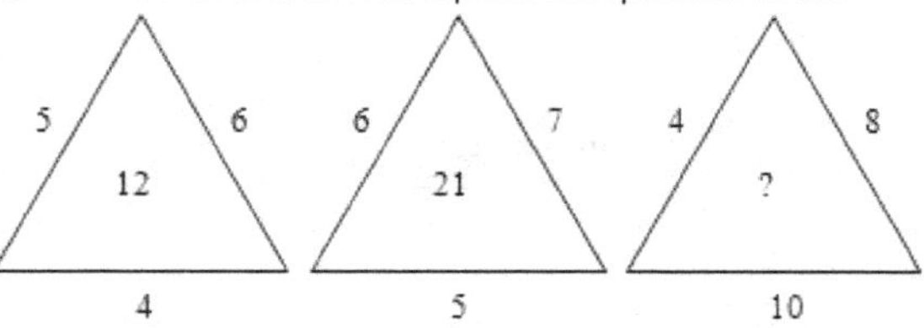

Q.18 Which number will replace the question mark?

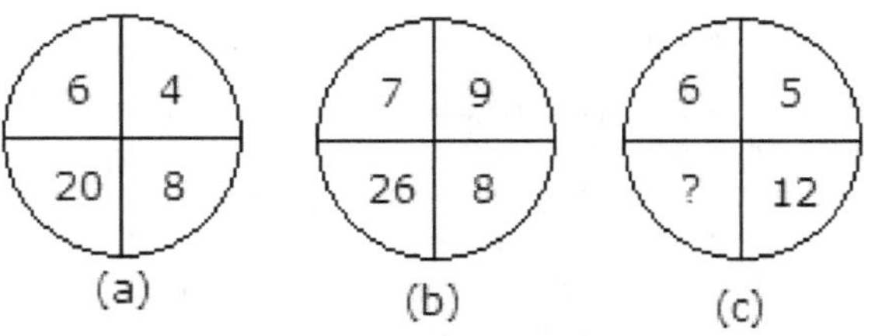

Multiple Select Questions (MSQ)

Q.19 Which of the following statements is/are true?

A. Alan Turing is known for having pioneered the concept of modern-day computers, by introducing the idea of a 'Turing Machine', which is simple, and yet capable of solving any form of algorithms that can be measured and quantified.

B. Avicenna was the most influential and renowned

philosopher and scientist of the Islamic world, popularly known as the father of modern medicine, he researched and came out with pioneering works in aromatherapy.

C. Edward de Bono is presently the world's foremost expert on conceptual thinking as the backbone behind structural innovation, tactical leadership, creativity and problem solving. He coined and introduced the concept of 'lateral thinking.'

D. Joseph Eugene Stiglitz is a noted German economist, who won the Nobel Memorial Prize in Economic Sciences for his work on asymmetric information.

Q.20 Select the statements below that are TRUE.

A. As everybody knows nowadays, the knowledge we possess of life before the beginnings of human memory and tradition is derived from the markings and fossils of living things in the stratified rocks.

B. The sedimentary rocks do not lay neatly stratum above stratum; they have been crumpled, bent, thrust about, distorted and mixed together and it is only as a result of many devoted lifetimes of work that the record has been put into order and read.

C. The earliest rocks in the record are called by geologists the Azoic rocks, because they show no traces of life. Great areas of these Azoic rocks lie uncovered in North America, and they are of such a thickness that geologists consider that they represent a period of at least half of the 1,600,000,000 which they assign to the whole geological record.

D. The Record of the Rocks is no more a complete record of life in the past. It is only when a species begins to speak and communicate, that it goes upon the Record.

Q.21 From the options below, select the Indian author/s writing in English whose works are represented below:

1. The Last burden
2. Weight Loss
3. Rich like us
4. The mammaries of welfare street
5. The day in shadow
6. A time to be happy

A. Sachin Kundalkar
B. Nayantara Sahgal
C. R. K. Narayanan
D. Upamanyu Chaterjee

Q.22 Nehru's was a many sided personality. He enjoyed reading and writing books as much as he enjoyed fighting political and social evils or residing tyranny. In him, the scientist and the humanist were held in perfect balance. While he kept looking at special problems from a scientific standpoint. He never forgot that we should nourish the total man. As a scientist, he refused to believe in a benevolent power interested in men's affairs. but, as a self proclaimed non-believer, he loved affirming his faith in life and the beauty of nature. Children he adored. Unlike Wordsworth, he did not see him trailing clouds of glory from the recent sojourn in heaven. He saw them as blossoms of promise and renewal, the only hope for mankind. Which of the statements reflects Nehru point of view?

A. Humanism is more important than science
B. Science is supreme and humanism is subordinate to it
C. Science and Humanism are equally important
D. There is no ground between science and humanism

Q.23 Question given below consists of a statement, followed by three arguments numbered I , II and III. You have to decide which of the arguments is a 'strong' argument. Statement: Should all the profit making public sector units be sold to privatecompanies?

Arguments:

I. Yes. This will help the government to augment its resources for implementing the development programmes.

II. No. The private companies will not be able to run these units effectively.

III. Yes. There will be a significant improvement in the quality of services.

IV. No. There would not be job security for the employees at all the levels.

A. Only II and III are strong
B. All are strong
C. Only III and IV are strong
D. Only I, II and III are strong

Q.24 Question below is given a statement followed by three assumptions numbered I, II and III. You have to consider the statement and the following assumptions and decide which of the assumptions is implicit in the statement.

Statement: This book is so prepared that even a layman can study science in the absence of a teacher.

Assumptions:

I. A layman wishes to study science without a teacher.

II. A teacher may not always be available to teach science.

III. A layman generally finds it difficult to learn science on its own.

A. Only I and II are implicit
B. Only II and III are implicit
C. Only I and III are implicit
D. All are implicit

Q.25 Have you ever wondered what keeps a hot air balloon flying? The same principle that keeps food frozen in the open chest freezers at the grocery store allows hot air balloons to fly. It's a very basic principle: Hot air rises and cold air falls. So while the super-cooled air in the grocery store freezer settles down around the food, the hot air in a hot air balloon pushes up, keeping the balloon floating above the ground. In order to understand more about how this principle works in hot air balloons, it helps to know more about hot air balloons themselves.

A hot air balloon has three major parts: the basket, the burner, and the envelope. The basket is where passengers ride. The basket is usually made of wicker. This ensures that it will be comfortable and add little extra weight. The burner is positioned above the passenger's heads and produces a huge flame to heat the air inside the envelope. The envelope is the colorful fabric balloon that holds the hot air. When the air inside the envelope is heated, the balloon rises The pilot can control the up-and-down movements of the hot air balloon by regulating the heat in the envelope. To ascend, the pilot heats the air in the envelope. When the pilot is ready to land, the air in the balloon is allowed to cool and the balloon becomes heavier than air. This makes the balloon descend.

Before the balloon is launched, the pilot knows which way the wind is blowing. This means that she has a general idea about which way the balloon will go. But, sometimes the pilot can actually control the direction that the balloon flies while in flight. This is because the air above the ground is sectioned into layers in which the direction of the wind may be different. So even though the pilot can't steer the balloon, she can fly or higher or lower into a different layer of air. Some days the difference between the direction of the wind between layers is negligible. But other days the difference is so strong that it can actually push the balloon in a completely different direction!

Using the passage as a guide, it can be inferred that which of the following statements is true?

A. Air goes up and out the top of a chimney when you light a fire.

B. Cool air collects about the ceiling when you open a refrigerator.

C. Smoke from a candle rises after you blow out the flame.

D. Cold air coming from an air conditioning vent settles about the floor.

Q.26 Which of these paintings is / are by Salvador Dali

A. 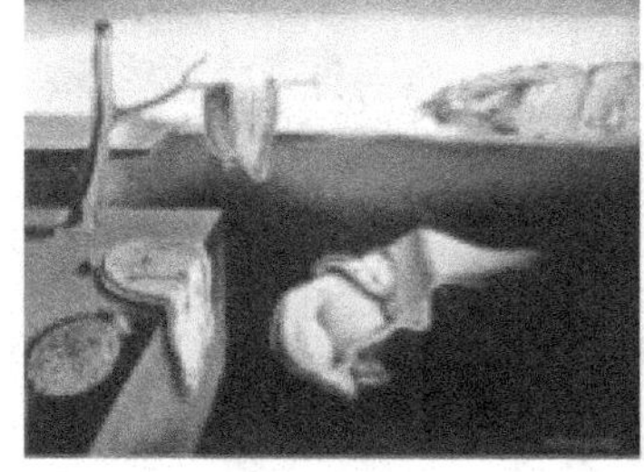

B. 

C. 

D. 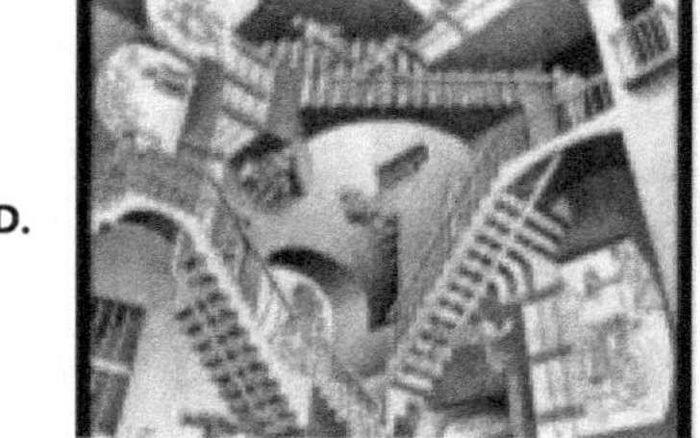

Q.27 From the following, which are the paintings by the famous artist M.F. Husain?

A. 

B. 

C. 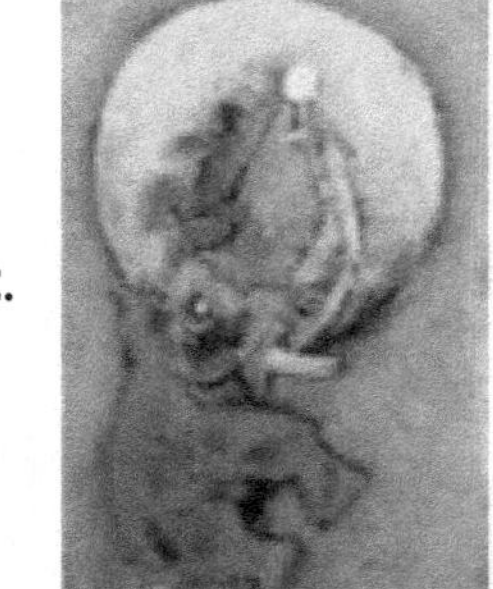

D. 

Q.28 Identify the Indian traditional Art below

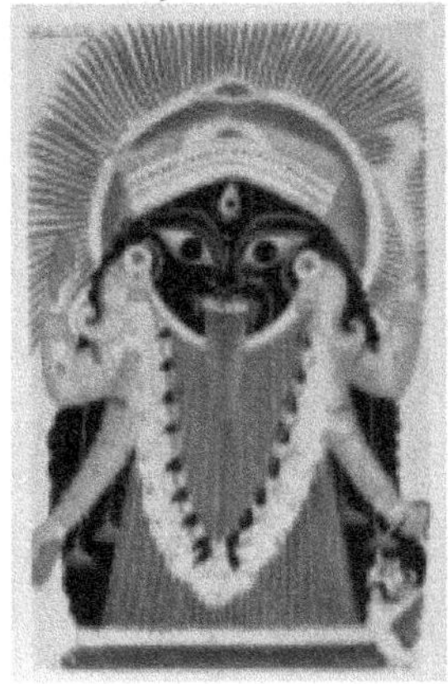

A. Kalamkari **B.** Kalighat
C. Tharu **D.** None of these

Q.29 In this question identify the new shape that could be constructed if the two example shapes were combined. No other change should be made to the two shapes other than combining them.

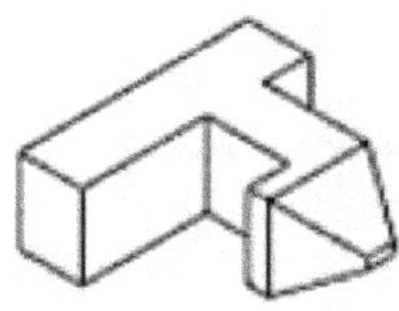
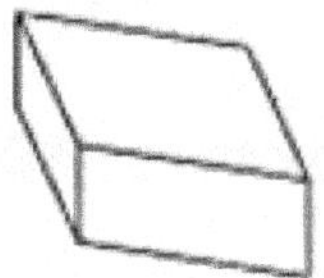

A. 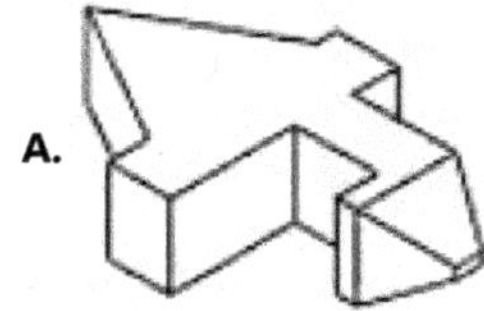

B. 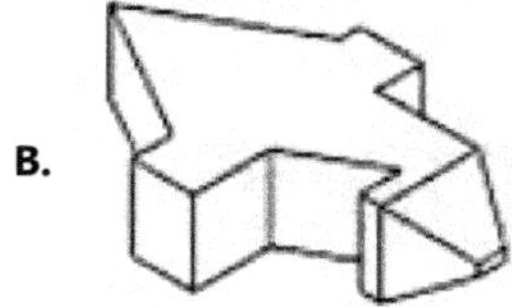

C. 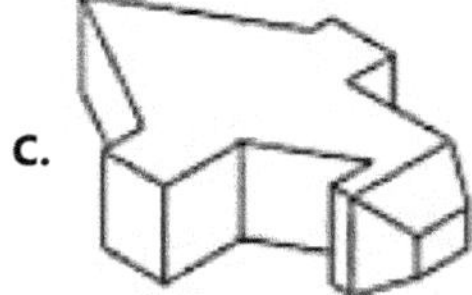

D. None of these

Q.30 Identify the 3D shape's net.

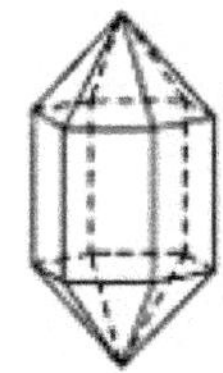

A. 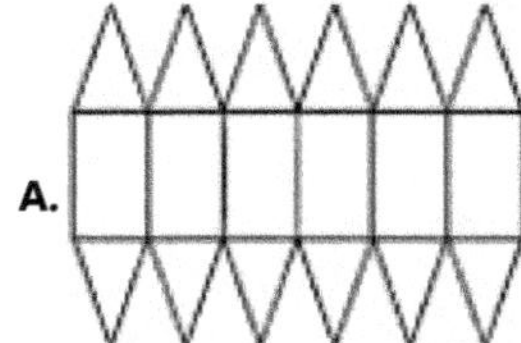

B. 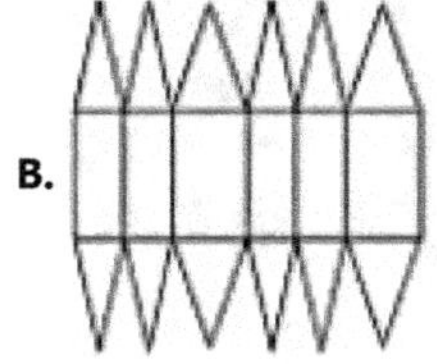

C. 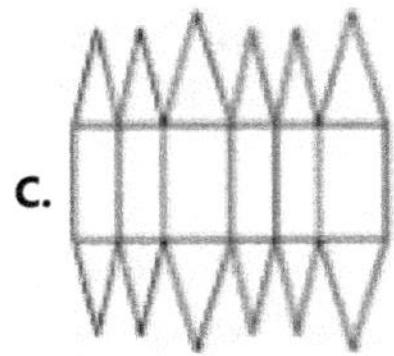

D. None of these

Q.31 Identify the answer shape, which has been rotated but is otherwise the same as the question shape

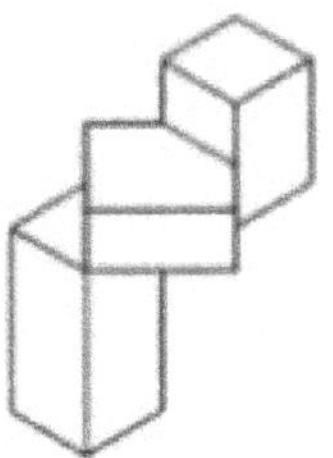

A. 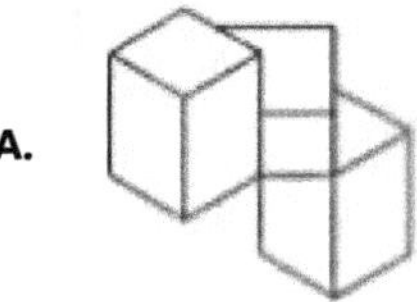

B. 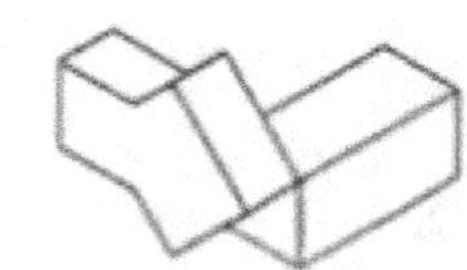

C. 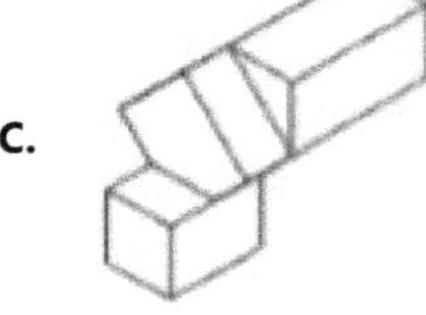

D. None of these

Q.32 Identify the mirror image of the question shape (reject any suggested answer in which any change other than reflection has occurred).

A. 

B. 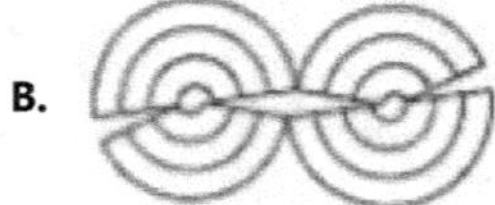

C. 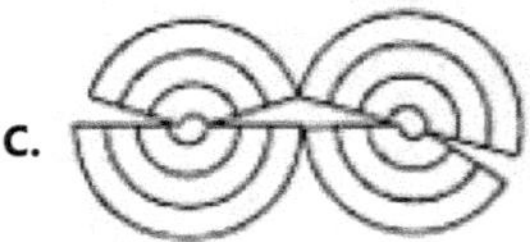

D. None of these

Q.33 Pick the TWO answer choices that will come together to make the figure shown. Pieces may be reflected and or rotated

A. 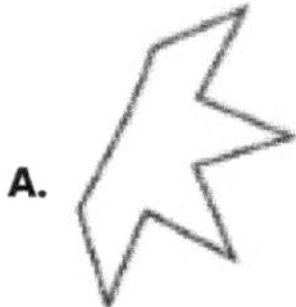 B. 

C. 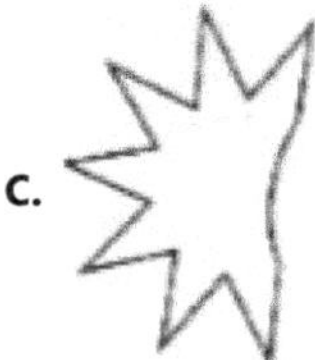 D. 

Q.34 4–5 pieces are given. Choose the answer choice that represents a figure comprised of ALL pieces. Pieces may be rotated and/or reflected.

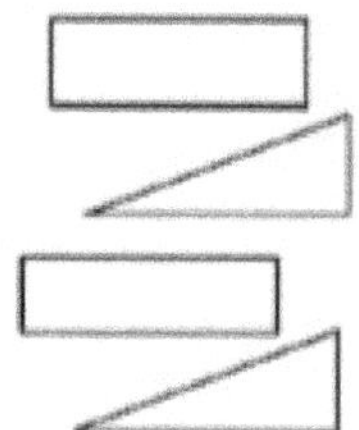

A.  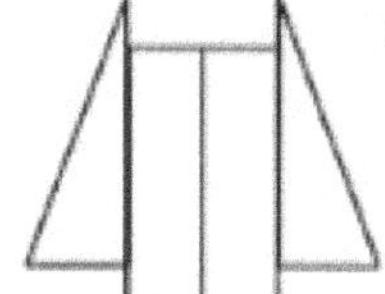 B. 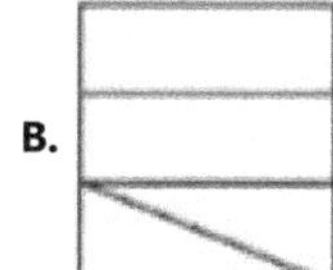

C. 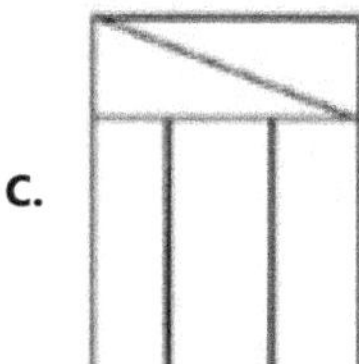 D. 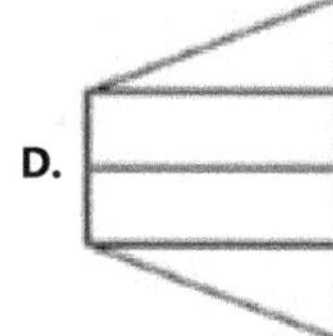

Q.35 A square is cut into 7 pieces as shown on the extreme left of the image. Identify which of the options can be made using all 7 pieces.

A.  B. 

C.  D. 

Q.36 Which of the following terms are related to Architecture?

A. Vernacular **B.** Pragmatic

C. Arcade **D.** Fenestration

Multiple Choice Questions (MCQ)

Q.37 Identify the correct art techniques with which the following paintings have been made.

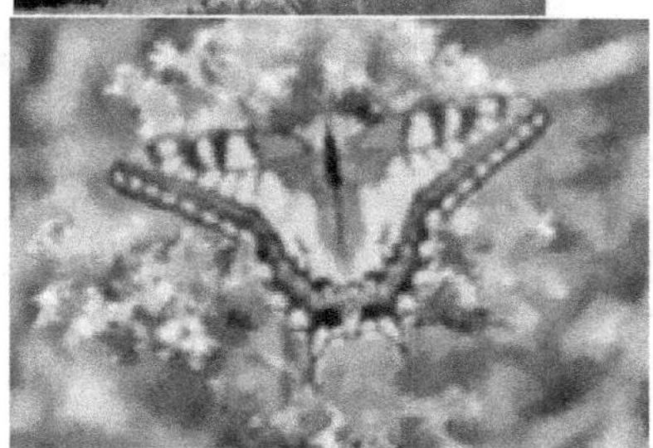

A. Watercolor, Crayon, Pastel, Oil

B. Watercolor, oil, Crayon, Acrylic
C. Acrylic, Crayon, Oil, Watercolor
D. Watercolor, Crayon, Pastel, Acrylic

Q.38 Identify the correct art techniques with which the following paintings have been made.

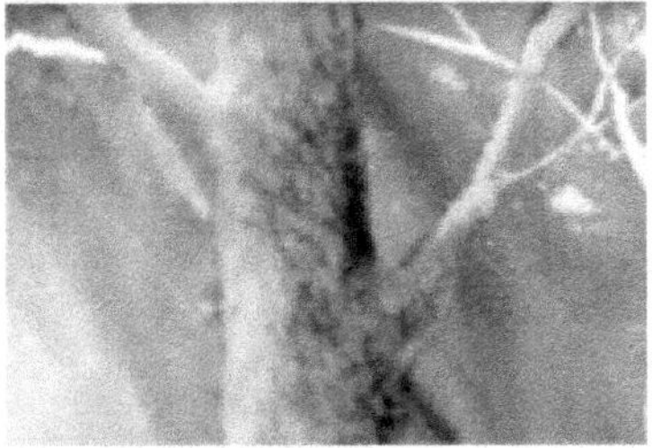

A. Oil, Pastel, Crayon, Watercolor
B. Pastel, Oil, Crayon, Acrylic
C. Oil, Watercolor, Crayon, Pastel
D. Oil, Watercolor, Pastel, Crayon

Q.39 To create a sense of depth in a painting using color, which of these do you need to execute:

A. Warm reds in the foreground, cool reds in the background
B. Light and de-saturated colors in the background
C. Cool colors in the middle to distant background
D. All of the above

Q.40 A convex lens will make an image appear _____ if the object is placed between the focal point and the lens.

A. Smaller and upside down
B. Smaller and right side up
C. Larger and upside down
D. Larger and right side up

Q.41 Which of the following parts of the camera has the same function as the lens in the eye

A. Shutter B. Diaphragm
C. Focusing ring D. Lens

Q.42 A pen placed into a glass of water does not appear as normal.
What property of light is responsible for the pen appearing as it does?

A. Refraction B. Dispersion
C. Reflection D. Combination

Q.43 Shown are the symbols for different functions. Identify the correct description sequence from the given choices.

A. Industrial vehicles, Biohazard, Oxidizing, Corrosive
B. Industrial vehicle, Oxidizing, Biohazard, Corrosive
C. Industrial vehicle, Corrosive, Flammable, biohazard
D. Industrial vehicle, Oxidizing, Corrosive, Biohazard

Q.44 Complete the series

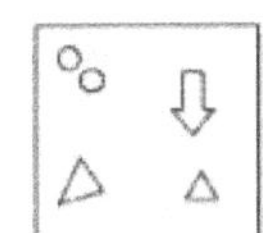 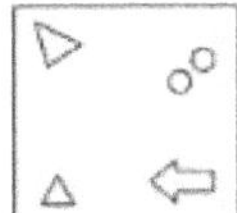 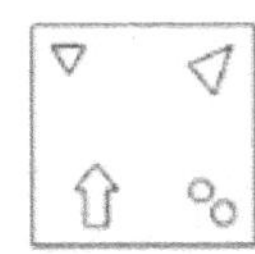 

A. 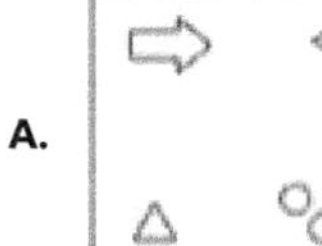

B. 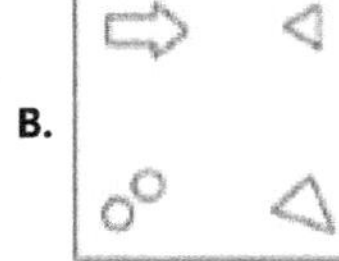

C. 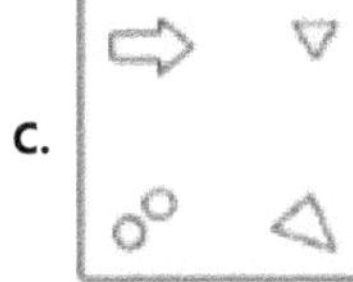

D. 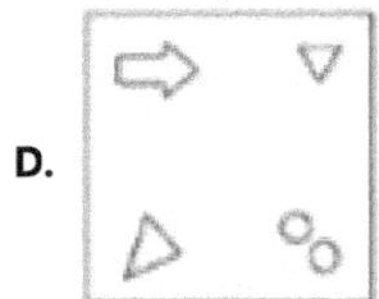

Q.45 Complete the series:

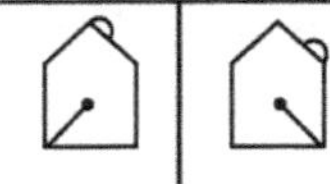 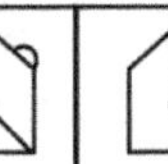 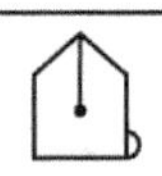  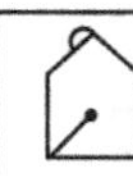 

A. 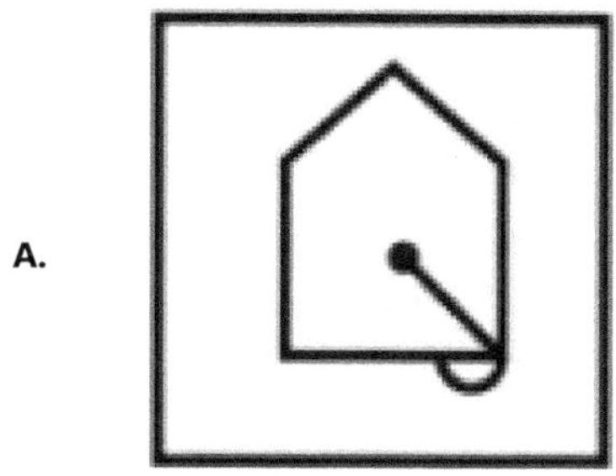

B. 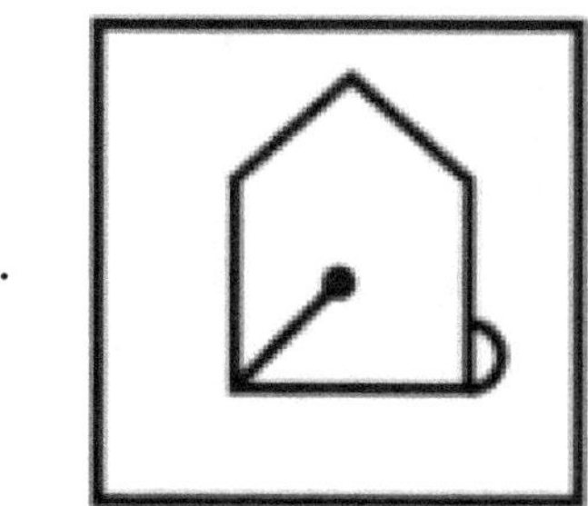

C. 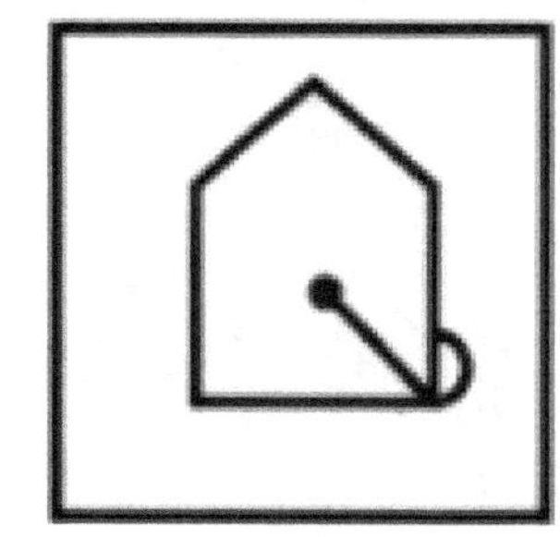

D. 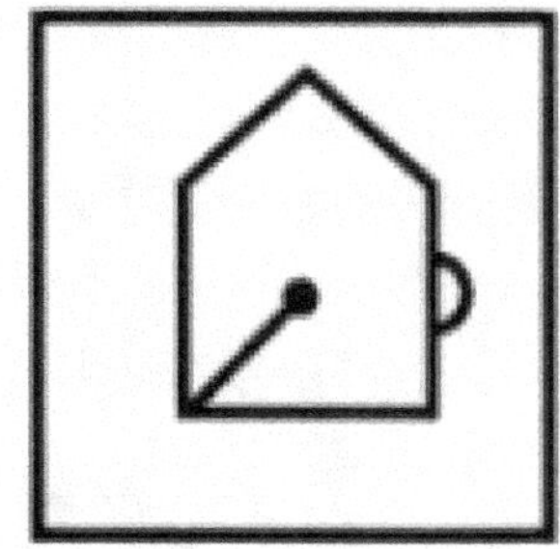

Q.46 There are eight rules which when applied to the sequence will transform it to one of the four options shown below. Identify the correct option.

AB Delete the last character

BC Replace the third character with the next in the alphabet

CD Insert the letter P between the third and fourth characters

DE Exchange the first and last characters

EF Replace the second character with the previous letter in the alphabet

FG Replace the fifth character with the next in the alphabet

GH Reverse the whole sequence of letters

HI Delete the third characterTTOHSP = BC + FG + DE + HI =

A. TTHTP **B.** PTHTP **C.** PTPHTT **D.** PTHTT

Q.47 In the following question, there is a specific relationship between the first and second figure. The same relationship exists between the third and fourth figure which will replace the question mark (?). Select the correct figure from the alternatives given.

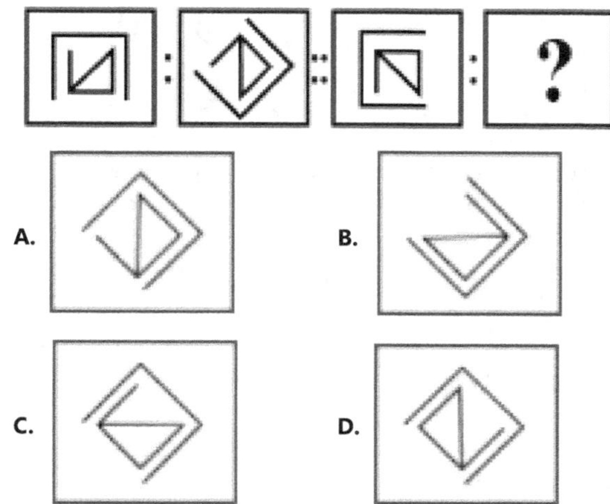

Q.48 Choose the alternative which closely resembles the water-image of the given combination.

D 6 Z 7 F 4

A. DeZ\E4 B. ᗡeZ\ᴲ4

C. DeZ\E4 D. ᗡeZ7ᴲ4

Q.49 Find out from amongst the four alternatives as to how the pattern would appear when the transparent sheet is folded at the dotted line.

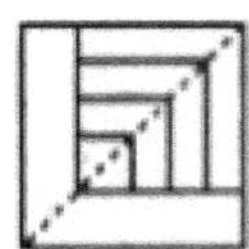

A. 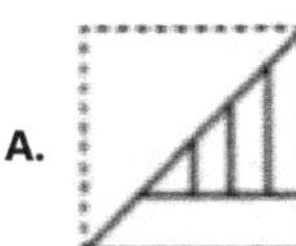 B. 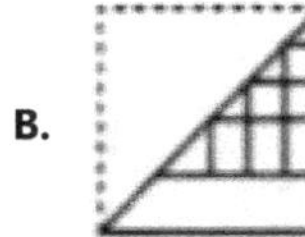

C. 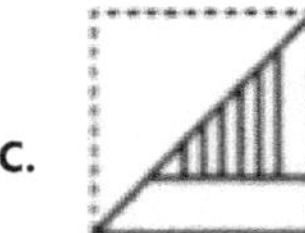 D. 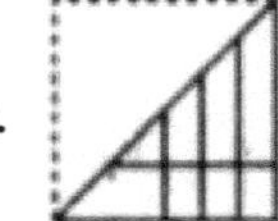

Q.50 Choose a figure, which would most closely resemble the unfolded form of Figure (Z).

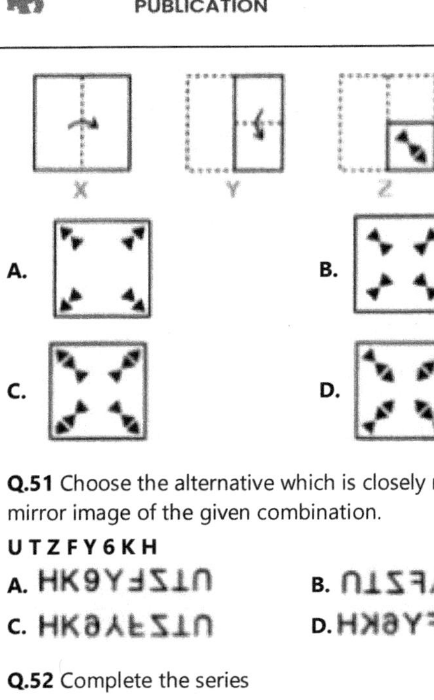

Q.51 Choose the alternative which is closely resembles the mirror image of the given combination.

U T Z F Y 6 K H

A. HK9YꟻZTU
B. UTZꟻY9KH
C. HK6YꟻZTU
D. HKƏYꟻZTU

Q.52 Complete the series

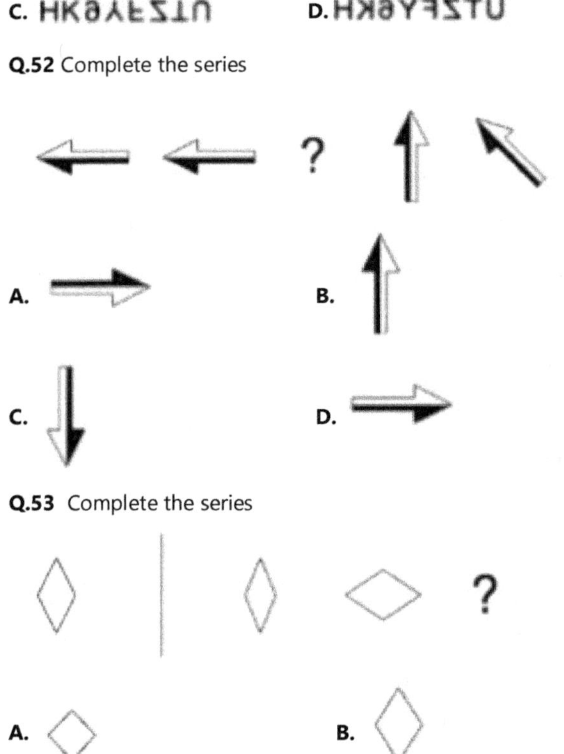

Q.53 Complete the series

Q.54 What will be the most probable pose at position 4 to complete the sequence below?

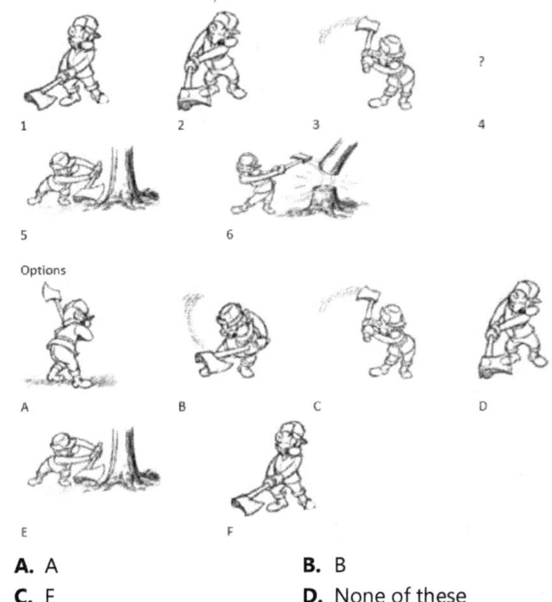

A. A
B. B
C. F
D. None of these

Q.55 Spot the difference.

Below are two apparently identical pictures. In fact, there are differences between the two—Spot them

A. 5 **B.** 6 **C.** 7 **D.** 8

Q.56 In each question, an incomplete statement (Stem) followed by fillers is given. Pick out the best one which can complete incomplete stem correctly and meaningfully.

The weather outside was extremely pleasant and hence we decided to ......

A. Utilize our time in watching the television
B. Refrain from going out for a morning walk
C. Enjoy a morning ride in the open
D. Employ this rare opportunity for writing letters

Q.57 Rearrange the following five sentences in proper sequence to form a meaningful paragraph, then answer the questions given below.

1. But by then it was too late to correct things.
2. It is impossible to steer such a large project to success without planning.
3. He had to standby and watch helplessly.
4. The whole scheme was destined, to fail from the beginning.
5. Bhaskar started realizing this only towards the end.

A. 25431 **B.** 24531 **C.** 12543 **D.** 12534

Q.58 Read the following five sentences in the proper sequence so as to form a meaningfull paragraph, then answer the questions given below them.

1. I reached office at 11 O' clock after sending the money.
2. Some money had to be sent to my parents.
3. After that, I spent almost an hour at the Post Office.
4. Therefore, I went to bank to withdraw some money.
5. However, I had no money with me.

A. 25431 **B.** 24531 **C.** 12543 **D.** 12534

Q.59 Pick up the one which is most nearly the same in meaning as the word printed in bold and can replaces it without altering the meaning of the sentence.

The visitor had a **bohemian** look

A. Hostile **B.** Unconventional
C. Sinister **D.** Unfriendly

Q.60 Direction: Choose the word which best expresses the meaning of the underlined word in the sentence.

The attitude of western countries towards third-world countries is rather callous, to say the least.

A. Cursed **B.** Kind
C. Unfeeling **D.** Passive

Q.61 Identify the product shown below.

A. Paper tube **B.** Candleholder
C. Wall paint roller **D.** Newspaper

Q.62 Arrange according to order (past to present) for the car pictures (A to D).

1.

2.

3.

4.

A. 1234 **B.** 4312 **C.** 3142 **D.** 4123

Q.63 A famous historic sculpture is shown in the picture, what it is called?

A. Thinking David **B.** Vinci at sea
C. The thinker **D.** Venus de Millo

Q.64 Identify the tools shown below and also state for what it is used for

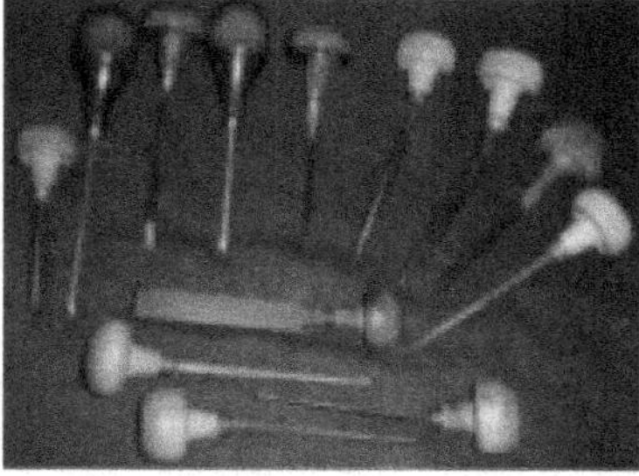

A. Wood carving **B.** Clay modeling
C. Wax engraving **D.** Painting

Q.65 Varaha temple is an example of which style of architecture

A. Rock cut architecture
B. Indo Islamic architecture
C. Colonial Architecture
D. None of the above

Q.66 Below given view is popularly known as

A. Dog eye view
B. Three-point perspective
C. Fish eye view
D. Worms eye view

Q.67 In the following question choose the word, which is the exact OPPOSITE of the given words.

ARTIFICIAL

A. Red **B.** Natural **C.** Truthful **D.** Solid

Q.68 In the following question choose the word, which is the exact OPPOSITE of the given words.

EXODUS

A. Influx **B.** Home-coming
C. Return **D.** Restoration

// Smart Answer Sheet //

Correct Indicates percentage of students who answered questions correctly.

Skipped Indicates percentage of students who skipped questions.

Q.	Ans.	Correct	Skipped
1	23	18.31 %	4.23 %
2	#	40.85 %	15.49 %
3	15	66.2 %	15.49 %
4	11	28.17 %	15.49 %
5	25	59.86 %	16.9 %
6	54	56.34 %	19.01 %
7	15	49.3 %	19.01 %
8	126	73.24 %	16.9 %
9	27	13.38 %	17.61 %
10	18	45.77 %	16.2 %
11	3	54.23 %	17.6 %
12	10	49.3 %	20.42 %
13	#	54.23 %	16.19 %
14	6	59.86 %	19.01 %

Q.	Ans.	Correct	Skipped
15	15	61.97 %	17.61 %
16	13	36.62 %	21.83 %
17	32	14.79 %	24.65 %
18	#	12.68 %	19.71 %
19	B, A, C	15.49 %	26.76 %
20	B, A, C	27.46 %	26.77 %
21	B, D	16.9 %	30.28 %
22	C	42.25 %	23.95 %
23	C	42.25 %	22.54 %
24	B	53.52 %	21.83 %
25	A, D, C	51.41 %	25.35 %
26	B, A, C	44.37 %	24.64 %
27	A, D, C	42.25 %	25.36 %
28	B	60.56 %	20.43 %

Q.	Ans.	Correct	Skipped
29	B	53.52 %	21.13 %
30	B	15.49 %	20.43 %
31	C	51.41 %	21.83 %
32	B	71.13 %	20.42 %
33	B, D	71.13 %	21.12 %
34	C	44.37 %	20.42 %
35	A, D	26.06 %	26.76 %
36	A, D, C	25.35 %	26.06 %
37	A	57.04 %	15.5 %
38	C	52.11 %	16.2 %
39	D	57.75 %	19.71 %
40	D	38.03 %	17.6 %
41	D	51.41 %	16.2 %
42	A	69.01 %	19.72 %

Q.	Ans.	Correct	Skipped
43	A	66.9 %	17.61 %
44	C	66.2 %	17.6 %
45	C	39.44 %	23.94 %
46	D	62.68 %	19.71 %
47	A	47.18 %	21.13 %
48	C	66.9 %	17.61 %
49	A	77.46 %	17.61 %
50	C	77.46 %	18.31 %
51	D	77.46 %	18.31 %
52	A	21.13 %	19.01 %
53	C	55.63 %	19.72 %
54	B	71.13 %	19.01 %
55	B	27.46 %	19.72 %
56	C	66.9 %	19.02 %

Q.	Ans.	Correct	Skipped
57	A	21.13 %	19.72 %
58	A	54.93 %	20.42 %
59	B	51.41 %	21.13 %
60	C	19.72 %	21.13 %
61	C	78.87 %	18.31 %
62	C	64.08 %	19.02 %
63	C	56.34 %	20.42 %
64	A	54.23 %	19.01 %
65	A	69.72 %	20.42 %
66	D	65.49 %	19.72 %
67	B	77.46 %	18.31 %
68	A	40.85 %	22.53 %

#

Q.	Answer
2	North
13	F
18	25

Performance Analysis	
Avg. Score (%)	45.42%
Toppers Score (%)	110.42%
Your Score	

//Hints and Solutions//

1.

1. ✥	9. ❉	17. ★
2. ✝	10. ❖	18. ●
3. ✳	11. ▼	19. ❍
4. ✳	12. ✪	20. ◆
5. ✿	13. ✥	21. ▲
6. ❄	14. ✡	22. ✷
7. ❆	15. ✹	23. ☆
8. ✱	16. ☮	

2.

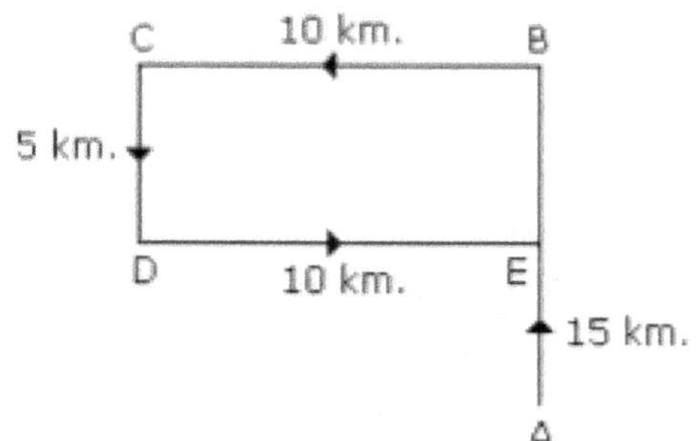

Therefore, it is clear that he is in the North from his house.

3. There are 15 lines.

4. There are 11 different circles.

5. TUB will have 25 surfaces.

6. One side of the big cube $-\sqrt[3]{125} - 5cm$

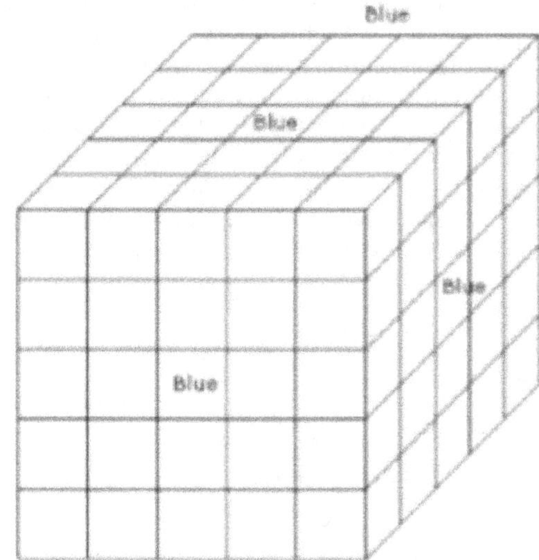

No. of small cubes having only one face coloured $=$

$(5-2)2 \times 6 = 9 \times 6$

$= 54$

7. In this case we have to equate the following:

$5^{*}21 = 7^{*}?$

$= 5^{*}21/7$

$= 15$ days.

8. There are 126 cubes.

6 ×6+6 ×5+6 ×4+6 ×3+6 ×2+6 ×1=126.

9.

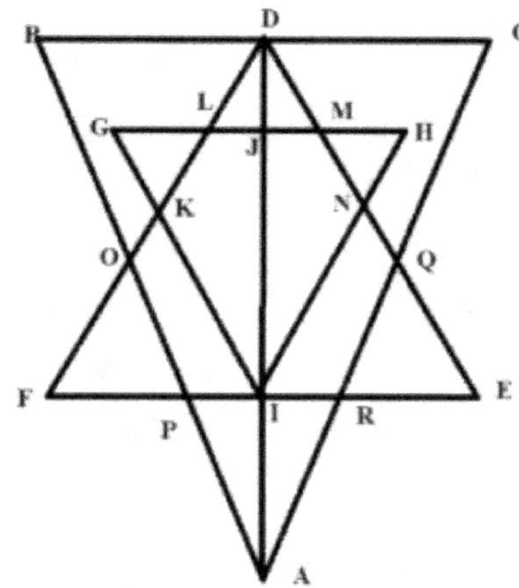

In the figure the triangles are GLK, DLJ, DJM, HMN, QRE, IRA, IPA, FPO, BDO, CDQ, DLM, PRA, KFI, NEI, HJI, GJI, DKI, DNI, DIE, DFI, DOA, DQA, GHI, DCA, DBA, DEF and ABC

Total number of triangles = 27

Hence, the correct answer is 27.

10. The figure may be labelled as shown.

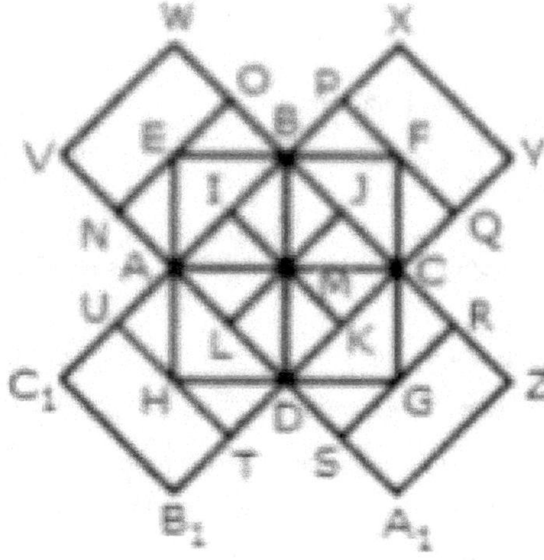

The squares composed of two components each are BJMI, CKMJ, DLMK and AIML i.e. 4 in number.

The squares composed of three components each are EBMA, BFCM, MCGD and AMDH i.e. 4 in number.

The squares composed of four components each are VWBA, XYCB, ZA1DC and B1C1AD i.e. 4 in number.

The squares composed of seven components each are NOJL, PQKI, RSLJ and TUIK i.e. 4 in number.

There is only one square i.e. ABCD composed of eight components.

There is only one square i.e. EFGH composed of twelve componenents.

11. The figure may be labeled as shown.

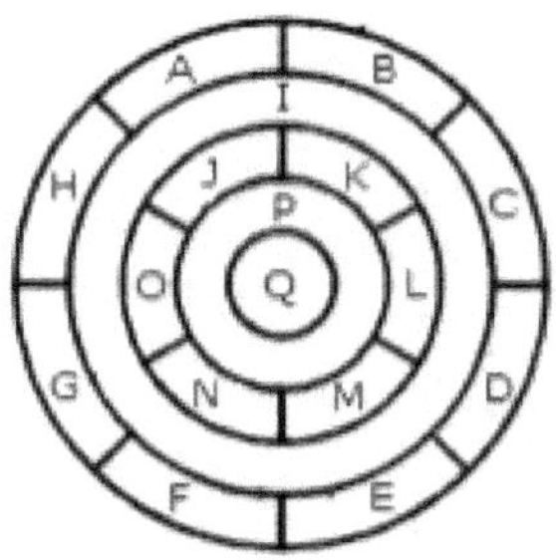

The regions A, C, E and G can have the same colour say colour 1. The regions B, D, F and H can have the same colour (but different from colour 1) say colour 2.

The region 1 lies adjacent to each one of the regions A, B, C, D, E, F, G and H and therefore it should have a different colour say colour 3.

The regions J, L and N can have the same colour (different from colour 3) say colour 1.

The regions K, M and O can have the same colour (different fromthe colours 1 and 3). Thus, these regions will have colour 2.

The region P cannot have any of the colours 1 and 2 as it lies adjacent to each one of the regions J, K, L, M, N and O and so it will have colour 3.

The region Q can have any of the colours 1 or 2.

Minimum number of colours required is 3.

12. Jack 10

13. The correct is F.

14. The total of the numbers in each column alternates 20, 30, 20, 30, 20, 30

15. There are 15 surfaces.

16. The numbers in each circle total 100.

17. The number inside the triangle is obtained by dividing the product of the numbers outside of the triangle by 10. Thus,

In I triangle, $(5 \times 6 \times 4) \div 10 = 12$

In II triangle, $(6 \times 7 \times 5) \div 10 = 21$

$\therefore$ In III triangle, missing number $\Rightarrow (4 \times 8 \times 10) \div 10 = 32$

Hence, the correct answer is 32.

18. From figure a: $6 + 4 + 8 = 18$

$18 + 2 = 20$

From figure b: $7 + 9 + 8 = 24$

$24 + 2 = 26$

From figure c: $6 + 5 + 12 = 23$

$23 + 2 = 25$

Hence, the correct answer is 25.

19. A,B,C are true

20. A,B, C are true

21. option B and D is correct.

22. Science and Humanism are equally important.

Hence option C is correct.

23. The government cannot sell off public sector units just to pool up funds for development. Besides, if it does so, these units shall be handed over to private companies which are fully equipped to run these units effectively. So, neither I nor II holds strong. Privatization shall surely ensure better services, but private companies adopt hire and fire policy and they are free to terminate the services of any employee as and when they wish to. Thus, both III and IV hold strong.

24. Clearly, the statement is made to impress the usefulness of the book. It does not mention the desire of a layman. So, I is not implicit. Also, the book is intended to guide one when a teacher is not available. So, both II and III are implicit.

25. In paragraph 1, we learn that "Hot air rises and cold air falls." Therefore, the cool air inside a refrigerator would fall to the floor when you open the door, not collect about the ceiling. This means (B) is not true. When you have a fire, the air inside the chimney is hot. Therefore, it can be inferred that air goes up and out the top of a chimney when you have a fire. (A) is correct. Smoke is hot. So it rises. Therefore, it can be inferred that smoke from a candle rises after you blow out the flame. (C) is correct. Cold air falls. Therefore, it can be inferred that cold air coming from an air conditioning vent settles about the floor. (D) is correct.

26. option A, B and C are correct.

27. option A, C and D is correct.

28. option B is correct.

29. In a) the rhomb has been truncated, and in c) the 'roof' shape has been truncated.

30. a) shows a different form with regular sides, and in c) the big triangles are too long.

31. In a) and b) one of the parallelepipeds has been shortened.

32. In a) the left shape has been moved to the right and the right shape to the left and both have been slightly rotated, and in c) only the left shape has been reflected.

33. b+d

34.

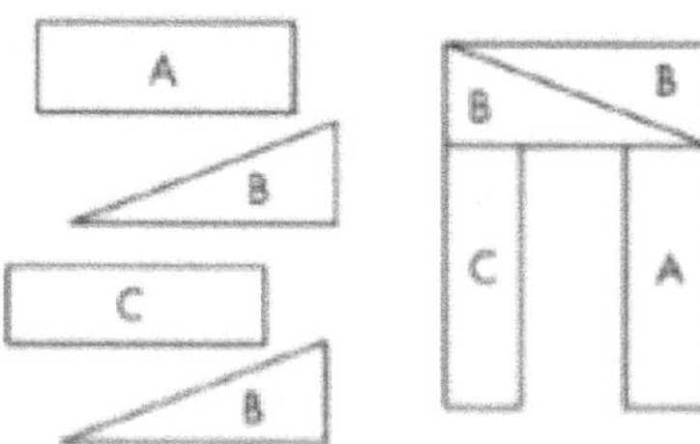

35. option A and D is correct.

36. option A, C and D is correct.

37. Watercolor, Crayon, Pastel, Oil

38. Oil, Watercolor, Crayon, Pastel

39. All of the above

40. A convex lens is also known as a converging lens. A converging lens is a lens that converges rays of light that are traveling parallel to its principal axis. They can be identified by their shape which is relatively thick across the middle and thin at the upper and lower edges. The edges are curved outward rather than inward. As light approaches the lens, the rays are parallel. As each ray reaches the glass surface, it refracts according to the effective angle of incidence at that point of the lens. Since the surface is curved, different rays of light will refract to different degrees; the outermost rays will refract the most. This runs contrary to what occurs when a divergent lens (otherwise known as concave, biconcave or plano-concave) is employed. In this case, light is refracted away from the axis and outward.

41. our Cornea behaves much like the front lens element of a lens. Together with the lens, which is behind the iris, they are the eye's focusing elements. ... As with the camera, if the "film" is bad in the eye (retina), no matter how good rest of the eye is, we will not get a good quality image or picture.

42. Refraction is the reason that pen does not looks normal.

43. Industrial vehicles, Biohazard, Oxidizing, Corrosive

44. option C is correct.

45. As it is evident from the diagrams, the line in the center of the pentagon moves 4, 3, 2, 1 spaces and the small semi-circle moves one space and in the last figure moves 2 spaces.

So in the next figure, the circle moves 2 spaces and the line moves four spaces.

Hence, the correct option is (C).

46. First replace the O with P and then the S with T, next exchange the first T and last P to give PTPHTT and finally delete the second P.

47.

In the first pair, the outer shape rotates 135° clockwise, and the innermost shape flips and rotates 45° clockwise.

So, the next pair will follow the same pattern.

Hence, the correct option is (A).

48. option C is water-image of D 6 Z 7 F 4.

49. option A is correct.

50. option C iscorrect.

51. option D is mirror image of U T Z F Y 6 K H.

52. option A will replace the ?

53. option C will replace ?

54. option B will come at position 4.

55. 6 differences

56. Enjoy a morning ride in the open

57. The correct order is-

2- It is impossible to steer such a large project to success without planning.

5- Bhaskar started realizing this only towards the end.

4- The whole scheme was destined, to fail from the beginning.

3- He had to standby and watch helplessly.

1- But by then it was too late to correct things.

The correct order is 25431.

Hence, the correct option is (A).

58. 25431

Hence option A is correct.

59. bohemian means Unconventional.

60. The underlined word 'callous' means an insensitive or cruel disregard for others. It refers to the character or nature of a person or a group.

Option (C): 'Unfeeling' means 'unsympathetic, lacking sensitivity. It expresses the meaning of 'callous'. So (C) is correct.

Option (A): 'Cursed' means 'damned or doomed'. It does not refer to a behavioral trait.

Option (B): 'Kind' is a positive trait that refers to someone who is generous and considerate. It's the opposite of 'callous'.

Option (D): 'Passive' means 'unresponsive, submissive'. It does not explain the underlined word.

Hence, the correct option is (C).

61. Wall paint roller

62. 3142

Hence option C is correct.

63. The Thinker

Hence option C is correct.

64. The above tools are used for Wood carving.

65. Rock cut architecture

Hence option A is correct.

66. Worms eye view

Hence option D is correct.

67. Natural is opposite of Artificial.

68. Influx is opposite of Exodus.

Mock Test 10

Numerical Answer Type (NAT)

Q.1 Umesh directly went from P, to Q, which is 9 feet distant. Then he turns to the right and walked 4 feet. After this he turned to the right and walked a distance, which is equal from P to Q. Finally, he turned to the right and walked 3 feet. How far is he now from P?

Q.2 How many circles contain a black dot?

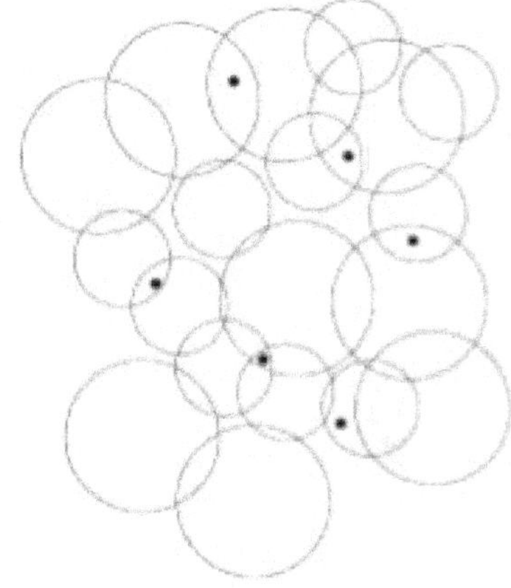

Q.3 Find the missing number:

6	9	15
8	12	20
4	6	?

Q.4 All the faces of a cube are painted with blue color. Then it is cut into 125 small equal cubes. How many small cubes will be formed having no face colored?

Q.5 A photograph measuring 9.5 cm by 7.5 cm is to be enlarged. If the enlargement of the longest side is 11.4 cm, what is the length of the smallest side?

Q.6 Count the number of cubes in the given figure.

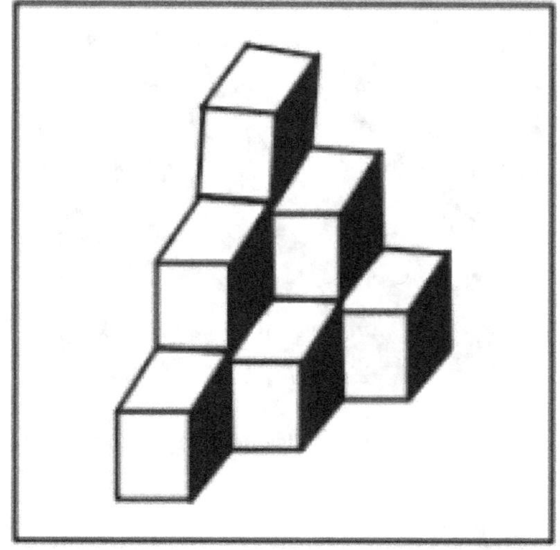

Q.7 Find the number that will replace ? in the figure given below:

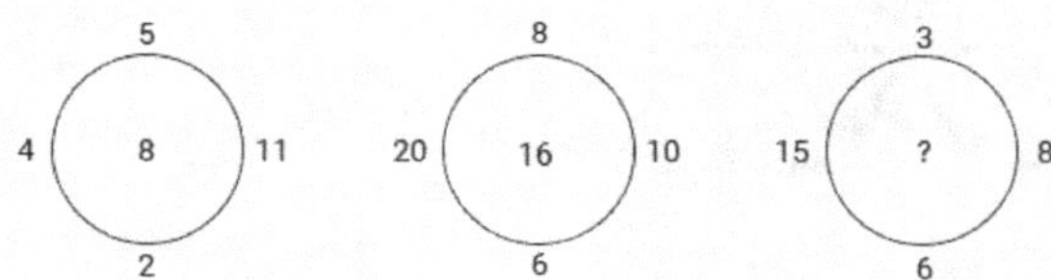

Q.8 Count number of unique patterns in the given grid.

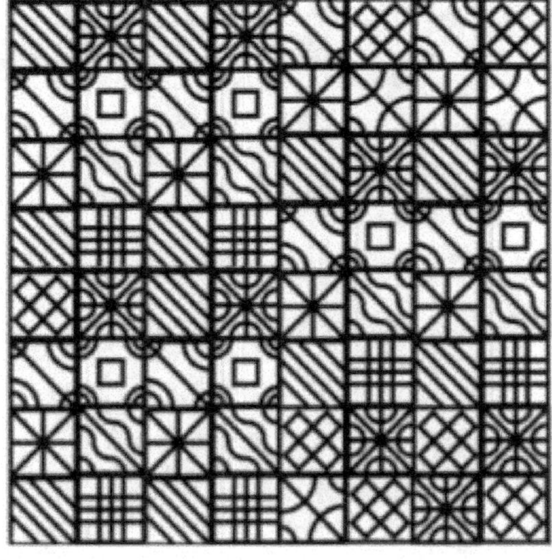

Q.9 Count the number of children reading open books.

Q.10 Count the number of parallelogram in the given figure.

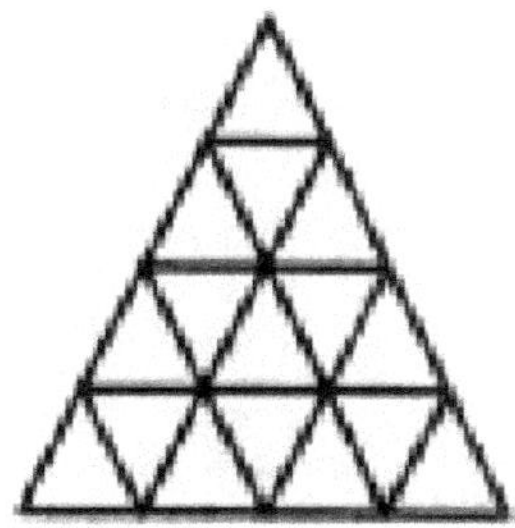

Q.11 In eight years time the combined age of me and my two sons will be 124. What will it be in five years time?

Q.12 What number should replace the question mark?
1000, 865, ?, 595, 460, 325

Q.13

A	B	C	D	E	
F	G	H	I	J	
K	L	M	N	O	
P	Q	R	S	T	
U	V	W	X	Y	Z

What letter is immediate to the left of the letter that is immediately below the letter two to the left of the letter I?

Q.14 What number should replace the question mark?

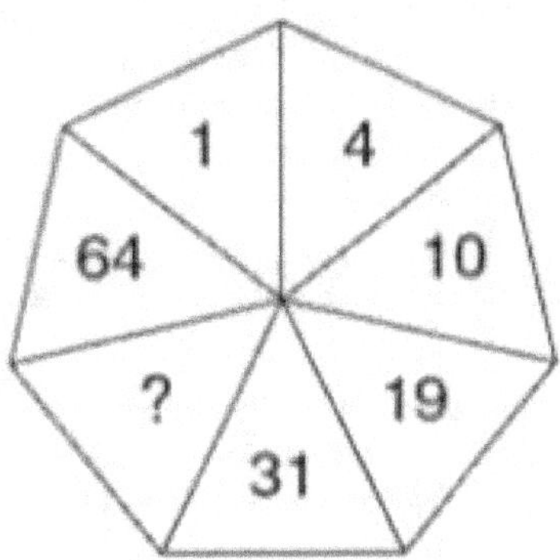

Q.15 SUNDAY MONDAY TUESDAY WEDNESDAY THURSDAY FRIDAY SATURDAY

What day comes three days after the day which comes two days after the day which comes immediately after the day which comes two days after Monday?

Q.16 What value of weight should be placed on the scales to balance?

Q.17 Row 1 shows a word with 7 partial letters. Row 2 contains the parts that complete the word in Row 1. The parts in Row 2 are arranged randomly. What should be the correct sequence in Row 2?

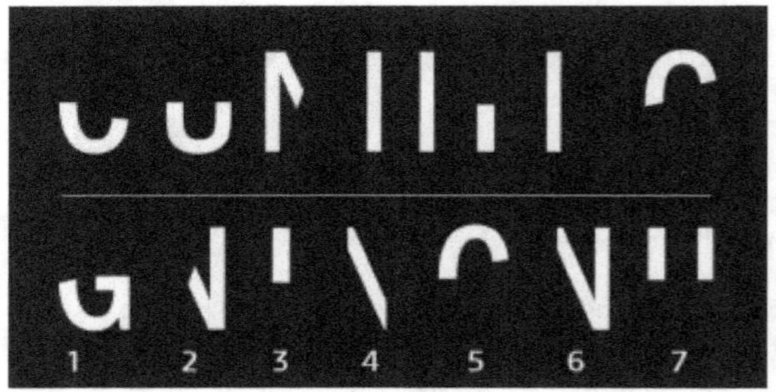

Q.18 Find out the total number of surfaces of the object, given below in the problem figure. Problem figure

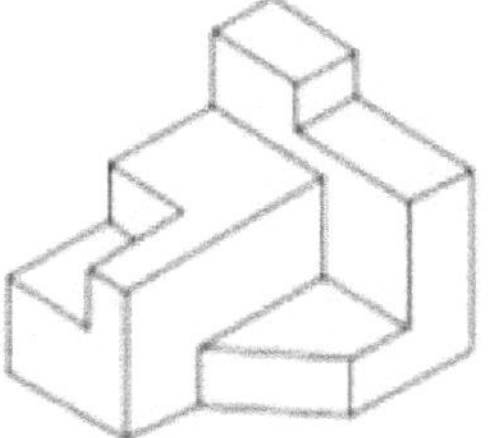

Multiple Select Questions (MSQ)

Q.19 Which of the following statements is/are true?

A. Ernest Hemingway was a Nobel Prize-winning American writer who touched the pinnacles of fame with his novel

'The Old Man and the Sea' which catapulted him to international glory.

B. Often remembered as the Father of Modern Astronomy, Galileo Galilee was one of the most celebrated and illustrious neurosurgeon in the history of mankind

C. Ustad Ali Akbar Khan was one of the most renowned Sarod maestros.

D. Aryabhata was an acclaimed mathematician-astronomer. At the age of 24, he wrote his famed "Aryabhatiya", was aware of the concept of zero. He was the first to calculate the value for 'pi' accurately to the fourth decimal point.

Q.20 Select the statements below that are TRUE.

A. The Big Bang Theory is the leading explanation about how the universe began. At its simplest, it talks about the universe as we know it starting with a small singularity, then inflating over the next 13.8 million years to the cosmos that we know today

B. Because current instruments don't allow astronomers to peer back at the universe's birth, much of what we understand about the Big Bang Theory comes from mathematical theory and models.

C. Astronomers can, however, see the "echo" of the expansion through a phenomenon known as the cosmic microwave background.

D. While astronomers could see the universe's beginnings, they've also been seeking out proof of its rapid inflation. Theory says that in the first second after the universe was born, our cosmos ballooned faster than the speed of light.

Q.21 From the options below, select the Indian author/s writing in English whose works are represented below:

1. Maximum city
2. Mountain echoes
3. The white tiger
4. Paro
5. Selection day
6. A Himalayan love story

A. Khushwant Singh **B.** Namita Gokhale
C. Aravinda Adiga **D.** Suketu Mehta

Q.22 Question given below consists of a statement, followed by three arguments numbered I , II and III. You have to decide which of the arguments is a 'strong' argument. Statement: Should the public sector undertakings be kilo wed to adopt hire and fire policy?

Arguments:

I. Yes. This will help the public sector undertakings to get rid of non-performing employees and reward the performing employees.

II. No. This will give an unjust handle to the management and they may use it indiscriminately.

III. Yes. This will help increase the level of efficiency of these organizations and these will become profitable establishments.

A. Only I and II are strong
B. Only II and III are strong
C. Only I and III are strong
D. All are strong

Q.23 Question below is given a statement followed by three assumptions numbered I, II and III. You have to consider the statement and the following assumptions and decide which of the assumptions is implicit in the statement. Statement: "Wanted a two bedroom flat in the court area for immediate possession." - An advertisement.

I. Flats are available in court area.

II. Some people will respond to the advertisement.

III. It is a practice to give such an advertisement.

A. All are implicit
B. Only II is implicit
C. None is implicit
D. Only I and II are implicit

Q.24 Modern economies do not differentiate between renewable and non-renewable materials, as its method is to measures everything by means of a money price. Thus, taking various alternatives fuels, like coal, oil, wood or water power: the only difference between them recognized by modern economics is relative cost per equivalent unit. The cheapest is automatically the one to be preferred, as to do otherwise would be irrational and 'uneconomic'. From a Buddhist point of view of course this will not do, the essential difference between non-renewable fuels like coal and oil on the one hand and renewable fuels like wood and waterpower on the other cannot be simply overlooked. Non-renewable goods must be used only if they are indispensable, and then only with the greatest care and the highest concern for conservation. To use them carelessly or extravagantly is an act of violence, and while complete non-violence may not be possible on earth, it is nonetheless the duty of man to aim at deal of non-violence in all he does. Which of the following statements may be assumed to be false from the information in the passage?

1. The writer finds the attitude of modern economists towards natural resources to be uneconomic.
2. Buddhist economists are in different to the cost of fuels
3. To use oil on non-essentials is contrary to the Buddhist economic philosophy.
4. To fell a tree is an act of violence not permitted by Buddhist economists?

A. 1 and 2 are false
B. 1, 2 and 4 are false
C. 3 and 4 are false
D. All 1, 2, 3, and 4 are false

Q.25 Which of the paintings below is from the artist Edward Munch?

A. 

B. 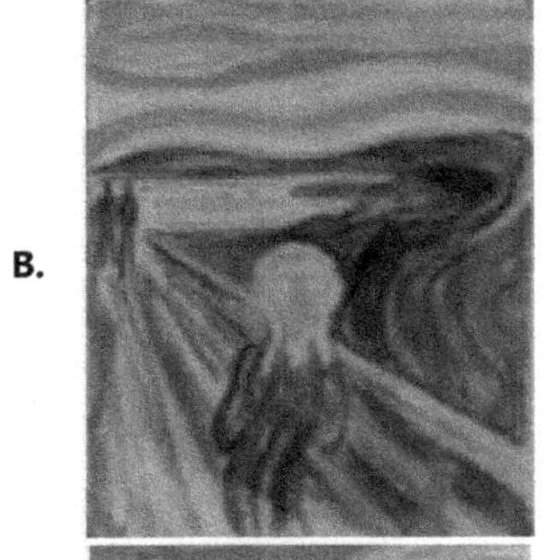

C. 

D. 

Q.26 Identify from the following, the paintings by Vilas Chormale.

A. 

B. 

C. 

D. 

Q.27 Name the states of the folk art forms below in their respective order

Kangra Painting

Tanjore painting

A. Himachal Pradesh and Tamil Nadu
B. Bihar and Maharashtra
C. Himachal Pradesh and Karnataka
D. Kerala and Karnataka

Q.28 Your hand will cast a shadow on a wall in the sunlight.

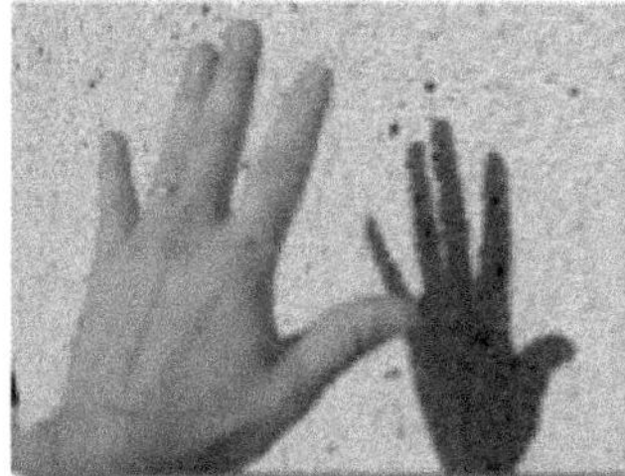

What statement is best describes the formation of the shadow?

A. Black rays of light emit from the area on the wall behind the hand.
B. Light rays are reflected from the wall where the shadow occurs.
C. Light rays are refracted from the wall where the shadow occurs.
D. The hand blocks the light rays striking it, result in the shadow on the wall.

Q.29 Which of the following statements is/are true?

A. Charles Mingus was one of the most important figures of 20th century American music. He was an eminent Rock musician and his music was impregnated with emotions.
B. Regarded as one of the 'most important thinkers of the last century', Sigmund Freud is considered the father of 'psychoanalysis', who revolutionized the study of dreams with his magnum opus, 'The Interpretation of Dreams'.
C. Bhaskara II, also known as Bhaskara or as Bhaskaracharya, was a 12th century Indian mathematician and a renowned astronomer who accurately defined many astronomical quantities, including the length of the sidereal year, discovered the principles of differential calculus and its application to astronomical problems and computations centuries before European mathematicians like Newton and Leibniz.
D. C.V. Raman was the first Indian to win the Nobel Prize for Physics. He won it for his discovery, 'The Raman Effect'.

Q.30 Which of the following statements is/are true?

A. Location is the major factor responsible for monsoon type of climate in India.
B. Thermal contrast is the major factor responsible for monsoon type of climate in India.
C. Upper air circulation is the major factor responsible for monsoon type of climate in India.
D. All of the above

Q.31 Shown are logos of different companies/organizations. Select the option(s) that identifies the designer of the logo.

A. Devashish Bhattacharya
B. Benoy Shankar
C. Vikas Satwalekar
D. R. K. Joshi

Q.32 Which of the following terms are related to industrial design?

A. Metering **B.** Jugendstil
C. PU / PUR **D.** Stereolithography

Q.33 A square is cut into 7 pieces as shown on the extreme left of the image. Identify which of the options can be made using all 7 pieces.

A. 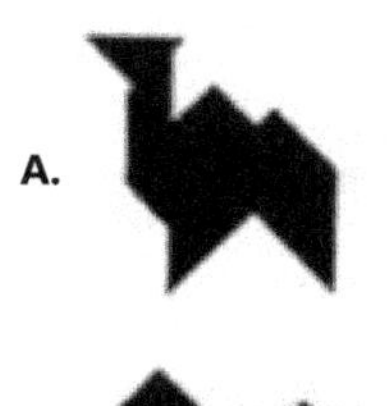 B. 

C.  D.

Q.34 4–5 pieces are given. Choose the answer choice that represents a figure comprised of ALL pieces. Pieces may be rotated and/or reflected.

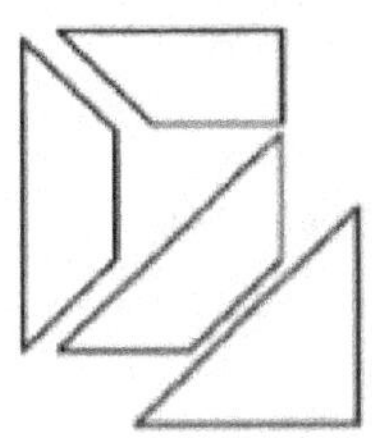

A. 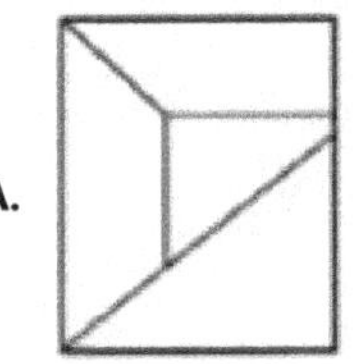 B. 

C. 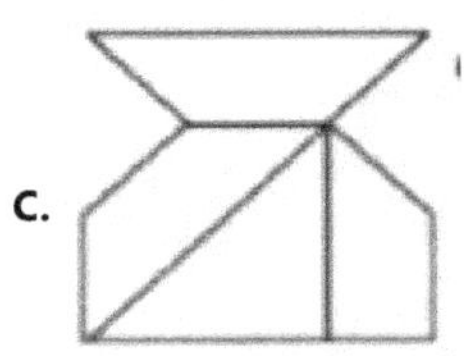 D. 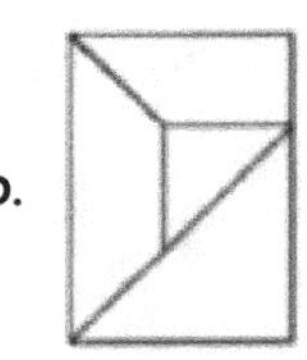

Q.35 Identify the mirror image of the question shape (reject any suggested answer in which any change other than reflection has occurred).

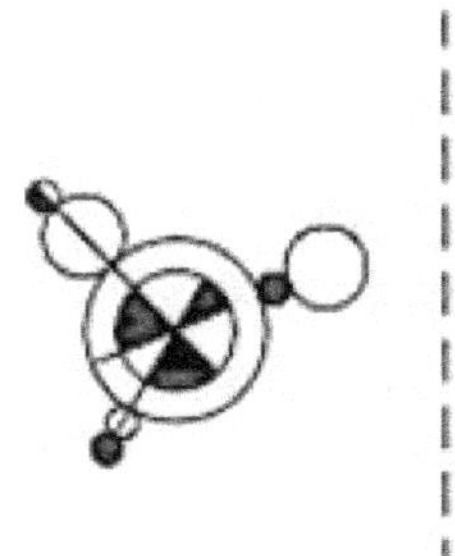

A. 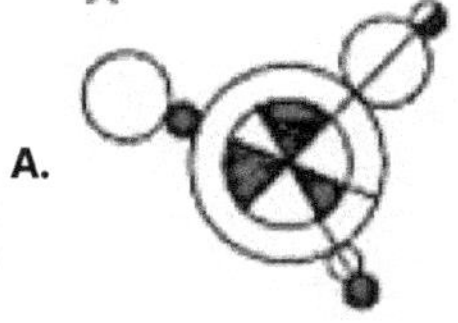 B. 

C.  **D.** None of these

Q.36 Identify the answer shape, which has been rotated but is otherwise the same as the question shape.

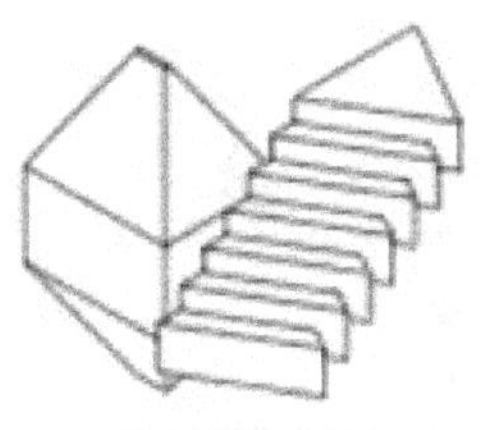

A. 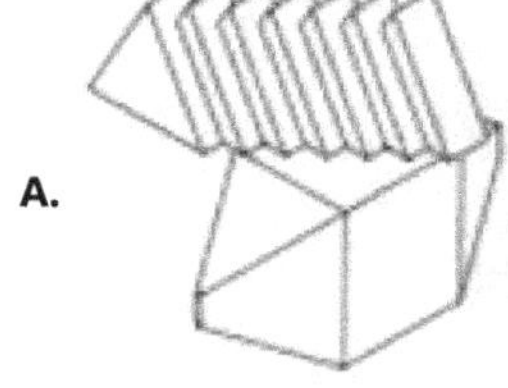 B. 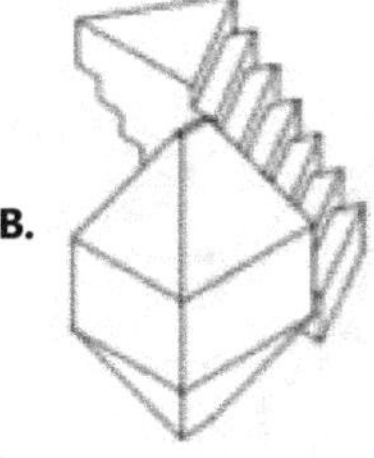

C. 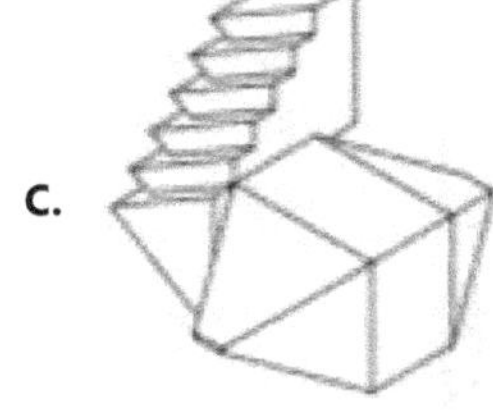 **D.** None of these

Multiple Choice Questions (MCQ)

Q.37 Complete the series

 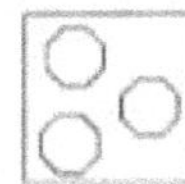 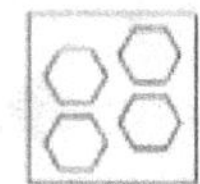  

A. 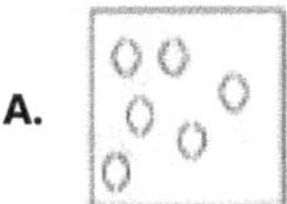 B. 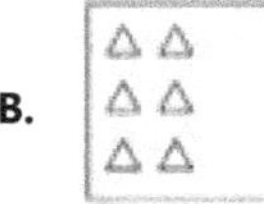

C. 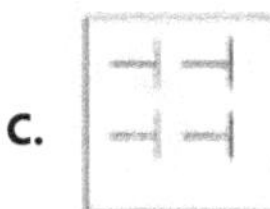 D. 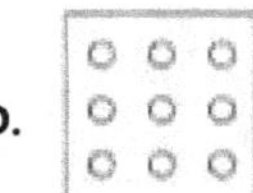

Q.38 There are eight rules which when applied to the sequence will transform it to one of the four options shown below. Identify the correct option.

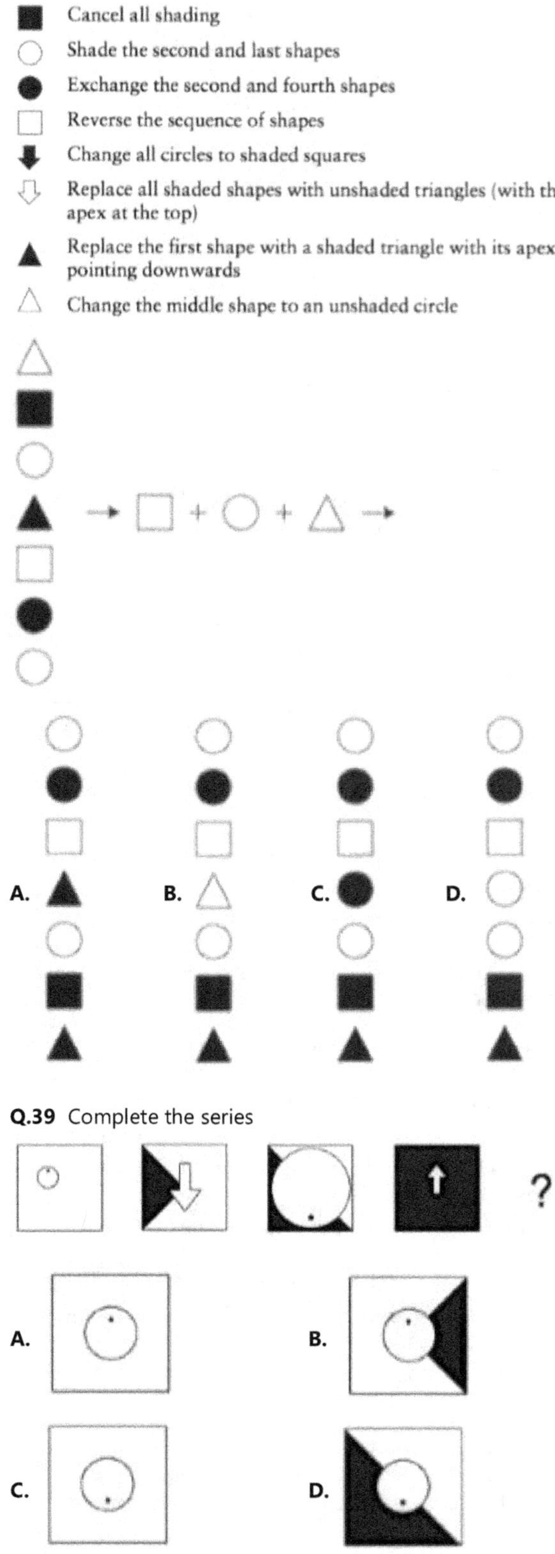

Q.39 Complete the series

Q.40 There are eight rules which when applied to the sequence will transform it to one of the four options shown below. Identify the correct option.

AB Delete the last character

BC Replace the third character with the next in the alphabet

CD Insert the letter P between the third and fourth characters

DE Exchange the first and last characters

EF Replace the second character with the previous letter in the alphabet.

FG Replace the fifth character with the next in the alphabet

GH Reverse the whole sequence of letters

HI Delete the third character RCCUMJA = GH + CD + EF + GH =

A. AIMUPCCA **B.** RICUPMMA
C. RCCUPMIA **D.** RICUMJA

Q.41 Choose the alternative which is closely resembles the water-image of the given combination.

bridge

(1) pɿ!qɡe (2) pʟ!qɡe
(3) pɿ!qɡe (4) pʟ!pɡe

A. 1 **B.** 2 **C.** 3 **D.** 4

Q.42 Find out from amongst the four alternatives as to how the pattern would appear when the transparent sheet is folded at the dotted line.

  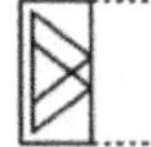 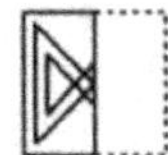 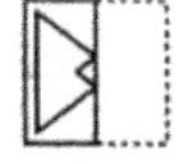

A. 1 **B.** 2 **C.** 3 **D.** 4

Q.43 Choose a figure which would most closely resemble the unfolded form of Figure (Z).

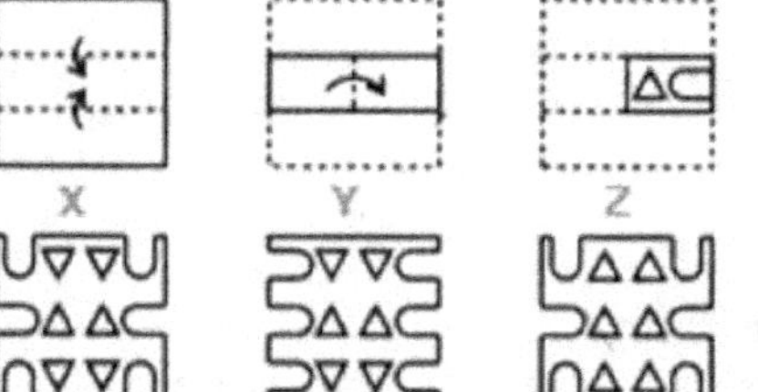

A. 1 **B.** 2 **C.** 3 **D.** 4

Q.44 Choose the correct mirror image of the given figure (X) from amongst the four alternatives.

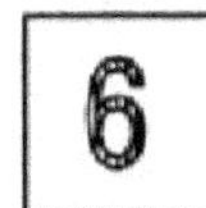   

A. 1 **B.** 2 **C.** 3 **D.** 4

Q.45 What will be the most probable pose at position 4 to complete the sequence below?

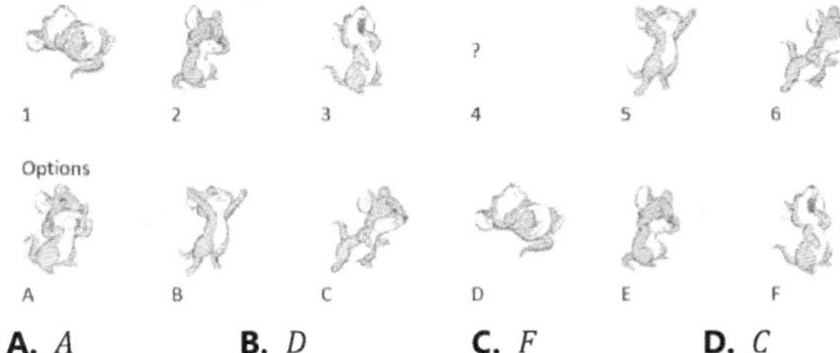

A. *A* **B.** *D* **C.** *F* **D.** *C*

Q.46 Spot the difference. Below are two apparently identical pictures. In fact, there are differences between the two—Spot them

A. 5 **B.** 6 **C.** 7 **D.** 8

Q.47 In each question, an incomplete statement (Stem) followed by fillers is given. Pick out the best one, which can complete incomplete stem correctly and meaningfully. Owing to the acute power shortage, the people of our locality have decided to...

A. dispense with other non-conventional energy sources
B. resort to abundant use of electricity for illumination
C. off-switch the electrical appliance while not in use
D. resort to use of electricity only when it is inevitable

Q.48 Rearrange the following five sentences in proper sequence to form a meaningful paragraph, then answer the questions given below.

1. Kiran received a call to attend the interview.
2. He applied for a new job.
3. Kiran was an ambitious boy.
4. But, he was not happy there.
5. His father had put him in a clerical job.

A. 35421 **B.** 34521 **C.** 32145 **D.** 35412

Q.49 Pick up the one which is most nearly the same in meaning as the word printed in bold and can replaces it without altering the meaning of the sentence.

It is very difficult to **retain** all that you hear in the class.

A. Keep **B.** Recall
C. Preserve **D.** Conserve

Q.50 Pick up the one which is most nearly the same in meaning as the word printed in bold and can replaces it without altering the meaning of the sentence.

The great artist life was full of **vicissitudes**.

A. Sorrows **B.** Misfortunes
C. Changes **D.** Surprises

Q.51 It was Sunday on Jan 1, 2006. What was the day of the week Jan 1, 2010?

A. Sunday **B.** Saturday
C. Friday **D.** Wednesday

Q.52 In the following questions choose the word that is the exact OPPOSITE of the given words.

ENORMOUS

A. Soft **B.** Average **C.** Tiny **D.** Weak

Q.53 In the following questions choose the word that is the exact OPPOSITE of the given words.

COMMISSIONED

A. Started **B.** Closed
C. Finished **D.** Terminated

Q.54 In the questions below the sentences have been given in Direct/Indirect speech. From the given alternatives, choose the one which best expresses the given sentence in Indirect/Direct speech.

"If you don't keep quiet I shall shoot you", he said to her in a calm voice.

A. He warned her to shoot if she didn't keep quiet calmly.
B. He said calmly that I shall shoot you if you don't be quiet.
C. He warned her calmly that he would shoot her if she didn't keep quiet.
D. Calmly he warned her that be quiet or else he will have to shoot her.

Q.55 In the questions below the sentences have been given in Active/Passive voice. From the given alternatives, choose the one which best expresses the given sentence in Passive/Active voice.

After driving professor Kumar to the museum she dropped him at his hotel.

A. After being driven to the museum, Professor Kumar was dropped at his hotel.
B. Professor Kumar was being driven dropped at his hotel.
C. After she had driven Professor Kumar to the museum she had dropped him at his hotel.
D. After she was driven Professor Kumar to the museum she had dropped him at his hotel.

Q.56 In the questions below the sentences have been given in Active/Passive voice. From the given alternatives, choose the one which best expresses the given sentence in Passive/Active voice.

I remember my sister taking me to the museum.

A. I remember I was taken to the museum by my sister.
B. I remember being taken to the museum by my sister.
C. I remember myself being taken to the museum by my sister.
D. I remember taken to the museum by my sister.

Q.57 Pick out the most effective word(s) from the given words to fill in the blank to make the sentence meaningfully complete.

Fate smiles ...... those who untiringly grapple with stark realities of life.

A. with **B.** over **C.** on **D.** round

Q.58 Pick out the most effective word(s) from the given words to fill in the blank to make the sentence meaningfully complete.

The miser gazed ...... at the pile of gold coins in front of him.

A. avidly **B.** admiringly
C. thoughtfully **D.** earnestly

Q.59 Direction: Select the most appropriate word to fill in the blanks.

Thomas did not ______ the vegetables because he was busy.

A. bringing **B.** bought
C. had bought **D.** bring

Q.60 Direction: Select the most appropriate word to fill in the blanks.

The teacher needs to find out ______ bag, is it?

A. who's **B.** who **C.** whose **D.** which

Q.61 In the questions given below, a part of the sentence is italicised. Below are given alternatives to the italicized part, which may improve the sentence. Choose the correct alternative. In case no improvement is needed, option 'D' is the answer.

The workers are *hell bent at* getting what is due to them.

A. Hell bent up getting
B. Hell bent for getting
C. Hell bent upon getting
D. No improvement

Q.62 In questions given below, a part of the sentence is italicised and underlined. Below are given alternatives to the italicized part, which may improve the sentence. Choose the correct alternative. In case no improvement is needed, option 'D' is the answer.

When it was feared that the serfs might go too far and gain their freedom from serfdom, the protestant leaders joined the princes *at crushing* them.

A. into crushing **B.** in crushing
C. without crushing **D.** No improvement

Q.63 Look at this series: 2, 1, (1/2), (1/4), ... What number should come next?

A. (1/3) **B.** (1/8) **C.** (2/8) **D.** (1/16)

Q.64

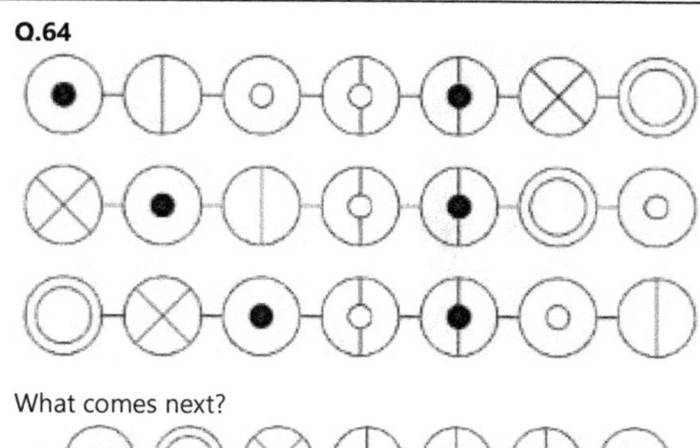

What comes next?

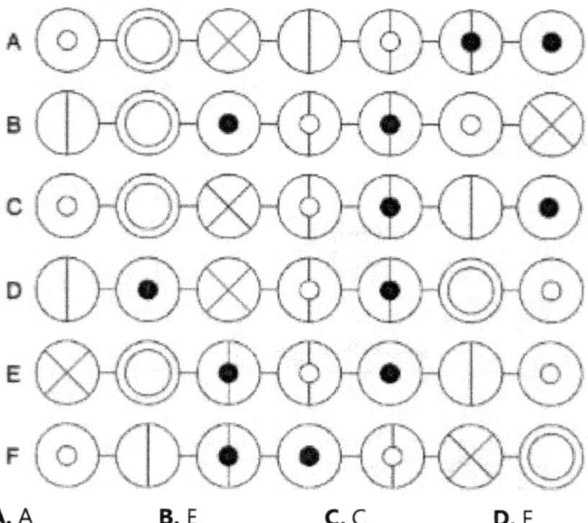

A. A **B.** E **C.** C **D.** F

Q.65

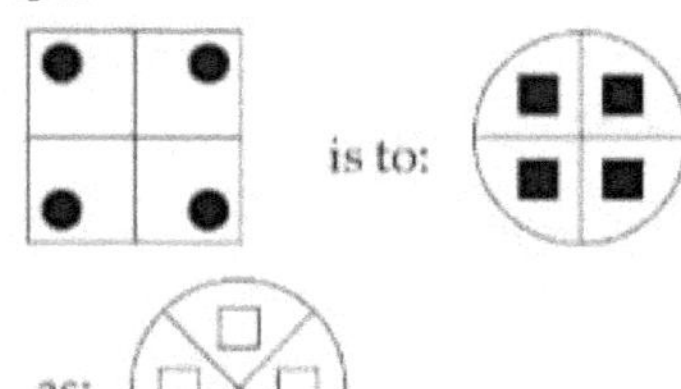

as:

is to:

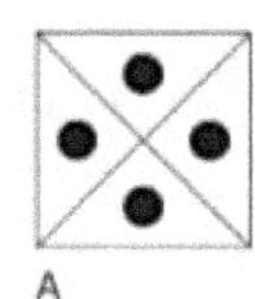
A

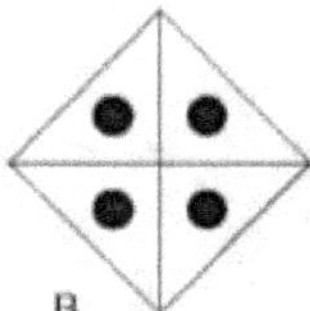
B

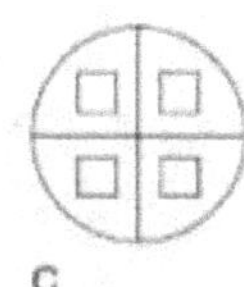
C

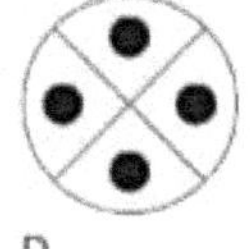
D

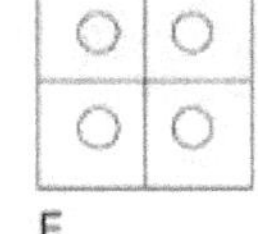
E

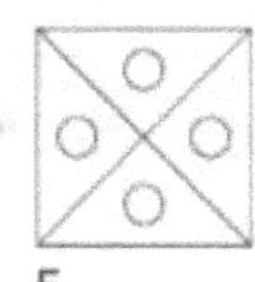
F

A. A **B.** C **C.** E **D.** F

Q.66 Identify the product

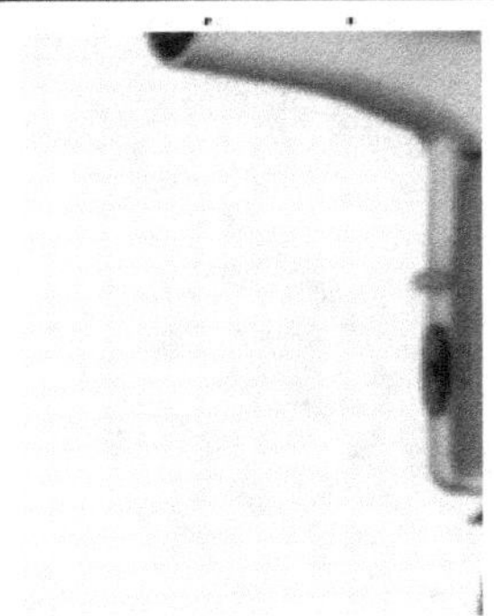

A. Hair dryer
B. Electric drill
C. Gamma sensor
D. None of these

Q.67 Identify the cartoon character.

A. Kendall Perkins
B. Kick Buttowski
C. Brad Buttowski
D. honey buttowski

Q.68 Identify animal from the texture

A. Zebra **B.** Tiger **C.** Giraffe **D.** Squirrel

// Smart Answer Sheet //

Correct Indicates percentage of students who answered questions correctly.

Skipped Indicates percentage of students who skipped questions.

Q.	Ans.	Correct	Skipped
1	1	75.33 %	4.67 %
2	12	72.67 %	15.33 %
3	10	52.67 %	18.0 %
4	27	54.0 %	20.67 %
5	9	47.33 %	21.34 %
6	10	71.33 %	18.0 %
7	14	13.33 %	22.67 %
8	9	51.33 %	18.0 %
9	12	5.33 %	17.34 %
10	45	10.67 %	18.66 %
11	115	39.33 %	21.34 %
12	730	71.33 %	16.67 %
13	#	52.0 %	19.33 %
14	46	62.0 %	20.0 %

Q.	Ans.	Correct	Skipped
15	#	20.0 %	17.33 %
16	7.5	42.67 %	17.33 %
17	5724361	9.33 %	32.67 %
18	16	54.0 %	17.33 %
19	A, D, C	42.0 %	30.0 %
20	B, D, C	12.0 %	30.0 %
21	B, D, C	22.0 %	30.0 %
22	C	24.67 %	28.0 %
23	B	24.67 %	27.33 %
24	B	14.67 %	30.66 %
25	B, D, C	58.0 %	24.0 %
26	B, D, C	44.67 %	29.33 %
27	A	48.0 %	24.0 %
28	D	60.67 %	24.0 %

Q.	Ans.	Correct	Skipped
29	B, D, C	26.67 %	32.0 %
30	D	46.67 %	26.66 %
31	A, D	33.33 %	28.0 %
32	B, D, C	14.0 %	29.33 %
33	B, A, D, C	54.0 %	28.0 %
34	B	22.67 %	22.66 %
35	B	68.0 %	23.33 %
36	B	19.33 %	24.67 %
37	A	35.33 %	21.34 %
38	D	56.0 %	26.0 %
39	A	44.0 %	21.33 %
40	C	62.67 %	26.66 %
41	B	70.0 %	20.67 %
42	B	68.67 %	22.66 %

Q.	Ans.	Correct	Skipped
43	B	68.0 %	21.33 %
44	B	74.0 %	21.33 %
45	A	72.67 %	22.66 %
46	D	13.33 %	22.67 %
47	D	28.67 %	27.33 %
48	A	62.0 %	24.0 %
49	A	21.33 %	24.67 %
50	C	27.33 %	28.67 %
51	C	40.67 %	28.0 %
52	C	58.0 %	23.33 %
53	A	21.33 %	24.67 %
54	C	52.67 %	28.0 %
55	A	36.67 %	27.33 %
56	B	48.67 %	26.66 %

Q.	Ans.	Correct	Skipped
57	C	27.33 %	26.67 %
58	A	31.33 %	28.0 %
59	D	34.67 %	26.0 %
60	C	53.33 %	24.67 %
61	C	17.33 %	28.0 %
62	B	41.33 %	28.67 %
63	B	67.33 %	24.0 %
64	C	52.0 %	24.0 %
65	D	55.33 %	22.67 %
66	A	66.0 %	24.67 %
67	B	58.0 %	27.33 %
68	A	68.67 %	22.66 %

#

Q.	Answer
13	K
15	TUESDAY

Performance Analysis	
Avg. Score (%)	41.25%
Toppers Score (%)	95.42%
Your Score	

//Hints and Solutions//

1.

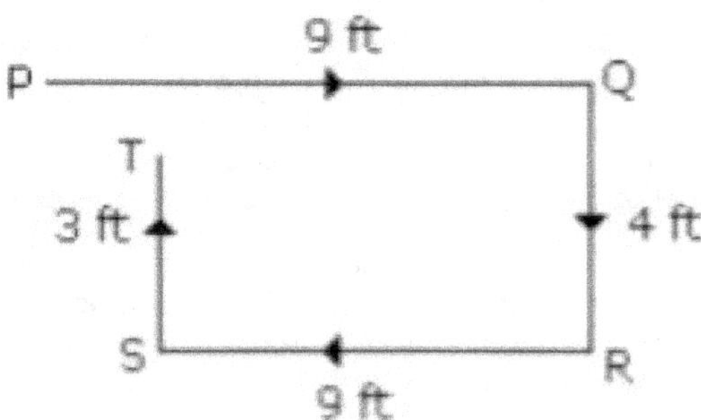

Required distance = 4ft-3ft = 1ft.

2. 12 circles have black dots.

3. First element + second element = Third Element.

6 + 9 = 15

8 + 12 = 20

4 + 6 = 10

Hence, the correct answer is 10.

4. One side of the big cube $= \sqrt[3]{125} = 5cm$

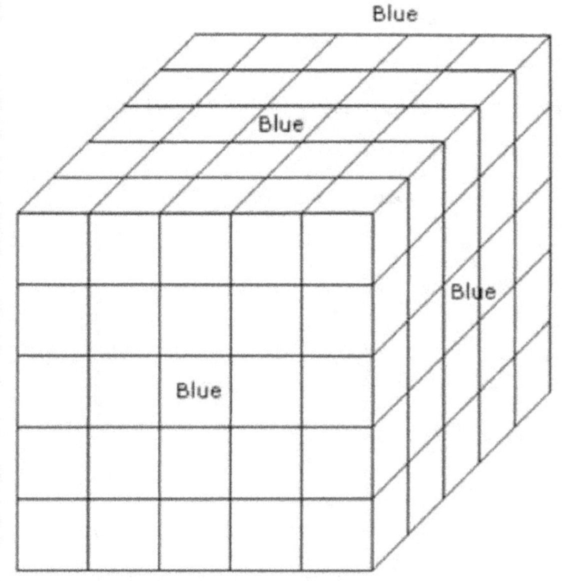

No. of small cubes having no face coloured = (x - 2)3

= (5 - 2)3

= 27

5. Size of shortest side = (11.4 ÷ 9.5) × 7.5 = 9 cm.

6. On the basis of the following pattern in given dices, we can say that six cubes are visible and four cubes are invisible.

Thus, there are 10 cubes.

Hence, the correct answer is 10.

7. In the first case,

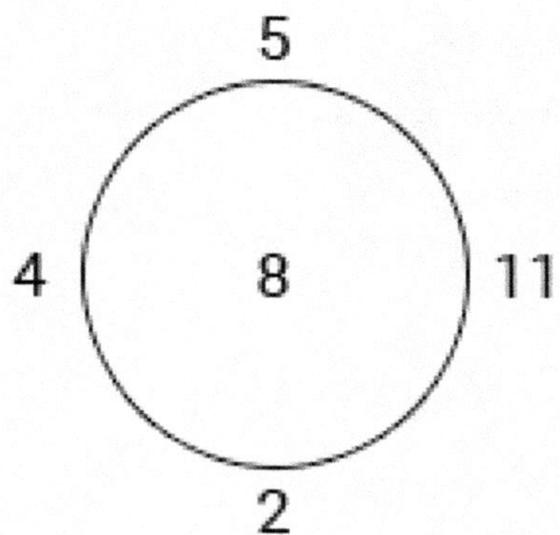

8 = (11+4)-(5+2)

In the second case,

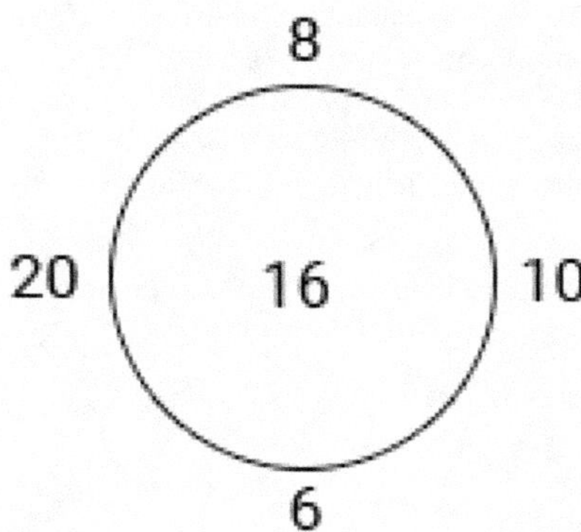

16 = (10+20)-(8+6)

We can see that the difference of the sum values of the horizontally placed numbers and vertically placed numbers is being taken to get the number that is placed inside the circle.

On applying this same logic,

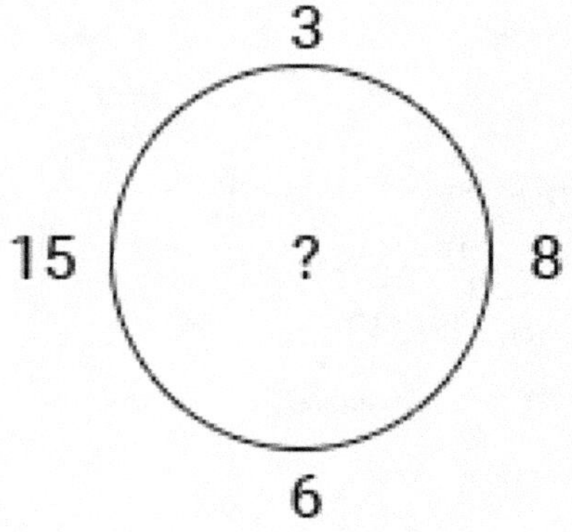

? = (8+15)-(3+6)

? = 14

Hence, the correct answer is 14.

8. There are 9 unique patterns.

9. 12 kids are reading open books.

10. The figure may be labelled as shown.

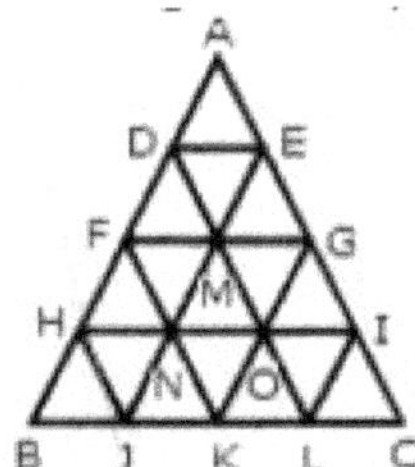

The parallelograms composed of two components each are ADME, DFNM, EMOG, FHJN, MNKO, GOLI, HBJN, NJKO, OKLI, FHNM, MNOG, DFME, HJKN, NKLO, OLCI, FNOM, MOIG and DMGE. i.e. 18 in number. The parallelograms composed of four components each are HOKB, NILJ, FGOH, HOLJ, NICK, FGIN, FMJB, DENH, MGKJ, MGCL, DEIO, FMLK, AENF, AGOD, DMJH, DOKF, EILM and EGKN i.e. 18 in number. The parallelograms composed of six components each are AEJH, DAIL, DECL, DEJB, HILB and HICJ i.e. 6 in number. The parallelograms composed of eight components each are FGKB, FGCK and AGKF i.e. 3 in number. Total number of parallelograms in the figure = 18 + 18 + 6 + 3 = 45.

11. in eight years the combined age is 124; the age nowis 124–(8×3)=100.Age in five years is 100+(5×3)=115

12. 730: deduct 135 each time

13. Two letters left of I is G.

Immediate below of G is L.

Immediate left of L is K.

Hence, the correct answer is K.

14. start at 1 and work clockwise adding 3, 6, 9, 12, 15, 18

15. Monday+2 = wednesday , wednesday+1 = Thursday , Thursday+2 = Saturday and last saturday + 3 = TUESDAY

So, Answer is TUESDAY.

16. 7.5 kg:

9 × 5 = 45 and 6 × 7.5 = 45

17. 5724361 should be the correct sequence in Row 2.

The forming letters are $: C, U, N, N, I, N, G$

Hence, the correct answer is 5724361.

18. There are 16 surfaces on above figure.

19. A,C, D are true

20. B, C, D are true.

21. Namita Gokhale - Mountain Echoes, Paro, A Himalayan Love Story

Aravinda Adiga - The White Tiger, Selection Day

Suketu Mehta - Maximum City

22. 'Hire and fire policy' implies 'taking up the performing employees and discarding the nonperforming ones'. Clearly, such a policy would stand out to encourage employees to work hard and devotedly to retain their jobs and thus enhance productivity and profitability of the organizations. So, both arguments I and III hold strong. Argument II seems to be vague in the light of this.

23. The advertisement depicts only the requirement, not the availability of flats in court area. So, I is not implicit. Such advertisements are given with the expectation of a response which can make such a flat available. So, II is implicit. Assumption III does not follow from the statement and so is not implicit.

24. 1, 2 and 4 are false

Hence option B is correct.

25. option B, C and D are correct.

26. option B, C and D are correct.

27. Himachal Pradesh and Tamil Nadu

Hence option A is correct.

28. The hand blocks the light rays striking it, result in the shadow on the wall.

29. option B, C and D are true.

30. All of the above

Hence option D is correct.

31. option A and D are correct.

32. option B, C and D are correct.

33. All of the above options are correct.

34.

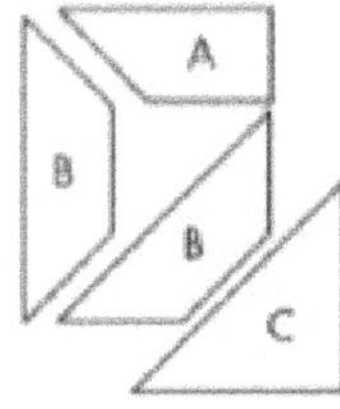

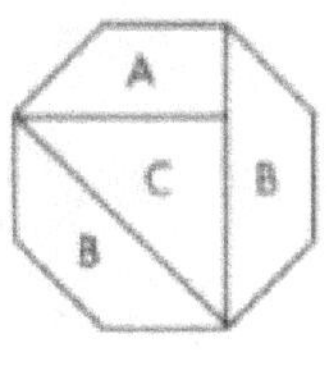

35. Explanation: a) has the right shape but the shadings are in wrong sectors, and c) is a rotation.

36. In a) the rectangular shape has been thickened, and in c) there is one 'step' missing.

37. Explanation: At each step the number of shapes increases by one, and the number of sides that the shapes have decreases by two.

38.

39. The background shading is increasing from none to a quarter to a half and finally to all shaded; the shapes are also alternating between circles and arrows, and the direction of the arrows and the position of the dots in the circles are also alter- nating between the top and bottom.

40. First reverse the sequence to read AJMUCCR, then insert a P between the M and the U, next replace the J with an I and finally reverse the sequence again to read RCCUPMIA.

41.

42.

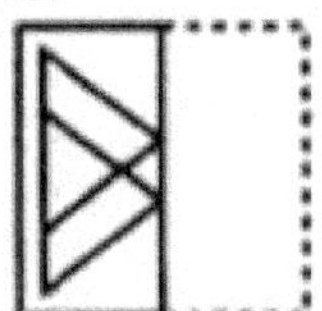

43.

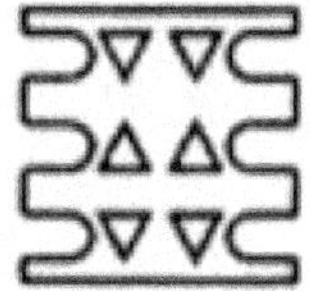

44.

45. Figure (A) will replace the $?$.

Hence, the correct option is (A).

8 differences

46. D

47. resort to use of electricity only when it is inevitable

48. 35421

Hence option A is correct.

49. Keep = Retain

Hence option A is correct.

50. Changes = Vicissitudes

Hence option C is correct.

51. On 31st December, 2005 it was Saturday.

Number of odd days from the year 2006 to the year 2009 = (1 + 1 + 2 + 1) = 5 days. On 31st December 2009, it was Thursday. Thus, on 1st Jan, 2010 it is Friday.

52. Tiny

Hence option C is correct.

53. Started

Hence option A is correct.

54. He warned her calmly that he would shoot her if she didn't keep quiet.

55. After being driven to the museum, Professor Kumar was dropped at his hotel.

56. I remember being taken to the museum by my sister.

57. Fate smiles **on** those who untiringly grapple with stark realities of life.

58. The miser gazed **avidly** at the pile of gold coins in front of him.

59. The sentence is in the past tense as 'did' is used.

Also, whenever 'did' is used, the verb that follows it must be in its base form.

So, we have to use 'bring' in the blank.

Hence, the correct option is (D).

60. 'Whose' means belonging to or associated with which person. Eg - Whose pen is this?

Here in the sentence, the teacher needs to find out who the owner of the bag is. So, 'Whose' is the correct answer.

Hence, the correct option is (C).

61. "Hell bent upon" is a suitable word to replace "hell bent at" in the given sentence. So the improved sentence will be "The workers are hell bent upon getting what is due to them".

Hence, the correct option is (C).

62. in crushing

Hence option B is correct.

63. This is a simple division series; each number is one-half of the previous number.

In other terms to say, the number is divided by 2 successively to get the next result.

4/2 = 2

2/2 = 1

1/2 = 1/2

(1/2)/2 = 1/4

(1/4)/2 = 1/8 and so on.

64. at each stage the third circle moves to the end and the sixth circle moves to the beginning

65. the circle becomes a square and the four white squares become white circles

66. Hair dryer

Hence option A is correct.

67. Kick Buttowski

Hence option B is correct.

68. Zebra

Hence option A is correct.

// Notes //

// Notes //

www.ingramcontent.com/pod-product-compliance
Lightning Source LLC
LaVergne TN
LVHW080058170826
845677LV00024B/1786
* 9 7 8 9 3 9 0 2 3 9 2 0 7 *